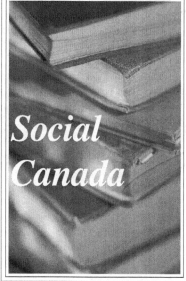

Disability and Social Policy in Canada

SECOND EDITION

EDITED BY

Mary Ann McColl

and

Lyn Jongbloed

Captus University Publications

Disability and Social Policy in Canada, second edition

Captus Press Inc.
Units 14 & 15
1600 Steeles Avenue West
Concord, ON
Canada   L4K 4M2
Phone: (416) 736–5537
Fax: (416) 736–5793
Email: Info@captus.com
Internet: http://www.captus.com

Library and Archives Canada Cataloguing in Publication
McColl, Mary Ann, 1956–
   Disability and social policy in Canada / Mary Ann McColl and Lyn Jongbloed. — 2nd ed.

First ed. written by Anne Crichton and Lyn Jongbloed.
Includes bibliographical references and index.
ISBN-13 978-1-55322-128-9
ISBN-10 1-55322-128-1

   1. Handicapped—Government policy—Canada. I. Jongbloed, Lyn, 1948–
II. Crichton, Anne Disability and social policy in Canada. III. Title.

HV1559.C3M33 2006   362.4'04561'0971   C2006-902679-3

Canada   *We acknowledge the financial support of the Government of Canada through the Book Publishing Industry Development Program (BPIDP) for our publishing activities.*

0 9 8 7 6 5 4 3 2
Printed in Canada

Contents

Introduction

This book is a compilation about disability and social policy in Canada. It is intended to serve as an analysis of the current state and future prospects of disability policy at the beginning of the 21st century. Unlike many accounts of disability policy, we give relatively little attention to history in this book, since it has been so thoroughly dealt with in a number of other books and articles. Instead, we focus on the present state of disability policy and attempt to look forward to identify directions for development and investment to ensure the best possible policy environment for disabled Canadians. We touch upon the recent past to the extent that it shapes the directions and issues of current policy.

We assume our readers of this book will be a mixed audience made up of consumers, professionals, students, decision-makers and researchers. While they may have a wide variety of particular interests, the common bond that unites them is a shared interest in disability, and in the structures and processes that shape the lives of people with disabilities. All our readers will, to a greater or lesser extent, be experts in the area of disability, but we do not assume that they are experts in policy studies or policy analysis. Thus, this book functions at a variety of levels. We assume no prior knowledge of disability policy, but rather try to make the arguments in each chapter stand on their own merits. Some chapters function on an experiential or narrative level, while others are highly empirical. Some quote specific statutes and programs, while others speak generally about a policy area. Hopefully, all will add to the reader's appreciation of the issues and complexities associated with disability policy.

To begin, let us put a few basic elements in place. First of all, language — in this book, we and our co-authors will use the terms disabled people and people with a disability interchangeably. While we understand that there are specific preferences in particular quarters for one or the other of these terms, and while we acknowledge that each may be associated with specific ideologies, we have chosen to avoid debates about language as an end in themselves (Human Resources Development Canada [HRDC], 1998; Titchkosky, 2001). This is not to say that we do not think language is important — quite the opposite in fact. We acknowledge that whole constellations of meaning can be communicated by the choice of a certain word or phrase. However, for the sake of this book, we cannot give our full attention to that debate and still do our job of discussing and analyzing policy. Therefore we choose to be inclusive of language about disability, so long as it meets a basic standard of respect and dignity.

DEFINITIONS

Next, let us advance a few definitions to serve us throughout our discussions. The first and most obvious definition that is needed here is one for disability. As you read on through the chapters, you will detect that different authors have preferences for different definitions. However, for the sake of a starting point, we must acknowledge that there are at least three definitions that prevail in modern discourse about disability. There is the *biomedical* definition, whereby disability is defined in terms of an illness, injury or other impairment of the individual, leading to the inability to DO certain things. There is the *socio-political* definition, sometimes referred to as the social construction of disability. This definition holds that all individuals are inherently different from one another, and the factor that defines disability is the context in which individuals attempt to act. Thus, disability is located in the environment that erects barriers to, provides inadequate supports for, or simply fails to recognize the abilities of individuals. The third definition is one that exists at the *intersection* of the previous two. It acknowledges both an individual biomedical contribution and an environmental contribution to disability — or as Shakespeare and Watson (2001) put it, "biology and sociology [are] simultaneously at play in disability". Common to all three definitions, however, is the notion of DOING — the basic human quality of being occupied in meaningful activity, and the impediments to it. Regardless of the reason specified in a definition, at the heart of the concept of disability is the notion of activities that humans wish to perform, need to perform or are expected to perform.

A second important definition for our discussions is the definition of policy, and more specifically of disability policy. Boyce (2002) defines policy as a purposeful set of actions aimed to address identified social problems with a specific set of actions. Policy may address *structures* (supports, institutions, resources), *processes* (access, roles, functions) or *outcomes* (justice, equality, service).

According to Bickenbach (1993), there are a number of possible motives for the development of social policy:

- Charity — voluntarily serving others who are deemed to be less fortunate;
- Need fulfilment — provision of goods or service to fill a perceived need in society;
- Compensation — seeking to obtain justice for someone who has accrued a loss;
- Welfare maximization — investing in people or institutions on the expectation that they will make a contribution to society in return;
- Equality — redistribution of wealth or capital to achieve a goal of equality.

All of these policy motives have been applied to policy relating to people with disabilities at one time or another, but perhaps the most compelling and most commonly employed in modern disability policy is the last motive, equality. However, we must be clear about what we mean by equality. Policy analysts talk about horizontal and vertical equity — horizontal equity refers to equal treatment of all, assuming that all are equal before the law; vertical equity refers to *unequal* treatment commensurate with needs, recognizing that all may not be equal with regard to access to certain goods and ser-

3
—

vices that society has to offer (www.tutor2u.net). Bickenbach (1993) looks at a variety of different meanings of equality:

- Equality of consideration, meaning equal ability to seek a benefit. In other words, were all individuals equally informed and advised about the opportunity to apply?
- Equality of opportunity, or equal access. Were all individuals afforded a chance to participate?
- Equality of participation, or the ability to participate in the same way or to the same extent as others. Were all individuals permitted to engage in all aspects of the activity?
- Equality of outcome, or equal result. Were all individuals treated in such a way that they wound up receiving the same amount of goods and services in the end?

Each form of equality has dramatically different requirements for the policy considerations aimed at achieving it.

Finally, one more word about policy in general that helps to frame our discussions. Again, according to Bickenbach (1993), there are at least four decisions that must be made in framing a policy:

- Whether to fill a need, or to fulfil an entitlement or a right;
- Whether to confer a benefit or to remove an obstacle;
- Whether to provide access to a process or to ensure an outcome; and
- Whether to offer something general to everyone or to provide something specific to an identified group or minority.

Our goal in this book is to talk about disability policy in particular, so we need to define what is meant by disability policy. According to Bickenbach (1993), it is policy that addresses two fundamental questions:

1. What does it mean to have a disability?
2. What is society obliged to do for those who have a disability?

He contends that the answer to the last question is to ensure that disabled people obtain *respect*, *participation* and *accommodation*. He further contends that in the ideal, disability policy would conform to the following expectations:

- It would integrate all aspects of disability — biomedical, economic and socio-political;

- It would set out clear criteria for entitlement, and a process to resolve disputes or appeals regarding entitlement;
- It would provide for one or more of the three policy goals specified above (respect, participation and/or accommodation); and
- It would be commensurate with the broader social policy; in other words, it would situate disability within the mainstream of society.

We use the term "disability policy" as if it referred to an entity that was widely recognized and acknowledged as such. The term invokes the idea of a disability system that is governed by disability policy (Boyce, 2002). However, the reality is a long way from that. Disability policy has been described as conflicting, fragmented, incoherent, not user-friendly, a "hit-or-miss" affair (Cameron & Valentine 2001; Holt et al., 2000; Prince, 2004). According to Lande (1998), disability policy has been the victim of vague statutory definitions and capricious judicial opinions leading to flawed case law. Policy governing issues of interest to people with disabilities ranges across jurisdictions, across sectors within government, and across programs within ministries. In fact, it is a patchwork of legislation, regulations, programs, providers and entitlements that requires considerable probing to reveal, and considerable patience to understand. We hope that this book will help the reader find his or her way through this complex topic, and understand some of the reasons it is as complex as it is.

JURISDICTION IN DISABILITY POLICY

The disability policy environment in Canada is dominated by several major statutes and programs at the *federal* level. Since its beginnings as a system aimed at providing for injured workers and veterans, the federal government has taken a leadership role in setting standards and providing for the necessities of people with disabilities (Crichton & Jongbloed, 1998; Torjman, 2001; Tremblay, Campbell & Hudson, 2005). Although legislation has been referred to as a "blunt tool" with which to remedy social problems (Holt et al., 2000), it is the skeleton of a system of policy. In Canada, statutes like the *Constitution Act*, the *Charter of Rights and Freedoms*, the *Canada Health Act*, the *Employment Equity Act* and the *Human Rights Act* form the basis upon which disability programs and entitlements rely (Cameron & Valentine, 2001). Layered on

5

top of those laws are a set of programs offered by government aimed at addressing the social and economic needs of people with disabilities. For example, the Canada Pension Plan Disability program provides a disability income benefit; Revenue Canada provides a disability tax credit; the Office for Disability Issues within Social Development Canada provides standards and ideological guidance about disability; Statistics Canada collects information about disability; Employment Insurance provides benefits to disabled workers. These are just a few examples of the web of services and programs concerning disability at the federal level.

However, according to the *Constitution Act* in Canada (and before that the *British North America Act* of 1867), most services to individual citizens are delivered at the *provincial* level. Therefore, in each province and territory, there are also laws and programs that have major implications for the lives of people with disabilities. Social security, health, education, housing, transportation, child care, adaptive equipment, personal care and vocational programs are all examples of provincial jurisdiction over issues affecting people with disabilities. It is beyond the scope of this book to deal in detail with legislation, programs or organizations at the provincial level.

The political scene in Canada has been dominated in recent years by tensions between the federal and provincial/territorial governments as to who does what and where the resources for specific commitments should come from. As far as disability policy is concerned, it has been designated as one of a small set of items over which federal-provincial tensions must be resolved (Cameron & Valentine, 2001). There is concern that a weakened position for the federal government relative to the provinces is not in the best interests of people with disabilities (Torjman, 2001).

Historically, the disability community has been served well by its relationship with the federal government. Several key successes have resulted in a legacy of legislation and political culture that have advanced the cause of disabled people (Crichton & Jongbloed, 1998; Torjman, 2001). The same cannot be said, however, for the provincial governments. Recent trends toward delisting insured health services, cutting welfare rolls, and decreasing commitments to home health services and to municipalities have adversely affected the social service net for provincial populations as a whole. Whenever this happens, it is a relative certainty that those who are the most disadvantaged, and thus the most dependent upon those services, suffer most. Arguably, many people with disabilities are among those most in need, and thus are disproportionately disadvantaged by such measures (Cameron & Valentine,

2001). A survey conducted by the Office for Disability Issues (Social Development Canada [SDC], 2004a) shows that Canadians believe that governments ought to be responsible for the provision of supports such as health, education, transportation, housing and special needs. Whereas families, informal networks and the voluntary sector can be expected to provide general supports, these specific programs are part of what Canadians believe is the government's job.

SCOPE OF THIS BOOK

In this book, we look at who the disability community is, and how they are seen and understood by policy-makers. We look at the current Canadian policy context to identify some of the issues that are most pressing and most strategic for people with disabilities. Next we look at disabled people as actors in the political environment, the organizations that represent them, and their relative success or failure as political actors. In the major section of the book, we look at a number of specific policy issues that are of particular importance to people with disabilities — employment and income, health and social services, culture and community services. We conclude with a summary of issues raised, obstacles yet to overcome, resources available and future directions.

Section I

Disability in Canada

In the first section of this book, we address the question: "What is meant by disability?" Views of disability have changed over the last century. Disability was viewed as an individual medical issue, an economic issue, and later, as a socio-political issue. It is now recognized that disability incorporates all these issues.

Definitions of disability have influenced who has been viewed or counted as disabled by policy-makers. The Special Committee of Parliament that investigated disability issues in the International Year of Disabled Persons in 1981 recommended that the government count the number of people with functional performance difficulties. This led to the Canadian Health and Disability Survey conducted in 1983–1984 and the Health and Activity Limitation Survey in 1986. Both surveys reflected the World Health Organization's definition of disability: "Any restriction or lack of ability to perform an activity in the manner or within the range considered normal for a human being." Numerous national surveys have been conducted since that time, and this chapter offers us a window on six of them.

The four chapters in this section focus on the definition and conceptualization of disability. They examine definitions of disability in national surveys in Canada between 1989 and 2001 — definitions that are primarily biomedical and economic in nature.

Chapter 1

Adele Furrie provides an overview of four national disability surveys: the 1983–1984 Canadian Health and Disability Survey, the 1986 Health and Activity Limitation Survey, the 1991 Health and Activity Limitation Survey and the 2001 Participation and Activity Limitation Survey. She identifies four issues that require consideration when using survey data collected on people with disabilities. These are: the conceptualization of disability, the identity of participants, the use of proxy respondents and the context of the survey. Survey questions to operationalize disability have changed over time. The way of identifying the population with disabilities has also evolved. Current sampling methods underestimate the prevalence of disability among children.

Chapter 2

In her second chapter, Adele Furrie offers a profile of the disabled population in Canada, derived from data collected in the 2001 Participation and Activity Limitation Survey. Factors influencing inclusion or exclusion of Canadians with disabilities depend to a large extent on age. Three age groups (0–14, 15–64, and 65 and older) are profiled, providing a picture of the main issues and barriers faced by each group.

Chapter 3

Mary Ann McColl compares the ways in which Canadians with disabilities are portrayed in five national surveys, namely the Health and Activity Limitation Survey in 1991, the General Social Survey in 1994, the Canada Election Survey in 1997, National Population Health Survey in 1998 and the Participation and Activity Limitations Survey in 2001. She focuses on the differences among surveys in terms of the proportion of people aged 20–64 who were classified as disabled. These differences could be explained by sampling method or by the definition of disability used in the survey. Implications of definitions for access to health services, income replacement/employment and human rights are explored.

Chapter 4

In the last chapter in this section, Titchkosky applies detailed text analysis to contemporary federal government position statements about disability produced between 1981 and 2004. She focuses on the most recent of these to explore how texts reveal a reciprocal relationship between people and policy. She shows how texts influence policy that affects people, but also how people, disabled people in particular, tell us something about our policy and our society.

1

Disability Surveys in Canada

ADELE FURRIE

INTRODUCTION

Over the last 20 years a number of national surveys have focused on Canadians with disabilities. This chapter identifies four issues that should be considered when using survey data that have been collected on the population with disabilities. These issues are then used as a framework to analyze four national surveys conducted between 1983 and 2001.

The chapter begins with a discussion of the factors that prompted the development of quantitative data collection regarding people with disabilities in Canada and comments on the fact that disability statistics have no ongoing place within the national statistical program. This is followed by identification of four issues that should be considered when using data concerning the population with disabilities. These issues are the conceptualization of disability, the identity of participants, the use of proxy respondents and the context of the survey. These issues are used as a framework to analyze the 1983–1984 Canadian Health and Disability Survey, the

1986–1987 Health and Activity Limitation Survey, the 1991 Health and Activity Limitation Survey and the 2001 Participation and Activity Limitation Survey.

BACKGROUND

Since the early 1980s, the Canadian government has been listening to Canadians with disabilities describe an environment that restricts or impedes their full participation in activities that are taken for granted by the non-disabled population (Canada, 1981). The articulate recollections of personal experiences provided by disabled Canadians to members of the Special Parliamentary Committee on the Disabled and the Handicapped were overwhelming. These experiences included a young couple trying desperately to learn how to cope with an autistic daughter but not knowing to whom they can turn to obtain information and support. They included a university graduate with an obvious disability who said she was denied employment because of the pervasive notion that an individual with a disability is not as productive as a non-disabled person. And they included a young man in a wheelchair who was frustrated that he was denied access to certain buildings because of stairs, and access to rooms within an accessible building because of narrow doorways.

When Committee members turned to Statistics Canada to provide the data on the nature and extent of these barriers, they were surprised to learn that there were no quantitative data concerning the population with disabilities available at Canada's national statistical agency. The Committee admonished Statistics Canada over their reluctance to include a question on the 1981 Census of Population. Through one of their 130 recommendations, the Committee directed Statistics Canada to develop and implement a long-term strategy that would generate comprehensive data on the population with disabilities.

More than two decades have passed since the tabling of the Committee's report. Canadian government officials are *still* conversing with Canadians with disabilities. Programs and services have been implemented to remove physical barriers, but barriers *still* exist. Many Canadians with disabilities are still confused as they attempt to find their way through the maze that exists at the various government levels, and unmet needs are still the norm for many. Attitudes are changing, but negative stereotypes *still* persist. These are reflected in, for example, the high numbers of Canadians with disabilities who have decided that looking for work is a useless exercise. More quantitative data concerning Canadians with disabilities exist but disability statistics *still* have no ongoing place within the national statistical program. Rather, they are treated as a special survey when additional funding becomes available. Such was the reason for the 10-year hiatus between the 1991 Health and Activity Limitation Survey and the 2001 Participation and Activity Limitation Survey.

Is the situation in Canada unique to Canada? Not at all! Faced with an increasing need to recognize and to address the barriers being faced by their citizens with disabilities, other countries have been following a path very similar to Canada's. Some are ahead of Canada; others are lagging behind. Some have developed mechanisms to maintain an ongoing dialogue between government and citizens with disabilities. Many have developed programs and services to "level the playing field". Some have developed a national strategy to collect ongoing statistical data against which to measure the progress toward the complete removal of barriers.

Countries are working together to develop a common framework within which to collect and disseminate statistical data. The World Health Organization's (WHO) 2001 publication, *International Classification of Functioning, Disability and Health* (ICF), provides a unified and standard language and framework of health and health-related terms. Statistical agencies and health officials are working together to develop tools using ICF concepts so that international comparisons can be facilitated. The United Nations Statistical Division (UNSD) is working with country officials to implement these tools in developing countries. A set of questions to identify the population with disabilities was included for the first time in their recommendations for censuses (United Nations [UN], 1998). DISTAT — Version 2 brings together disability statistics that have been collected by countries, but the UNSD cautions the user that prevalence rates should not be compared across countries because of different concepts and data-collection methods (unstats.un.org). In 2005, they will initiate a systematic and regular collection of basic statistics on human functioning and disability by introducing a disability statistics questionnaire to the existing Demographic Yearbook data-collection system (unstats.un.org).

UNDERSTANDING THE QUANTITATIVE DATA

There are four issues that should be considered when using data concerning the population with disabilities that has been collected in a survey environment. These include how the concept of disability is operationalized, how the population with disabilities is identified, the use of proxy respondents, and the context of the survey.

(a) Conceptualization of disability

As a starting point, it was agreed that in a survey environment, the only logical approach to identifying the population with disabilities was to use a subjective approach — asking individuals with disabilities to self-report on the nature and extent of their disability. Based on this decision, it was agreed that the concepts embedded in the *International Classification of Impairments, Disabilities and Handicaps* (ICIDH) were appropriate (Canada, 1986c). Statistics Canada officials were fortunate to be able to build on the work completed by the Organisation for Economic Co-operation and Development (OECD) working group that operationalized the functional definition of disability. These questions provided the starting point for developing the screening questions that were used to identify the adult population with disabilities. While these questions worked well in identifying those individuals who were limited in their activities as a result of a physical or sensory impairment, they did not work well in identifying those adults who experienced a limitation in their activity because of a developmental anomaly, or a mental health condition, or as a result of labelling by others because of a disability (McWhinnie, 1981). Through consultations with Canadians with disabilities, advocates, and organizations of and for persons with disabilities, questions were added to identify these populations.

(b) Identification of persons with disabilities

Locating the population with disabilities living in private households so that an interview can be conducted is not a simple task, and it is very expensive. Persons with disabilities are spread across the country, and the majority of households do not include an individual with a disability. This is particularly true for children and young adults; only five in 100 households, on average, would have a child or young adult with a disability. Because disability increases with age, it becomes less of an issue to identify adults and seniors with disabilities. All four disability-specific surveys used a two-stage approach to identify the potential population with disabilities — an initial screener with one person responding on behalf of all members of the household — followed by the detailed survey questionnaire that was completed with the individual.

(c) The use of proxy respondents

The use of proxy respondents to collect data that are subjective in nature is problematic. While persons who have significant limitation in their activities will be identified both through the initial screen and the more detailed survey questionnaire, experience has shown that persons who have a mild or moderate limitation in their activities might not be identified through the initial screen.

(d) The context of the survey

The context within which disability screening questions are asked or the order in which they are asked may also affect the prevalence rates of disability. Experience has shown that disability questions included in a health survey that follow questions on presence of chronic conditions, for example, are more likely to result in a higher prevalence rate than those asked in a survey that deals with employment.

ANALYZING THE SURVEYS

What follows is an overview of these four issues for each of the four surveys that comprise the national database on disability issues. One will see from the overview that although the concept of disability has remained unchanged, the questions used to operationalize the concept have evolved over time, with new categories being added and questions being refined. How the population with disabilities is first identified has also evolved. It began with a household-based survey and the use of a proxy respondent to identify the population with disabilities; it then changed to allow for false negatives in the initial screen by selecting a sample of persons who were not identified as having a disability; and in 2001, it returned to the original design that did not allow for false negatives. These ongoing changes highlight the need for Statistics Canada to develop a standardized approach to both the operationalization of the concept of disability and the methodology used for the initial screening. This is a necessary requirement to measure progress and the impact of programs and services.

The 1983–1984 Canadian Health and Disability Survey (1983 CHDS)

The CHDS was the first attempt to collect national data on the prevalence of disability in Canada. The survey was completed

in two stages. The initial stage was conducted as part of the regular monthly labour force interview that provided at that time —
and continues to provide today — the monthly employment figures
on the size and composition of the Canadian labour force. The
disability questions were added to five-sixths of the monthly sample
of households in October 1983, and in June 1984 they were added
to five-sixths of the monthly sample of households in six of the
ten provinces. This was done so that provincial estimates could be
produced.

The respondent who completed the labour force survey questionnaire also completed the supplementary questions on behalf
of all household members. For adults aged 15 and older, 19 screening questions were added as a supplement to the regular labour
force survey questionnaire, including 12 questions that covered
activities of daily living as indicators of physical disability, five
questions concerning hearing, seeing and speech problems, one
question dealing with general limitation in activity, and one question that was included to identify persons with developmental
delays. This last question was only asked when a proxy respondent
was completing the questionnaire. No attempt was made to explicitly cover persons with a disability as a result of a mental or emotional condition because of concerns that such questions might
negatively affect the response rate to the labour force survey in
subsequent months.

For children aged 0 to 14, the approach was somewhat different. A child was considered to have a disability if he/she used
technical aids, was limited in activities considered normal for a
child of his/her age, attended a special school or special classes
within a regular school, or had a specific chronic condition or
vision or hearing trouble. The household respondent was asked
these questions.

All persons for whom a positive response to one or more
screening questions was obtained during the initial interview were
contacted approximately one week after the initial contact. A parent responded on behalf of a child. Proxy responses were accepted
only if the adult was unable to respond for him/herself.

The screening questions were asked again, and those respondents who answered positively to one or more of the questions
during the interview were classified as having a disability. They
were asked additional questions to explore the accommodations
obtained from society to eliminate or reduce barriers to full participation, and as well, questions about barriers that had not been
removed (Canada, 1986c).

The 1986–1987 Health and Activity Limitation Survey (1986 HALS)

The 1986 HALS was the second major disability survey undertaken by Statistics Canada. It was also the first post-census survey conducted by Statistics Canada. The two disability questions added to the long questionnaire of the 1986 Census of Population — the one completed by every fifth household in Canada — were used as the sampling frame for persons residing in households. The first disability question on the Census asked about general limitation in activity at home, at school or at work, or in other activities such as transportation to and from work or leisure activities. The second question asked if the individual had any long-term disabilities or handicaps.

The results of the testing of the two Census questions prior to their inclusion on the 1986 Census questionnaire indicated that not all persons with disabilities would respond positively to the Census disability questions. Therefore, the 1986 HALS sample included a sample of persons who responded positively to one or both of the Census disability questions as well as a sample of individuals who answered negatively to both disability questions.

The 1986 HALS used the same 12 questions covering activities of daily living as indicators of physical disability as well as the same five questions concerning hearing, seeing and speech problems that were used in the 1983 CHDS for adults. In response to the limitations in the data identified by users of the 1983 CHDS, the 1986 HALS split the general limitation question in two — with one question dealing with limitation in activity because of a physical condition or health problem, and the second question dealing with limitation in activity because of a long-term emotional, psychological, nervous, or mental health condition or problem. Two other questions were added: one to identify individuals with a learning disability, and the other to identify individuals with developmental disabilities or a disability as a result of a mental health condition. Two questions were also added to the child's screening questions — one dealing with ability to speak and be understood, and the second to identify emotional, psychological, nervous and mental health conditions.

A parent responded on behalf of a child. Proxy responses were accepted only if the adult was unable to respond for him/herself.

If a respondent answered positively to one or more of these screening questions, they were asked additional questions to explore both the accommodations obtained from society to eliminate or reduce barriers to full participation and the barriers encountered that had not been removed.

Because the sample was selected from the 1986 Census, the resulting database includes not only the information from the 1986 HALS questionnaire, but also all of the Census data for the individuals. Some family and household income data from the Census were also included.

Of the 100,265 who participated in the survey, approximately 112,000 individuals who answered "Yes" were selected to participate in the 1986 HALS. Of those, 11,735 were non-respondents. There were 22,040 (22%) who answered "No" to all of the 1986 HALS screening questions (false positives to the Census disability questions) and, as a result, were classified as non-disabled. The remaining 78,225 were classified as having a disability.

Of the 67,230 individuals who answered "No", 3,910 (5.8%) answered "Yes" to one or more of the 1986 HALS screening questions (false negatives to the Census screening questions) and, as a result, were classified as having a disability. The remaining 63,320 were classified as non-disabled (Statistics Canada, 1988).

The 1991 Health and Activity Limitation Survey (1991 HALS)

The same sample design and sample allocation used in the 1986 HALS was used for the 1991 HALS. The 1991 Census question that was used for the initial screen for the 1991 HALS was identical to the one used as the initial screen from the 1986 Census for the 1986 HALS.

The majority of the screening questions remained the same as in the 1986 HALS, with some minor changes to the adult questionnaire. There was continued criticism that persons with learning disabilities, developmental disabilities and/or disabilities as a result of a mental health condition could not be differentiated in the survey. As a result, the learning disability question was expanded to include some examples of learning disabilities. Two additional questions were added after extensive consultation with the Canadian Mental Health Association, the Canadian Association for Community Living and People First. Both examined the issue of labelling — one in the context of difficulty learning, and the other because of a specific mental health condition.

If a respondent answered positively to one or more of these screening questions, they were asked additional questions to explore both the accommodations obtained from society to eliminate or reduce barriers to full participation and the barriers encountered that had not been removed. Employment was of particular interest in the 1991 HALS since these data formed the basis for the availability data that were used to monitor employers' compliance with the relatively new *Employment Equity Act*.

Again, because the sample was selected from the 1991 Census, the resulting database included not only the information from the 1991 HALS questionnaire, but all of the Census data for the individual as well. Also, some family and household income data from the Census were included.

Approximately 35,000 individuals who answered "Yes" were selected to participate in the 1991 HALS. Of those, 7,000 answered "No" to all of the HALS screening questions (20%) and were classified as not having a disability (false positives to the Census disability questions). The remaining 28,000 were classified as having a disability.

Approximately 113,000 individuals who answered "No" were selected to participate in the 1991 HALS. Of those, 5,600 (5%) responded "Yes" to one or more of the HALS screening questions (false negatives to the Census disability questions) and, as a result, were classified as having a disability. The remaining 107,400 were classified as non-disabled (Statistics Canada, 1992).

The 2001 Participation and Activity Limitation Survey (2001 PALS)

PALS is also a post-census survey that used the 2001 Census of Population disability questions as an initial screen. Because of the new, more refined disability questions that were included in the 2001 Census, it was decided that the PALS 2001 sample would be selected only from those individuals who responded positively to one or more of the disability questions on the 2001 Census of Population long questionnaire.

The majority of the screening questions remained the same as in the 1991 HALS, with some minor changes. The questions on labelling — one in the context of learning difficulty and the other because of a specific mental health condition — were removed, and a question on limitation as a result of pain was added.

Of the 43,275 individuals who were selected to participate in PALS, 22% answered "No" to the PALS screening questions (false positives to the Census disability questions). Interviews were conducted over the telephone. Proxy responses were obtained for children aged 0 to 14 and for adults who was unable to respond for him/herself or was unavailable during the survey period.

As in the previous post-census surveys, if a respondent answered positively to one or more of the screening questions, they were asked additional questions to explore both the accommodations obtained from society to eliminate or reduce barriers to full participation and the barriers encountered that had not been removed. Also, because the sample was selected using the 2001 Census of Population, a link between the two data sets was established, and data are available, as in the previous post-census surveys, from both the survey questionnaire and the Census (Canada, 2002b).

Initial feedback concerning the 2006 Participation and Activity Limitation Survey indicates that the questions used to identify the population with disabilities — both the initial screening on the 2006 Census and the more detailed questions on the survey questionnaires — will not change from 2001. There are also indications that the method used to identify the population with disabilities will also not change. This means that there will be no sample taken to identify the false negatives to the Census screening questions. The good news is that measurement of change between 2001 and 2006 will be possible. The bad news is that the population with disabilities will continue to be underestimated, particularly among children and youth. Because of the changing landscape with respect to coverage of the population with disabilities, the 2001 PALS data is used with no comparisons being made to the previous disability surveys. While this limits the analysis, there are such differences between the previous surveys and the 2001 PALS that Statistics Canada cautions that such comparisons should not be attempted.

CONCLUSION

This chapter has analyzed how survey questions have conceptualized and operationalized disability, and how identification of the population with disabilities has evolved in national surveys. The need for Statistics Canada to develop a standardized approach is stressed, since this is necessary to measure progress as well as the impact of programs and services.

2

Profiling Canadians with Disabilities

ADELE FURRIE

INTRODUCTION

Using data from the 2001 PALS, this chapter profiles the activities and the challenges faced by people with disabilities. It begins with a description of the Canadians who were included in the survey, followed by a description of activities of people with disabilities aged 0 to 14, adults aged 15 to 64 and adults aged 65 and older, including their income, employment rates, support with everyday activities and barriers to accessing health and social services.

Unless otherwise noted, the data presented in this section of the chapter has been produced from the PALS micro-data files. Access to these files was obtained through a contract with Statistics Canada.

According to the 2001 PALS, 3.6 million Canadians or 12.4% of the population were persons with disabilities and were residing in private households and collective dwellings within the 10 provinces (excluding residents of First Nation communities). PALS did not collect data in the three territories or in institutions. The exclu-

Table 2.1: Age specific prevalence of disability.

Age group	# persons with disabilities	% with a disability
0–4	26,210	1.6
5–9	70,370	3.7
10–14	84,350	4.2
15–24	131,035	3.9
25–64	1,817,460	11.4
65–74	649,180	31.2
75 and older	802,670	53.3
All ages	**3,601,265**	**12.4**

sion of residents in institutions means that there is an undercount of seniors with disabilities. This is particularly true among those aged 85 and older, where 9% of males and 35.4% of females in this age group reside in institutions (Canada, 2001a).

Table 2.1 shows that the prevalence of disability increases with age, from 1.6% among children aged between birth and four to 71% for seniors aged 85 and older. The only exception is for young adults aged between 15 and 24, with only 3.9% reported to have a disability as compared to the 4.2% reported for children aged 10 to 14. This difference could be attributed to a change in the way disability is defined between children aged from birth to 14 and adults aged 15 and older. It could also be a reflection of the proxy reporting issue. While a parent or guardian would respond on behalf of children under the age of 15, young adults in most instances respond for themselves. There are only slight differences between males and females in all age groups.

Social and economic exclusion continues to be an integral part of the lives of many Canadians with disabilities. These exclusions manifest themselves in many of the same ways as were articulated in the early 1980s. Many young Canadians with disabilities and their families experience the economic impact as a result of one parent having to stay home to care for the child with the disability. Some children with disabilities do not have the aids that they need; for many, this limits the kind or amount of activities they can do and causes frustration and difficulty with social relationships. Some young adults with disabilities continue to face barriers within the

23

workplace. And many seniors with disabilities, even those who are receiving support with daily activities from family and friends, report that they need more support, and many are unable to afford that support. Attitudes toward Canadians with disabilities are changing but still have a long way to go (Social Development Canada [SDC], 2004b). Many non-disabled Canadians feel, for example, that an individual with a disability should not consider certain types of occupations, and that children with learning disabilities or behaviour problems should not be integrated into the public school system.

PROFILES OF CANADIANS WITH DISABILITIES

How Canadians with disabilities are included or excluded in their community varies according to age. Therefore, the profiles that follow have been segmented into three age groups: children between birth and 14, adults aged 15 to 64, and seniors aged 65 and older. Within each profile is an overview of the demographics of the age group, some information about the nature and extent of their disabilities, and an overview of the impact that living with a disability has on these Canadians.

Children Aged between Birth and 14

Among children aged between birth and four, only 1.6% (26,210) are reported to have a disability.

- For slightly more than half of these children (53.2%), the parent reported that the main condition causing the disability existed at birth, or was due to a premature birth, or to an accident during the birthing process. Another 20.9% reported "other", with the majority of the write-in responses being "genetic", or "hereditary" or "inherited"; 8.9% of parents reported that the disability was due to a disease or an illness; and 12.7% said they did not know the cause.

- One of the first barriers encountered by parents with a disabled child occurred when trying to get a diagnosis for their child's health problem or condition: 33.6% reported a long waiting period before the diagnosis was provided; 33.4% said the doctor took a "wait and see" approach; and 20.7% reported difficulty getting referrals or appointments.

- Getting the help that is needed to do everyday activities, such as house cleaning or meal preparation, or getting help so that other family responsibilities can be attended to, or just having some personal time, is a problem for 45% of parents with a very young child with a disability. Among these who need help but do not have it, 27% reported that they were on a waiting list.

- Having a very young child with a disability impacts the economic status of the family. Almost one-third of these families (31%) reported that one parent had not taken a job in order to take care of the child; 31% reported changing working hours to a different time of day or night to accommodate the needs of the child; and 23% reported that one parent quit their job to care for the child. An overwhelming 26% of families reported that in the 12 months prior to the 2001 PALS was conducted, there were financial problems as a result of the child's condition.

For children aged 5 to 9 and those aged 10 to 14, the disability rates are 3.7% and 4.2%, respectively.

- Cause of the disability for 5- to 14-year-olds was reported as "existed at birth", or as a result of a premature birth, or of an accident during the birthing process. Almost one in five parents (18.6%) reported that they just did not know the cause of the disability, and about the same number answered "other cause" and provided the explanation of "hereditary", "genetic" or "inherited".

- Similar to the younger children with disabilities, getting information from a health professional was difficult. More than one-third of parents (36%) said the doctor took a "wait and see" approach; 33% reported a long waiting period before the diagnosis was provided; and 23% reported difficulty getting referrals or appointments.

- The parent of three of every ten children aged 5 to 14 with a disability reported that his/her child needed aids that they did not have and that not having these aids impacted him/her. Within this group of 45,585 children, 56% reported that the child's everyday activity was reduced, 62% reported that the child was frustrated, and 54% reported that lack of these aids affected the child's self-esteem.

- Almost all children with disabilities in this age group (95%) attend school. Among those, 6% attend a special education school. Of those who attend regular schools, 29% have a mix of regular classes and special education classes, and 9% attend only special education classes. The Environics survey asked about integration versus segregation of children with disabilities within the school system. Opinions varied. When considering a child with a physical disability, 55% of Canadians said the child should be integrated. Only one-third felt that integration is the best approach for a child with a mental or learning disability.

- Among parents of children with disabilities who attend regular schools that do not have special education classes, seven out of every ten reported that their child almost always looked forward to going to school. Only 51% of parents whose child went to a regular school with special education classes reported this level of feeling, and this dropped to 45% for children attending special education schools.

- After-school activities are the norm for most children; these activities can be organized or unorganized, including physical activities such as dance/gymnastics/martial arts classes, or non-sport-related activities such as music/art, church groups, Girl or Boy Scouts. Among parents of children with disabilities, 13% report that their children never take part in these types of activities, and 21% reported that their child took part in only one type.

- Getting along with their peers is often seen as a measure of being socially well-adjusted. The parents of children with disabilities (59%) reported that their child got along very well or quite well with friends or classmates. However, 13% reported the opposite, saying that there were frequent or constant problems with interactions between their child and his/her classmates or friends.

- Similar to the families that have younger children with disabilities, getting the help that they need to support them in everyday family-related activities and getting respite to have some personal time are also problems for almost half of the families that have children with disabilities aged 5 to 14. Almost three out of four (71%) say that help from family and friends is not available, and 16% say that their child is on a waiting list for the needed help.

- Dual wage earner families have become the norm in Canada. For many families with children with disabilities, this is either not an option, or the nature or extent of their work has changed. Almost two out of ten families (19%) reported that one parent had quit work to care for the child, and 34% reported that one parent has had to reduce the number of hours worked because of these caring responsibilities. For 18% of families, there were financial problems reported in the 12 months prior to the conduct of PALS as a result of their child's condition.

Adults Aged 15 to 64

The 2001 PALS included questions that allowed Canadians aged 15 and older to identify 11 different types of disabilities (see Table 2.2). These included seeing, hearing, speaking, mobility, agility, memory, learning, developmental, learning, pain and unknown (limitation in activity at home, school/work and in other activities).

Limitation in activity as a result of pain is an addition to the screening questions, and it resulted in the addition of 148,755 individuals who reported only limitation in activity due to pain. When asked about the underlying condition that caused the pain, 12.6% said it was arthritis or rheumatism with no specific site mentioned, 13.4% reported pain in the back or spine or related specifically

Table 2.2: Reasons for reporting an activity limitation.

Type of disability	% aged 15 and older reporting a disability
Mobility	71.7
Pain	69.5
Agility	66.6
Hearing	30.4
Seeing	17.4
Psychological	15.3
Learning	13.2
Memory	12.3
Speaking	10.6
Developmental	3.5
Unknown	2.8

to disc issues, and 14.4% cited specific diseases such as Crohn's disease, diabetes, heart disease and migraines. Almost one-quarter (23.6%) who reported only limitation because of pain were aged 45 to 54 years.

Mobility was the type of disability most often reported by 3,420,340 Canadians aged 15 and older who reported a disability (71.7%). This type of disability is more predominant among seniors, with 83.4% of seniors with a disability aged 75 and older reporting this type of disability, as compared to 38.7% of young adults with a disability aged 15 to 19. Contrast this to persons who report a learning disability and those individuals who report a developmental disability. For these two types of disabilities, the younger you are, the more likely you are to report a learning or a developmental disability. Overall, 13.2% of the population with disabilities reported having a learning disability; however, 53.1% of disabled Canadians aged 15 to 19 reported having a learning disability, as compared to 5.9% of seniors with a disability aged 75 and older. The same is true for persons reporting a developmental disability. Overall, the percentage is 3.5%; but among youth with disabilities aged 15 to 19, the rate is 22.4%, and it is less than 1% among seniors aged 75 and older.

Young Adults Aged 15 to 24

The challenges facing young adults in the new millennium differ significantly from those faced by young adults in the 1980s and 1990s. The economic environment is different, resulting in fewer jobs and, as a result, more competition for those jobs (Statistics Canada, 2003). The cost of post-secondary education has been steadily increasing over past decades (Canada, 2005). So, who are these young adults with disabilities, and how do they fare in meeting these challenges when compared to their non-disabled peers?

- About 3.9% (151,035) of Canadians aged 15 to 24 reported at least one type of disability in PALS. Almost one in three young adults with disabilities (30.4%) reported that their limitation in activity began prior to their entrance into the school system — between birth and four.

- Pain (50.9%), learning (44.1%) and mobility (42%) are the three types of disabilities most often reported by these young adults.

- Barriers to receiving the health care and social services that they needed were reported by 22.7% of young adults with disabilities. The reasons given by these 34,275 young adults included "not covered by insurance" (28.9%), "don't know where or how to obtain them" (18.1%), and "they were not available in the area" (15%).

- The cost of obtaining the medication or drugs was a problem for 13.6% of young adults with disabilities; 10.9% reported that they used their medications or drugs less often than they were supposed to because of the cost.

- In 2001, the majority of 15- to 19-year-olds were attending school full time regardless of whether they reported a disability — 76% for youth with a disability, 75.3% for non-disabled youth. There was, however, a significant difference between the school attendance for 20- to 24-year-olds who had a disability and those reporting no disability — 46.6% of non-disabled youth were attending school, while only 30.7% of youth reporting a disability were still attending school.

- Among the 19,730 young adults with a disability who aged between 15 and 19 and were not attending school full time, only 32.8% were employed, while 58.2% of their non-disabled peers were employed.

- For youth aged 20 to 24, the employment difference was even greater. Only 51.5% of youth aged 20 to 24 with a disability reported that they were employed, while 72.6% of non-disabled youth in this age group were employed. Even at this early age, youth with disabilities are not even attempting to look for work — a staggering 31.5% are neither employed nor looking for work. Contrast this to their non-disabled peers, where only 12.7% are not active labour force participants.

- There was little difference in the employment income reported by youth aged 15 to 19. Among those non-disabled youth who reported employment income in 2000 (58.2%), 12.9% reported employment income of $10,000 or more. For their peers with disabilities who reported employment income (43.3%), 10.6% reported that level of employment income.

- The differences became more pronounced between disabled and non-disabled youth aged 20 to 24. For the 85% of non-disabled youth in this age group who reported employment income, 10.5% earned $30,000 or more in 2000. Among the 65.3% of 20 to 20 year-olds with a disability who reported employment income in 2000, only 6.4% reported that level of income.

• Youth with disabilities are more likely to be part of a family whose income is classified by Statistics Canada as low income. Among youth aged 15 to 19 who reported a disability, 22.5% were a member of a low-income family. For non-disabled youth, only 15.9% were members of low-income families. For youth aged 20 to 24 who reported having a disability, 32.5% were members of a low-income family compared to only 22.1% of youth aged 20 to 24 who were not disabled.

Adults Aged 25 to 64

The rate of disability prevalence increases as age increases, and females have a slightly higher rate of disability across all of the five-year age groups between 25 and 64 (Table 2.3). Limitation in activity caused by pain was reported by 77.7% of adults aged 25 to 64, and it was the type of disability reported most often by all five-year age groups with this age range. Mobility and agility disabilities were reported by 74.9% and 71.6%, respectively, of adults in this broad age group. These two types of disabilities were also second

Table 2.3: Age-specific prevalence rates for adults with disability.

Age group	Males	Females
25–29	4.2	5.0
30–34	5.5	5.9
35–39	6.8	7.9
40–44	9.3	10.2
45–49	11.3	12.2
50–54	14.0	16.5
55–59	19.4	20.7
60–64	23.3	24.5
25–64	**10.8**	**11.9**

and third most often reported by each of the five-year age groups within this age range.

For young adults within this broad age group (ages 25 to 29 and 30 to 34), learning disabilities followed pain and problems with mobility agility in terms of the frequency reported — 29.8% and 25.9% respectively. For middle-aged adults (those aged 35 to 49), it was psychological disabilities (24.5% for persons aged 35 to 39, 26.7% for persons aged 40 to 44, and 24.7% for persons aged 45 to 49). For the older adults (those aged 50 to 64), it was hearing disabilities (26.3% for persons aged 50 to 54, 29.2% for persons aged 55 to 59, and 32.7% for persons aged 60 to 64).

A disability touches on all aspects of one's life. An adult with a disability is more likely to be living without a spouse and more likely to be living with his/her parents. The economic impact is significant. Not only do many more adults with disabilities have out-of-pocket expenses related to their disabilities, they also earn less, have lower family income and are more likely to live in a low-income family.

- Adults with disabilities across the broad age group (from 25 to 64) and within the five-year age groups (25 to 29, 30 to 34, etc.) included in the broad age group are more likely to be divorced than their non-disabled peers. Young adults with disabilities aged 25 to 29 are almost four times more likely to be divorced than their non-disabled peers; for the other five-year age groups, the ratio ranges from 1.5 more likely to twice as likely. Adults with disabilities are less likely to be married, with ratios ranging from 0.7 to 0.9.

- Adults with disabilities across the broad age group (25 to 64) and within the five-year age groups (25 to 29, 30 to 34, etc.) included in the broad age group are more likely to still be living with their parents than their non-disabled peers. The same holds true when one compares the proportion of disabled and non-disabled individuals living alone — the ratio ranges from a low of 1.1 for persons aged 25 to 29 to a high of 2.0 for persons aged 45 to 49. Being a lone parent is more likely for adults with disabilities than their non-disabled peers across all of the five-year age groups — for young adults with disabilities aged 25 to 29, the ratio is 3.1.

- Among adults with disabilities who aged 25 to 64, 31.4% do not have all of the support that they need to help them with their everyday activities. Among those who needed more help (571,045 adults), 64% stated that the help cost too much and they could not afford it, and 33.6% said that the help that they needed was not covered by insurance.

- Among adults with disabilities and aged 25 to 64, 22.6% reported that they needed more health care or access to social services, and that they did not get what they needed. Cost, again, was the primary factor; 45.9% stated that the help cost too much and they could not afford it, and 55.1% said that the help that they needed was not covered by insurance.

- Most adults enjoy a network of family and friends with whom they keep in touch. For most adults with disabilities, this is the case. However, talking on the telephone with family and friends is an activity that is rarely done, if ever, by 12.2% of adults with disabilities aged 25 to 64. Visiting family and friends is an activity that is rarely or never done by 16.9% of adults with disabilities. Shopping, an activity that seems to be a regular activity done by most adults, is rarely or never done by 14.3% of adults with disabilities.

- More than half (53.5% or 972,540) of the adults with disabilities would like to do more in their spare time. Among those, 41.4% say that what they would like to do costs too much; 6.4% stated that they need other aids and equipment to do so; 13.4% said that they would need someone's assistance and that that support is not available; and 12% stated that the transportation services available to take them out to these activities were either inadequate or not accessible.

- Regardless of age or gender, adults with disabilities are less likely to be employed than their non-disabled peers. This holds true for the youngest in this age group (those aged 25 to 29) as well as the oldest (those aged 60 to 64). For males aged 25 to 29, 83.7% of the non-disabled population are employed, while only 56.5% of young males with disabilities are employed. For females in this age group, the difference is less pronounced but exists nonetheless — 74% versus 61.8%). For males aged 60 to 64, 52.4% of the non-disabled population are employed, while only 25.7% of young males with disabilities are employed. For females in this age group, the difference is even greater — 33.1% versus 13.5%.

- The unemployment rate for male adults with disabilities is twice that of non-disabled male adults. This holds true for each of the five-year age groups up to and including the 45 to 49 age group. For females, the difference is less pronounced across all of the five-year age groups, but there still is a disparity.

- Many adults with disabilities are neither employed nor looking for work. This group includes those individuals who are concerned about losing all or some of their current income if they went to work.

- Just over eight of every ten (84.2%) non-disabled adults aged 25 to 64 reported having employment income in 2000, compared to just over half (52.8%) of adults with disabilities. Among those who reported employment income, 14.4% of the population with disabilities reported employment income of less than $5,000, while only 7.7% of their non-disabled peers reported this level of employment income. Almost half (46.9%) of the non-disabled population reported an employment income of $30,000 or more, while only 36.9% of the population with disabilities fell into this employment income bracket.

- Adults with disabilities are slightly more than twice as likely to be part of a family whose total family income is classified by Statistics Canada as low income. For the youngest in this age group (those aged 25 to 29) and for the oldest (those aged 60 to 64), the ratio is 1.6. For all of the other five-year age groups, the ratios exceed 2.1, with the highest being 2.7 for the age groups 45 to 49 and 50 to 54.

Adults Aged 65 and Older

As noted earlier, the 2001 PALS did not include individuals who were residents of institutions. While across all age groups this only accounts for 3% of the Canadian population, the exclusion is far more significant for seniors aged 85 and older. Institutions include senior residences and long-term care homes, and these types of facilities are home to 9% of males and 35.4% of females who are aged 85 and older.

Among those adults aged 65 and older who were living in private households at the time of the 2001 PALS interviews, slightly more females than males reported having a disability — 42% as compared to 38.5 (see Table 2.4). The disability rate increases rap-

Table 2.4: Age-specific prevalence ratio for seniors with disability.

Age group	% reporting disabilities	
	Male	Female
65–69	27.4	27.2
70–74	33.6	37.2
75–79	45.5	45.4
80–84	55.5	56.0
85 and older	69.3	71.8
65 and older	**38.5**	**42.0**

idly as age increases, going from just over one in four males and females reporting a disability who were aged 65 to 69 years to seven out of ten seniors aged 85 years and older.

Many seniors who report having a disability and who are living in the community need the support of others to assist them with their daily activities, and this need increases as age increases. Some do not have all of the support that they need. More seniors with disabilities live alone, and their contact with others is limited.

- Seniors with disabilities are more likely to live with other family members than non-disabled seniors — 9.5% versus 5.1%. This difference increases as age increases; for example, among young seniors (those aged 65 to 69), 6.2% with disabilities live with other family members, compared to 4.8% for non-disabled. Among the very old seniors (those aged 85 and older), the ratio is slightly more than double — 16.7% as compared to 8.3%.

- When total income for adults with disabilities and non-disabled adults are compared, one sees large differences between these two groups in the younger ages, but the gap narrows as the population ages. For example, comparing total income for persons aged 45 to 49, the percentage of non-disabled persons reporting a total income of less than $20,000 in 2000 was 28.3% as compared to 55.2% for the persons with disabilities. This same comparison for persons aged 70 to 74 is far less —

59.3% for non-disabled and 62.2% for disabled. This shows that seniors, regardless of disability status, live with lower total incomes.

- While most seniors who need help with everyday activities are getting all the help that they need, there are still some who have unmet needs — 5.5% need help, or more help, with everyday housework, 7.9% need help or more help with heavy housework and 6.6% need help or more help with running errands. Reasons given for not having all the help that is needed vary: 8.9% claimed that it is too expensive (8.9%); 4.4% said that they could not get it because it was not covered by insurance; and 3.9% said they did not know where to go to find the additional help that they needed.

- Among seniors with disabilities, 7.7% (112,395) reported that they needed additional health care or social services but they were not able to get what they needed. Reasons given by these 112,395 seniors for not getting this care included services not covered by insurance (37.9%) and cost (43.9%).

- There were 2.8% of seniors with disabilities feel that they have no control over the decisions made concerning their everyday activities. This percentage increases as age increases from less than 1% of seniors aged 65 to 69 reporting this lack of control to 5.3% among seniors aged 85 and older.

- About 24.2% of seniors would like to do more activities. Of those 351,605 seniors who would like to do more, 77.9% reported that they cannot do more because of their health condition(s), 26.9% said they could do more but they need another person's help and that help is not available, 19.9% reported that transportation services were either not available or inadequate, and 25.7% reported that the activities that they wanted to do were too expensive.

- Many seniors are isolated, having little contact with family or friends — 8.5% report that they never or less than once a month talk with family or friends on the telephone; 28% report that they never or less than once a month visit with family or friends; 62.7% report that they never or less than once a month play cards or bingo outside the home; and 20.1% report that they never or less than once a month go shopping.

CONCLUSION

The 2001 PALS paints a portrait of the lives of Canadians with dis-abilities and identifies barriers to full participation in the commu-nity. Improvement or lack of progress cannot be calculated because a comparative set of data does not exist. If the 2006 PALS uses the same questions as the 2001 PALS, analyses will be able to identify change over a five-year period. Ideally, data on disability should be part of the data regularly collected by Statistics Canada.

3

Portraits of Disability in National Surveys

MARY ANN McCOLL

INTRODUCTION

We are fortunate in Canada to have a wealth of population-based information about people with disabilities for use by policy-makers, researchers and advocates. There is a remarkable storehouse of national, provincial and regional level data available to Canadian researchers to study a variety of issues and conditions associated with disability. Some of these data are available in public access files, and can be readily obtained at no cost. Other data sets require secure premises, security checks for users, and extensive processes of permission and authorization. This chapter focuses on the former — public access databases.

Analysis of the disability policy-making process in Canada suggests that research data is one of a number of sources of evidence used by the policy community (Boyce et al., 2001). However, in order to effectively use the available data to the best advantage, we need to understand the caveats of the data-based approach, the

limitations of the data source and the generalizability of the findings. In this chapter, we address three objectives:

1. To examine definitions of disability used in national, population-level survey data;
2. To compare the characteristics of disabled people and the
   portrait of disability according to each survey;
3. To discuss policy and service implications of subscription to
   different definitions of disability.

BACKGROUND

The first issue in examining population-level databases for their
ability to contribute to policy is the need to know to whom the
data are referring. In other words, when the data refer to people
with disabilities, whom do they include? Prior to any methodological discussion of how disabled people were sampled or how accessible the data-gathering approach was, we must be clear what we
mean by disability. When we make a statement based on the data
about what disabled people do or do not do, what their preferences
are, or what conditions characterize them, we must be clear about
who we are talking about.

The definition of disability has undergone a fascinating and
contentious period of development over the past 40 years. Numerous authors have discussed different definitions of disability, and
argued for the benefits of one over another (Donoghue, 2003;
McColl & Bickenbach, 1998; Michaelakis, 2003; Roulstone, 2003).
However, all agree that the biomedical definition that held sway
prior to the 1970s is limited in its application beyond the health
care environment, for which it was intended. More modern definitions of disability have recognized the full spectrum of disabled
people's participation in society, and have not restricted consideration to the underlying impairment or health condition. Instead
they have located the origin of disability partially or wholly outside
of the individual; that is, in the environment, in a society built to
serve the average or majority mode of moving, thinking, understanding, sensing and reacting. This definition is typically associated
with the social model of disability. However, the social model has
recently also been criticized. Dewsbury and colleagues claim that
the social model merely replaces the biomedical discourse with a
sociological discourse, and still fails to deal with the real issues facing people with disabilities, such as housing, employment and
human rights (Dewsbury et al., 2004).

The current gold standard for defining disability, according to several commentators, is WHO's 2001 definition (Chatterji, Ustun & Bickenbach, 1999; Mehlmann & Neuhauser, 1999). The ICF published by WHO in 2001 defines disability as a component of health (rather than a consequence of disease), a determinant of health or a risk factor. It is an umbrella term for impairments, activity limitations and participation restrictions (WHO, 2001a, p. 3). This definition incorporates two ideas: that disability is associated with health, and that it manifests as activity limitations and participation restrictions.

It also includes a number of other ideas that are beginning to permeate the consciousness of health professionals, researchers, policy-makers and, perhaps more slowly, the public. For example, the WHO definition incorporates some aspects of the social construction of disability — in other words, the idea that disability is not an objective biomedical reality, but rather a product of our culture and social institutions. On the other hand, the WHO definition, because of its reliance on the presence of a diagnosable health condition, has been accused of "unrelenting positivism" and "naïve realism" (Michaelakis, 2003; Roulstone, 2003). Some authors believe that by placing the definition of disability in the realm of health, it unnecessarily limits the scope of disability, and perpetuates the biomedical culture that has historically applied the sick role to people with disabilities and treated them as a segregated minority group.

This debate has important implications for measurement and data collection on disability. For example, is it appropriate in survey data to ask people with disabilities about specific health conditions, and to make assumptions about the relationship of those conditions to disability? Even more fundamental, is information about health conditions and activity limitation a suitable indicator of population levels of disability? Should we depend on individuals as the source of information about disability, or should data about disability focus on the structures and institutions that socially construct our potentially disabling society? Should disability information be collected at a higher level of analysis, such as the community, the health region or the legislative jurisdiction?

Another feature of the WHO definition is its resistance to the notion that disability is a minority concern. Instead it casts disability as a universal concern of varying degrees (Chatterji, Ustun & Bickenbach, 1999). This idea also has important implications for data collection about disability. Historically, disability has been treated dichotomously by survey methodologists. On the basis of a screening question (or series of questions), individuals are classified as either having a disability or not having one (Cwikel, 1999; Mehlman & Neuhauser, 1999; Joslyn, 1999). As was mentioned above, many Canadian national surveys contain a data field that acts as a screen or flag for disability. However, this approach has been criticized for inaccuracy and misrepresentation of disability. The Canadian Council on Social Development (CCSD, 2001) contends that this threshold approach grossly underestimates the presence of disability, while Cwikel (1999) and Chatterji and colleagues (1999) argue the opposite. Mehlmann and Neuhauser (1999) advocate instead for an ordinal approach to measurement; that is, one that recognizes that there are varying degrees of disability, not simply its presence or absence.

While it is almost impossible to marshal a credible argument against the ordinal approach, the reality faced by people with disabilities in interacting with social institutions is the dichotomous approach. The dichotomous approach responds not to the heterogeneity of disability, but rather to the dichotomy of the policy response — for example, pension/no pension; service/no service; benefit/no benefit. People with disabilities are repeatedly required to fulfill eligibility requirements, to seek the label of disability, in order to qualify for program and policy entitlements. Thus, the dichotomous approach pervades the reality of Canadian social and political institutions and, therefore, must be dealt with and understood if it is to be administered fairly and equitably, and ultimately if it is to be changed.

PORTRAITS OF DISABILITY

In this chapter, I have sought to understand what existing data tell us about living with a disability in Canadian society, and how those data and their interpretations vary depending on how the questions are asked. To that end, public access data files on five national surveys spanning 10 years were obtained from Statistics Canada through the Social Science Data Centre at Queen's University in Kingston, Ontario:

- The 1991 HALS;
- The 1994 General Social Survey (GSS);
- The 1997 Canada Elections Survey (CES);
- The 1998–1999 National Population Health Survey (NPHS); and
- The 2001 PALS.

The 1991 HALS and its successor, the 2001 PALS, are arguably the international gold standard for disability data. At the time that the HALS was initially conceived and administered, there was no other country in the world that attempted population-based data collection on disability, conforming to the WHO definition of disability. Table 3.1 gives more information about the specific objectives of each of the five surveys.

The sample from each survey consisted of all respondents between 20 and 64 years of age. The 20–64 age range was chosen in order to capture adult disability, and to avoid mixing those with disabilities acquired in old age.

Table 3.2 shows the number of disabled people and the sampling proportion of each survey. It can be readily seen from the table that sample sizes varied dramatically across surveys, from 207 on the CES to more than 18,000 on the HALS. In all instances, sampling weights were applied to correct for sampling proportions, as recommended in the survey documentation. Sampling weights are intended to increase the generalizability of findings to the Canadian population, and are used in all subsequent analyses.

Sampling strategies differed by survey, as shown in Table 3.1. There are a number of particular factors to note when assessing sampling strategy. First, it is important to note if the sampling strategy targets the entire population (e.g., census) or particular geographic clusters. Second, it is important to note how respondents were sampled — as individuals or households. Finally, it should be noted if there were particular exclusions in a sampling frame. For example, the NPHS excluded Aboriginal reserves, Armed Forces, remote areas, and the three northern territories. The CES only included Canadian citizens over the age of 18. Most notably, the HALS and PALS were population-based surveys, since they accompanied the census. All of the others used a cluster sampling technique.

The primary variable of interest is the classification of disability and the underlying definition or construction of disability implied by the operational definition used in the survey. Table 3.1 shows the actual screening questions used in each of the surveys to classify individuals as disabled or not. While very similar, the questions contain some combination of four elements:

- Presence of a long-term disability or handicap;
- Limitation in kind or amount of activity;
- Presence of a physical condition, mental condition or health condition; and

Table 3.1: Description of the five surveys.

	Purpose	Sample	Definition of disability
HALS ('91)	"… to collect data on the nature and severity of disabilities; barriers that persons with disabilities face; the use of and need for assistive devices; and the out-of-pocket expenses related to disability"	Census–based, individually mailed, subsequent telephone survey	"Are you limited in the kind or amount of activity you can do because of a long-term physical condition, mental condition or mental problem … at home, at school, at work or at other activities"; "Do you have a long-term disability or handicap?"
GSS ('94)	"… to gather data on social trends in order to monitor temporal changes in the living conditions and well-being of Canadians."	Household telephone survey, random digit dialing (RDD), all persons >15 years	"Are you limited in the amount of activity done at home?"
CES ('97)	"… to collect information on vote intention and party identification, interest in election, knowledge and rating of parties and leaders"	Household, telephone, RDD, Canadian citizens >18 years, probability sampling within household	"Do you have any long-term disability or handicap?"
NPHS ('98–'99)	"… to collect information related to the health of the Canadian population."	Labour Force sampling frame, household, telephone, cluster sample	"Are you limited in the kind or amount of activity you can do because of a long-term physical condition, mental condition or mental problem … at home, at school, at work or at other activities"; "Do you have a long-term disability or handicap?"
PALS ('01)	"… to provide essential information on the prevalence of various disabilities, the supports for persons with disabilities, their employment, income and participation in society."	Same as HALS	"Does a physical condition, mental condition or health problem reduce the amount or the kind of activity you can do at home? At school/work? In other activities (transportation or leisure)?"

Table 3.2: Proportion of sample classified as disabled.

	GSS ('94)	NPHS ('98–'99)	HALS ('91)	PALS ('01)	CES ('97)
Disabled-unweighted	16.2	15.6%	31.4	27.2	6.9
(n)	(7,156)	(1,703)	(18,384)	(20,710)	(207)
Disabled-weighted	14.5	14.5	14.1	9.6	6.3
Non-disabled-weighted	85.5	85.5	85.9	89.4	93.7

- Location of limitation — home, school, work, or other (e.g., transportation).

Prevalence of Disability

The most basic implication of the definition of disability used in population survey research is the proportion classified as disabled based on that definition. Table 3.2 shows that the prevalence of disability varied significantly between the five surveys used, with CES having the smallest proportion of disabled individuals (6%), PALS showing about 10%, and GSS, HALS and NPHS all being approximately 14%. The table is organized by increasing prevalence from left to right. It does not appear that a temporal trend exists to explain these differences. The very low prevalence on the CES is surprising, given that the sampling frame and question construction were similar to the other surveys. It may be that the method of probability sampling within households somehow systematically decreased the likelihood of participation for disabled household members. In any case, the small sample for the CES makes the estimates produced less stable and less reliable than those from the other surveys.

The remainder of the analyses presented focus on the group labelled as disabled in each of the surveys of interest. Table 3.3 compares the information provided about the types of **impairments and activity limitations** experienced by respondents who self-identified as having a disability. The most notable observation about the table is the dramatic differences that occur from survey to survey. Whereas more than half of the disabled respondents on both HALS and PALS reported mobility impairments, less than 10% of

43

Table 3.3: Impairments and activity restrictions (in %).

	HALS ('91)	CES ('97)	NPHS ('98–'99)	PALS ('01)
IMPAIRMENTS				
Cognitive/Learning	31.5		36.6	35.3
Emotional	26.1		8.5	
Hearing	25.8	4.8	5.3	24.3
Mobility	55.1	43.6	9.9	69.1
Seeing	9.6	10.1	3.9	15.2
Agility/Dexterity	52.8	13.6	3.5	64.8
Speaking	6.7		2.0	11.4
Pain			50.9	77.7
Other		27.7		
ACTIVITY RESTRICTIONS				
Heavy Housework	65.2		44.7	13.0
Meal Preparation	49.6		9.4	2.5
Housework	28.1		19.3	7.3
Shopping for Necessities	24.2		15.4	3.1
Personal Care	4.9		4.5	1.3
Moving about Indoors	2.2		5.3	0.6

respondents on the NPHS reported these types of problems. Pain was reported by over half the respondents in the two instances where it was directly asked (PALS and NPHS). Cognitive and learning disabilities were consistently reported by about 35% of the disabled participants (except on the CES, where this impairment was not addressed).

With regard to **activity limitations**, the same six questions were asked on PALS, NPHS and HALS. Respondents on all three surveys agreed that the most troublesome activities were instrumental activities of daily living, especially heavy chores, like yard work, home maintenance and snow shoveling. Personal care and mobility difficulties affected less than 5% of those who included themselves among the disabled population.

Three of the surveys asked about **self-assessed health** — PALS, NPHS and GSS. Figure 3.1 compares the results of these sur-

Figure 3.1: Proportion of sample in various states of self-reported health.

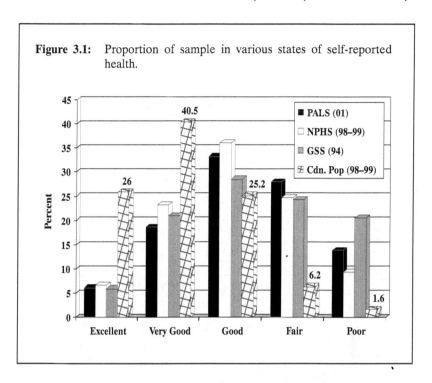

veys, including the general Canadian population rates derived from NPHS. The general population, shown by the "checkered" bars, has a curve that is highly skewed to the right, with over 90% rating their health between good and excellent, and a mode in the very good range. The disabled populations on all three surveys were more inclined to rate their health poorly. The modal response for disabled people was good heath, rather than very good health.

Demographic Characteristics

Table 3.4 compares the gender distribution of disabled samples on all five surveys. The HALS and CES show the most extreme and, interestingly, opposite distributions of males and females. Most of the surveys show the disabled population being dominated by women, with the exception of the CES, which shows a preponderance of males.

Figure 3.2 looks at the age distribution of the disabled samples on the five surveys; that is, the proportion in each age group within the disabled sample. Most notable in this figure is the fact that

Table 3.4: Gender.

	HALS (91)	PALS (01)	NPHS (98–99)	GSS (94)	CES (97)
Males	43.1	44.6	46.1	47.3	54.9
Females	56.9	55.4	53.9	52.7	45.1

Figure 3.2: Proportion of population in each age group.

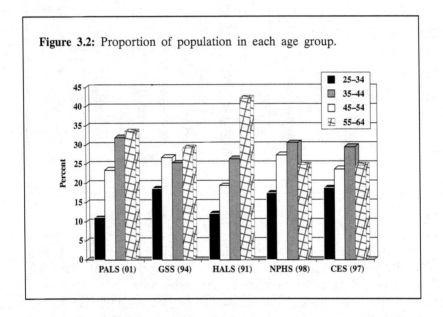

there are two distinct shapes of the age distribution curve. For the PALS, GSS and HALS, the shape of the curve is as expected — the prevalence of disability increases with age, with the mode in the highest age group. However, for the NPHS and CES, the mode is in the 45–54 age range, suggesting that there is a drop off in the prevalence of disability after about 50 years of age. This finding warrants further exploration.

Socio-economic Characteristics

Table 3.5 provides information about education, income and employment for people with disabilities in the five surveys. With

Table 3.5: Educational attainment, employment and household income (in %).

	HALS (91)	GSS (94)	CES† (97)	NPHS (98–99)	PALS (2001)
EDUCATIONAL ATTAINMENT					
Less than secondary	45.7	35.5	33.6	23.9	17.2
Graduated secondary	13.0	15.9	23.3	14.9	15.7
Some post-secondary	34.9	12.2	28.6	29.4	28.5
University/College degree	6.5	36.3	14.6	31.8	38.5
EMPLOYMENT					
Employed	47.9	49.5	41.9	55.1	69.1
Unemployed	7.5	5.4	15.6	7.8	5.0
Not in labour force	44.6	45.1	42.4	37.1	25.9
school		4.5	3.4		6.9
housekeeping		18.8	7.8		13.3
retired		7.3	14.1		3.5
disabled		14.2	17.1		2.2
INCOME					
< $10,000	38.3	10.5	36.8	6.8	4.1
$10–$19,000	21.3	13.4	36.8	14.3	9.0
$20–$29,000	15.6	16.3	15.8	12.7	10.6
$30–$39,000	24.8	15.1	5.3	13.9	13.8
$40–$49,000	24.8	15.2	23.7	12.0	13.2
$50–$59,000	24.8	10.4	7.9	8.9	11.6
> $60,000	24.8	19.0	10.5	31.4	37.7

† CES has small cell sizes, estimates may be unstable.

regard to educational attainment, between 25 and 45% of respondents report not having completed high school, and only between 40 and 60% attained any post-secondary education, compared to about 70% in the general Canadian population. Again, the explanation of a temporal trend cannot be invoked to explain these findings. Much as we might have hoped that access to higher education had improved for people with disabilities in recent decades, these results do not show a steady increase in either secondary or post-secondary educational attainment. They do, however, show a steady decrease in the proportion who do not complete high school.

The surveys are fairly consistent that employment hovered somewhere around the 50% mark for people with disabilities in Canada in the decade between 1991 and 2001. Unemployment varies between 5 (close to the population norm) and 15% over the five surveys, while the number reported as not in the labour market declined over the period. With regard to income, the surveys agree that people with disabilities are over-represented at the low end of the scale, and under-represented at the high end.

DISCUSSION

In summary, when we compare the descriptive information about the disabled population in Canada afforded by the five surveys, several similarities emerged:

- All agreed that the prevalence of disability was, on average, between 10 and 15%;
- With the exception of the CES, the surveys showed that disability is consistently more prevalent among women;
- People with disabilities were less likely to have post-secondary education and more likely to lack a completed high school education;
- There was a lower percentage of people with disabilities in the labour force; and
- People with disabilities were generally over-represented in the low-income categories.

However, the surveys were also dissimilar in a number of respects, such as the prevalence of particular impairments in the disabled population.

- Whereas several of the surveys showed the disabled population having about half of its members with physical disabilities (HALS, CES and PALS), the NPHS showed that the most prevalent conditions were pain and learning disabilities. Generally, prevalence of particular impairments was high on the disability-related surveys, and low on the NPHS.

- There is some interesting variation between surveys in the relationship of age to disability within the adult population.

- There were also differences in self-reported health, with the GSS (a survey not focused on health) reporting poorer self-reported health among the disabled population than the NPHS.

- The importance of particular activity restrictions also varied between samples, with HALS generally reporting higher values than the NPHS.

- Finally, there were differences between surveys on the extent of socio-economic disadvantage. HALS portrays the bleakest scenario, with significantly more of the population in the low-income groups, while NPHS and PALS report the most favourable portrait, with only slightly smaller percentages in the high income groups than the Canadian population as a whole.

While the different portraits of disability depicted by each of these surveys are important conceptually, they become crucial when we realize that decisions about service and policy may be based on these numbers, and the impressions and assumptions that accompany them. In the final section of this chapter, I offer several examples of the ways that the data associated with these varying portraits of the disabled population might affect policy and the delivery of goods and services to people with disabilities in Canada. I offer both positive and negative implications for three types of policy issues: access to health services, income replacement/employment and human rights. These three policy areas were chosen for their relevance to people with disabilities.

Access to Health Services

Those portraits of disability that give detailed information on impairment and illness, when applied to health service and policy, have the advantage of promoting a high degree of attention and specificity to health issues for people with disabilities. Data derived from the HALS and the NPHS offer detailed information to health planners for the development and evaluation of health services that meet specific needs of disabled Canadians.

However, on the negative side, this same emphasis on underlying health conditions is the very feature for which the biomedical definition of disability has been roundly criticized in recent years. The medicalization of disability has served to distance professionals from people with disabilities, focus on limitations rather than potentialities, and undermine the political power of people with disabilities. By reducing every concern to one of medical diagnosis and treatment, the opportunities for full participation of people with disabilities in Canadian society are limited to their participation in the health care system.

A focus on economic issues, on the other hand, also provides information that guides policy relating to access to health services, such as resources available to individuals with disabilities to respond to out-of-pocket service costs, extra-billing, costs of adaptive equipment and supplies, and opportunity costs due to lost productivity. To the extent that people with disabilities are economically disadvantaged, they are in a poor position to absorb these costs and to access services that require out-of-pocket expenditures. Despite the federal disability tax credit, which is intended to compensate for extraordinary costs associated with the disability, non-insured health costs represent an undue hardship on those who need the services most but are least able to pay.

By focusing on poverty and unemployment in the disabled population, one is able to derive a true picture of the potential vulnerability of disabled people as regards the social determinants of health. In addition to the impairment-based health problems the person experiences, there may also be socially derived problems that have health consequences. Thus, an economic approach to access to health services for the disabled people may magnify the complexity of health issues in this population and, hopefully, result in more expedient and timely access.

Finally, also on the negative side, the focus on economic issues may underestimate the need for service, by inadequately describing the complex health picture of people with disabilities. It may provide insufficient data to plan services that address the complex, multi-dimensional health and social problems that people with disabilities often face. I will discuss this issue further in my chapter on access to health services (Chapter 19).

Income Replacement

The data provided in the surveys agree that people with disabilities are typically disadvantaged economically, but disagrees about the extent of that disadvantage. A broad range of services and policies exist at both the federal and provincial levels, as well as in the public and private sectors, to provide economic benefits to people with disabilities, and to ensure equity in the workplace. For most of these programs and benefits, a crucial issue is the establishment of eligibility. As seen in the preceding discussion, the data differ substantially both on the biomedical and socio-economic parameters that might be drawn upon to establish eligibility.

Dependence on biomedical information for developing and implementing economic policy may have the advantage of offering a degree of specificity to the establishment of eligibility. In addition, it may shine some light not only on the physical problems, but also on problems of an emotional or cognitive nature. Instead of focusing exclusively on observable and diagnosable conditions, the information from the surveys appears to take greater consideration of important issues like pain and learning difficulties.

On the other hand, the focus on a broad definition of disability — one that includes invisible and less easily defined disabilities — has the potential also to limit economic considerations. If the broader definition results in a considerably higher prevalence of disability, it may mean that a finite resource pool has to be shared among many more people. Larger numbers of potential beneficiaries make the prospect of income replacement appear very costly indeed, and may decrease both political and public support for these programs. Further, the more inclusive definition of disability means that the pool of recipients represents a broader range of need, and thus schedules of benefits need to be more complex and detailed in order to ensure fair distribution of resources so as to meet the needs of the neediest.

If policy-makers were to focus on economic indicators associated with disability for policy around income replacement, there would at least be the advantage of focusing attention where it belongs. The economic indicators of disability argue that there are systematic inequities in Canadian society that specifically disadvantage people with disabilities. Income replacement programs are one of a variety of strategies designed to redress these inequities. On the negative side, however, the economic approach is sometimes seen as portraying competitive employment as the only legitimate productive goal, to which all should strive. To those for whom competitive employment is not a realistic outcome, this approach may be experienced as promoting two classes of citizens. Furthermore, the focus on low employment among people with disabilities may also have a negative outcome, in that the adult disabled population may become stereotyped with low expectations of productive capacity and economic independence. In some political climates, society invests in adults in order to return them to productive employment and active taxpayer status. A perception that people with disabilities are not typically employable could lead to a general undervaluing of the population, and a subsequent reluctance to invest in their needs.

Human Rights

The portrayal of disability in the five surveys also has the potential to impact the consideration of human rights issues. Looking exclusively at the biomedical indicators, the data have the advantage of legitimizing claims for consideration by lending to them the authority conferred by medical validation. In our society, medical testimonials and expert opinions are virtually incontrovertible sources of evidence of the need for consideration. However, the price of this support is the necessity to adopt the "sick role" and to become a "patient", rather than a citizen with full rights and participation.

If instead we consider economic and social descriptors of disability available from the surveys, the data provide a clear indication of inequities in rights-based sectors like education. This focus on socio-economic inequities, rather than personal characteristics, is consistent with a citizenship approach to service entitlements, rather than a charitable or biomedical approach. It assumes a structural level of analysis of social inequities, rather than a personal level. On the negative side, however, it provides little guidance in terms of the types of accommodations needed or the particular problems faced by people with disabilities.

CONCLUSION

In summary, this chapter has used data from five national surveys to describe and compare portrayals of the disabled community in Canada. We have noted that each of the five surveys provides a slightly different picture of disabled Canadians. We have discussed the positive and negative aspects of each of these portrayals for three areas of policy and service that are of particular concern to people with disabilities: access to health services, income replacement and human rights.

These analyses have shown the power of data to create a portrait, and the importance of that portrait for subsequent decisions about access to goods and services. They have emphasized the need to understand the underlying assumptions upon which data are collected and the methodological decisions that flow from those assumptions. While evidence-based positions are arguably the strongest form of advocacy, it is essential to understand the sources and conditions under which data were collected in order to most effectively marshal a case or present an argument. Hopefully, these analyses have shown that different cases can be made on a variety of issues, all on the basis of high quality, national population-based data. This chapter emphasizes both the benefits and the caveats of evidence-based advocacy.

What then is recommended to those wishing to make the situation of disabled Canadians more advantageous and equitable? First and foremost, I recommend using the abundant, high-quality data that exist. Second, I recommend using these data with a degree of knowledge and sophistication, an awareness of their inherent strengths and limitations. Third, I recommend a healthy level of skepticism when examining numbers that are meant to characterize the situation of people with disabilities. The chapter has shown how variable these numbers can be, and the necessity of understanding them relative to conditions of sampling, definition and question construction around disability. Finally, I recommend using multiple sources of data for the fullest possible picture of the conditions of life for people with disabilities in Canadian society.

4

Policy, Disability, Reciprocity?

TANYA TITCHKOSKY

We interpret, therefore we are. (Iser, 2000, p. 1)

Texts and ... relations [disability policy] must be explored as they are 'in action' and constitute media of action. Their conceptual dimensions must be held ... as 'organizers' packaged in texts that transmit 'organization' invented in one site of ruling to multiple sites, regulating the local activities of particular people. (Smith, 1999, p. 93)

INTRODUCTION

Policy texts and our reading of them are a form of interpretation. Interpretation is a social activity through which our conceptions and relations to each other are built. Interpretation is the form of social action that this chapter analyzes. My aim is to uncover the active social character of policy texts on physical, mental and sensory disability issues. I ask: How do policy texts on disability regulate readers' conceptions of disability? In order to explore what policy *does to* conceptions of disability, and what conceptions of disability *do to* policy, I make use of recent Canadian government documents that textually package disability issues. This chapter then considers the issue of reciprocity. Given that we are interpretive beings, we have a chance to influence the productive force of policy by critically attending to what it is making of us.

TEXTS IN CANADIAN DISABILITY POLICY

Texts are action, thus active. Texts do not merely talk about the world; they are also part of the world. Dorothy Smith suggests above that texts act upon readers and so, through reading, meaning is made. Texts organize experience even in simple ways such as serving to call out to readers, "Pay attention to this. This is interesting." Still, texts don't make sense on their own — they need readers and writers to make them sensible. The sensibility of the text is a form of social action that occurs between the text and the reader, and this includes policy texts and the readers of those texts.

Texts are active, thus sensible. Texts are made sensible through the transmission of conceptual organization. For example, we can read many things about disability: policy documents regarding disability rates and disability issues; texts promoting disability initiatives and practices; or texts reporting on the progress of these initiatives and practices. Our reading is made possible by having a concept of disability. Text relies on and reproduces such conceptions, turning on and tuning in to a regulated form of social organization of "disability".

One primary activity of the Canadian government in relation to disability is policy-text production and its distribution. As many authors in this collection make clear, the history of the textual packaging of disability is complex. Since the *Obstacles* (Canada, 1981) were charted, a *National Strategy* (Canada, 1991) has been announced and the *Will to Act* (Canada, 1996) established. The government of Canada has also provided a "vision" for federal, provincial and local governments to work *In Unison* (Canada, 1998) toward the full participation of citizens with disabilities; that vision, put into the shape of a "blueprint" (Canada, 2000a), has been followed up by an account of best practices and a *Strategic Plan 2002–2007* (Office for Disability Issues [ODI], 2002) for its implementation. Surrounded by numerous background documents and reports, all of these textual orderings of disability culminate in *Advancing the Inclusion of Persons with Disabilities* (HRDC, 2002a, [hereafter called *Advancing*]), which proclaims:

> This first [sic] comprehensive report on disability in Canada describes where our country has made progress, how the Government of Canada has contributed, and where work remains to be done. (p. 2)

It is this *Advancing* document, its surrounding literature, and data presentations that I analyze in this chapter. Elsewhere, I (Titchkosky, 2002, 2003a, 2003b) have addressed how the documents published prior to *Advancing* are governing our ways of conceptualizing embodiment. Here, I turn my attention to documents produced in 2002–2003 and released by 2004 that explicitly address disability policy issues. *Advancing* appears as the culmination of much policy activity and it also claims to represent future policy initiatives: "where work remains to be done". *Advancing*, and its surrounding materials, allows us the opportunity to unpack the conceptions of disability that not only inform the production of the document, but also regulate the meaning of disability for readers.

Policy as Social Action

Exploring what policy *does to* conceptions of disability, and what conceptions of disability *do to* policy requires us to conceive of policy (like we would any text) as a form of "social action".

Max Weber (1947) says that "[a]ction is social insofar as, by virtue of the subjective meaning attached to it by the acting individual(s), it takes account of the behavior of others and is thereby oriented in its course" (p. 88). Policy takes into account, and orients to, the meaning that can be attached to disability. Policy thereby orients readers, asking us to think about disability in particular ways. Treating text as social action means resisting the idea that policy is merely the basis, or plan, or preparatory sketch for future activities. Policy — its words, plans, ideas; that is, its sensibility — makes an appearance in our lives. Policy appears in social life by acting upon that life. Regardless of what a policy text claims that it might eventually implement, its existence influences the here and now by packaging our relations to disability.

Understanding policy as a form of social action is not the same as documenting the historical or ideological generation of policy, nor is it the same as attempting to predict a policy's potential worth, nor is it the same as agreeing or disagreeing with it. Conceiving of policy as a form of socially "organized discursive-action" (Foucault, 1977, 1978) means uncovering how it gives rise to and depends upon particular conceptions of disability as we read it. Even if policy plans for programs and practices never come to pass, or never realize anything new, the social fact remains that policy has generated a conception of disability. Policy interprets disability, thereby giving readers a version of what it is and is not. The consequences of this definitional process are important to consider since we are today living with these conceptions.

Through policy, conceptions of disability become part of our lives, and the ways we live with these conceptions are connected to future policy development and implementation. One way to live self-reflexively with policy as a form of social action is to ask, "What does this policy say disability *is*?", or, "How does this policy provide an answer to the question: Who am I?" These questions are everyone's questions insofar as all people (disabled or not) live in relation to conceptions of disability, and how we do so has something to teach us about who we are both individually and collectively.

The government of Canada too is aware that there are differing conceptual models through which disability policy is forged, e.g., "medical", "functional", or "Social and Human Rights" models (Canada, 2003a, p. 38). Like the rest of us, the government lives with its conception(s) of disability. For example, the government is making note of these different conceptions of disability as if there are no major conflicts among them. However, identifying the ideological model that policy represents is not enough since what is made of disability is always more than the model in which the making is done.

Henri-Jacque Stiker says in *A History of Disability* (1999), "We are always other than what society made us and believes us to be" (p. 51). Policy based on, for example, a medical model of disability acts on people's lives. This activity asserts, yet again, the sense in which a medicalized conception of disability is legitimated. Individuals must live with the sense in which disability is repetitively conceived of as nothing other than a negative (medical) condition of lack, e.g., "a physical or mental condition or impairment that restricts them in their ability to perform activities that are normal..." (HRDC, 2002a, p. 73). This conception enters people's lives. But nobody can be fully contained by the singular reductive packaging of disability as a medical issue of lack, limit, and restriction. People must interpret and live with the fact that they have been defined medically; people must live with the fact that it is part of common-sense reasoning to conceive of disability as nothing other than a problematic condition of restriction. People also live with the fact that they are other than, or more than, what society makes and believes people to be. *

Perceiving policy as a form of social action means orienting to the present tense; it is to uncover the dimensions of the concept of disability as we read policy texts, situated where we find ourselves in everyday life. Such an orientation means understanding that anything stated about disability in a policy document is an organizer of our experience of disability, yet one conception is never able to assume total control over the meaning of disability. Policy as social action takes place in the midst of social actors reading these texts, and in between readers and text the potential unpredictable "spark" of new meaning can arise (Asenjo, 1988, p. 62; McRuer, 2003; Titchkosky, 2003a, p. 217).

This possibility of something new means that there must be a kind of active reciprocity between bureaucratically informed policy-texts and readers. The fact that disability is surrounded by *both* texts and readers means that the relation between them is helping to constitute ways to conceive of disability as something for thought and action. Guided by the question, "What are we making of policy as it makes something of us?", I turn now to a particular text. I use *Advancing the Inclusion of Persons with Disabilities* and surrounding documents in order to examine the powers of these policy statements to produce a version of disability.

Policy Activity as Productive Power

Obstacles, *Will to Act*, *In Unison*, and the rest of the policy documents previously referred to, demonstrate that much of the work of the government, especially as it pertains to disability, is text mediated. Indeed, *Advancing* provides a "Chronology of Legislation and Initiatives" (p. 71). The majority of the initiatives are documents for public consumption. Among different government agencies, such as HRDC, Statistics Canada, Canada Customs, etc., there are differing conceptions of disability set out in policy and/or displayed through procedure. Putting disability into text is an interesting social fact involving the activity of conceptualizing and defining disability. Thus, Len Barton (1998) repeatedly suggests that it is important to be interested in how "... disability is defined, by whom, in what contexts and with what consequences" (p. 88).

Advancing (pp. 10–11) tells us that defining disability is "not an easy task", and that it is also "... important to distinguish between definitions and eligibility criteria ...". A variety of definitions, criteria, forms and medical certificates mediate the relationship the government has with people who may or may not be deemed to be a "person with a disability". Qualifying for disability supports or services most typically involves demonstrating one's embodied reflection of one of the many conceptions of disability at work in any particular government department, agency, or ministry. More-over, writing and reading about this difficulty itself produces a con-ception of disability as difficulty.

Disability as a "definitional difficulty" is mentioned in many government documents. This is especially the case in the publica-tion of the 1998 *In Unison: A Canadian Approach to Disability Issues*. *In Unison* (Canada, 1998) made use of an oversimplified definition of disability and made it appear as if the whole of the government followed WHO's definition of disability: "Any restric-tion or inability to perform an activity in the manner or within the range considered normal for a human being" (p. 33). It has since become obvious to the government that this is not the only concep-tion or model of disability at work. Thus *Advancing* (p. 10) says "... no single definition can cover all disabilities...." The government now believes that their conception of disability "goes beyond a medical approach" (p. 11) since, alongside their medical definition of disability, they also make use of the new framework of the ICF established by WHO in 2001. At the same time, some people engaged in disability studies scholarship and activism have made it clear that any use of the WHO definition should be questioned since it "... identifies impairment as the determining factor in explaining disability ..." (Barnes, 1998, p. 67; Barnes & Oliver, 1995; Oliver, 1996; Williams, 1998). Treating impairment as the defining feature of disability ignores the power of social life to con-stitute the meaning of people while producing the illusion that dis-ability is an individual issue.

Still, there has been growing public interest in definitional debate, as well as changes in survey methodology at both the national and international levels, and there are shifts in who is and is not to be served by existing programs. All these, combined with a host of other factors, led the government of Canada to decide, in response to The House of Commons Standing Committee on Human Resources Development and the Status of Persons with Disabilities (HRDC, 2002a, p. 11), to document the different bases and biases of these conflicting definitions of disability (see also, *A Common Vision*). The resulting publication, *Defining Disability: A Complex Issue* (Canada, 2003a, [hereafter, *Defining*]), concludes that

> [d]isability is a multi-dimensional concept with both objective and
> subjective characteristics. A single harmonized 'operational' defi-
> nition of disability across federal programs may not be desirable
> or achievable. And, the scope of solutions to address the broader
> issues identified [goes] beyond definitions. (p. 44)

This conclusion asks the reader to go beyond definition since
the issue of seeking a harmonized definition of disability is dis-
satisfying and, thus, uninteresting. However, going beyond definition prevents us from exploring how disability *is* being defined
and packaged and how this packaging powerfully organizes current
relations to disability. So, let us return to the text itself in order
to understand the ways in which this policy statement is a productive power packaging the meaning of disability in the here and
now.

Regardless of whether it is desirable to have a single harmonized operational definition, or whether this is even achievable,
we still have documents producing the meaning of disability by
organizing a unified, sensible, working conception of disability
that is assumed to be obvious to readers of the text. For example,
it is regarded as obvious that disability is a concept and, just as
obvious, that this concept has both objective and subjective characteristics. The concept — disability — can refer to both a thing in the
world (object) and that with which people have a variety of interpretive relationships (subjective). Indeed, when *Advancing* (p. 4)
offers a profile of disability in Canada, it begins by noting that the
data is "based on subjective responses ... based on people identifying themselves as having one or more limitations on their activities." This subjective/objective rendering of disabled people is made
into a Canadian disability rate, 1 in 8 [PALS]. This rate is framed
as "only an estimate ..." (p. 4) since it involves subjective responses
to the body as an object of limit.

But note that the uncertainty granted to disability is deemed
to be caused only by our subjective responses to disability. The
text produces a sense that the social scientific objectification of
embodiment is clear and certain. Without ever having to make an
argument for it, these documents powerfully put forward the idea
that there could be true and certain knowledge on disability if it
were not for subjectivity (people) getting in the way. Moreover, the
policy text makes "limitation" appear as if it is an objective account
of disability, and so it appears *as if* no subjects were involved in
organizing a conception of disability as mere limit.

Narrating disability in this way suggests that to conceive of disability is to imagine a certain kind of object (e.g., embodied limitations) to which one may have many kinds of subjective responses (e.g., identification or non-identification as disabled). Whatever one's subjective relation, *Defining* (p. 44) assumes that it is relatively easy to know there is disability in the world, and that disability is objectively a limit and thus a problem that needs solutions, since "the broader issues identified go beyond definitions". It is not, however, so easy, nor even desirable, to have a single, harmonized working definition of all the different things that can be called disability and subjectively oriented to as such. Finally, in order to achieve a solution to the problem that *disability is*, government policy recommends that readers go beyond definitional issues.

Producing Disability as Problem

We can now address questions that will draw us closer to the issue of reciprocity. How is disability defined and packaged by *Advancing* and its surrounding documents? What meaning is being given to our particular relations with disability? How is this textual packaging of the problem organizing our particular relations with disability in the here and now?

The documents I have been interrogating suggest that disability is a concept that people use in order to refer to problems. But, referring to disability is itself a problem, given that defining it is "a complex issue", and "not an easy task" (HRDC, 2002a, p. 10). Disability is a way of conceiving of problems that require solutions. There are desirable and undesirable, achievable and unachievable, relationships to disability conceived of as a problem. These texts assume that we all know that disability is a problem. Moreover, these texts assume that readers recognize the importance of the need to get beyond definitional conflicts if the problem of disability is to be addressed and solved.

It turns out that to be "objective" about disability is to be certain that it is a problem. Thus, when *Advancing* proceeds to profile disability, it profiles problems: disabled people in Canada face a labour non-participation rate, an unemployment rate, a rate of education, and a level of income that are about half of what non-disabled persons face. The problem is more devastating if one is an Aboriginal person. These are rates on "people with disabilities" who are first and foremost defined as "problem" people. The "problem" that disability is imagined to be is located nowhere but

in individuals — "It is estimated that some 3.6 million Canadians —
1 in 8 — have a disability" (HRDC, 2002a, p. 2). While what
should be done may be in question, *it is beyond question that disability is being packaged as a problem.*

Even though solutions to disability are yet to be developed, the
concluding remarks of these texts suggest that whatever sort of
problem disability is, it is not one that is tied to the definitional
jam that publications such as *Defining Disability* (2003) or *Advancing*
(2002, pp. 10–12; and 2004) clearly delineate and also, eventually,
dismiss. That disability is a problem is taken for granted. Disability
as *"problem"* is not even regarded as one definition in conflict with
all the other definitions. Readers are simply invited to "go beyond"
definitional conflicts by regarding disability as *objectively* a problem,
as if this is not a human-made definition of disability.

Despite warning against a unified definition of disability, the
policy text uniformly defines disability as a problem, and this definition is used across all federal programs, policies and their texts. Put
differently, one way we can get beyond the definitional jam is by
assuming that "problem" is the whole "defining" reality of disability
— its essence, its transcendental unity, and its nature. All other definitions are surpass-able since they are framed as inadequate subjective responses to the clear problem that disability is. That this
ruling definition ought to make us uninterested in all other definitions is, however, more complex and interesting than it may at
first appear. While it is easy to take for granted "problem" as a
reasonable way to package the total meaning of disability, this
packaging is still a form of social action worthy of critical attention.

Consider, for example, the social fact that in texts and through
our lived experience within which we work, or procure services
from, government departments and programs, disability comes to us
as a host of differing conceptions as seen by conflicting definitions,
eligibility criteria, etc. These scenarios demand that people attend
to the ruling conception of disability in order to demonstrate
whether one qualifies for services. To qualify means to measure up,
or somehow exemplify the conception used to determine what will
count as disability in this particular government program and at
this time. Much of the social and physical environment is neither
accessible nor welcoming toward disabled people. Yet, in Canada,
disability supports and services are almost exclusively credited to
individuals who "measure up". Thus, individuals need to be interested in definition since being in possession of a clearly definable
problem condition is necessary to access individualized supports and
services.

But now there is a new problem — how to make differential embodiment definable as disability while holding on to the belief that getting beyond definition is where the solution lies. *Defining Disability* suggests that we should organize our relationship with this definitional conflict so as to be uninterested in it, and so as to conceive of conflicting definitions as not part of the problem that is disability. Through text, disability is being achieved under the totalizing concept "problem". This "total problem" is also packaged as a problem "on its own", outside of the conceptual world of federal policy and procedures. Disability is made to belong only to individuals and not to environments, definitional procedures, or to medical discourse. Policy is thus advancing the inclusion of disability conceived of *as* a problem, which regulates the practices of people in the locality of their lives with disability. Through the action of policy, disability is reproduced as a problem even while seemingly separate from this productive process. This mystified relationship with our own productive activity as readers and writers of disability policy begs the question: What does it mean to produce a statement on disability that denies that it is relying on and reproducing the dominant societal ideology — disability is, as the saying goes, *totally* a problem?

This is a fascinating aspect of the productive power of policy. The statement is suggesting, in the here and now, how readers ought to organize relationships with disability. The text offers readers a recommended subjective relationship. It suggests that readers will find the activity of definition neither interesting nor desirable and should find some other relationship with disability. The recommended relationship is for readers to seek solutions to the *problem that is disability* "as if" this problem is unrelated to the ways in which we define it as such; the ways we program ourselves to respond to it as such; and the ways we measure, write, and report on it as such. In this way, the social fact of disability is being treated as if it is asocial. The text's power lies in its active suggestion to regard as normal the idea that disability is a problem on its own; as normal to grasp individuals as the embodiment of problem; and thus as normal to orient to disability as somehow beyond the definitional quandaries that have made disability what it is today. Unmoored from the social activity of definition, disability is not imagined as something that is made by, and belongs to, collectivities. Neither is disability imagined as something we make together through social interaction, such as through the act of policy production and distribution.

Advancing the inclusion of this sort of understanding of disability is thus advancing a productive force: a force that produces — on the back of disability, so to speak — a sense of the ordinariness of ignoring, or even denying, the power of people to make up the meaning of excluded persons. If it is true that a society can only ever exclude those it has construed as exclude-able (Titchkosky, 2003b, p. 518), then the way in which excludable people are brought into policy and brought up as a definitional issue has everything to do with what will and will not come to our collective attention. For example, advancing the idea that disability is a problem unrelated to societal packaging procedures makes it difficult to begin to bring to collective attention the complex sense in which disability is "social". The social processes that help to constitute disability "as if" it is not social are further enhanced by requiring individuals to prove their personal eligibility, thus reconfirming an individualized conception of disability.

To, instead, advance the idea that disability is *social* requires that we attend to disability as a reality that, simply put, *only ever appears in the midst of people*. Disability *is* processes of social action and interpretation. At bottom, we do not have access to disability outside of social contexts within which and through which we conceptualize it (Michalko, 2002). There is a hidden reciprocity in any act of noticing, defining, or discussing disability. There are no minds, bodies, or senses that are problems on their own — we make some people in possession of problematic embodiment in some locales some of the time. Yet, we imagine and act otherwise. These particular policy statements on definitional difficulties serve as one way we construe disability as if it is problem on its own. Ironically, there is no possible perception of disability outside of conceptions, yet one dominant conception of disability is that it is a "thing", a condition, unrelated to interpretation. Through the inescapable activity that is social life, disability is being made to appear as an asocial problem-thing possessed by individuals. Insofar as we pass over the constitutive power of the social action of policy, we will remain trapped within an unimaginative relationship with disability that rules it as problem while enslaving us all to a singularly uninteresting version of disability as that which never matters beyond limit.

Advancing the Inclusion of Disability as Limit

The *Advancing* document ends with a statement that is echoed through many government documents. The statement appears to be

quite contrary to my depiction of the government's asocial conception of disability. The final statement of the conclusion reads: "By
working together, Canada can move forward toward full inclusion
of persons with disabilities in society" (HRDC, 2002a, p. 69).
"Working together toward full inclusion" certainly seems as if disability is a collective social issue, and is thus an issue that belongs
to the community. Is disability social then, and is it so recognized
by government policy? I turn now to an analysis of *Advancing*'s
overt statements on the "social" character of disability.

Advancing (p. 10) says, "For many decades, disability was seen
as a set of characteristics of the individual — a person *was* disabled
or *had* a disability." The text implies that we have advanced past
the idea that a useless limb makes for a useless individual; that a
flawed sense makes for a flawed individual, etc. For at least the
past decade, the government has produced pamphlets and charts
aiming to teach the general public to conceive of disability as an
add-on to a person and as not tied up with, thus diminishing, being
a person. Following the adage "See the person, not the disability",
these materials aim to teach anyone who speaks of disability to say
"person with a disability", and not to say "disabled person" (see
Titchkosky, 2001). An unquestioned belief in disability as negative
limit, void of human potential, requires that person and disability
must be separated. Consistently, all Canadian policy publications
are united in the act of referring to all disabled Canadians as "people with disabilities". This "evolved" form of reference is as consistent as it is omnipresent. Yet this singular form of expression is
not treated as a harmonized definitional act being accomplished by
all government agencies in and through all policy and all publications. The concept of disability can remain as negative as it ever
was, but the government has helped Canadians evolve a form of
perception that can see a person "despite" the devalued disposition
of disability.

The evolution that brought forth the idea that it is good to
conceive of disability solely as an add-on condition to personhood
provoked yet more changes. Sometime during 2002, government
policy texts began to include the idea that disability can *also* be
conceived of as a "social phenomenon". *Advancing* (pp. 10–11), for
example, says,

> But in the past two decades, as the disability rights movement
> has emerged, the concept of disability has shifted from individual
> impairment to a more social phenomenon. In this social view,
> persons with disabilities are seen as being restricted in perform-

ing daily activities because of a complex set of interrelating factors, some pertaining to the person and some pertaining to the person's immediate environment and social/political arrangements.

This explicit recognition that disability is "more social" or "also social" is occurring in a document that regards disability as a non-social problem and as a problem located in the bodies, minds and senses of some people. Never is disability regarded as something that a collective imaginatively generates and systematically organizes. So, *Advancing* can explicitly present disability as an individualized problem. For example, the opening words of *Advancing* (p. 2) read: "Disabilities affect people of all ages and backgrounds. Some people are born with one or more disabilities. Many others develop disabilities through illness, injury or aging". How, then, can the objectively defined non-social problem condition of disability also be social?

Perhaps these texts merely make a mistake, e.g., confusing impairment with disability. To call what the government is doing a "mistake" wilfully ignores the actual concept of disability at work in the text. To call this a mistake would be an error since it would impose a reality on the reality that the document is producing. Understanding that words actively produce a world, a version of which I may not like, but nonetheless a world, requires that we continue with an analysis without defining what the government texts are doing as accident or a mistake. Thus my questions: How can disability be conceived of as both social and non-social at the same time? How can that which is regarded as existing, regardless of human activities of any kind, also pertain to the person's immediate environment, and social and political arrangements? How can that which merely happens either at birth or as we age also be a political and social happening? Put differently, when we are prompted by policy initiatives to work toward the inclusion of persons with disabilities, what version of disability are we being asked to include, and what kind of reciprocity between Canada and its citizens with disabilities are we being asked to seek and advance? By addressing these questions, we might learn something about the type of reciprocity that exists between government documents and the problem populations addressed in these documents, as well as between readers and the notion of disability in the here and now.

Let us try to uncover the sensibility behind regarding disability as the "asocial-condition-that-is-also-social". The government's new found recognition of the emergence of the disability rights movement where "disability has shifted from individual impairment to a more social phenomenon" (HRDC, 2002a, p. 10) is the recognition of a "view". The phrase, "In this social view ..." accomplishes the understanding that disability is an object that is subject to a variety of views. One of the views arises from the disability movement, or from what government documents also refer to as the "disability community".

While profiling disability in Canada, *Advancing* also includes a statement on the disability community in the final "other issues" section. After providing a narrative that statistically profiles the low education, employment, and income rates faced by disabled people, the document also mentions "other issues". These other issues include a brief list of what can be conceived of as the actual social contexts in which disability actually appears (transportation, housing, communication). One final "other issue" is the fragmentation of government services:

> ... [T]he disability community has argued that fragmentation of government services, both within and across government jurisdictions, is one of most important obstacles preventing persons with disabilities from participating fully in society. (HRDC, 2002a, pp. 8, 68)

Despite the government's absolutely unified definition of disability as a problem managed through the equally unified procedure of imagining disability as a limit that is merely added on to an otherwise "normal life", the disability community is accusing the government of fragmentation. Policy is forcefully packaging disability as a condition of limit, thereby separating limit from the essential social fact that limits are "of" and "in" life. Limits, to be limits, must also imply possibilities (Cohen & Weiss, 2003). But just as disability is being fragmented from life, limit is being fragmented from possibility. Fragmentation then not only lies in government services but is the grounds for how to deal with disability. Disability is fragmented from life since it is conceptualized merely as a limit one may experience; disability is being conceptualized as somehow separate from, even in opposition to, life.

Still, the inclusion of the notion of a disability community that has a point of view from which arguments can be launched highlights the reality that disability is now being regarded in two distinct ways within a single government document. We are given a conception of problem people (people with disabilities), and we have views, opinions, and arguments made by a "disability community". Disability is thus being granted an identity as something other

67

TANYA TITCHKOSKY

than a problem since it is also being depicted as a movement, as a community that makes arguments, and as something more than a body of problems causing restriction, limit, and inability. We have here the first hint that disability can be conceived of as a way of being-in-the-world that bears a self-reflective relationship with it.

Between disability understood as nothing but a problem and the new references to disability as a community or a movement lies a conflict mediated through the idea of "a view". People who are members of the disability community offer a view or an argument; an argument not only that disability is social, but also that the government has something to do with the social character ascribed to disability. This is the view of people who have been defined as interesting only as problem, resulting in a subjectivity originating from an objectified essence as problem. In the end, what the document is including is yet another subjective response. This "view" is presented so as to suggest that disability is still "restriction in performing daily activities", but that such restriction is caused by "a complex set of interrelating factors". The complexity lies in the fact that restriction is not just "pertaining to the person" since some restrictions also pertain "to the person's immediate environment and social/political arrangements." People with problems also experience their problems in environments, and the nature of their problem is affected by social and political arrangements. While this is hardly a social view of the body, it is acknowledging that so-called restricted bodies appear in environments arranged by social and political interests that may further restrict and limit these restricted and limited bodies.

The inclusion of the view that leads to the argument that disability is "also social" is, ironically, a re-assertion that disabled people are people with restrictions regardless of societal response. This way of making disability meaningful serves to empower the *status quo* since it denies the need to problematize the taken-for-granted formulation of disability as problem (Slee, 2004, p. 46). At best, restricted people may be of the view that they are further restricted by the immediate environment (but this is a view coming from people already defined as problem people). The arrangements, that is, the environment — the social and political milieu — are nowhere charted, profiled, statistically measured, or depicted in *Advancing*. A view belonging to disabled people who belong to a disability community (a coalition of problem people) makes the view more or less "their problem". After all, the government offers no comment on the view; the view is merely reported. There is no policy given to support or service this view.

68

In the end, the view of a disability community that understands the government as producing fragmentation and barriers serves only as the occasion for the government to reiterate that it has "agreed to work together to meet the needs of all Canadians" (HRDC, 2002a, p. 8). The issue of the disability community's view is othered, so to speak. To assert that "disability is also a social phenomenon" is representative of a view that is incorporated almost as if it is a view by nobody from nowhere, thus requiring no response.

Reciprocity?

The view is presented; the argument given; a unique form of reciprocity arises. Just what sort of reciprocity does this exchange represent? In responding to the political response of the government, the disability community, conceived of as the coalition of people with problems, is transformed into the trouble that disability was all along depicted to be, even as this community attempts to highlight the trouble caused by framing disability as nothing but a problem. By including disability as nothing but a problem faced by some people, government policy makes absent its own power to form the meaning of disability. The text makes present the view that turns on the idea that disability is socially constituted and organized through attempts to solve the "problem". But this different view is presented as one more subjective view and is corralled; thereby, the boundaries around the notion that disability is an asocial problem are re-asserted. A kind of reciprocity of absence is thus established. Disability as a life, as community or as a movement, or as that which is born of our interpretive relationships with others, is continually made absent while the singular unified "objective" definition of disability as a problem is made present.

Precluded as a critical voice; excluded as a space for reflection; rejected as a name for difference, or for a movement, or for valued diversity; disability is nonetheless made present as a condition of limit. The utterance "It is also social", or the utterance "This more social view", dissolves the sociality of disability in favour of the singular definitional reality of disability as problem. Disability is drained of life, and the only social thing granted to disability is the recognition that some people "with disabilities" have views and make arguments.

Insofar as it is true that current policy is mediating "disability" as a problem-thing beyond human interpretation and interaction, people will be enabled only to respond to policy by evaluating the policy's potential to assist the "thing" it intends to assist. This definition and packaging of disability restricts people from developing a response to how disability is being made meaningful in and through policy and its subsequent programs. This sort of reciprocity requires that whatever evaluative response arises, it will only be sensible if it reconfirms that policy is a form of giving; policy *gives ways* to establish future practices and programs. While policy may be evaluated from time to time as a lousy or precious gift, it is not to be imagined as a form of making. As soon as we begin to engage policy as itself a form of social action, we then need to consider how policy acts to constitute the meaning of disability, and such consideration gets in the way of evaluating whether or not the policy will be helpful. Policy is thus to be regarded as not making up the meaning of people. Thus we "ought" to continue to imagine policy *as if* it merely provides a plan of action to address pre-existing problems.

But as policy makes future action plans for populations of problem people, it cannot escape from representing "who" the policy intends to help. There is, in other words, a reciprocal production between plans for help and the types of people for whom the help is intended. Current policy has made disability appear as mere limit, a restriction of an asocial nature. To attempt to encounter policy as an activity is to grapple with policy text as a creation of that world that wants to imagine disability in this way. It follows then that what has *already* been said and done, such as putting differences into policy texts as the problem of disability, must be analyzed for the taken-for-granted values against which disability is typically made to show up as lack and limit. In this way, policy can be read as performing the meaning of disability, since both policy and its analysis are forms of discursive social action. Simply put, texts on disability, including mine, call out a meaning for disability.

Brian Pronger (2002) says, "To call is also to summon ... That which is called is brought nearer by virtue of being shown within the conceptual universe ... as the kind of being that it has been called" (p. 150). In the face of policy, we need to continue to ask: What is being called and packaged here? To what is the reader brought near? While it is obvious that policy sets up programs of future action to serve, to aid, to include, etc., it is not so obvious that policy, in the here and now, is already a doing. Policy calls on us to be a certain type of person; it calls on us to imagine problems in a particular way, and policy brings near some imagined relationship between people and problems. I have called all this "social action", and have shown that such action is integral in constituting the meaning of disability today.

CONCLUSION

In this chapter, I analyzed policy documents that attempted to render disability objectively. My analysis tried to grasp this objective rendering of disability as a subjective move — as a form of interpretation. Understanding the interpretive character of policy means that instead of addressing what policy might do "for" people, we can address policy as a form of oriented social action that does something "to" how communities conceive of disability. Such an approach requires an inquirer who commits to the concrete idea that disability makes no objective sense on its own. When disability appears, it always appears in the human-made world and appears to, by, and through people. This is why disability has much to teach about the organization of contemporary society.

But strangely enough, these very concrete ideas are not so easy to imagine, let alone to dwell on. Once again, and not for the first time, current government documents on disability singularly depict it as "essentially" a problem. And so an abstract reality is built that places people under the demands of an active reciprocal engagement with disability *as if* it is a thing, *as if* it has nothing to do with human acts of noticing, interpreting, and living with disability. The problem that is disability can take many, apparently objective, forms. In some government documents, disability takes shape as the problem of embodiment where there are different rates of severity, longevity, cause and consequence of bodies, minds or senses that make a person depart from ways of doing things considered normal for a human being; in others, the problem is depicted as lack of knowledge as to what extent "people with disabilities" are missing supports and facing barriers. But "problem" remains an unquestioned definitional fact.

Understanding policy as a productive organizing force, producing the meaning of people, *requires reading policy as itself an "activity"*. Policy is not just set principles, values, best practices, or definitions that can eventually be used to guide future action. Whatever future it might make possible, policy organizes, even produces, the meaning of persons in the here and now and deserves to be studied as a form of power that packages people in ordered relationships with themselves, with others, and with problems. This is why the reciprocal *meaning making* that occurs through the productive activity of writing and reading policy is no less worthy of study than whether or not a policy "got the job done".

Section II

The Disability Policy Context

In the second section of this book, we examine the disability policy context; that is, the environment in which disability policy exists and seeks to improve the lot of people with disabilities. Societal values influence the development of social policies, and disability policies are part of overall social policies. In Canada, our overall social policy is influenced by our historical colonial links to Britain and Europe, and associated beliefs about the importance of collectivism. Until recently, Canadians have historically enjoyed consensus regarding a collectivist welfare state, when to some people, the cost seemed to have become too onerous.

While we do not propose to offer a detailed history of disability policy development in Canada, it is useful to have some broad historical trends within which to situate the developing disability policy. Most authors agree that the earliest public concern about disability arose in the late 19th century, when asylums were built to house disabled individuals and residential institutions constructed for the education of disabled children (Boyce et al., 2001; Neufeldt, 2003). This is referred to as the institutional period

(Cameron & Valentine, 2001) or the law and order period (Crichton & Jongbloed, 1998).

This was followed in the early 20th century by a period of income supports for veterans and injured workers, and by the dominance of the medical profession in defining the state of disability and the needs of disabled people. This stage lasted to the 1960s, and was characterized by dramatic advances in medical and rehabilitation technology, leading to a belief that the professions held the key to a better life for people with disabilities.

The growing civil rights movement had a dramatic effect on society in the 1960s and 1970s, challenging virtually every aspect of established society, and questioning every form of authority. The disability community was not exempt from this sweeping social movement (Driedger, 1989). In a climate of socio-political reform, people with disabilities began to see their issues not simply as personal problems, but as social problems; not simply as misfortunes, but as injustices (Peters, 2003). In 1975, the United Nations passed their Declaration of Human Rights for Disabled People, paving the way for Canada and other developed nations to begin to reconsider the policy environment pertaining to disability. In 1981, the International Year of Disabled Persons marked the beginning of a watershed period for disability rights in Canada.

For a brief period in the 1980s and early 1990s, the pace of change accelerated in disability policy development. The concept of the welfare state was challenged as being too concerned with financial redistribution and not enough with promoting equality of citizenship. The crowning achievement of this period was the identification of disabled people as a group whose rights were enshrined in the *Charter of Rights and Freedoms* — a document that has become a touchstone for much of the disability policy that has followed since. When the Constitution was repatriated in 1982, and the *Charter of Rights and Freedoms* was appended, it was generally accepted that equalization not only involved ensuring a minimum income and providing collectivist social services, but also involved changed attitudes toward disadvantaged groups.

Disability-related reforms proceeded in parallel in Canada and the United States throughout this period. Differences in the definition of disability in Canada and the United States reflect value differences — in the United States individualism is highly valued, whereas in Canada, there is greater commitment to collectivism. This section offers three chapters that discuss the policy environment for disability reforms in the late 20th to early 21st century.

74

Chapter 5

The chapter by Jerome Bickenbach examines how discrimination is viewed in rights legislation in Canada and the United States. He points out that Canada and the United States have focused on anti-discrimination legislation as a tool for achieving equality. He compares the definitions of disability used in the Canadian *Charter of Rights and Freedoms* and the *Americans with Disabilities Act* (ADA). Whereas the definition in the ADA focuses on individual functional status, Canada's *Charter of Rights and Freedoms* does not define disability. Canadian courts have viewed discrimination as the social response to disability; not as an individual functional problem. Equality is not simply the absence of discrimination. Equality and full participation depend on the existence of resources to meet needs. Social inequality associated with disability is marked by the absence of resources and opportunities and is thus an issue of distributive justice.

Chapter 6

Joiner addresses the question of what it means for people with disabilities to be treated equally. He examines aspects of universalism and minority approaches to disability in relation to equality and argues that a combination of the two approaches is desirable for addressing what is involved in being treated equally.

Chapter 7

One of the changes that has occurred in Canada's welfare state over the last 35 years is decreased government commitment to low-income groups. Michael Prince states that in terms of expenditures at the level of the federal government, there was a decline in commitment to people with disabilities between 1990 and the present time. Spokespersons for people with disabilities rank disability supports as the first priority for helping people with disabilities gain access to quality of life. Prince argues that a national strategy of disability supports should be introduced. He describes current intergovernmental transfers for disability and proposes a revised plan for transfer and federal investment.

Chapter 8

The last chapter in this section outlines seven trends that influence the context within which disability policy exists. Rioux and

Samson take a historical approach to understanding how these trends have unfolded over time, and how the Canadian situation exists within the wider international context. The chapter shows the evolving human rights framework for disability policy in light of trends in economics, culture, technology and society.

5

Canadian Charter v. American ADA: Individual Rights or Collective Responsibilities

JEROME E. BICKENBACH

INTRODUCTION

In the 1990s, it was presumed that anti-discrimination legislation was the best way to achieve equality for people with disabilities. This chapter focuses on the law as an instrument of equality for people with disabilities. It first compares definitions in the *Americans with Disabilities Act 1990* (ADA) and the *Canadian Charter of Rights and Freedoms* and examines the significance of the differences. It then analyzes the model of disability in WHO's 2001 ICF and its three levels of human functioning — body, personal capacity and social functioning.

In this chapter, the importance of clearly identifying the purpose of a law is stressed. The definition of disability needs to be consistent with the purposes of the law. It is argued that anti-discrimination laws and laws related to the provision of services and medical equipment should be based on different definitions of disability (or rather, different dimensions of a single, multidimensional notion). The role played by anti-discrimination legislation in combating inequality is clarified; inequality associated with disability as a matter of corrective and distributive injustice, as well as the types of laws that address corrective justice and distributive justice, are examined.

The minority model of disability is critiqued and it is argued that disability is a universal phenomenon, as it is reflected in the ICF. It gives examples of ways in which environments can be designed to address distributive inequality.

THE LAW AND PEOPLE WITH DISABILITIES

How can the law serve the interests of equality for persons with disability? Is the law the best, or the only social instrument for achieving equality? Is it of modest usefulness, or worse, an outright hindrance? Although these are not easy questions, for much of the 1990s it was presumed that law had an essential role to play, and in particular that enforceable anti-discrimination legislation was the best legal tool for realizing equality. Disability advocates around the world set about convincing their local jurisdictions to enact legislation modeled on the ADA, arguing that wide-ranging protection against discrimination was the sine qua non of equality for persons with disabilities.

These days the situation is not as clear. Although complete data are not available, and precise statistical tools for measuring the impact of the ADA have yet to be developed, many researchers agree that its effect, at least on employment rates for persons with disabilities, has been disappointing. Recent U.S. Supreme Court decisions further limiting the application of the ADA can only make matters worse, and there is no reason to think the court's sympathy with the ADA will improve in the future. The ADA is hardly a failure, but judged from the perspective of achieving equality, it cannot be called an unqualified success either.

The legal definition of disability used in the ADA is obviously part of the problem. As many have argued, by entrenching a definition of disability (even an expansive one that includes "history of disability" and "perceived as disabled"), drafters of the ADA created a judicial step of complainant eligibility that has deflected judicial scrutiny away from disadvantageous treatment toward the complainant's actual functional status, in particular, its severity. Many complainants lost because they were not "disabled enough", irrespective of the treatment that moved them to complain in the first place. Arguably, the jurisprudence stated in section 15(1)

78

of Canada's *Charter of Rights and Freedoms* has fared better since "disability" is not defined and Canadian courts have seen that discrimination is a function of the social reception of disability, not the functional state of the complainant's body or mind.

But why is the definition of disability of such legal significance? The answer is that, from its inception, the disability rights movement in the United States joined forces with social scientists, many of whom were themselves disabled, in arguing that people with disabilities are disadvantaged by misunderstandings about what disability is. Disability, they insisted, is not a feature of a person's body; it is a complex interaction between the person and his or her physical, social and attitudinal environment. In order to make out this argument, the heyday of the disability rights movement in the 1960s and 1970s was marked by a proliferation of "models" and "paradigms" of disability, and legal academics have interjected these into their scholarship on anti-discrimination law ever since. These conceptualizations were highly successful as political slogans, and in that arena they got results, even though they were neither new nor models in any strict, scientific sense.

WHO's 2001 ICF is the first fully worked-out and operational model of disability that stands any chance of transforming political slogans (e.g., "My world disables me more than my impairment") into verifiable and measurable propositions. The ICF identifies three levels of human functioning — body, person and social functioning. Difficulties at each of these levels constitute (aspects of) disability, and no one level is more fundamental or basic than another. Nor is any presumption made that one level of difficulty leads inexorably to another — since the experience of disability is determined in part by features of the individual's environment, which is neither stable nor uniform. Both as a conceptual model and as a scientific tool, the ICF has a multiplicity of potential uses — statistical, administrative, clinical, research and social policy. But, in addition, the ICF teaches a couple of important lessons for law and the equality agenda.

The first lesson is straightforwardly definitional: If the law is to serve the interests of equality of persons with disabilities, we must be utterly clear about what dimension of the complex notion of "disability" our legal instruments are addressing. The legal definition must be appropriate to and consistent with the purposes of the law at issue. And laws of necessity have different purposes.

In the case of anti-discrimination law, there is wide consensus that its purposes are to ensure that persons with disabilities enjoy full citizenship, are treated with respect and dignity, and are not subjected to social disadvantage, abuse or negligence by virtue of individual or social reaction to their impairments. Achieving these purposes is the rationale of anti-discrimination law, and part of the equality agenda. On the other hand, it is *not* the purpose of anti-discrimination law to determine the eligibility of individuals for social benefits or resources that are provided in direct response to, or in compensation for, their functional status. These are legitimate aims of social welfare law generally — including social assistance, insurance, pensions, and workers compensation — but not of anti-discrimination law.

In short, anti-discrimination law should be grounded on a social conception of disability (in which disability is the outcome of an interaction between features of the person and the person's social, physical and attitudinal environment), rather than a biomedical conception (in which disability is an attribute of a person's body or mind). Anti-discrimination law should focus on individual and social response to impairments, not on the impairments themselves. Consequently, a statutory definition of "disability" for anti-discrimination should address the social problem of discrimination by specifying the kind of social disadvantage, disrespect or indignity people with disabilities experience; or in the words of a recent Canadian Supreme Court decision,

> ... [the focus of anti-discrimination law] is not on the impairment as such, nor even any associated functional limitations, but is on the problematic response of the state to either or both of these circumstances. It is the state action that stigmatizes the impairment, or which attributes false or exaggerated importance to the functional limitations (if any), or which fails to take into account the [remedial and ameliorative purposes of the anti-discrimination provision] that creates the legally relevant human rights dimension to what might otherwise be a straightforward biomedical condition. (*Granovsky v. Canada*, 2001, 1 S.C.R., p. 703)

It follows, as well, that when the law serves purposes other than preventing discrimination, it may need to rely on different aspects of disability. For example, a legal regime designed to provide medical or rehabilitative services, durable medical goods, or assistive technology will sensibly require that the recipient demonstrably possess the impairment-related needs the provision of these services and resources is designed to ameliorate. This suggests a statutory definition embodying our best biomedical information about impairments. Alternatively, laws that facilitate the development and provision of environmental accommodations in education, employment, transportation, communication or some other domain of human life must characterize disability in light of those aspects of the natural or built environment that either limit participation or enhance it for persons with disabilities.

It is evident that providing resources to meet the medical and rehabilitative needs of persons with disabilities and requiring environmental accommodation to ensure higher levels of social participation are legitimate and valuable purposes the law can serve. More to the point, these purposes are essential to the realistic achievement of equality and full participation for persons with disabilities. Anti-discrimination law has its part to play in the equality agenda for law; but there are other, equally vital, roles for the law to play.

The need for a broad and creative use of social welfare policy to achieve equality for persons with disabilities is a given in Europe and elsewhere, but not so much in the United States, with its relative aversion to rights- or entitlement-based "positive action" on the part of the state and its agencies. Recent scholarship in the United States has suggested that disability advocates may have undermined prospects for improvements in social welfare law by, unintentionally, catering to a neo-conservative agenda by selling the ADA as a tool for lowering the costs associated with disability and obviating the need for positive action. Advocates argued that the ADA would be a cost-saver, since, once discrimination was gone, people with disabilities would be able to get off welfare and join the workforce. Mandated workplace accommodation, it was argued, would require employers to incur only nominal costs. In light of this rhetoric, it is not surprising that the present U.S. Supreme Court, not ideologically aligned with the equality agenda in any event, would refuse to enforce the ADA when costs to employ or educate complainants would increase, due to accommodation and the provision of additional resources.

The rhetoric of the disability rights movement contained another time bomb. Disability advocates, following the lead of many social scientists, argued that people with disabilities form a "discreet and insular minority" and share a common "disability experience" that shapes their understanding of the world and creates a kind of culture that is uniquely theirs. The so-called "minority model" of disability, bolstered by a rhetoric of identity politics, was useful for creating solidarity to mobilize for social change. Yet the minority approach is based on a startlingly naïve, and factually false, perception about disability — that it is something that only happens to a few people.

This, indeed, is the second lesson we can learn from the model of disability embodied in the ICF. The classification is built on the premise that disability is not the mark of a separate group or class of people, but is rather a universal human phenomenon. Disability is universal because functional capacity is universal, and each human being exhibits some level of functional capacity across the spectrum of body functions and person-level activities. If there is a common "disability experience", it is one that every human being shares, at one time in their life, to one degree or another. In blunt epidemiological terms, disability is normality: it is intrinsic to the human condition.

The universality of disability, far from undermining the rationale of anti-discrimination law, greatly enhances its legitimacy. As a universal human condition, one that all people to one degree or anther share, disability ought to be a profoundly integrating feature of humanity, not a segregating one. When, because of prejudice, ignorance, or ulterior motive, disability is taken as a reason for unequal treatment — in employment, education, housing, or some other area of human social participation — the appropriate legal tool is anti-discrimination law. A situation or treatment that is disrespectful, one that creates disadvantage, abuse or negligence on the basis of disability, is unequal treatment that warrants a corrective social response. Although it is debatable whether the machinery of anti-discrimination law in force in any jurisdiction is adequate to this purpose, that anti-discrimination law is a legitimate legal tool in the service of equality, as a matter of corrective justice, is obvious once disability is seen as an intrinsic feature of the human condition.

Still, there is no reason to think that anti-discrimination law is sufficient for the equality agenda. Equality and full participation of all people, whether they have disabilities or not, depend on the provision of resources to meet needs, as well as environmental modifications and other accommodations to remove barriers to full participation. Of course, there are those who argue that failing to provide these resources and accommodation is itself discriminatory and so, at least in theory, within the proper purview of anti-discrimination law. Certainly, in Canadian, U.S. and other jurisdictions with robust anti-discrimination legislation, cases have been successfully litigated obliging the state to provide services and accommodations in specific circumstances for persons with disabilities (signing translators for deaf patients in hospitals, elevators to serve subway users with mobility impairments, more time for test-taking for students with learning disabilities, and so on).

Yet, no one could seriously argue that the complaint-based, reactive and remedial procedure characteristic of anti-discrimination law is the best, or only, way to pursue an equality social agenda. Even if anti-discrimination law worked smoothly, and economically, the condition of inequality that people with disabilities face cannot always fit into the conceptual mold, or legal test, of discrimination. Discrimination is a wrongful limitation of someone's freedom that denies them access to full participation and equal benefit. The wronged party has a claim of redress against whoever has done the discriminating. Redress is warranted if it can be shown that the individual was disadvantaged because of a trait or feature that was morally irrelevant and did not justify the treatment. A discriminatory action is offensive because it is disrespectful and assaults the dignity of an individual or a group. These are the inherent conceptual boundaries of the notion of discrimination. Because discrimination is an indignity, compensation to the victim of the insult is meaningful and appropriate as a matter of **corrective justice**.

By contrast, the characteristic feature of social inequality experienced by people with disabilities around the world is the unjust limitation of their equal right to participate in the full range of social roles and ways of living. This may be the consequence of neglect, lack of political clout, or some other systemic social failure to fairly distribute needed resources. Inequality is exemplified, concretely, not by the attitudes or even behaviours of others, but by the patent absence of resources, accommodations and opportunities that would make it realistically possible for a person with disabilities to participate in all areas of human social life, consistent with their own goals and aims.

Social inequality associated with disability, in a word, is not just a matter of corrective injustice; it is also a matter of **distributive injustice** — an unfair distribution of social resources and opportunities resulting in limitations of participation in all areas of social life. The most obvious social disadvantage linked to disability is an inequality in the satisfaction of basic human needs. In particular, resources are allocated to satisfy the repertoire of functional capacities of some people, but not of others, creating a distributive imbalance. This is not a matter of discrimination, but of political economy (market-based or otherwise): the size of a potential market for a product strongly predicts both availability and cost. As a result, people with low prevalence but high-need disabilities will have difficulties acquiring assistive devices and other resources while those with high prevalence conditions, such as myopia, will have a wide selection of affordable options to choose from.

The causes of distributive imbalance against disability are various and densely embedded in social and economic structures — and it is fair to say we know precious little about how they actually work (although theories abound). What is clear, though, is that the multifaceted phenomenon of inequality, as experienced by people with disabilities, cannot be forced into the conceptual mold of discrimination without risking the kind of judicial retrenchment that is now occurring in the United States. Without health services, assistive technology, or accommodations, people with disabilities are distinctly disadvantaged in all areas of life. This is a patent distributional inequality, and an injustice; but conceptually, it is not an instance of discrimination.

Anti-discrimination legislation, long the darling of the disability movement, must in the end be seen as playing an essential, but limited, role in the equality agenda. Attempts to extend and expand anti-discrimination law in order to remedy inequality in all of its manifestations will ultimately be futile, and may completely undermine the effectiveness of this law in its proper domain. To better serve the disability equality agenda, the spotlight must be turned from anti-discrimination to social welfare law — that complex and highly political domain of law and policy designed to facilitate the transference of resources, accommodations and opportunities for persons with disabilities. Here, fortunately, there is considerable room for legal creativity.

Consider two examples from the United States. The first is the federal *Assistive Technology Act, 1998*, which targets research and development, information transfer, and efficient distribution of all forms of assistive technology. Given the wide disparity in assistive technology programming among states, the primary function of the Act is to transfer federal funds to states so that they will create, or sustain, permanent and comprehensive programs for the development and distribution of assistive technology. The Act conditions funding on the involvement of individuals with disabilities in the maintenance, improvement and evaluation of whatever state program the Act funds. In addition, the Act creates industry standards for assistive devices, and sets up information services to enable consumers to find the products they need.

A second example addresses the fact that people with mobility and sensory disabilities are often disadvantaged by design standards and building codes for the built environment, thereby creating a "standard" that accommodates a range of variability in human functioning that is unrealistically narrow. In 1988, the U.S. Congress responded to this need by passing the *Fair Housing Act.* Growing out of the anti-discrimination tradition, the Act begins by prohibiting discrimination in the rental or sale of dwelling units to a person on grounds of disability. But the regulations passed under the Act move beyond the anti-discrimination pattern by setting out detailed design and construction requirements for all multi-family housing built after 1991. These requirements put into place what the Act terms a standard of "modest accessibility" for all new housing. These requirements "raise the bar" on accessibility, so that a "standard home" will be, as a matter of course, modestly accessible. Although a long way from the ideal of "universal design" — a design suitable for all people, whatever their level of functioning — the Act starts the process of extending the range of "normal functioning" that a "standard house design" must accommodate.

These innovative laws — and others that might be cited in areas of telecommunications, transportation, and education — address distributional inequality, the inequality implicit in "standard" products and "standard" architectural design. Using a wide range of policy techniques, these laws encourage, facilitate, or mandate a shift in our social response to variations in levels of functioning. Functional limitations may be chronic and beyond our capacity to fix or improve. But the lived experience of these limitations can be improved by altering the social and built environment, which may needlessly create disabling barriers or, again needlessly, fail to provide environmental facilitation. Removing barriers and providing environmental changes that facilitate functioning are ways of addressing distributional inequality. And the law can be an important social tool in making this possible.

How then can the law serve the interests of equality for persons with disability? The law can serve equality by addressing inequalities arising from both corrective and distributive injustice, through a variety of legal instruments and remedies. Anti-discrimination law is one of those legal tools, there is no doubt. But to be effective as an instrument of corrective justice, anti-discrimination law must be substantively focused and procedurally relevant to its remedial purposes. Nothing is gained — and much is lost — by extending the scope of anti-discrimination law to include inequalities arising from distributive injustice, or characterizing disability in a manner irrelevant to the phenomenon of discrimination. But again, although it is a necessary tool, anti-discrimination law is by no means sufficient. If the law is to more fully serve the equality interests of persons with disabilities, it must gingerly approach the complex, political arena of distributive justice. The law must seek creative ways of increasing full participation in employment, education, and family and community life for all people with disabilities by providing the resources, accommodations and opportunities that make meaningful participation possible.

CONCLUSION

This chapter has examined the law as an instrument to achieve equality for those with disabilities. Anti-discrimination laws such as the ADA address issues of corrective justice for people with disabilities. Social inequality, or lack of resources, is also a matter of distributive injustice. Laws such as those that promote universal design of buildings facilitate a social response to variations in levels of functioning and thereby address distributive justice.

6

Obscuring Disability: The Impact of a Universalism/Minority Group Dichotomy on Assessing Equality

IAN JOINER

INTRODUCTION

To be treated equally in society is an ideal and desirable goal for disabled people. However, discussions about this quest are often mired in theoretical ambivalence and rhetoric and frequently obscured by debates surrounding the varying conceptual models of disability and society. This chapter addresses the question: "What would it mean for people with disabilities to be treated equally?"

The chapter reviews three broad themes in the historical treatment of disability. This is followed by the argument that a blend of universalism and minority group approaches is suitable, if not necessary, for understanding and further advancing disability issues.

BACKGROUND

Historical and evolving views of disability are relevant to the parallel quest for equal treatment. Thus, a brief summary of key themes relating to these views is presented in this chapter. Many historical accounts of disability are organized in chronological order, presenting the progression of documented attitudes, policies and actions from antiquity to the 21st century (Braddock & Parish, 2001; DePoy & Gilson, 2004; Stiker, 1999). However, given the focus of this chapter, this section is organized along three themes as they relate to equal treatment and equality: ostracism, paternalism and inclusion. A preliminary reference to UN's *Standard Rules on the Equalization of Opportunities for Persons with Disabilities* (hereafter, Standard Rules) provides some general context.

The United Nations endorsed the Standard Rules in 1993 to serve as a guide for policy making by member countries in addressing the quest for equal participation by disabled people in various aspects of society (UN, 2003). The purpose of the Standard Rules is to promote the necessary preconditions for disabled people to exercise their rights, freedoms and obligations generally, and in eight target areas: accessibility; education; employment; income maintenance and social security; family life and personal integrity; culture; recreation and sports; and religion (UN, 2003). This international approach to consensus on the required directions for addressing barriers facing disabled people is based largely in a minority group rights perspective, which is discussed in more detail throughout this chapter. Discussion and debate on the extent to which the Standard Rules have (or have not) influenced equality for disabled people on a global scale is scarce in the academic literature.

The Standard Rules represent broad ideals and list general statements about the primary societal barriers and areas of disadvantage encountered by disabled people. In the absence of meaningful international legal mechanisms to compel countries to abide by and address the areas highlighted in the Standard Rules, it appears that any progress directly related to the document has been limited at best. However, the listing of target areas does provide a useful reference for this chapter by identifying aspects of life to be enjoyed by all people, which can reasonably be extrapolated to this discussion on equal treatment of disabled people. In Canada, this is exemplified by the ultimate goal of the disability community "as nothing short of complete inclusion with 'full citizenship' " (Cameron & Valentine, 2001, p. 23).

Ostracism has been a common theme in the history of disability. From the earliest recorded time, variation in human structure and function, or "atypicality" (DePoy & Gilson, 2004), has resulted in figurative and literal exclusion from the majority in society. In ancient Greece, for example, the presence of certain impairments was viewed as inhuman or immoral and dealt with by exposure — passively through neglect, or actively through execution (Ravaud & Stiker, 2001; Stiker, 1999). This discretionary and unequal treatment of disabled people is evident to varying degrees in the longstanding tradition of institutionalization (Braddock & Parrish, 2001; Oliver & Barnes, 1998) and, in the extreme, through targeted extermination and experimentation by the Nazi regime (Barnes & Mercer, 2003; Linton, 1998; Marks, 1999). One could also include here the practices of euthanasia for reasons related to disability and, in the era of rapidly advancing medical investigative technologies, selective abortion and other eugenics activities (Asche, 2001; Barnes & Mercer, 2003; Oliver & Barnes, 1998; Wolbring, 2003). To be treated equally along this theme would require the disassociation of all such acts from the label(s) of disability. The condoning of such acts by a society's institutions, whether by official policy decree or by legislative voids, has certainly varied over the course of history (Bickenbach, 1993; Jongbloed, 2003). However, the underlying support of such ostracism or selective elimination can be said to represent somewhat disturbing levels of intolerance or dehumanization (Enns, 1999) lending support to unequal treatment of disabled people.

Paternalism is a second theme under which to comment on equal treatment of disabled people. The rise of religious tolerance and awareness of broad social responsibilities gave rise to charity, which has resulted to some extent in a more paternalistic treatment of disabled people (DePoy & Gilson, 2004; Stiker, 1999). Whether in Victorian-era poorhouses or modern-day charity telethons, disabled people have been objectified in order to stimulate donations and to instill obligations in able-bodied counterparts. This has often been viewed as a negative treatment in disability literature, but as DePoy and Gilson (2004) point out, there have been benefits in this approach for promoting civil rights and for accessing much needed financial resources to advance disability issues. Paternalism has also been linked to the rise of the medical and rehabilitation approaches to disability, through which health professionals control access to, and benefit from, the relative dependence of disabled people alluded to earlier in this chapter. For the most part, a long history of being viewed as inadequate, incapable and vulnerable members of society has led to calls for empowerment and self-determination by disabled people (Charlton, 1998) and by advocacy organizations led by people with disabilities (C. Barnes, 2002; Stienstra & Wight-Felske, 2003). Being treated equally under this theme would result in autonomy and control over life decisions

(Cardol, DeJong & Ward, 2002), not only related to the physical aspects of impairment, but also across all the areas highlighted in the Standard Rules.

Although variations on the theme exist (Oliver & Barnes, 1998; Priestley, 2003; Ravaud & Stiker, 2001), inclusion can be seen as a third broad theme in the history of equal treatment of disabled people. This relates closely to equity, in that different people may require varying accommodations in order to achieve a reasonably equal level of participation in society. As seen for other minority groups, this includes, for example, affirmative action policies and anti-discrimination legislation for employment (Baker, 1990; Ravaud & Stiker, 2001). Equal treatment under this theme could be demonstrated in various ways: by integrated classrooms, where disabled children attend the same schools and classrooms as able-bodied children; by equal opportunity employment programs; and through the independent living movement, whereby disabled people participate as consumers with control over their own life decisions. Often, but not necessarily, there are economic benefits underlying such approaches, which align with a view of disability based in theories of capitalism where disabled people are viewed as consumers or as potentially exploitable human resources (Braddock & Parrish, 2001; DePoy & Gilson, 2004; Priestley, 2003). Of relevance here is an underlying stated aim of the UN Standard Rules to address global human resources issues (UN, 2003).

A MYSTIFYING DICHOTOMY

Various disability theorists and authors have paired off minority group (civil rights) approaches with universalism (human variation) approaches as contrasting models of disability (Bickenbach, 2001; Bickenbach et al., 1999; Scotch & Schriner, 1997; Zola, 1989). Although both are refinements of a broader social model of disability, universalism is positioned as offering more potential benefits for addressing the disadvantages faced by disabled people with respect to their interaction with society or with their environment. From a review of the literature for this chapter, it appears that the minority group approach has strong roots in disability protest and activism during the 1960s and 1970s and is supported more passionately by authors who are themselves disabled (for example, see Barnes, 2003a). Universalism, on the other hand, appears to be positioned as a more modern alternative with which to advance the drive toward full inclusion in society — something that some proponents of this approach feel the minority group has failed to accomplish (Bickenbach et al., 1999). A brief summary of each approach is provided in the remaining sections, followed by some thoughts on the utility of the debate for commenting on equal treatment for disabled people.

Minority Group Approach

A minority group approach, in which discrimination is a primary barrier, has been a dominant paradigm of the disability movement in asserting rights to full participation in society (Baker, 1990; Bickenbach, 2001; Scotch & Schriner, 1997). This paradigm embraces a pursuit of equality as demonstrated by racial and cultural minorities and by women in their varying success at achieving emancipation from an affluent/white/male/able-bodied hegemony. When viewed as members of a labelled minority group, disabled people experience prejudice, discrimination, oppression and segregation, as well as limited opportunities for education, employment and political influence, more often than members of the majority or privileged group(s) (Barnes & Mercer, 2003; Bickenbach et al., 1999; Braddock & Parish, 2001; Oliver & Barnes, 1998; Scotch & Schriner, 1997). Linking this to equality and equal treatment, Hahn (as cited in Bickenbach et al., 1999) states that discriminatory practices "seem to signify conscious or unconscious sentiments supporting a hierarchy of dominance and subordination between nondisabled and disabled [people] ... that is fundamentally incompatible with legal principles of freedom and equality" (p. 1180).

To be treated equally from this perspective is to achieve community control, empowerment and self-determination (Scotch & Schriner, 1997), often through legal mechanisms of civil rights, affirmative action and anti-discrimination legislation (Bickenbach et al., 1999; Kanter, 2003; Marks, 1999) and through political action (Barnes & Mercer, 2003; Stiker, 1999). To quote Oliver and Barnes (1998), this approach often aims to transform disability "from a commodity to a political weapon" (p. 56). Examples of the implementation of this approach include the independent living movement, which advocated consumer control and rejected professionals' power over disabled people's lives (Boyce et al., 2001), and the ADA, which has had some success in protecting disabled people against discrimination in employment, public accommodations, public transportation and telecommunications (Hinton, 2003; Scotch, 2000).

Universalism Approach

An alternative model is based on the universal nature of disability as it impacts all people. It focuses on variation in human nature, rather than identifying a minority group. Instead of seeking to demarcate disabled and able-bodied people as two separate and distinct categories, a universalism model of disability views functioning and the relative ease with which one interacts with the environment along a continuum. In other words, this approach incorporates the multidimensional variability of disability by critiquing the limits placed on people when society and its institutions have been built to deal with a narrow range of variation (Scotch & Schriner, 1997), or with a very limited definition of normal. This concept can be demonstrated in universal design architecture, whereby buildings and community locations are designed and built to meet the needs of many people with varying motor, vision, hearing or other impairments. A universalism approach still places the onus on the social creation of disability. However, the overarching goal would be to develop societal institutions, policies and practices that are neutral with regard to difference of any sort, including culture, age, sex, language, economic status or (dis)ability.

From a pragmatic perspective, universalism could be used to address the "incapacity of social systems to respond to individual variation" (Scotch & Schriner, 1997, p. 157) rather than to implement specific remedies for a multitude of identified minority groups. Often, under a minority group approach, an individual has to identify as a member of a particular defined (and labelled) group in order to receive benefits or remediation that have been allocated or assigned to that group based on their demonstrated or perceived disadvantage. In a pluralist liberal democracy, such as Canada, this may immediately place the individual (as a member of a designated group) at odds with other minority/oppressed/ disadvantaged groups for limited resources or accommodations. Also, a disabled person will most likely be a member of any number of other minority groups simultaneously, each with their justifiable claims for group rights (Green, 1995).

To be treated equally under universalism, from the perspectives in this chapter, would mean that societal institutions and opportunities would be accessible to more people, regardless of the extent of impairment. In this sense, one would not have to identify explicitly with a particular group in order to access special services assigned to or made available to that group. Although they should never be taken for granted, the scope of unquestioned civil liberties available to all people in many countries, such as freedom of association, religion or expression (Ravaud & Stiker, 2001), would be expanded and, more importantly, operationalized under universalism to cover even more elements of civic participation.

Addressing the Dichotomy

As alluded to in the introduction of this chapter, discussions about inclusion are often obscured by debates in the disability literature about distinctions between minority group and universalism approaches, with various authors advocating for one approach over the other (Barnes, 2003a; Bickenbach, 2001; Bickenbach et al., 1999; Scotch & Schriner, 1997). Although the debate appears valuable for the ongoing theoretical maturation of the sociology of disability, it detracts somewhat from a discussion of what it means to be treated equally as a disabled person. Paraphrasing Stiker (1999) by substituting *ability* for *sex* as a secondary difference in relation to common membership in the human species demonstrates a potential danger in focusing on distinctions in disability concepts: "[I]f we emphasize the difference, breaking the unity of the human, we make [ability] the fundamental one and make the two protagonists into two natures" (p. 193). Being treated equally infers sameness at some level. Focusing on the distinction, rather than this sameness, may detract from the ability to view the quest for equality in a productive and combined fashion. This method is similar to one adopted by Koch (2001) in seeking some common ground between social and physical constructions of disability, and it addresses the perceived disciplinary divide between disability studies and medical sociology (Thomas, 2004).

Much of the recent literature focusing on universalism as it relates to disability appears to promote WHO's ICF as an improved framework on which to measure and classify human functioning. In contrast to its predecessor that focused on the consequences of disease, the 2001 ICF focuses on the components of health, which can be viewed as a more universalist approach. By broadening its potential application, the ICF has alternatively been heralded as an overwhelming international success (Bickenbach, 2001; Bickenbach et al., 1999; Dahl, 2002; Hurst, 2003; Ustun et al., 2003) or as the further entrenchment of an impairment-focused, medical model approach to viewing disability (Barnes, 2003a; Wade & Halligan, 2003). Although beyond the scope of this chapter to provide a critical analysis of the ICF, it is valuable to note that the debate over ICF's potential value also appears to obscure the potential of a mutual viewpoint from which to consider equality.

Attempting to reconcile and balance personal reflections and critical analyses of various themes in the disability literature, it appears that minority group rights and universalism are not necessarily incompatible. Even though it articulates a narrow view of disability as a mobility issue, a quote by Ignatieff (2000), in his book *The Rights Revolution*, encapsulates the potential interconnectedness of the two approaches for viewing equality. It also succinctly illustrates the mutual impacts on those who identify themselves as disabled and those who do not, while hinting at the underlying other notion of *us and them* as another injurious, if not contradictory, dichotomy:

> Even when the rights that are gained are exclusively for the use of a particular group, all may benefit indirectly ... Thus only the disabled specifically benefit when their rights of access and mobility are granted, but the rest of us benefit in a general way too. We benefit because the disabled are freed from dependence relationships that embarrass them and us. Once their mobility rights are guaranteed, they can look after themselves and establish relationships with the rest of us on a basis of genuine equality. (p. 117)

Using this point of view as a transition, the next section of this chapter examines Section 15 of the 1982 *Canadian Charter of Rights and Freedoms* as an example of a constitutional mechanism that appears to blend the varying notions exemplified in the minority group and universalism approaches to viewing disability.

Fusing Divergent Perspectives in the Charter of Rights and Freedoms

Included in the patriation of the Canadian Constitution in 1982 was the *Charter of Rights and Freedoms* (hereafter, the *Charter*), which has particular relevance to this discussion of equal treatment for disabled people. The *Charter* sets out to guarantee broad rights and freedoms of all people and applies to activities of the federal, provincial and territorial parliaments and governments. As such, it represents the second of four basic types of legal expression of human rights as outlined by Bickenbach (2001): "(1) enforceable antidiscrimination legislation, (2) *constitutional guarantees of equality* [italics added], (3) specific entitlement programs, and (4) voluntary human rights manifestos" (p. 568). Included in the opening sections of the *Charter* are the basic fundamental freedoms mentioned earlier in this chapter, such as the freedom of religion and the freedom of association. One particular section of the *Charter*, however, is of critical importance to disabled people and to the notion of blending minority and universal approaches in discussing equal treatment.

Section 15 of the *Charter* "gives explicit recognition to the injustice of discrimination based on mental and physical disability" (Boyce et al., 2001):

> Every individual is equal before and under the law and has the right to the equal protection of the law without discrimination and, in particular, without discrimination based on race, national or ethnic origin, colour, religion, sex, age or mental or physical disability. (*Charter*, 1982, s. 15)

Being named as a particular characteristic in an overarching constitutional document that serves the purpose of articulating fundamental rights for all people holds promise for blending group identity and universal variation. There are pros and cons to explicit references in constitutional documents such as the *Charter* (Bickenbach, 2001), and a thorough review of challenges and references to the *Charter* on the issue of disability is certainly beyond the scope of this chapter. For better or worse, however, the *Charter* inclusion as a particular characteristic raises the profile of disability to a more entrenched level in Canadian society, while simultaneously identifying it as a target for affirmative action laws and programs (Rioux & Prince, 2002). As stated by Torjman (2001): "[T]he inclusion of physical and mental disability as a proscribed ground of discrimination was a pivotal moment in history for the disability community" (p. 155).

Because disability is referenced as a particular *characteristic* that has been associated with unequal treatment and discrimination rather than as a defined and finite *group*, the potential for universal application appears more feasible. The complex operationalizing of what the term "mental or physical disability" encompasses is left to various court decisions and public policies, but the key value of Section 15 lies in the neutrality of the language. For example, the *Charter* does not prohibit discrimination targeted at the very young or to the elderly. It generally states that age is just one of many characteristics shared by all people in varying and interrelated ways across our life continuum. To be explicitly named in a short list of many potential characteristics, even though it was not necessarily easily achieved (Boyce et al., 2001), holds promise for a universal viewing of disability with a minority group flavour. The challenge for disabled people, disability researchers and others is to ensure that disability, having been named in the *Charter*, is not "viewed to some extent as a 'niche concern' [which could yield] a much more limited, lower profile policy discourse" (Cameron & Valentine, 2001, p. 3).

CONCLUSION
This chapter integrates elements of universalism and minority approaches to disability with aspects of equality and equal treatment of disabled people. Through reference to historical and constitutional elements, it has argued that a blend of the two divergent approaches is suitable, if not necessary, for understanding and further advancing disability issues and for addressing what it entails to be treated equally. It concludes that apparent contradictions can, in fact, be valuable to discuss equality for disabled people and as guiding frameworks to hopefully counteract the opinion that "society's wish, as expressed through the treatment of disability, is to make identical, *without making equal* [italics in original]" (Stiker, 1999, p. 150).

7

A National Strategy for Disability Supports: Where Is the Government of Canada in This Social Project?

MICHAEL J. PRINCE

INTRODUCTION

Canadians with disabilities face many barriers in everyday life. In 1996, first ministers identified disability issues as a national priority for renewing social policy. The Government of Canada is on record as being committed to helping people with disabilities participate as fully as possible in Canadian society. However, as yet, we do not have a national strategy on disability supports, raising the questions: where is the federal government on this issue? And what might it do in the near term to put in place a national agenda and framework for action?

This chapter presents a case for the development of a national strategy of disability supports, identifies that existing arrangements are not working and describes the existing intergovernmental transfers in Canada for disability supports, and then outlines a revised transfer and federal investment plan as next steps to realize a vision of full inclusion for Canadians with disabilities. It critiques the declining commitment of the federal government to disabled people. Finally, it presents a proposition for moving forward with a national strategy for investments in disability supports by building on the Multilateral Framework for Labour Market Agreements for Persons with Disabilities.

BACKGROUND

Canadians with disabilities have long been disadvantaged, marginalized and stigmatized. While some important advances have occurred over the last 20 years — including some program reforms recently introduced at both the federal and provincial/territorial levels — there also have been many setbacks and erosions in supports, as well as continued challenges in everyday living and barriers to participation in schools, work, community activities, public services and facilities. Research and experience show that both generic and disability specific community services are inadequate in meeting existing needs.

Large numbers of Canadians with disabilities are not receiving the essential supports and services they require, whether the need is for aids and devices, support with daily activities, specialized housing features or work-related supports. In 2001, the most recent year surveyed, of the adults with disabilities who have some requirement for aids and devices, most have those needs met; that's the good policy news — but 497,000 people living with disabilities in Canada had a level of unmet need, and a further 160,000 adults with disabilities had *none* of the aids and devices they require. Similar patterns of service gaps and unmet needs exist for support with daily activities and specialized housing features (Crawford, 2005). And, the survey suggests that children with disabilities in Canada may be worse off than their adult counterparts in having their needs for aids and devices met. Those Canadians with disabilities most likely to experience unmet needs for supports and service are the most vulnerable among us; they are people with severe and very severe disabilities and low incomes (Fawcett and associates, 2004). Consequently, people with disabilities and their families experience undue hardship and are restricted from full and active participation in economic, educational and social life. Studies show that individuals and their families in Canada bear a disproportionate share of the costs, work and responsibilities associated with addressing the everyday needs of living with disabilities.

Research by Statistics Canada and other agencies, such as the Roeher Institute, identifies persons with disabilities as one of the groups at risk of persistent poverty, a situation that refers to the existence of multiple barriers to participation and where income assistance is absolutely essential yet, by itself, is insufficient to effectively combat poverty (Williams, 2004). Other groups identified by Statistics Canada as at risk of persistent poverty are recent immigrants, Aboriginal peoples, lone parents, and unattached individuals under age 45.

No doubt then, a critical need exists for improved and enhanced supports and services. Today, services and supports are fragmented, often unavailable or unaffordable, not portable across life transitions or places, and all too often disempowering or stigmatizing to those seeking a modicum of assistance to live in dignity and be active citizens.

We know that the needs of Canadians for disability supports and for more inclusive general services will grow and change due to:

- Our aging population;
- Pressures on smaller sized families to provide informal care;
- Public expectations of more flexible service provision and stronger accountability;
- Further de-institutionalization of persons with disabilities from facilities into communities; and
- Labour market needs for well-educated and skilled people.

Disability supports is an issue of employment — indeed, that has been the prime focus of much programming of late. Disability supports is also an issue of mobility and human rights; of independent living, learning and community participation; of personal and social development; of supporting families and caregivers; and in a definitive way, an issue of inclusion, citizenship and dignity.

EXISTING ARRANGEMENTS ARE NOT WORKING

A recent special report by *The Globe and Mail* demonstrates, powerfully and disturbingly, that current arrangements are not desirable, effective or likely sustainable. In a set of articles, *The Globe and Mail* documented the plight of more than 8,500 young and middle-aged people with disabilities across the country who are "stagnating" in nursing homes for the elderly. As the reporter expressed it:

> For Canada's physically and developmentally disabled, who have fought for the past two decades against institutionalization, it

> must seem as if they are stuck in neutral. With too few commu-
> nity supports, scant affordable housing or aged parents who can
> no longer care for them, they may find they have no option but
> a nursing home. (Priest, 2004a, p. A13)

According to the national director of programs and services for muscular dystrophy, "There's a lack of accessible disability supports. There's not enough of them, and when there are government-provided programs, they are very hard to access" (Priest, 2004a, p. A13).

The federal Conservative Party's health critic, Steven Fletcher, paralyzed from the neck down as the result of a car accident when he was 23 years old, recounts that at the time, "I was faced with a nursing home, which is basically a ghetto for people with severe disabilities. I had to fight like crazy to stay out of the institution" (Priest, 2004a, p. A13). Mr. Fletcher, elected as a Member of Parliament in the June 2004 federal election, lives in his own home and has health care aides 24 hours a day, paid in part by automobile insurance. Upon his arrival in Ottawa as an MP, accommodations have been undertaken, quite properly, to accommodate Mr. Fletcher, his wheelchair and attendant. For many other Canadians with disabilities, such financing and support systems are unavailable. Because they cannot afford and access attendant care or other home supports, many persons with disabilities are unable to live independently, who might otherwise be, and often are, maneuvered or compelled into institutions. While for some, the experience in an institution may be positive, for far too many young people with a disability, life in a nursing home can be degrading and depressing (Priest, 2004b).

What observations can we draw from this set of recent articles? As a social issue, with a complex mix of factors, this situation seems to be relatively low on the political and public radar of awareness. As well, there has been a loss of progress and even some slippage in the de-institutionalization of persons with disabilities in Canada, with the adverse result that the expedient of nursing home placements diminishes the human and social development of people, due to segregation, isolation and increased vulnerability.

It is little wonder that investing in a national strategy on disability-related supports is the top priority of the disability community, a goal expressed in various consensus statements and consultation meetings over the last decade (Council of Canadians with Disabilities [CCD], 2003b; CCD & Canadian Association for Community Living [CACL], 2005; Roeher Institute, 2001b). As well, federal, provincial and territorial governments have expressed commitment to this shared goal since 1998, and newly reaffirmed it in the November 2004 communiqué of social service ministers.

On its own, the federal government of Paul Martin also declared in the Speech from the Throne of October 2004 that Ottawa will "be a steadfast advocate of inclusion". And in December 2004, the Standing Committee on Finance, in their annual pre-budget consultation report, recommended that "the federal government meet with provincial/territorial governments and groups representing the disabled [sic] with a view to concluding a federal/provincial/territorial national disability strategy" (Canada, 2004b, Recommendation 28).

"To leave a lasting and distinctive mark on social policy," Jim Rice and I have recently noted, "Martin must identify a key policy area and focus on transformational reform" (Rice & Prince, 2004, p. 128). We suggested that a Canadian disability strategy could well serve as a new national social project, as one of the few bold new initiatives that the Martin Liberals might and could undertake during his tenure as Prime Minister, thus making a historic contribution and leaving an important policy legacy.

Recent federal budgets make one pause, however, and wonder where the federal government really is on this issue.

The 2005 Federal Budget and Liberal Commitments to Canadians with Disabilities: Delivering, Dithering or Declining?

Immediate media reaction to the 2005 federal budget tagged it as a "something for everyone" budget, a political spin most likely welcomed by the Martin Liberals. This characterization, while predictable, given the government's minority status in Parliament, was dangerously misleading for what the budget meant (and did not mean) for disadvantaged and marginalized groups in Canadian society, such as persons with physical and mental disabilities.

It was once said that with this budget then Prime Minister Martin had opened the floodgates of spending, showering billions around the country. *The Globe and Mail* editorial states: "Mr. Martin put aside his tightwad days and spread money around the country like a broken garden hose" (2005, p. A18). The truth was that what Canadians with disabilities would receive from this budget in new spending could only be described as a mere trickle. Of the $6.3 billion in new social spending planned over the five-year period announced in that budget, just over 4% (or $300 million) was specifically earmarked for Canadians with disabilities and family caregivers (Finance Canada, 2005a).

The 2005 budget surprisingly failed to deliver on Liberal commitments to Canadians with disabilities made over previous months and years. The actions that were undertaken reflect only partially Canadian values and Liberal pledges on removing barriers, advancing inclusion, fostering security and widening opportunity. While the Martin government's agenda for Canada's future was described as "ambitious", the claim ringed hollow with respect to disability issues. There was a total absence of a long-term plan and vision, as well as a lack of significant investments across a range of programs, services and transfers in that budget.

What we were seeing was an apparent decline in commitment in the 2005 budget, a postponement of attention to this group of Canadians and, perhaps of greater concern, a waning of sustained interest in matters of priority concern to Canadians living with disabilities. This is more worrisome and serious than rhetorical charges of dithering, which at least imply that a government knows the issues and options on the agenda that are before it, but hesitates and wavers prior to acting.

The new disability measures included in the 2005 federal budget were a series of modest changes to tax measures that would make an important difference, but only to a relatively small proportion of persons living with disabilities. The main initiatives were:

- Extending eligibility for the disability tax credit (DTC) to individuals who face multiple restrictions that together have a substantial impact on their everyday lives.
- Extending the DTC to more individuals who require extensive life-sustaining therapy on an ongoing basis.
- Increasing the maximum annual Child Disability Benefit to $2,000 per child.
- Expanding the list of expenses eligible for the disability supports deduction and the medical expense tax credit.

As well, the budget doubled, to $10,000, the maximum amount of medical and disability-related expenses that caregivers could claim on behalf of their dependants. From the perspective of the overall fiscal plan, obvious social needs, and expressed intergovernmental priorities, the measures for Canadians with disabilities were really minor steps in delivering on commitments to Canadians with disabilities and their families.

National disability organizations responded to this federal budget with what may be called polite yet profound disappointment. The Council of Canadians with Disabilities (CCD) stated:

> The improved tax measures are a positive step in the right direction in addressing the need for investments in supports. But, they are of no benefit to the vast majority of Canadians with disabilities who live in poverty and have no taxable income. (2005b, p. 1)

Marie White, the chairperson of the CCD, asked, "What will it take to get governments to address the real need? What will it take to get governments to address our priority — the investment in disability related services and supports?" (CCD, 2005b, p. 1). The Canadian Association for Community Living (CACL), while welcoming the implementation of the tax reforms, expressed frustration and regret that the Martin government did not move ahead on other commitments to Canadians with disabilities.

Disappointment by the disability community over the 2005 federal budget was conditioned by a number of factors: first, that "the tax system is limited in its ability to address the systemic issues of poverty, unemployment and exclusion effectively" (CACL, 2005, p. 1; Prince, 2001d); second, that the research evidence clearly documents significant gaps in needed services and supports by children and adults with disabilities in Canada; third, that House of Commons committees, public attitudes, and federal/provincial/territorial Ministers of Social Services have all recognized the importance of new investments in disability supports to advance the full participation of persons with disabilities; and fourth, that the 2004 federal budget, which was fiscally more cautious, included investments in employment, disability supports and income, and thus had been interpreted by many disability activists as laying the platform for a national disability strategy (CACL, 2004).

In addition, what *text* there was in the budget speech on issues of disability, and there was not very much, was problematic in what it said and in what was not said (Finance Canada, 2005b, p. 7). Implicit in the language used and in the issues highlighted in the budget speech was the old view of disability as a personal tragedy and biomedical phenomenon, resulting in a situation that intrinsically is burdensome for family caregivers. Absent was any reference to the more contemporary social model of disability that addresses attitudinal, institutional and environmental factors; absent, too, was any reference to equality rights and full citizenship, a terminology and philosophy apparent in previous budget speeches.

So, what to do? In his budget speech, Finance Minister Ralph Goodale declared, "This government will deliver!" For "[t]he disabled and their caregivers," among others, "[t]his government will deliver" (Finance Canada, 2005b, pp. 4–5). The immediate and obvious question for Canadians with disabilities was: when will the government deliver, on what exactly, and through which policy instruments?

The budget did contain a favourable fiscal context and some design elements for a possible strategic approach to disability supports. Budget surpluses were projected in each of the next five years, along with steady economic growth, low and stable inflation and a declining national debt. A number of other policy areas in the budget were guided by general goals and the pacing of implementation over several years, using a five-year fiscal framework to provide reliable and long-term funding. As an approach to innovating social policy, these are aspects of "directed incrementalism" — the setting of bold goals and working toward them step-by-step over the medium to long term (Prince, 2002b).

I want to turn to sketching the outlines of an approach to formulating a national strategy on disability supports using the federal spending power of direct expenditures, more specifically, intergovernmental transfer payments.

Why a Federal Transfer?

Federal grants in aid of particular expenditures in disability services have a fairly long and evolving history. The transfer of funds from the federal government to the provinces has been an important aspect of disability supports and intergovernmental relations in Canada for about 50 years.

Arrangements in the 1950s were formalized with legislation in 1961 on the Vocational Rehabilitation of Disabled Persons (VRDP), a program that ran from the early 1960s to the late 1990s when it was replaced with the Employability Assistance for Persons with Disabilities (EAPD). The EAPD was a multilateral agreement in effect from 1998 to 2003, which was succeeded by the Multilateral Framework on Labour Market Agreements for Persons with Disabilities (hereafter, the Multilateral Framework), with bilateral agreements in effect from 2004 to 2006.

There has been, then, a solid history of governments working in partnership, based on the use of the federal spending power and a shared commitment to improving opportunities for Canadians with disabilities — specifically for working age adults and increasingly on employment-related activities.

It is of more than mere historical interest that while other shared cost transfer arrangements in social policy disappeared or declined in the 1990s, this mechanism was preserved and subsequently revised with successive arrangements. This policy choice is politically significant, telling us something of the values that Canadians hold and their belief in a continued role by the federal government in the field of disability services and supports.

The rationale for a continued federal role in this field through intergovernmental transfers includes the following ideas:

- To address the core mandate and underlying mission of the Department of Human Resources and Social Development Canada;

- To support the portability of services and the mobility rights of Canadians with disabilities within and across jurisdictions and life situations;

- To encourage the further development and enhancement of the current patchwork of disability-related supports across the country;

- To assist provinces and territories, with their varying degrees of fiscal capacity, to undertake the provision of a range of accessible and responsive supports; and

- To advance equality rights under the *Canadian Charter* by sponsoring programs and activities that aim to ameliorate conditions of disadvantaged individuals because of mental or physical disability.

By increasing the size and nature of transfers to the provinces for disability supports, the federal government can directly contribute to closing the gaps between needs and services and thus truly advance the economic inclusion and social citizenship of Canadians with disabilities (Boadway, 2004).

Options for a Federal Transfer on Disability Supports

In transferring funds to the provinces and territories for disability supports, three basic options seem available in theory.

One option is to create an entirely new federal transfer arrangement for this initiative. There seems little appetite or support for this approach by some federal officials and by some provinces and territories. It would also likely add to the complexity of an already multifaceted system of fiscal federalism.

A second option is to add a fund within either the Canada Social Transfer or the Canada Health Transfer, in effect an earmarked supplement for financing disability supports. A concern with using either of these transfers is that given their large expenditures for other policy matters, disability issues could easily be dwarfed within them in terms of public support, political attention, and future investments. Another concern, with respect to the CST is that few accountability mechanisms are associated with this transfer arrangement. And, with respect to the CHT, a concern is that it would reinforce a medical model of disability rather than the social model preferred by most in the disability community.

Rather than using either the CST or CHT for disability-specific supports, another approach would be to ensure that these transfer arrangements reflect in their goals, values and administrative principles that vision of inclusion and empowerment expressed by *In Unison* and other policy statements.

A third option is to adapt and build on the federal transfer that already exists for disability supports. This approach involves engaging the disability community and other governments in a process of planning for a successor agreement to the Multilateral Framework.

Although this option raises issues of its own, such as the fact that Quebec and the territories are not signatories to the Multilateral Framework, these issues do not amount to insurmountable problems. (Quebec has participated in past intergovernmental agreements for persons with disabilities under bilateral arrangements with Ottawa; and the issue of participation by the territories is linked with resolving the relation between territorial financing and territorial-own source revenues — a matter, quite frankly, for political leaders to resolve.) What is more, this option has a number of advantages: there is a record of intergovernmental collaboration; it is a transfer familiar to groups in the disability community; it recognizes that provinces have primary responsibility in this area; administrative and accountability systems are in place; and the arrangement is up for review in any case in 2007.

What Is the Multilateral Framework?

With some input from the disability community as well as other stakeholders (business, labour, Aboriginal organizations),

Ministers responsible for Social Services endorsed the Multilateral Framework for Labour Market Agreements for Persons with Disabilities in 2002.

The goal of the Multilateral Framework is to improve the employment status of Canadians with disabilities. Behind this goal are the three objectives of enhancing the employability of persons with disabilities, increasing employment opportunities, and building on the existing knowledge base of people and employers. Thus, the focus is on working age adults with disabilities.

Several principles, agreed to by governments, underlie this initiative. The first, and perhaps overarching, one states that "[p]ersons with disabilities should be fully included in Canada's social and economic mainstream." Other principles speak of the need for a diverse set of approaches; access to mainstream and targeted programming; and the importance of supports and services that are "individualized, holistic, linked to other needed support systems" as well as "easy to access, portable across life situations, timely and inclusive" (Prince, 2002a, p. 61).

The Multilateral Framework has a cost-shared funding model. The federal government funds 50% of costs incurred by provinces for programs identified as priority areas under the Framework, up to an amount allocated in bilateral agreements negotiated with each province (except Quebec).

We can further describe the Multilateral Framework as a semi-conditional and closed-ended grant. That is, there are some general parameters regarding the areas and ways in which the funds can be spent, though leaving considerable discretion to the recipient government to decide. And, as a closed-ended transfer, there is an upper limit specified beyond which the federal government does not transfer further funds for costs incurred by provinces in providing eligible services or supports. So, under the previous agreement, the EAPD, in 2002–2003, governments contributed $477 million to labour market programs for persons with disabilities, of which $288 million was provincial funding and the other $189 million was federal funding. The 2003 federal budget renewed the Government of Canada's funding commitment under EAPD and its successor at $193 per year.

In practice, in recent years this has meant that the federal share of contributions on employment-related disability supports has actually declined from about 50% to 39.6% in 2002–2003. The 2004 federal budget announced a $30 million increase to the Multilateral Framework, raising the annual federal contribution to $222 million in the 2004–2005 fiscal year.

Five priority areas are identified as eligible for funding by the federal government: education and training; employment participation; employment opportunities; connecting employers and persons with disabilities; and building the knowledge base.

In terms of accountability requirements, provinces are to report on objectives, descriptions, target populations, and planned expenditures for programs and services. Baseline reports with this information were released by each jurisdiction on 3 December 2004. Reporting is also to include program indicators that specify the number of participants in programs and services; the number of participants completing a program or service where there is a specific start and end point to the intervention; and the number of participants obtaining or maintaining employment, where the program or service supports this activity. Beginning in 2005 and annually thereafter, governments have agreed also to report on a set of "societal indicators" that include the employment rate of working age persons with disabilities, employment income, and education attainment.

The Multilateral Framework as a Platform for Reform

The Multilateral Framework can readily serve as the platform for a new national strategy on disability supports. A new national strategy can build on the goals, objectives and principles, and the accountability and reporting features of the existing transfer program.

This is a key message: it is not a huge leap from the existing framework and transfer arrangement to a more comprehensive and substantial federal investment in supports and service for Canadians with disabilities.

A revised multilateral framework builds on the idea that employment-related supports are central to the success of persons with disabilities in the economic mainstream by adding other equally critical areas that require further public investments. The concept of supports would therefore be broadened to include an intervention, service, benefit or assistance provided to a person with a disability to assist the person and or their family in activities of everyday living and caregiving, in learning and education, and in preparing for, or attaining or maintaining, employment.

Expressed in relation to the strategic outcomes of social development, our proposal is to build on the goal of enhancing the economic participation of adult Canadians with disabilities, extending it to include promoting economic and social inclusion, participation, and well-being within inclusive communities for Canadians with disabilities of all ages.

Desired outcomes from such a collaborative intergovernmental initiative, that would form the basis for the accountability and reporting system, could include:

- Expanded quantity of existing supports to alleviate major gaps in coverage;
- Improved quality of supports;
- Reduced costs to individuals and families; and
- Enhanced portability of supports.

The actual number, nature and measures for desired outcomes would be, as expected, the subject of negotiations and consultations both within and across governments and the disability community. A parallel process would take place with national Aboriginal and community organizations.

Funded priority areas would span the life course and various life transitions, such as educational supports for children and youth; information and respite services for parents and other informal caregivers; and for all persons with disabilities, personal care, home supports, home modifications, local transportation arrangements, and service planning and service brokerage/co-ordination. These are the areas research consistently points to as essential for addressing gaps in unmet needs for supports, overcoming barriers, enabling inclusion and independent living, and supporting consumer control and improving the quality of life for Canadians with disabilities.

Federal funding under a new policy framework would be available to provinces and territories for this kind of array of personal supports for Canadians with disabilities and their families. Since the intent is to increase the supply and quality of much needed disability supports, it would need to be agreed that there would be no "clawback" of new federal investments in disability supports by recipient governments.

In recognition and respect of the fact that disability supports and services is an area of primarily provincial jurisdiction under the Constitution, the actual mix of areas funded in a given jurisdiction would be determined by that provincial or territorial government, in the context of shared goals and principles, and in consultation with representatives of the disability community in the jurisdiction. The approach I propose is not a national *system* with a standardized design with commands and controls by Ottawa; rather, I envisage a national *strategy* with shared policy objectives and desired outcomes informed by guiding principles and jurisdictionally based accountabilities.

The federal government would also offer adequate funding to enable national and provincial/territorial disability organizations to have the capacity to engage effectively in such consultations. A related question for the community and government to ponder is the necessity and potential effectiveness of a national council on disability, like the ones in health or learning that would act as a mechanism both to do public reporting and give some profile to the federal role. Over time, this initiative, with new, predictable and stable federal investments, will build a more secure base for the full age range and life situations of Canadians with disabilities, creating the foundation for their fuller participation in, and contribution to, all facets of Canadian society.

CONCLUSION

The case for the development of a national strategy for disability supports has been presented. The lack of disability supports — any good service or environmental adaptation that assists people with disabilities and their families to overcome limitations — results in poverty, exclusion, unemployment, discrimination and despair. To tackle these issues, this chapter described a revised transfer and federal investment plan. It also examined the possibility of developing a national strategy for disability supports by building on the Multilateral Framework for Labour Market Agreements for Persons with Disabilities.

Disability supports are a major need for people with disabilities and must be a priority for government action to improve the lives of Canadians with disabilities. To guide future action, both in the near term and the longer term of a decade or more, an overarching policy framework with measurable targets and a schedule is crucial to ensure that warm words do not result in cold comfort but rather produce authentic, meaningful and positive changes in people's life circumstances and opportunities. Given that disability issues are horizontal in nature, touching various policy fields and domains of life, a comprehensive and strategic approach that also includes a partnership approach among governments and between governments and individuals with disabilities, families and community groups is absolutely essential.

With the Martin Liberals defeat in the 2006 Canadian general election and a new Conservative government led by Stephen Harper, the political and policy context for disability issues is definitely altered. Of particular interest is the Conservative Party of Canada's commitment to a *National Disability Act* through which, they claim, reasonable access to health care, medical equipment, education, housing and transportation would be guaranteed to persons with disabilities. This legislative promise presents mixed signals for the disability community in Canada. On one hand, a new Act might strengthen enforcement of activities within areas of federal jurisdiction such as telecommunications, employment equity and human rights. On the other hand, a new Act is unlikely to tackle issues of poverty, literacy and the lack of disability-related supports, which are issues that largely fall within provincial areas of jurisdiction.

The 2006 federal budget of the Harper government did not include a broad strategy for disability issues but did contain specific tax measures and some vague intentions for further programming on employment supports and workforce participation. The maximum annual value of the Child Disability Benefit increased by 12.5% to $2,300, and eligibility was extended to more families, effective July 2006. The yearly maximum amount for the Refundable Medical Expenses Supplement rose 30% to $1,000 for the 2006 taxation year. The new Children's Fitness Tax Credit, announced in this budget, will seek to ensure that programs for children with disabilities qualify.

Thus, in this context, the Multilateral Framework approach remains an attractive option for comprehensive reform. Achieving an accessible and inclusive Canada, therefore, remains an elusive national social project.

8

Trends Impacting Disability: National and International Perspectives

MARCIA H. RIOUX
AND RITA M. SAMSON

INTRODUCTION

The disability policy context has changed significantly over the last few decades. This chapter provides a brief overview of important trends that affect disability policy:

1. New conceptualizations of disability;
2. Increasing recognition by bodies in the UN system and the international community of disability as a human rights issue;
3. Changing law and policy relating to disability at the national level;
4. Development of a grassroots disability rights movement and national and international organizations led by people with disabilities themselves;
5. Greater incidence and shifting causes of impairments;
6. Globalization; and
7. Biotechnology and genetics.

112

TRENDS AFFECTING DISABILITY POLICY
New Conceptualizations of Disability

The past few decades have witnessed the development of new conceptualizations of disability. By identifying different determinants of disability, the various conceptualizations impact the allocation of social responsibility for disability, the nature and scope of disability policy, legislation, programming and research, societal attitudes toward people with disabilities and the role of people with disabilities in all of these processes.

Conceptualizations of disability as an individual pathology have framed much of disability policy, legislation and programming in the past century and, until recently, have formed the dominant theoretical lens for the interpretation of disability (Rioux, 1997, 2003). Under this view, "[t]he impairment becomes the defining feature of the disabled person's self-identity and expectations" (Barnes, Mercer & Shakespeare, 1999, p. 41). Disability is treated as a form of deviance and a social burden. In research and policy, the focus of analysis is on the individual. Medical, social and other interventions focus on the individual whose qualities are seen as falling outside of established norms. The onus is on the person with a disability and his or her family to find ways to be included in society, and the imperative for social responsibility is charity and benevolence. Individual pathology approaches can be subdivided into biomedical and functional models.

The biomedical model assumes that disability is caused primarily by a disease, disorder, physical or mental condition that is aberrant or abnormal, but that can be prevented or ameliorated through biological, medical or genetic intervention by suitably skilled and qualified professionals. Disability is medicalized. Under the biomedical model, people with disabilities have been positioned as "other" to an established norm. In many instances, people with disabilities have been considered dangerous and/or non-contributing members of society without potential (Cohen, 1985; Cohen & Scull, 1983; Sutherland, 1976). Historically, this association of disability with pathology and danger formed the rationale for institutionalized exclusions of the population of people with disabilities in hospitals, workhouses or within their homes, and justified their exemption from mainstream education, employment, and other rights enjoyed by citizens who reflected the normative ideal (Foucault, 1976). In its harshest form, the biomedical model treated people with disabilities as inferior; in its kinder form, it treated them as helpless victims requiring care and protection. Proponents of the biologi-

113

cal model found people with disabilities both undeserving and incapable of managing the same rights and responsibilities as the rest of the population.

While still locating disability at the level of the individual, the functional model focuses not on the biological impairment but, rather, on the impact that impairment may have on a person's functional capacity. Interventions extend beyond medical cures and rehabilitation to include strategies aimed toward making the individual as socially functional as possible. Services developed from a functional approach (e.g., physiotherapy, occupational therapy, nursing and health visiting) have gone beyond therapeutic programs to include options such as life-skills training, pre-vocational training, functional assessments, counselling and job training, as well as skills for independent living. Such therapies are aimed at increasing peoples' independence and social productivity by developing skills and abilities regardless of impairment. The goal is for the individual to live as "normally" as possible, with skills comparable to those of people without disabilities (Meyer, Peck & Brown, 1991; Wolfensberger, 1972). The onus remains on the individual to change, while the power and expertise remains in the hands of professionals.

Toward the end of the 1960s, disability and human rights activists and theorists began to formulate new conceptions of disability in response to the oppressive and restrictive nature of the biomedical and functional discourses (Oliver, 1990; Rioux, 1997, 2003). They noted that by focusing solely on the biological and functional condition of the individual, these models fail to address the role played by society in limiting and enabling people. Disability is not inherent in the individual but rather is a function of social and economic conditions within society (Rioux, 2001). Social change is emphasized through interventions directed at political, social, economic and physical environments and systems rather than through cures or therapies for individuals. In contrast to the biomedical approach, the social pathology paradigm requires that people with disabilities have the opportunity to participate fully in society, and not be isolated in institutions with segregated services. The inclusion of people with disabilities is considered a public responsibility, since the characteristics associated with disability are interpreted as normal occurrences within the range of human diversity and difference rather than as deviant anomalies. Social pathology approaches to disability can be subdivided into the environmental and human rights models.

The environmental model of disability refutes the notion that disability is inherent in the individual, holding that personal abilities and limitations are determined by the interaction between an individual and his or her environments which may or may not accommodate that individual's differences. The policy and program focus is placed on the way that environments are arranged (Bercovici, 1983). Barriers in society that restrict the participation of people with impairments in economic, social and political life are identified and become sites for state intervention. Policy responses to these barriers emphasize the adaptation of physical and social environments to enable participation of people with a diversity of physical and mental characteristics through strategies such as implementing accessibility in building codes, principles of barrier-free design, adapted curricula, targeted policy and funding commitments. As distinguished from the individual pathology paradigm where decisions were made on behalf of people with disabilities, the environmental model requires that criteria for support programs prioritize individual determination of their own needs and individual control of services and supports.

The human rights model of disability builds on the conceptualization of the environmental model, extending the notion of disability as a result of environmental barriers to look at the overriding social causes of inequities and framing disability issues using human rights principles. In a human rights framework, disability is a consequence of social organization and individual status within larger social arrangements (Beresford & Campbell, 1994; Fougeyrollas, 1991; Oliver, 1990; Rioux & Bach, 1994; Roeher Institute, 1993b; Roth, 1983). Research, policy and law from a human rights approach look beyond particular environments to focus on the broad systemic factors preventing some groups from participating in society as equals. Determinants of disability from the human rights perspective are very wide-ranging and include many aspects: income and social status, social support networks, education, employment and working conditions, social environments, physical environments, biology and genetic factors, personal health practices and coping skills, health services, gender and culture. It is significant to note that the human rights approach does not ignore biological or genetic "impairment". However, in contrast to individual pathology approaches, it considers impairment as only one of the many determinants of disability. There is a presumption under the human rights model that public policy and programs should reflect a social responsibility to reduce civic inequalities and address social and economic disadvantage. Whereas the imperative

115

of social responsibility is derived from charity and benevolence under the individual pathology paradigm, it is a matter of justice and equality under the human rights model.

The human rights model includes disability rights within a paradigm of rights that have gained recognition since the adoption of the *Universal Declaration of Human Rights* (UDHR) by the UN General Assembly in 1948. The UDHR recognizes that all people are entitled to certain civil, political, economic, social and cultural rights, based on their status as humans and regardless of differences between individuals. Quinn and Degener have noted:

> [T]he human rights perspective means viewing people with disabilities as subjects and not as objects. It entails moving away from viewing people with disabilities as problems toward viewing them as rights holders. Importantly, it means locating any problems outside the person and especially in the manner by which various economic and social processes accommodate the difference of disability or not as the case may be. The debate about disability rights is therefore connected to a larger debate about the place of difference in society. (2002, p. 1)

A rights model of disability perceives variation in human characteristics associated with disability, whether in cognitive, sensory or motor ability, as inherent to the human condition. Whereas the quality of life of people with disabilities is measured according to the degree to which they are able to "normalize" under the individual pathology models, differences are not masked but are recognized and given priority under the human rights model. Variations do not limit potential contributions to society, but rather diversify the range of potential contributions and the mechanisms necessary to ensure that individual potential is realized.

The rights model acknowledges that in order to realize their potential, people have a right to supports such as personal services or aids and devices that they may need. There is a presumption that all people have the right to access, participate in and exercise self-determination as equals in society. It also recognizes that the ways in which institutions are organized must be changed to take into account the diversity of those who will be participating. For example, labour practices are as important as ramps in enabling people with disabilities to be employed. Flexibility of institutional policy is essential to the exercise of rights.

With the recent development of social pathology conceptualizations of disability, individual biology and functional capacity are no longer the only lenses through which disability is viewed. All four approaches to disability can be found in contemporary policy, law, and programs. Governments' efforts to adapt to shifting conceptualizations of disability are, in some cases, reflected in hybridized laws, programs and policies that include aspects of two or more of the models of disability. While individual pathology models continue to play a role in diagnosing disability, determining eligibility for programs and benefits and influencing access to rights and full participation, disability organizations, activists and experts have made tremendous progress in achieving a paradigm shift toward the social pathology models.

Increasing Recognition of Disability as a Human Rights Issue

Evidence of the paradigm shift from the individual to social pathology models can be seen in the activities and statements of bodies within the UN system and the wider international community wherein recognition of disability as a human rights issue is significantly increasing.

During the first three decades of UN's existence, people with disabilities were virtually ignored. When the *International Bill of Rights* (UN General Assembly, 1948, 1966a, 1966b) was drafted, disability was not included as a prohibited ground of discrimination in the equality provisions, indicating that, at that time, people with disabilities were not considered a group vulnerable to human rights violations. To the extent that disability issues were addressed by the United Nations, they were viewed from a biomedical and functional perspective, with efforts focused on prevention and rehabilitation measures, operationalized through technical assistance and information campaigns (UN Department of Economic and Social Affairs [UNDESA], 1997). Little attention was paid to obstacles to the full participation of people with disabilities created by social institutions and society in general (UNDESA, 1997).

It was not until the 1970s that people with disabilities were explicitly rendered subjects of human rights declarations in the *Declaration of the Rights of Mentally Retarded Persons* and the *Declaration on the Rights of Disabled Persons* (UN General Assembly, 1971, 1975). While both declarations recognize people with disabilities as rights bearers, these early instruments reflect the biomedical and functional models of disability, viewing people with disabilities principally as people with medical problems, dependent on social security and welfare and in need of segregated services and institutions. Moreover, both declarations purport to set limits on the rights of people with disabilities that are inconsistent with the provisions of the Bill of Rights. For example, paragraph 1 of the 1971 *Declaration of the Rights of Mentally Retarded Persons* states, "The mentally retarded person has, *to the maximum degree of feasibility*, the same rights as other human beings" [emphasis added].

While instruments in the Bill of Rights do place limitations on the exercise and/or enjoyment of certain rights, these instruments do not question the *entitlement of all humans to all rights* (civil, economic, social, cultural, political), *without discrimination*. Moreover, the extent to which the disability-specific declarations purport to limit the exercise of rights by people with disabilities far exceeds those limitations set out in the instruments of the Bill of Rights. Paragraph 7 of the 1971 *Declaration of the Rights of Mentally Retarded Persons* refers to situations in which it may "become necessary to restrict or deny some or *all* of these rights" [emphasis added]. After stating that people with disabilities have the same civil and political rights as other human beings, paragraph 4 of the 1975 *Declaration on the Rights of Disabled Persons* states that paragraph 7 of the 1971 *Declaration of the Rights of Mentally Retarded Persons* "applies to any possible limitation or suppression of those rights for mentally disabled persons". As such, the declarations leave open the possibility of limiting or denying the exercise and enjoyment of *any* and *all* rights by people with mental disabilities. This is directly contrary to the level of protection afforded by the Bill of Rights instruments, which recognize that there are certain rights that are non-negotiable: for example, the right to life; freedom from torture, cruelty, inhuman or degrading treatment or punishment; no medical or scientific experimentation without free and informed consent; freedom from slavery and involuntary servitude; and the right to recognition as a person before the law. At no time and for no reason may a state limit or deny the exercise of these rights for *any* human being. While explicitly recognizing people with disabilities as rights bearers, by offering fewer entitlements and protections than people with disabilities already held under the Bill of Rights, the disability declarations arguably pushed the cause of the recognition of human rights for people with disabilities backward several steps.

In 1976, the UN General Assembly declared that 1981 would be the International Year for Disabled Persons (IYDP). A major outcome of the IYDP was the General Assembly's 1982 adoption and call for implementation of the World Programme of Action concerning Disabled Persons (the Programme) (1982a, 1982b). The Programme recognized the responsibility within the UN system of addressing the human rights of people with disabilities, in the following recommendation:

> Organizations and bodies involved in the United Nations system responsible for the preparation and administration of international agreements, covenants and other instruments that might have a direct or indirect impact on persons with disabilities should ensure that such instruments fully take into account the situation of persons who are disabled. (UN Advisory Committee for IYDP, 1982, para. 164)

The first two goals of the Programme — prevention and rehabilitation — reflected the individual pathology model of disability. However, the Programme's third goal — equalization of opportunities — marked the beginning of a shift to a human rights approach to disability. The Programme defined "equalization of opportunity" as

> ... the process through which the general system of society, such as the physical and cultural environment, housing and transportation, social and health services, educational and work opportunities, cultural and social life, including sports and recreational facilities are made accessible to all. (UN Advisory Committee for IYDP, 1982, para. 12)

Also, significantly, the relationship between disability and the environment was officially recognized in the definition of "handicap":

> Handicap is therefore a function of the relationship between persons with disabilities and their environment. It occurs when they encounter cultural, physical or social barriers, which prevent their access to the various systems of society that are available to other citizens. Thus, handicap is the loss or limitation of opportunities to take part in the community on an equal level with others. (UN Advisory Committee for IYDP, 1982, para. 7)

The Programme recognized the applicability of existing human rights instruments to people with disabilities and required states, among other actors, to ensure opportunities for people with disabilities by eliminating barriers to full participation and to create, through legislation, the necessary legal bases and authority for measures to achieve the Programme's objectives (UN Advisory Committee for IYDP, 1982, paras. 71 and 162–169). It explicitly recognized the responsibility of the organizations and bodies in the UN system to address the human rights of people with disabilities (UN Advisory Committee for IYDP, 1982, para. 164). In addition, the Programme called for the proactive promotion of the participation of people with disabilities in decision-making and the establishment and empowerment of organizations of people with disabilities (UN Advisory Committee for IYDP, 1982, para. 92).

To facilitate the implementation of the Programme, in 1982, the General Assembly proclaimed the period between 1983 and 1992 the UN Decade of Disabled Persons (1982b). During this decade, the international community made significant progress toward enabling the full participation of people with disabilities in all spheres of society.

In August 1984, the Sub-Commission on Prevention of Discrimination and Protection of Minorities appointed a Special Rapporteur, Mr. Leandro Despouy, to conduct a comprehensive study on the relationship between human rights and disability. In his 1993 report, *Human Rights and Disabled Persons*, Mr. Despouy made it clear that disability is a human rights concern in which UN treaty monitoring bodies should be involved. Included among his recommendations was the following:

> After the Decade has ended, the question of human rights and disability should be kept on the agendas of the General Assembly, the Economic and Social Council, the Commission on Human Rights and the Sub-Commission as an item of constant concern and on-going attention. (Despouy, 1993, para. 274)

Together with another report issued during the decade (Daes, 1983), the Despouy report assisted in gaining recognition for people with disabilities not only as recipients of charity, but as the subject of human rights.

In 1989, the first specific reference to the rights of people with disabilities in a binding international human rights treaty was included in Article 23 of the *Convention on the Rights of the Child* (UN General Assembly, 1989).

Further evidence of the endorsement of the rights-based approach to disability by the international community was signalled by the General Assembly's 1993 adoption of the *Standard Rules on the Equalization of Opportunities for Persons with Disabilities* (hereafter, Standard Rules). The Standard Rules provide concrete and direct advice on disability policy. By mandating individual empowerment, independence and increased structural access, the Standard Rules address the exclusion of people with disabilities from participation in their communities (Lindqvist, 2002). The Standard Rules are designed to ensure that children and adults with disabilities enjoy the same rights and obligations as other people and participate fully in their societies, without obstacles. The 22-rule instrument reflects a strong human rights perspective, outlining a process for national governments, in partnership with people with disabilities and disability organizations, to identify and remove obstacles to full participation.

While not legally binding, the Standard Rules serve as guidelines for policy development and a tool for advocacy. They also demonstrate a strong moral and political commitment on behalf of states to enabling the human rights of people with disabilities through the equalization of opportunities. Beginning in 1998, and continuing in subsequent resolutions, the UN Commission on Human Rights has reinforced the importance and significance of the Standard Rules as an evaluative instrument to be used to assess the degree of compliance with human rights standards concerning people with disabilities:

> The Commission on Human Rights ... *Recognizes* that any violation of the fundamental principle of equality or any discrimination or other negative differential treatment of persons with disabilities inconsistent with the United Nations Standard Rules on the Equalization of Opportunities for Persons with Disabilities is an infringement of the human rights of persons with disabilities. (para. 1)

Unlike other non-binding international disability instruments, the Standard Rules have a Special Rapporteur and a panel of experts with the mandate to promote and monitor their implementation. The first person to be appointed as Special Rapporteur, Dr. Bengt Lindqvist, notes that the Standard Rules are being applied for advocacy, policy making, legislation and evaluation in all regions of the world and by many governments and disability organizations (Lindqvist, 2002).

The Standard Rules also informed one of the most important international human rights documents in the disability field — the 1994 General Comment No. 5 of the UN Committee on Economic, Social and Cultural Rights (CESCR, the body of independent experts that monitors the International Covenant on Economic, Social and Cultural Rights). General comments are issued by treaty monitoring bodies to provide detail regarding procedures relating to monitoring and to explain the content of specific rights guaranteed under the treaty. While other UN treaty monitoring bodies have referred to disability in various statements and documents, General Comment No. 5 is the only detailed analysis outlining how general human rights guarantees apply to people with disabilities. In this General Comment, the CESCR analyses disability as a human rights issue. The General Comment states:

> The Covenant does not refer explicitly to persons with disabilities. Nevertheless, the Universal Declaration of Human Rights recognizes that all human beings are born free and equal in dignity and rights and, since the Covenant's provisions apply fully to all members of society, persons with disabilities are clearly entitled to the full range of rights recognized in the Covenant. In addition, in so far as special treatment is necessary, States parties are required to take appropriate measures, to the maximum extent of their available resources, to enable such persons to seek to overcome any disadvantages, in terms of the enjoyment of the rights specified in the Covenant, flowing from their disability. Moreover, the requirement contained in article 2(2) of the Covenant that the rights "enunciated ... will be exercised without discrimination of any kind" based on certain specified grounds "or other status" clearly applies to discrimination on the grounds of disability. (UNCESCR, 1994, para. 5)

Clear endorsement by the international community of a human rights approach to disability is evidenced in a series of resolutions adopted by the UN Commission on Human Rights (CHR). Beginning in the early 1990s, the CHR has adopted almost yearly resolutions specifically regarding the human rights of people with disabilities. Each new resolution has included more provisions and used stronger language than the last to recognize both the rights of people with disabilities and UN's role in the protection and promotion of those rights. The CHR has often been criticized for its political bias — its members are appointed by member states and, as a result, their positions on issues often simply reflect state views. However, Alston notes that the CHR "has firmly established itself as [the] single most important United Nations organ in the human rights field" (1992, p. 126). The very fact of the CHR's politicization means that its clear and continued endorsement of a human rights approach to disability can be seen to represent the wide acceptance of this point of view by the international community.

Moreover, inclusion of the human rights of people with disabilities as specific policy concerns in such documents as the *Vienna Declaration and Programme of Action* adopted by the 1993 World Conference on Human Rights, the *Copenhagen Declaration on Social Development and Programme of Action* of the 1995 World Summit for Social Development and the *Beijing Declaration and*

Platform for Action adopted by the Fourth World Conference on Women in 1995, provide further evidence of international recognition and support for a broad human rights approach to advance the status of persons with disabilities in mainstream development.

In its 2000 resolution, the CHR called for an examination "of measures to strengthen the protection and monitoring of human rights of persons with disabilities" (para. 30). This led to a study commissioned by the UN Office of the High Commissioner for Human Rights evaluating "the current use and future potential of United Nations human rights instruments in the context of disability" (Quinn & Degener, 2002). The report found that while some steps have been taken by the existing UN treaty monitoring bodies to include the consideration of disability, the rights of people with disabilities are, on the whole, ignored by these processes. In addition, the study found that when disability is addressed, it is not addressed coherently or consistently, and that the individual pathology model of disability often prevails in the attitudes and actions of States parties.

Calls from disability rights experts and disability organizations for binding protection and promotion of the rights of people with disabilities led to the General Assembly's adoption of resolution 56/168 in December 2001. The resolution establishes an Ad Hoc Committee "to consider proposals for a comprehensive and integral international convention to promote and protect the rights and dignity of persons with disabilities" (para. 1). The Ad Hoc Committee has held seven sessions and with others planned.

Once negotiated and ratified by a sufficient number of countries, a disability rights treaty would create legally binding human rights obligations specific to the needs and situation of people with disabilities. As demonstrated by the experiences of the 1981 UN *Convention on the Elimination of All Forms of Discrimination against Women* and the 1989 UN *Convention on the Rights of the Child*, a disability-specific convention would play a crucial role in ensuring that disability is recognized and accepted as a human rights issue. In addition, a convention could create a specific mechanism to monitor the progress of States parties in protecting and promoting disability rights. However, learning from the experience of the disability declarations, the drafters of the new convention must be wary that the provisions agreed to do not purport to detract, in any way, from rights entitlements already guaranteed to people with disabilities in the Bill of Rights instruments.

Concurrently with the process to draft a disability-focused convention, opportunities exist to develop and enhance the disability dimension in existing international, regional and national human rights systems. At a meeting in 2002, hosted by the UN High Commissioner for Human Rights, with the participation of Special Rapporteur on Disability Lindqvist, over 30 State representatives, nongovernmental organizations and UN agency participants agreed on a multifaceted approach to disability. They endorsed a "twin-track approach" whereby "the drafting of a new convention should not be seen as an alternative to strengthening attention to disability within the existing international human rights system" (Special Rapporteur on Disability [SPD], 2002).

Other bodies in the UN system have shifted their conceptual approach to disability. In the case of WHO, this shift may be seen through the systems it has developed to classify disability and its role in community-based rehabilitation. Adopted by the World Health Assembly in 1980, the *International Classification of Impairments, Disabilities and Handicaps* (ICIDH) proposes concepts and definitions of "impairment" (abnormality in function), "disability" (not being able to perform an activity considered "normal" for a human being) and "handicap" (inability to perform a "normal" social role) (Barnes, 1991; Oliver, 1990). A causal linear progression is assumed from impairment to disability to handicap. With disability and handicap flowing from the starting point of intellectual or physical "abnormality" (impairment), a strong individual pathology focus is maintained.

In 2001, WHO approved a new system of classification, the ICF, to replace the ICIDH. The ICF retains the mixed models of disability, but strives to place more emphasis on non-medical determinants by focusing on "components of health classification" instead of "consequences of disease classification". The new model replaces the ICIDH's linear connection between impairment, disability and handicap with bi-directional arrows linking these and other elements of health, functioning and disability. The ICF also explicitly recognizes the role of environmental and personal factors as determinants.

While moving closer to the social pathology paradigm by removing the causal link and including consideration of personal and environmental factors, the ICF still maintains a fundamentally biomedical approach (Hurst, 2000). Disability remains primarily a health rather than a political concern, and individual functioning remains the starting point of the analysis (C. Barnes, 2003b).

WHO's reconceptualization of disability can also be observed by studying the development of its community-based rehabilitation programs. WHO first introduced the concept of community-based rehabilitation in the late 1970s as a strategy to address the medical and functional needs of people with disabilities within their communities. Over the course of the 1980s, the International Labour Organization (ILO) and United Nations Educational, Scientific and Cultural Organization (UNESCO) also adopted community-based approaches to their work with people with disabilities in the areas of occupational and educational inclusion. In 1994, WHO, the ILO and UNESCO collaborated to produce a joint position paper to promote a common approach to their community-based initiatives. The paper refers to the entire approach as "community-based rehabilitation" (or "CBR"), which it defines as

> ... a strategy within general community development for rehabilitation, equalisation of opportunities and social inclusion of all children and adults with disabilities. CBR is implemented through the combined efforts of people with disabilities themselves, their families and communities, and the appropriate health, education, vocational and social services. (ILO, UNESCO & WHO, 1994, p. 5)

Through its recognition of the need to secure the equalization of opportunities, social inclusion and participation of people with disabilities, CBR, as defined in 1994, can be seen to move beyond the biomedical approach to disability. Continued use of "rehabilitation" as an umbrella term for all activities under this approach, however, indicates that the primary focus remains to be on the ability of the individual to fit into society rather than the role played by society in limiting and enabling people.

In 2004, the ILO, WHO and UNESCO issued a new joint position paper entitled: *CBR: a Strategy for Rehabilitation, Equalization of Opportunities and Poverty Reduction and Social Inclusion of People with Disabilities.* The stated purpose of the joint paper is "to describe and support the concept of CBR as it is evolving, with its emphasis on human rights and its call for action against poverty that affects many people with disabilities" (ILO, UNESCO & WHO, 2004, p. 2). As noted in its statement of purpose, the document explicitly references actions taken to protect and promote human rights, and states that the UN Standard Rules address the steps needed to ensure these rights (pp. 3, 4 and 10). The paper also refers explicitly to the social model of disability, recognizing the existence of environmental barriers to participation and stating that "[d]isability is no longer viewed as merely the result of impairment" (p. 3). Further, emphasis is placed on the expanding role of organizations of people with disabilities. The 2004 position paper appears, therefore, to take a significant step toward the adoption of a social pathology and even human rights approach to disability. The wisdom of continuing to refer to this approach as a type of "rehabilitation", however, is not clear. This certainly remains a major point of contention among leading disability organizations.

In addition to its activities in the area of CBR noted above, a paradigm shift in ILO's approach to disability issues can be traced by examining an ILO convention, recommendation and code of practice developed over the last few decades. In 1983, the General Conference of the ILO adopted the binding Convention No. 159 concerning *Vocational Rehabilitation and Employment (Disabled Persons)*. While specifically referring to the World Programme of Action's call for full participation and equality for people with disabilities, the convention appears to adopt a principally functional approach to securing that participation — focusing on rehabilitation and ways in which the impaired individual can be assisted to fit into the existing workplace. Of note, however, is nonbinding Recommendation No. 168, adopted at the same time as Convention No. 159, which sets out guidelines for national policy and action under the convention. In addition to elements reflecting an individual pathology model, the recommendation also refers to the elimination of general physical, communications and architectural barriers and obstacles to the employment of people with disabilities. In 2002, an ILO tripartite meeting of experts adopted a code of practice entitled *Managing Disability in the Workplace*. While defining disability in terms of a medical impairment and calling for measures to address the functional capacity of workers, the code of practice arguably goes further than the 1983 convention and recommendation to incorporate aspects of the environmental approach to disability by, for example, calling for adjustments in systems of advertising and interviewing for recruitment and promotion of people with disabilities. Discrimination against people with disabilities is condemned; however, significantly, the right to work of people with disabilities is not mentioned.

In addition to activities at the international level, there have been a number of regional developments reinforcing the rights of people with disabilities. Europe had a Year of the Disabled in 1981 and a second one in 2003. The UN Economic and Social Commission for Asia and the Pacific proclaimed the period 1993 to 2002 the Asian and Pacific Decade of Disabled Persons and then renewed it with a second decade from 2003 to 2012. African (2000–2009) and Arab (2003–2012) Decades of Disabled Persons have also been established.

126

Regional human rights instruments have also explicitly addressed disability. See, for example,

- Organization of African Unity: Paragraph 18(4) of the 1981 *African Charter on Human and Peoples' Rights*;
- Organization of American States: Article 18 of the 1988 *Additional Protocol to the American Convention on Human Rights in the Area of Economic, Social and Cultural Rights "Protocol of San Salvador"*;
- Council of Europe: Article 15 of the 1996 revised *European Social Charter*; and
- Organization of American States: the 1996 *Inter-American Convention on the Elimination of All Forms of Discrimination Against Persons with Disabilities*.

These mechanisms are important complements to those at the international level since issues and activities can be tailored to the specific regional context. In addition, they provide opportunities for intra-regional co-operation and technical assistance.

While neither complete nor uniform, the shift within the UN system and international community toward a social pathology conceptualization of disability and, specifically, a human rights approach, is significant. The increasing recognition of disability as a human rights issue is extremely important for improving the quality of life of people with disabilities and achieving equality and justice. This recognition comes at a time when a rights-based approach to development is also emerging as a new area in the human rights field. A human rights approach to development identifies the structural causes that marginalize particular groups, effectively depriving them of the benefits of development. Combining the human rights approaches to disability and to development will be important for people with disabilities in developing countries.

Changing Law and Policy Relating to Disability

The shift from the individual pathology to the social pathology conceptualization of disability has also resulted in a wave of changes in law and policy at the national level. Whereas disability issues were once addressed solely as matters of social security, health, welfare and guardianship, they are increasingly being recognized as the subject of human rights (Degener, 2003). As such, people with disabilities are recognized as rights-bearers rather than objects of charity (Quinn, 1999).

Some countries now have constitutional guarantees for disability rights and equality. These include Austria, Brazil, Canada, Finland, Fiji, Gambia, Ghana, Germany, Malawi, New Zealand, South Africa, Switzerland and Uganda (Degener, 2003). In many countries, governments are in the process of drafting, passing or implementing new laws prohibiting discrimination based on disability. Most of the laws currently in force were enacted during the last decade. In some cases, these laws are very broad and cover all aspects of life; in other cases, the laws are specific to certain sectors, for example, employment. Some of these laws are general anti-discrimination laws, prohibiting discrimination on the ground of disability in addition to other grounds such as gender, age, religion and others; other laws focus on disability specifically (Degener, 2003).

Most of the disability-specific laws have been modelled after American anti-discrimination legislation and, specifically, the 1990 *Americans with Disabilities Act of 1990* or the 1993 UN Standard Rules (Degener, 2003). In fact, Standard Rule No. 15 encourages the adoption of national disability discrimination legislation:

> States have a responsibility to create the legal basis for measures to achieve the objectives of full participation and equality for persons with disabilities ... States must ensure that organizations of persons with disabilities are involved in the development of national legislation concerning the rights of persons with disabilities, as well as in the ongoing evaluation of that legislation ... Any discriminatory provisions against persons with disabilities must be eliminated. National legislation should provide for appropriate sanctions in case of violations of the principle of non-discrimination. (UN, 2003)

The fact that the Standard Rules are enforced by a special monitoring system has contributed to countries' adherence to Rule 15. Notably, General Comment No. 5 of the CESCR also emphasizes the clear need for anti-discrimination legislation, stating that "[i]n order to remedy past and present discrimination and to deter future discrimination, comprehensive anti-discrimination legislation in relation to disability would seem to be indispensable in virtually all State parties" (1994, para. 16).

In addition to anti-discrimination laws, reforms to other types of legislation indicate a shift from the individual to the social pathology conceptualization of disability, with the goal of establishing equal opportunities for people with disabilities. For example, many countries have laws that aim to ensure the participation of people with disabilities in community and public life: building codes that require new buildings to be fully accessible; education laws that establish the principle of full integration; and social welfare laws that ensure that people with disabilities have a minimum income (Degener, 2003).

The past decade has also seen the development of national disability policies on an unprecedented scale. A considerable number of countries throughout the world have now adopted national policies on disability consistent with the guidelines provided by the Standard Rules (SPD, 2002).

The wave of national disability legal and policy reform is certainly positive. However, it must be recognized that the actual effectiveness of anti-discrimination and other disability legislation is often determined by the decisions of courts and tribunals called upon to interpret and enforce it. Moreover, the power of policies to bring real change to the lives of people with disabilities depends significantly on sustained political will. A considerable challenge lies ahead to ensure that guarantees for the protection and promotion of the human rights of people with disabilities on paper translate into the actual enjoyment of human rights by people with disabilities in reality.

Development of a Disability Rights Movement

A very significant development over the last few decades has been the mobilization of people with disabilities into disability organizations at the grassroots, national and international levels. These organizations have led the development of the conceptualization of disability as a social pathology, including both the environmental and human rights models. Advocating that empowerment and self-direction are the key to achieving equality and citizenship, they have demanded and participated in the drafting of new disability law, policy and programming at all levels.

The general dissatisfaction with disability services began in the late 1960s, leading to the politicization of disability by activists with disabilities and disability organizations in different parts of the world. The American independent living movement is a notable example from that period. Marking the beginning of the shift to the social pathology conceptualization of disability, the independent living movement advocated that the barriers confronting people with disabilities are less related to individual impairment than to social attitudes, interpretations of disability, and architectural, legal and educational barriers. Conventional thinking about the causes of disability was increasingly challenged, and the organization and structure of services on which the majority of people with disabilities had to depend came into question. People with disabilities in many countries began to demand greater participation in the organization and management of these services. They also began to run services independently, putting their own ideas into practice. Independent living centres became places where people with disabilities could come together to compare experiences and build relationships. Roberts, a founder of the movement, identified four core principles of independent living: self-determination; self-image and public education; advocacy; and service to all (Roberts, 1989).

A second movement with considerable impact was the Swedish Self-Advocacy Movement. In the late 1960s, Dr. Bengt Nirje, director of the Swedish Association for Persons with Mental Retardation, began leisure clubs composed of members with and without intellectual disabilities. National conferences of club members were held in 1968 and 1970, and the participants developed statements regarding the way they wanted to be treated. By 1972, the movement had spread to the United Kingdom, Canada and the United States. In each country, groups of individuals with intellectual disabilities were formed with members insisting upon their right to speak and act on behalf of themselves regarding issues that affect them. One of these groups was People First — so named in response to the view expressed by one of its members that he wanted to be known "as a person first", with disability being considered secondarily, if at all. Today, the Self-Advocacy Movement is truly international in scope, with a presence in 43 countries and an estimated membership in excess of 17,000 people (People First of Oregon, n.d.).

The first international cross-disability organization run by people with disabilities, Disabled Peoples' International (DPI), was established in 1981. For several years, people with disabilities had sought equal representation in the professional organization Rehabilitation International (RI). In 1980, at the RI World Congress (a meeting of 3000 rehabilitation experts and service providers), a resolution that would have required the equal participation of people with disabilities in each country's RI organization was defeated. As a result, the decision was taken by a group of delegates to establish DPI as a cross-disability organization for and run by people with disabilities. Four hundred people with disabilities from 51 countries attended DPI's first World Congress in Singapore. Congress participants demanded that people with disabilities assert "a voice of our own" (Drieger, 1987). The DPI movement has made significant progress in bringing disability issues to the international stage. By 1987, it had obtained consultative status with the United Nations, the ILO and UNESCO. It had successfully raised questions of human rights violations against people with disabilities before the UN Human Rights Commission and served as a catalyst for the formation of organizations of and for people with disabilities in 100 countries around the world (Drieger, 1987). In order to be a DPI member, an organization must be national in scope and the majority of decision-making positions must be held by people with disabilities.

In addition to the cross-disability DPI, international organizations focusing on particular disabilities have been established. In 1999, the International Disability Alliance (IDA) was formed in Cape Town, South Africa. The IDA is composed of eight international disability organizations: Inclusion International, International Federation of Hard of Hearing People, World Blind Union, Disabled Peoples' International, Rehabilitation International, World Federation of the Deaf, World Federation of the Deafblind and World Network of Users and Survivors of Psychiatry. The IDA aims to be a voice for the international disability movement in global policy matters and to facilitate co-operation and exchanges of information between the international disability organizations, primarily in relation to multilateral organizations (IDA, n.d.).

The adoption of the Standard Rules in 1993 provided a significant impetus for the further growth of disability organizations and an opportunity for those organizations to influence the development of disability law and policy nationally and internationally. As previously mentioned, unlike other non-binding human rights instruments, the Standard Rules are monitored by a Special Rapporteur and a panel of experts. The panel of experts consists of 10 representatives from six major international non-governmental organizations in the disability field. There are five women and five men from around the world, each with different disabilities. The panel of experts has had a significant influence on the development of disability law and policy at the international level. In addition to serving as a consultative body monitoring the Standard Rules, the panel of experts has been involved in consultations with other UN bodies and specialized agencies such as WHO, the ILO, the World Bank and UNESCO (SPD, 2002, para. 16).

Also, as noted above, Rule 15 of the Standard Rules encourages the creation of structures for government and disability organizations to co-operate in policy and planning and the evaluation of laws, programs and services. This has led to the mobilization of a large network of national disability organizations around the world. In 2002, there were over 600 national affiliates of the six international non-governmental disability organizations represented on the panel of experts (SPD, 2002, para. 96). These national disability organizations have played a key role in ensuring that their respective governments participate in the Standard Rules processes. The fact that so many countries have now adopted anti-discrimination laws and disability policies can be attributed, in large part, to the advocacy efforts of these national disability organizations (Degener, 2003, p. 162).

Disability organizations have also played important roles during the first phases of the current process to draft and negotiate a new UN disability convention. Pressure from disability organizations significantly influenced the General Assembly's 2001 decision to initiate the convention process. For many years, members of the disability community advocated strongly for the creation a binding international convention to protect and promote the rights of people with disabilities. In March 2000, for example, the World NGO Summit on Disability adopted a declaration (Beijing Declaration) pointing to the systematic discrimination faced by people with disabilities and the marginalization of disability rights in the monitoring procedures of existing UN human rights treaty bodies. The declaration called for the immediate initiation of a process to draft an international convention.

In addition to influencing the General Assembly's decision to consider a new convention, people with disabilities and disability organizations have been extensively involved in the convention drafting and negotiation processes. Following significant pressure from disability organizations, the General Assembly adopted a generous accreditation system permitting significant attendance by non-governmental organizations, including disability-specific organizations, at Ad Hoc Committee (AHC) sessions (UN General Assembly, 2002a, para. 1). The General Assembly also recognized the need to provide non-governmental organizations from developing countries with the financial assistance necessary to enable their participation in the AHC sessions (UN General Assembly, 2002a, para. 3). At its first session (29 July to 2 August 2002), the AHC adopted modalities for the participation of accredited non-governmental organizations, permitting them to attend all public meetings of the AHC, to make statements (by selecting — when time is limited — spokespersons from among themselves), to receive copies of all official documents, to make written or other presentations, and to make their materials available to state delegations in accessible areas designated by the Secretariat (UNAHC, 2002, para. 10). In December 2002, the General Assembly endorsed the provisions made by the AHC for the active participation of non-governmental organizations in its processes (UN General Assembly, 2002b, para. 9), urging that further efforts be made to ensure that active participation is achieved and stressing "... the important contribution of non-governmental organizations to the promotion of human rights and fundamental freedoms of persons with disabilities" (UN General Assembly, 2002b, preamble). To support the participation of non-governmental organizations and experts from developing countries, the General Assembly established a voluntary fund and invited governments, civil society and the private sector to contribute (UN General Assembly, 2002b, para. 14). In addition, the General Assembly encouraged Member States to include people with disabilities in their delegations to the meetings of the AHC (UN General Assembly, 2002b, para. 13). Subsequent resolutions of the General Assembly in 2003 and 2004 have reiterated these statements and commitments (UN General Assembly, 2003, 2004).

Disability organizations have not only attended AHC meetings but have also been actively involved in the convention drafting process. In its second session (16–27 June 2003), the AHC established a Working Group to prepare a draft text of a convention to act as a basis for negotiation. In an unprecedented move, the AHC decided that 12 of the 40 members of the Working Group would represent

> ... non-governmental organizations (NGOs), especially organizations of persons with disabilities, accredited to the Ad Hoc Committee, to be selected by those organizations, taking into account the diversity of disabilities and of NGOs, ensuring adequate representation of NGOs from developing countries and from all regions. (UN General Assembly, 2003, para. 15)

In his presentation at the 2004 World Bank Disability and Development Conference held at the World Bank offices in Washington, D.C., on 30 November 2004, then AHC Chair, H.E. Ambassador Luis Gallegos of Ecuador, remarked upon the extensive participation by people with disabilities and their organizations in the drafting and negotiation of the convention. He noted that the United Nations has never before witnessed this level of engagement by civil society actors in the drafting of the previous seven international human rights treaties.

The last few decades have witnessed exponential growth in the number of grassroots, national and international organizations of and for people with disabilities. These organizations have successfully secured a place on the international agenda for the issue of the human rights of people with disabilities. They have led the paradigm shift from the individual to the social pathology conceptualizations of disability and gained significant recognition for the fact that people with disabilities and their organizations must be active participants in all matters that affect them.

Greater Incidence and Shifting Causes of Impairment

A further trend affecting disability involves changes in the incidence and causes of impairment. As noted previously, biological or genetic impairment is one of the many determinants of disability. Other determinants include income and social status, social support networks, education, employment and working conditions, social environments, physical environments, personal health practices and coping skills, health services, gender and culture.

The United Nations estimates that 600 million people, at least 10% of the world's population, have some form of disability (Quinn & Degener, 2002, p. 1). WHO has found that incidence of impairment is increasing, and causes are changing. Life expectancy in general, and of children with disabilities in particular, is increasing due to advances in medical technology that preserve and prolong life (WHO, n.d.-a). Improved perinatal care, for instance, has resulted in better survival rates for children with disabilities. Longer life expectancy has also contributed to a growing population of older people and a consequent increase in the population of people with age-related disabilities (WHO, n.d.-a). The causes of impairments are also changing. Impairments stemming from socio-political causes rather than biomedical factors are increasing. Each day, poverty, accidents, natural disasters, violence, war and its aftermath, result in impairments in people of all ages. The last decades have seen a shift in the major causes of impairment from communicable diseases and maternal and perinatal causes to chronic, non-communicable ones (WHO, 2002).

Moreover, while disability is a global phenomenon, the incidence and experience of impairment is not uniform across the various parts of the world. Eighty percent of the world's people with disabilities live in low-income countries (WHO, n.d.-b). In southern countries with developing or transitional economies and in some areas of northern countries where there are significant populations of Aboriginal peoples or where poverty is endemic, the major causes of impairments are malnutrition, communicable diseases, low quality of perinatal care, environmental damage, accidents (including violence and industrial conditions) and war and its aftermath. Some estimate that these conditions are responsible for 70% of impairment. Many developing countries, where infectious disease epidemics persist, also see a rise in the number of people with chronic conditions related to infectious diseases like tuberculosis, HIV/AIDS, and leprosy, which result in a need for long-term care (WHO, 2001b). In those northern countries considered to be more economically developed, accidents, rheumatic conditions, cardiovascular diseases, pulmonary and psychiatric illnesses and chronic pain are significantly more likely causes of impairment than malnutrition, communicable diseases and poor perinatal care.

The above trends have various implications for the future of rehabilitation and health care services. The estimated number of people who require rehabilitation services at any point in time is 1.5% of the population, that is, about 90 million people (WHO, n.d.-a). WHO's Disability and Rehabilitation Team (DAR) recognizes that the increase in the total number of people with acquired impairments has led to a greater need for rehabilitation services. This need has not been met; instead, greater dependence has been placed on institutional solutions (WHO, n.d.-a). DAR notes that this situation is gradually being rectified by the development and implementation of rehabilitation services that enable people with disabilities to live in communities (WHO, n.d.-a). Ending the institutionalization and segregation of people with disabilities is critical to the realization of and respect for their human rights.

Moreover, the organization of health care services has failed to keep pace with the increased prevalence of chronic over acute conditions. Historically, health care services have been developed and organized to respond to acute illnesses and conditions such as those caused by epidemics of infectious diseases, or injuries requiring health care services for limited periods. These medical services are not designed to answer the needs of persons with chronic conditions requiring long-term care. A chronic care paradigm will require a longer-term focus from multiple providers and supports that permit patients to assume more active roles through self-care.

The significant part played by non-biomedical factors in causing and exacerbating impairment should also be addressed. Throughout the world, the most serious illnesses and diseases are attributable to insufficient or inappropriate food, contaminated water, hazardous

135

work and living conditions, lack of access to vaccinations and inadequate health care (Hubbard, 1995). Moreover, the realities of modern warfare lead to impairments experienced by both combatants and civilians. Injuries resulting from the detonation of landmines can occur years after the cessation of hostilities. Natural disasters, domestic and gang violence, traffic and other accidents all play a role in creating impairment. Where impairment exists, moreover, factors such as poverty, conflict, violence and natural disasters serve to increase barriers to full societal participation and the realization of rights. With this in mind, efforts to ensure economic and social justice, domestic and international peace, adequate humanitarian assistance and, in short, the full realization of all human rights for all people, must be issues of concern in the field of disability.

Globalization

In recent years, the global movement toward information exchange, movement of people and freer markets has had major impacts on all people, including those with disabilities.

One result of this occurrence has been increased contact between people with disabilities, regardless of country of residence. The development of accessible Internet technologies and increased Internet services worldwide has fostered the creation of networks of people with disabilities at all levels. Through the Internet, people with disabilities have been able to share experiences, build relationships and engage in substantive dialogue on policies, legislation and programs. The strength and scope of the disability movement has gained tremendously through this phenomenon.

Economic globalization has had a significantly more negative effect on the situation of people with disabilities. Social justice, equality, basic rights and human dignity have been subordinated to the narrow constraints of globalized economics (Rioux, 2002). This process is usually attributed to the increasing interdependence of national economies within the world market and the idea that this has constrained the ability of national governments to follow the economic, and therefore social, policies of their choice. Interdependence is seen to result from the increased volume of trade, foreign direct investment and cross-border financial flows. As social policy is bound by economic policy, this leads to budget constraint and privatization. Governments are no longer total masters in their own countries, and welfare developments are, to some extent, at the mercy of globalizing influences. There is some disagreement as to the extent to which globalization actually compels governments to adopt certain social policies. Some would argue that national elites are using the threat of globalization to present their policy preferences as inevitable (Moran & Wood, 1996). Though globalization may require states to adapt to changing circumstances, in so doing, state power has not been lost but rather transformed, with the most powerful capitalist states being active agents in shaping the processes of globalization (Holden & Beresford, 2002). For example, where there is a political will to do so, competition between states can be regulated and human rights protected through multilateral treaties. Yet, this argument clearly has less relevance to developing countries still under the yoke of structural adjustment and deficit reduction policies imposed by international financial institutions and bilateral lenders.

Globalization is being used to justify shifting responsibility for social well-being as evidenced in basic health and education, culture, equality and equity from the public domain (government) to the private (markets, family and community) (Rioux, 2002). Neoliberal governments argue that deficit reduction is a greater common good than social justice and the availability of support services necessary for the equal participation of people with disabilities in society, even going so far as to suggest that global financial and capital markets make full employment, strong unions and generous welfare states institutions of the past with no future since they undermine profit maximization and result in lost investment. Social well-being is increasingly market-driven and privatized as the boundary between public and private responsibility is redefined. Social welfare is considered to belong primarily to the private domain, and only when it cannot be achieved in this way should the state intervene and guarantee a social minimum using public resources.

In the context of reduced social responsibility, governments return to considering disability as an individual pathology. If individual biology, for which the state allegedly had neither culpability nor influence, is the determining factor in disability, minimal state involvement is justified. Integral, comprehensive and universal policies addressing determinants of disability other than biological or genetic impairment are not implemented. Inequalities and the limitation of citizenship are the result.

Already people with disabilities are much more likely to live in poverty than other Canadians. Of adults with disabilities, 43% have an individual income of less than $10,000 per year, and 26% have income of less than $5,000 (HRDC, 1999b). These figures do not take into account the high costs associated with living a disability (HRDC, 1999b citing: Federal Task Force on Disability Issues, 1996; Perrin, 1991; Roeher Institute, 1994). Reduced social supports and lack of real employment opportunities resulting from globalization serve to exacerbate this problem. While some welfare states have chosen to emphasize education in their social policy as a means to promote labour flexibility, this has yet to translate into recognition of the need for full inclusion of people with disabilities in education (Holden & Beresford, 2002). Policies intended to increase labour supply by widening opportunities for participation in the workforce, moreover, have not provided the comprehensive supports necessary to ensure that those people with disabilities able to secure employment are not relegated to the lowest-paying positions (Holden & Beresford, 2002). Further, by placing the work ethic at the centre of social policy, there is a significant danger that those unable to participate will be ostracized and penalized, leading to further marginalization and exclusion of people with disabilities (Jordan, 1998).

Finally, despite the negative impact that economic globalization is having on the lives of people with disabilities, they remain invisible in the process; they are not consulted by either government actors or transnational corporations. Moreover, the concerns of people with disabilities are not included in the platform of civil society's anti-globalization movement (Sampson, 2003).

There is a tension, therefore, between the positive and negative impacts of globalization on people with disabilities. While the globalization of communications has opened the door to increased dialogue between and among people with disabilities around the world and facilitated the formation of extensive support and advocacy networks, economic globalization threatens to shift responsibility for social well-being from the public to the private domain, leading to increased privatization, neglect of determinants of disability other than biological or genetic impairment, and increased marginalization and exclusion of people with disabilities worldwide.

Yet, as noted previously, the perception that globalization compels governments to adopt certain social policies is not necessarily accurate. As evidenced by the history of the movement of people with disabilities, conventional ideas can be challenged through political and legal action. The need for increased activism and engagement of people with disabilities and disability organizations in the debates shaping the processes of globalization at both the national and international levels is clear.

Biotechnology and Genetics

Over the last decade, discoveries in biotechnology and genetics have occurred at an accelerated rate, with major implications for people with disabilities and their human rights. The concerns of people with disabilities can be grouped around five human rights issues: non-discrimination, justice, diversity, autonomy/informed consent and participation (Avard, 2001; Roeher Institute, 1999). There is an increasing recognition of the need to monitor these developments to ascertain that they do not undermine individual rights.

The identification of genetic variants is vastly expanding our understanding of how certain illnesses and diseases are developed. Much of the rhetoric promises that these discoveries will result in a decrease in disability and disease in society. However, at this time, gene therapy has not reached a developed phase. As such, the prenatal detection of genes connected with major impairments currently can only reduce disability in society through the termination of the pregnancy. Effective cures and therapeutic interventions are not available.

For many people in the disability rights movement, genetic research and its application is not so much about science as the place of difference in society. It raises fundamental issues about the place of people with disabilities in society and the potential for discrimination based on genetic characteristics. To date, for example, people have been denied driver's licences, insurance coverage, employment and the right to adopt on the basis of genetic prediction of future illness (Hubbard, 1993).

It is argued that the use of selective termination of pregnancy devalues certain individuals and reinforces society's discriminatory attitude toward them (Cole, 2001; Hubbard, 1993; Roeher Institute, 1999; Wolbring, 2003). The perception of those with disabilities and the definition of "normalcy" shifts with genetic understanding and with the belief that people with disabilities are preventable or avoidable through the use of genetic services. Evolving perceptions about disabilities are then constructed from a base determination that it is a positive achievement to eliminate that "condition".

There is a fear that the rapid increase in genetic knowledge, the history of eugenics and forced sterilization in this century, and the widespread discrimination and negative social attitudes about disability, including the devaluation of those perceived to be unable to participate in the globalized labour market, may lead to pressure for a new eugenics movement (Cole, 2001; Rioux, 2000). Shakespeare distinguishes between strong and weak eugenics (Shakespeare, 1998). Strong eugenics is state-controlled and motivated by social judgment that people with disabilities are unworthy of life and/or that society should not have to bear the financial costs of supporting non-productive members. Weak eugenics involves the promotion of technologies of reproductive selection as a matter of individual free choice motivated by the medical judgment that the lives of people with disabilities involve unacceptable suffering. Based on this distinction, Shakespeare posits that the current British genetic practices are "weakly eugenic". He notes, however, that a shift could be made toward "strongly eugenic" practices, recognizing that there already is a tendency to frame screening policies in terms of cost-benefit analyses and that certain genetic professionals have expressed strong eugenic statements (Cole, 2001; DPI Europe n.d.; Hubbard, 1993; Shakespeare, 1998).

Some commentators hold that a woman's right to choose must permit her to terminate her pregnancy for any reason, including for "genetic abnormality" (DPI Europe, n.d.; Shakespeare, 1998). They note however that, currently, there are a number of pressures placed on women both to undergo prenatal screening and diagnostic testing and to abort foetuses with identified "genetic abnormalities". These include: social or cultural pressures resulting from the tendency to portray impairments as "overwhelming tragedies" in the press; institutional pressures wherein the genetic counselling provided portrays only negative views of living with an impairment; and financial pressures resulting from the fact of insufficient supports available to parents of children with impairments, often leading families into poverty (Shakespeare, 1998). While supporting a woman's right to choose, this group of commentators emphasize that the choice should be freely made and fully informed. They state that there must not be any pressure to undergo prenatal testing, that genetic counselling for prospective parents must be widely and freely available and include positive information about the experience of impairment, provided preferably by the experts in the field — that is, people with disabilities themselves, and that women must be able to have confidence that, if they decide not to terminate, their child will be welcomed into society and provided with the levels of social, practical and financial support necessary for full participation (DPI Europe, n.d.; Shakespeare, 1998).

Others take the position that to permit terminations on the basis of potential impairment, or "disability selection", is equivalent to sex selection and should not be permitted (Wolbring, 2003). To prohibit the one choice and permit the other would lead to what Wolbring refers to as an "animal farm" philosophy in which some (the unwanted sex) are more equal than others (people with disabilities). Shakespeare responds to this argument by stating that there are some very severe impairments that society justifiably should want to avoid completely, whereas this is never the case with sex. Wolbring would respond by citing the difficulties in making determinations regarding the relative "severity" of various impairments. Hubbard notes that similar negative societal attitudes that lead to sex selection in countries such as India and China lead to disability selection in the West; the targets reflect societal judgments regarding who should and should not be a part of this world.

The possibility that people with disabilities will increasingly become the focus of genetic research and experimental treatments poses yet another concern (Avard, 2001). Given the huge financial implications of new discoveries for scientists and for biotechnology and pharmaceutical companies, the temptation to take advantage of vulnerable groups will be strong. In all research, the free and informed consent of participants must be secured. Where the research involves people with cognitive impairments and mental disorders, special safeguards must be in place.

There is also a real concern that the new genetics signal the return to the traditional medical model of disability, undermining the recent gains made by the social pathology models (DPI Europe, n.d.; Roeher Institute, 1999; Wolbring, 2003). Reducing disability to a genetic flaw perpetuates and reinforces a view of disability as simply a medical abnormality and individual pathology. People with disabilities are defined only by their impairments. While there is a biological reality to disability (an impairment), to suggest that genetic codes are the primary determinants of disability inadequately accounts for other determinants, such as economic, social, political and environmental factors (Hubbard, 1995; Lippman & Bereano, 1993; Roeher Institute, 1999; Wolfe, 1995). Medicalization of disability has the potential to lead to heightened discrimination against people with disabilities and to justify increased investment in genetic research at the expense of investments to address other determinants of disability (DPI Europe n.d.; Hubbard, 1993).

It must be emphasized that genetics and biotechnology will never be able to completely eliminate impairments. Over 80% of people with disabilities were not born with their impairments but rather acquired them during their life course as a result of, for example, poverty, accidents, war, or environmental hazards (British Council of Disabled People, n.d.; Hubbard, 1995). Arguably, resources are much better spent on ensuring the equal enjoyment of rights by people with disabilities in a society in that respects and values diversity.

From a human rights perspective, persons with disabilities must be consulted, represented and systematically involved in committees, debates and counselling about genetics and biomedical technologies. Currently, debates occur at many levels — academia, policy making, government and civil society; however, a disability rights perspective has often been excluded from or rejected by all of these discussions (Wolbring, 2003). The participation of people with disabilities will provide insights into the experience of disability and impairment, thereby helping to correct many of the current misconceptions. Vigilance will be required to ensure that the new genetics do not lead to the new eugenics.

CONCLUSION

The past few decades have witnessed significant trends in the disability policy context. Developed and championed by a growing disability movement, the reconceptualization of disability as a social pathology, including the adoption of a human rights approach, has led to widespread change. There is now an increasing recognition of the social responsibility for disability that has impacted the nature and scope of disability law, policy, programming and research at all levels. Current efforts to draft and negotiate a binding UN convention for the protection and promotion of the rights of people with disabilities and the active and positive role played by people with disabilities in that process provide evidence of the significant progress made.

However, challenges remain. These include securing the necessary consensus among disability organizations and national governments representing diverse interests regarding the terms of a disability convention, ensuring that new international and national disability laws, policies and programs translate into actual improvements in the daily lives of people with disabilities, crafting appropriate responses to the greater incidence and shifting causes of impairment, opposing attempts to shift social responsibility for disability from the public to the private domain, monitoring developments in the field of biotechnology and genetics to ensure that the rights of people with disabilities are not undermined and increasing the recognition among all actors that people with disabilities must be active participants in all matters that affect them.

Section III
Advocacy and Consumer Participation

The earliest advocacy organizations in Canada emerged in the early part of the 20th century, were aimed at ensuring some degree of consideration and service for injured veterans and workers. Disability groups proliferated in the 1960s, in a climate of civil unrest and relative economic prosperity. For the Canadian disability movement, the first meeting of Disabled Persons International in Winnipeg in 1981 — the International Year of Disabled Persons — was highly formative. Not only was Canada seen as pivotal in the world disability movement, but also, by bringing the world to its doorstep, the Canadian movement coalesced in an unprecedented fashion.

Since 1990, however, there seems to be general agreement that the disability advocacy sector has become stalled (McColl & Boyce, 2003). Stienstra (2003) suggests that disability advocacy is trapped in a cycle of consultation that leads only to further consultation, and not to action. Prince (2004) coins the term *"déjà vu discourse"* to describe this vicious cycle. He characterizes the mood of the movement as one of disappointment and frustration at the steady decline of benefit levels and the erosion of programs for people with disabilities.

A number of possible reasons for this have been advanced, and some are dealt with in the following four chapters. Bickenbach (1993) characterizes disability policy as being at an impasse due to the lack of a clear end point and the absence of a well-formulated action plan. Cameron and Valentine (2001) note a general retrenchment in government in the 1990s, in response to economic pressures. As a result, they observe that disability programs tend to resort to the more traditional biomedical definition of disability in their screening and eligibility criteria as a means of restricting resource commitments. Neufeldt (2003) observes that government attention has simply shifted elsewhere in response to pressing economic issues. The general downloading of social programs to smaller jurisdictions, such as regions or municipalities, and in some provinces to the private sector, has meant that the pot of money for services and support has dwindled. Pedlar and colleagues (2000) point to the rise of the for-profit private sector in the provision of health and social services. He notes that private concerns are typically insensitive to advocacy from grassroots organizations, and tend to be concerned more with the views of their investors than their clients.

There have also been a number of changes within advocacy organizations in the late 20th to early 21st century that have influenced the focus and impact of disability advocacy. Whereas prior to the 1990s the disability movement appeared to be increasingly politicized, radicalized and empowered, the more recent history may not be so positive (McColl & Boyce, 2003). Table III.1 shows three views of the life cycle of organizations or social movements such as the disability advocacy movement.

Although Boyce et al. (2001) characterize the disability movement as an "emerging" movement, not yet sufficiently developed or connected to be considered institutionalized, Neufeldt (2003) claims that the movement is in decline — that is, in the latter stages of these cycles, regardless of whose conceptualization one prefers. He notes that energy has flagged for disability advocacy, leadership has burned out, and disability organizations have been co-opted by government as a result of their dependence for financial support. He also suggests that the potential exists for a backlash against disability advocacy, if a public perception were to arise that the gains made to date were not adequately appreciated. He warns against a "never satisfied" public perception of the disability community.

Table III.1: Three views of the life cycle of organizations and social movements.

Crichton & Jongbloed	Turner & Killian	Mauss
Organizational development, including assembling of resources and streamlining of procedures	General unrest, perception of a social problem	Incipiency — perception of problem, but no formal membership or leadership
	Identification of needed change	
	Formal organization of a movement	Coalescence — development of processes and resources
	Institutionalization of the movement	Institutionalization
Mandate review, reconsideration of goals and strategies		Fragmentation — differentiation of factions within the movement
		Demise — decline and dissolution of the original movement and its purposes

The following four chapters explore aspects of the disability movement in Canada in the early 21st century. They provide perspectives on the state of disability advocacy and political participation in Canada, and offer possibilities for a re-energized advocacy initiative.

Chapter 9
In his second chapter, Joiner provides an introduction to the policy-making process in Canada, focusing on various ways in which people with disabilities can take part in the process. He offers a discussion of three levels of participation, from consultation to engagement, as well as a brief discussion of the barriers to policy participation. He concludes with a recommendation that disability advocacy groups work toward greater political and organizational sophistication in order to enhance their success in influencing policy.

Chapter 10
In his second chapter, Prince considers four possible identities for the disability community: as a service sector, as a new social movement, as a constitutional category of citizens, and as a political lobby. He identifies a number of issues that need to be addressed in order for the disability community to have a stronger and more effective voice, such as strengthening organizations, building coalitions, increasing capacity for social critique, increasing public awareness of disability and improving political connections.

Chapter 11
In this chapter, Wight-Felske and Krassioukova-Enns discuss partnerships of organizations representing people with disabilities with government, the private sector, voluntary organizations, educators and researchers. They offer five examples from the experience of the Council of Canadians with Disabilities (CCD), and extract six lessons learned.

Chapter 12
In Chapter 12, Boyce and colleagues reflect on challenges faced and strategies used by disability organizations over the past two decades to respond to consumer needs, resource constraints and ideological shifts in the disability advocacy movement in Can-

146

ada. They conclude by analyzing these changes in light of social movement theory — a perspective that has been advanced by a number of authors in this volume.

Chapter 13

Stienstra and D'Aubin look at a variety of ways in which people with disabilities participate as citizens in the democratic process. From a discussion of the struggle for accessible polling stations, so that disabled people can participate as voters, they go on to discuss strategies for attracting attention to disability issues at election time. They conclude with a discussion of the experience of disabled candidates seeking public office, and some of the barriers faced in securing and holding positions as elected officials.

Chapter 14

Finally, to round out this section on the participation of consumers in disability policy in Canada, McColl uses the 1997 Canada National Elections Survey to compare the electoral participation of disabled people to the population as a whole, and to focus on the issues of importance to the disability community. The chapter also identifies barriers and enablers of democratic participation, and discusses reasons for differences.

9

Perhaps Not Yet: Policy Making Through Citizen Engagement

IAN JOINER

INTRODUCTION

This chapter assesses citizen engagement in policy making and its potential benefits and limitations for individuals and organizations within the disability community in Canada. Although Prince, in Chapter 10, argues that there is no one conception or organization form of it, the term *disability community* is used in this chapter as a general reference to disabled people and their organizations. Voluntary citizen participation in governance has long been a valued concept in Western democratic societies (Boyce et al., 2001). Citizen engagement, as a more recent notion of participation, is often positioned as an alluring remedy to a perceived democratic deficit (Abelson & Eyles, 2002; Cheyne & Comrie, 2002; Delli Carpini, Cook & Jacobs, 2004; Dickinson, 2002). However, the ongoing maturation of institutional structures and processes to operationalize such engagement, the diversity within the disability community, and the evolution of disability advocacy represent significant challenges to effective citizen engagement.

This chapter begins with a discussion of the nature of policy making in Canada, followed by a review of literature on the evolving notions of public participation, consultation and citizen engagement. This is followed by a commentary on the potential of citizen engagement for advancing disability-related issues.

BACKGROUND

In order to situate the argument that citizen engagement is limited for advancing disability issues in the current policy making environment, it is useful to provide some context on the nature of policy making. Policy, for the purpose of this chapter, is a purposive course of action or inaction by government or another public body that addresses a specific issue and that may represent some underlying stated intention (Boyce et al., 2001; Drake, 1999; Inwood, 1999; Malcolmson & Myers, 1996).

Citizenship, participation, policy making and disability are viewed in the context of a pluralist theory of the state for this discussion. From this perspective, states comprised a variety of groups who use their power and influence to negotiate for their own interests (Drake, 1999). As summarized by Dunleavy and O'Leary (1987), and of relevance to this chapter, "political pluralism recognizes the existence of diversity in social, institutional and ideological practices, and values that diversity" (p. 13).

Historically and constitutionally in the Canadian regime, public policy decisions are primarily influenced by three branches of government. Generally, major policy and regulatory decisions are directed by the executive branch, which, in Westminster-style democracies, constitutes a majority of the elected members in a parliamentary assembly. The parliament, or legislative branch, in its role as the citizens' representative, reviews and debates proposed legislation while scrutinizing the executive. Finally, federal and provincial courts (the judicial branch) play the role of judging whether a policy is legal with respect to key governing principles and precedents (Inwood, 1999; Malcolmson & Myers, 1996). This synopsis might be construed as naïve simplification, given others' views on the central concentration of power or the rarity of "policy participants" in cabinet (Savoie, 1999, p. 244), or even given the diverse models of state organization (Dunleavy & O'Leary, 1987); however, it provides a basis for issues discussed later in this chapter.

Bureaucrats and related actors play a key role in policy making in that they advance options on various policy instruments and strategic directions at the request of the executive. These options are often based on consultation with citizens and stakeholder groups. It is this intersection between the government, as represented by the bureaucracy and the elected officials, and the public that is at the heart of this discussion on citizen engagement in policy making.

The work of Hogwood and Gunn (1984) and Drake (1999) outlines a number of general stages in the policy development process, which appear consistent with a pluralist theory of the state. The stages range from deciding that an issue exists and deciding on definitions and the development of methods, through the analysis of options, to implementing the selected course of action and evaluating any policy outcomes. Citizen engagement addresses not only the early stages of issue definition, but also assumes some accountability for monitoring any related outcomes (Mendelsohn & McLean, 2002; Phillips, 2001).

Inwood (1999) suggests five characteristics that ought to be considered when approaching public policy making: (a) environmental factors, such as geography and demography; (b) the distribution of power, influence and competition; (c) social attitudes and ideas; (d) institutional structure; and (e) procedural factors. As argued in this chapter, analyzing the institutional and procedural infrastructure that supports policy making is key to understanding the extent to which engagement can be operationalized to effectively address disability issues.

PARTICIPATION, CONSULTATION AND ENGAGEMENT

For the purpose of this chapter, increased *participation* by citizens in policy making is positioned as a desirable ideal (Contandriopoulos, 2004; Morone & Kilbreth, 2003), although others have commented on the rhetoric and limitations of this goal (Aronson, 1993). In light of the political and sociological complexities inherent in the construction of citizenship (thorough analysis of which is beyond the scope of this chapter), a definition from Drake (1999) is proposed:

> To be a citizen is to be able to take part in the decisions that create or re-create the contours of society, and to be able to participate in functions such as work, leisure, political debate, travel and religious observance. (p. 41)

It is useful to view citizen involvement in policy making along a continuum. At one end of the continuum is the unidirectional transfer of information from government to the public or vice versa. At the other end of the continuum is a two-way dialogue between government and the public — dialogue that has a genuine influence on policy (Drake, 2002; Phillips, 2001). Citizen engagement, as discussed in this chapter, would be situated near the latter end of the continuum.

Public participation, in the broadest sense, can relate to any attempt to include the perspectives, opinions and recommendations of the general populace in policy development and decision making. More specifically, Boyce et al. (2001, p. 23) summarize various conceptualizations of citizen participation either as a means to an end (instrumental participation) or as the end in its self (transformational participation). They state that instrumental participation includes such activities as presenting briefs, serving on advisory committees and lobbying government, while transformational participation aims to develop and strengthen capacities in social development over the long term.

Using health services planning as an example, public participation provides many advantages:

(a) Improved decision making and health system performance;
(b) A more active, engaged and public-spirited citizenry;
(c) Systems that reflect the needs, values, culture and attitudes of the community;
(d) More efficient use of resources;
(e) Increased support for resulting programs and services;
(f) Greater access to local skills and resources;
(g) Increased community awareness of health issues; and
(h) An enhanced sense of control and empowerment (Abelson & Eyles, 2002; Pivik, 2002).

However, various authors have also questioned the feasibility and desirability of such grand romantic views of participation in health services policy making (Aronson, 1993; Frankish et al., 2002; Morone & Kilbreth, 2003).

Moving from participation, generally, to the more specific term *consultation* will facilitate the ultimate discussion of citizen engagement as a more recent phenomenon. As stated by Contandriopoulos (2004), "whereas participation usually encompasses all possible ways in which the public can influence a decision, consultation usually describes a situation in which the public can voice its

opinion without any direct possibility of decision in the end"
(p. 325). Such consultative approaches as one-on-one discussions,
advisory councils or committees, legislative hearings, multi-stake-
holder roundtables, public meetings, opinion polls, stratified focus
groups, Web sites and 1-800 numbers, while at the least involve
some interaction between citizen and government, do not necessarily reflect a meaningful contribution to policy making. Writing on
the history of disability advocacy in Canada, Stienstra (2003) provides a framework for assessing the type and quality of different
forms of consultation. As discussed in the following section, many
of the evaluative questions in this framework relate directly to limitations of traditional consultative methods and allude to some of
the promises of more deliberative citizen engagement techniques.

Criticisms of traditional consultative approaches appear frequently in the literature. For example, it has been written that
these approaches reflect a lopsided balance of power, are often by
invitation only, provide limited exchange of views and genuine dialogue and seldom make an impact on civil society (Phillips, 2001).
Also, traditional models of consultation tend to provide a snapshot
of public opinion at a particular moment in time (Mendelsohn &
McLean, 2002) and provide very truncated citizen involvement and
accountability to citizens (Cheyne & Comrie, 2002). Reddel and
Woolcock (2004) state that traditional consultative methods "reinforce centralized and passive models of decision-making" (p. 85).
Specifically relating to the policy participation of people with disabilities, Stienstra (2003) succinctly asserts some of these criticisms
and limitations: "While consultation has been the primary framework for including people with disabilities in policy development, it
has not been an effective tool to make policy change and resulting
positive changes in the lives of people with disabilities" (p. 34).

Disenchantment with the substantive outcomes of traditional
consultation has lead many academics and policy-makers to seek
alternative and more promising mechanisms for *citizen engagement*
(Cheyne & Comrie, 2002; Delli Carpini, Cook & Jacobs, 2004;
Mendelsohn & McLean, 2002). The expectations of citizen engagement as an enhanced framework for public input in policy making
are immense. As Phillips (2001) states:

> ... [It] is meant not simply to reproduce traditional forms of con-
> sultation, but to promote a more deliberative form of democracy
> ... [where] parties are treated as equals.... This does not imply ...
> that citizens ... have the final say on policy, but it does require
> established and credible mechanisms, processes or protocols, in

order for the results of such deliberation to have an institutionalized impact on political decision-making. (p. 11)

Much of the recent emergence of the term "citizen engagement" and its use in Canadian academic literature occurred around
the 1999 Social Union Framework Agreement (SUFA) (Lazar,
2000; Mendelsohn & McLean, 2000; Mendelsohn & McLean, 2002;
O'Hara, 1997; Phillips, 2001) and also related to local government
(Graham & Phillips, 1998). Other recent and international literature on citizen engagement has focused on various issues, such as
its relationship to participatory governance (Reddel & Woolcock,
2004), to health care restructuring and rationing (Abelson & Eyles,
2002; Dickinson, 2002; Maxwell, Rosell & Forest, 2003; Pivik, 2002;
Redden, 1999; Ruether, St. Claire & Coffman, 2001), to local governance (Pearce & Mawson, 2003), and to the impact of globalization and new information technologies (Smith, 2001).

Although the SUFA marked "the first time that the federal
and provincial governments have made explicit joint commitments
about engaging citizens in the governing process" (Phillips, 2001,
p. 3), the related literature appears fixated on reconciling the distinct concepts of citizen engagement and intergovernmental relations. However, comments relating to the SUFA are applied here
to disability and policy making where appropriate. For example, in
an article on Canadian federalism and disability policy, Prince
(2001c), states that the SUFA gives "new recognition and opportunity for various public interest groups to participate more directly
in intergovernmental policy making" (p. 814).

Methods of cultivating citizen engagement include study circles, constituent assemblies, citizens' juries, focus groups, strategic
social planning, citizen-based summits, framework agreements and
deliberative opinion polling through random selection (Cheyne &
Comrie, 2002; Mendelsohn & McLean, 2002; Phillips, 2001; Roberts, 2004). Details of these different methods are not provided
here, other than to say they share a goal of facilitating "deliberative dialogue between citizens (and/or their organizations) and government officials that contributes meaningfully to specific policy
decisions in a transparent and accountable manner" (Phillips, 2001,
p. 10).

Citizen engagement mechanisms involve citizens in each stage
of the policy making process and consist of ongoing dialogue and
interactive, co-decisional processes that are publicly accountable for
stated outcomes (Mendelsohn & McLean, 2002). The model of
public administration through which the engagement is viewed (e.g.,

representative, administrative, pluralist) ought to be taken into account, as it may influence such mechanisms (Roberts, 2004). As Roberts (2004) states, "because direct citizen participation most often rests on the shoulders of public administrators for successful execution, it is important to know how the citizen and his or her direct involvement are viewed within a particular framework" (p. 317).

At this point, it is fitting to consider the various roles that the citizen as participant may assume in the policy making process. Across all sectors and communities, an individual may be called upon or may volunteer for any number of roles. As stated by Mendelsohn and McLean (2002), "genuine citizen engagement must begin with a clear conception of what role citizens will play" (p. 24). Following are some examples of possible roles:

(a) A consumer/customer of government services;
(b) A client of government programs;
(c) An interest group advocate;
(d) A voter;
(e) A bearer of rights vis-à-vis the *Charter of Rights and Freedoms*; or,
(f) A democratic actor (collated from Boyce et al., 2001; Drake, 1999; Mendelsohn and McLean, 2002; Roberts, 2004).

The concurrent diversity of roles experienced by people with disabilities and the labels and perceptions attributed to those roles are discussed later in the chapter.

Commenting on citizen engagement commitments in the SUFA, Phillips (2001) states that the pressure to participate is likely to come through coalitions "from the bottom up, financially supported and partly enabled by government" (p. 28). This prediction appears to be similar to the known evolution of disability advocacy in Canada, which, at times, has been vulnerable to the ebb and flow of government support (Boyce et al., 2001; Neufeldt, 2003; Rioux & Prince, 2002). Also, disability advocacy groups have collaborated with others to form coalitions (e.g., the Council of Canadians with Disabilities) to more effectively employ the power of the group against other powerful interests (Neufeldt, 2003) such as medical and rehabilitation professionals, government bureaucrats and charities headed by non-disabled people (Drake, 2002; Imrie, 1997).

Citizen engagement, as a means of achieving further democratization of participatory deliberation in policy making, appears to have some limitations. For example, Cheyne and Comrie (2002), in evaluating the search by local authorities in New Zealand for meaningful and manageable mechanisms of citizen engagement, cite some issues with citizens' juries. The issues include inadequate representation, high costs and fiscal limitations, potential for manipulation by the commissioning body, and the often politicized decision-making process.

In a comprehensive review of empirical literature on public deliberation and its impact on citizen engagement, Delli Carpini, Cook & Jacobs (2004) summarize the strengths and limitations of mechanisms such as deliberative forums. They state that "public deliberation has been singled out as a unique mechanism for producing collective results" yet also conclude that "the traditional tools of electoral and legislative avenues to collective decision-making remain essential" (p. 321). This is mirrored in the idea that there may be dangers in promoting networks, engagement and partnerships as alternatives to other established and legitimate political and policy institutions (Reddel & Woolcock, 2004).

Some of the promises of citizen engagement alluded to earlier continue to be scrutinized as various jurisdictions around the world evaluate recent initiatives. In summarizing research findings, Delli Carpini, Cook & Jacobs (2004) conclude that the impact of deliberation and other forms of discursive politics is highly context dependent. They state that the impact varies with: the purpose of the deliberation; the subject under discussion; who participates; the connection to authoritative decision-makers; the rules governing interactions; the information provided; prior beliefs of sponsors and participants; and other real world considerations.

Relating to initiatives in Australia, Reddel and Woolcock (2004) emphasize that one must keep in mind the distinction between citizen engagement (i.e., efforts to expand citizen participation into decision making) and the broader and longer-term concept of participatory governance (i.e., active partnerships and collaboration between civil society, the private sector and governments). They further state that the "long-term impact of citizen engagement on the key political and policy drivers of the state government remain uncertain" (p. 84).

Some questions for further research on citizen engagement mechanisms include determining the impact of such factors as socio-economic status, gender, race, and education on the impact of the deliberative dialogue (Delli Carpini, Cook & Jacobs, 2004). One could add disability to this list of factors. Disability, when viewed as a complex and evolving construct, is often intertwined with other identities that have historically been the target of oppression and that have been excluded from or minimally involved in the policy making process (Charlton, 1998; Drake, 1999; Marks, 1999; Prince, 2004; Rioux & Prince, 2002).

Perhaps Not Yet: Citizen Engagement and Disability

This chapter argues that although citizen engagement offers certain innovations for policy making related to disability, it appears premature to expect major transformational change from such mechanisms in the foreseeable future. Citizen engagement appears to demonstrate promising rhetoric, yet is lacking in tangible infrastructure (Phillips, 2001) and conclusive evaluations as to the outcomes and efficacy of such mechanisms for enhancing participation and consultation (Delli Carpini, Cook & Jacobs, 2004). At the risk of appearing pragmatic, this chapter suggests that various traditional approaches, including advocacy, representation, consultation and formal lobbying, ought to be combined with any new engagement opportunities in order to continue to advance disability issues broadly, and in policy making processes specifically.

Increasingly, the extent to which the disability community participates in public policy making is being assessed, theorized and critiqued in the academic literature. This literature has addressed varying subjects, including: Canadian federalism and legislative initiatives (Boyce et al., 2001; Prince, 2001c; Prince, 2004; Rioux & Prince, 2002); Canadian disability advocacy (McColl & Boyce, 2003; Stienstra, 2003); local governance and voluntary organizations in Britain (M. Barnes, 2002; Drake, 2002; Scott-Hill, 2002) and disability policy in general (C. Barnes, 2002; Drake, 1999). This literature reflects the increasing politicization of the disability community away from historical roots of oppression and disenfranchisement, whilst identifying and articulating the institutional, societal and attitudinal barriers to such emancipation. The remainder of this chapter provides a commentary on factors limiting the potential of citizen engagement for disabled people and is organized in three subsections.

Engagement, Minority and Disadvantage

In assessing the potential opportunity for citizen engagement, disability can be viewed through a lens of minority culture or relative disadvantage. Regarding new information and communication technologies, Smith (2001) stresses that they will strengthen the ability of citizens to relate horizontally to government. However, approaches for enhancing citizen engagement must consider the impact of inequity experienced by oppressed groups regarding access to such technology and information, as reflected by Roberts' (2004) cautious optimism:

> There has been some success in bringing disadvantaged groups into public deliberations with public officials through the use of interactive surveys that draw random samples of the population ... [however] ... inviting everyone to the table as coequals in a learning process, and giving them the tools and resources they need to be successful, is one of the greatest challenges of direct citizen participation. (p. 338)

Although it varies among individuals, disability is associated with disproportionate societal impacts and relative disadvantage. Disability is also associated with greater levels of absolute poverty (Barnes & Mercer, 2003; Marks, 1999), lower self-reported general health (Rioux & Prince, 2002) and lower educational attainment (Barnes & Mercer, 2003; Oliver & Barnes, 1998). It thus appears reasonable to infer that such inequities might impede access to new forms of consultation, if suitable and comprehensive physical and technical accommodations are not put in place. This issue has been further explored in relation to the impact of power differentials on the ability of disabled people to access deliberative forums:

> People do not have equal opportunity to attend and participate in decision-making forums. Nor does everyone meet the standards of cognitive and lingual competence set within forums dominated by professional/bureaucratic norms of debate. We need a practice of deliberation which explicitly recognises and encompasses inequalities of power and diversity of experience and expression, rather than assuming that such inequality and diversity will be accommodated within processes governed by universalist notions of fairness and competence. (M. Barnes, 2002, p. 324)

These concerns are not necessarily unique to deliberative engagement, but they foreshadow potentially negative outcomes if the power differentials, inequalities and cultural assumptions are not addressed (Drake, 2002). For example, Church (1996) describes barriers to psychiatric survivor participation in the consultations of a legislative subcommittee in Ontario. The consultation experience was negative for many consumer participants, in part because of the lack of accommodation and the professional/bureaucratic character-ization of participant actions as "bad manners" (p. 27).

Engagement, Identity and Multiple Roles

As mentioned earlier in this chapter, mechanisms of citizen engagement depend upon the explicit and shared understanding of a participant's role in the deliberation, which, in the case of policy making, is often determined by the government (Drake, 2002) or bureaucratic sponsor of the engagement process. This parallels the typology of roles alluded to in a comparative summary of rehabili-tation service delivery models (McColl, Gerein & Valentine, 1997), whereby disabled participants may be expected to take on one or more roles such as passive patient, empowered client, or informed consumer, depending on the specific interaction. This potentially reactive metamorphosis on the part of the participant to meet the externally imposed requirements of their participation may pose sig-nificant challenges for a disabled person, especially if the partici-pant and the sponsor have diverging ontological, cultural or political foundations for their views of disability.

All people have a multitude of roles and identities at any par-ticular moment in time. This multiplicity is shaped by each individ-ual's own values and assumptions, as well as the values and biases of others. Relating to disability, much has been written about iden-tity as a critical factor in assessing and understanding the experi-ence of disability and the impact of identity on social participation, disability rights advocacy and equality (Barnes & Mercer, 2003; Charlton, 1998; Marks, 1999; Oliver & Barnes, 1998). Just as Charlton (1998) states that many disabled people do not always identify with each other as a group, one should not expect that a disabled person would necessarily want to be identified as repre-senting the views of the disabled as a perceived homogenous group in engagement mechanisms.

Without established infrastructure and consistently applied pro-cesses to ensure the random selection of a person who *happens* to have a disability (among other identities) as a member of a large diverse population, the potential for true citizen engagement will be limited. It is more likely in the current environment of consultation that disability will be framed as a particular target demographic from which to solicit specific input on disability-specific issues, as defined and controlled by policy-makers.

Engagement and Disability Advocacy

Finally, this chapter argues that citizen engagement does not appear to be a panacea for issues that have been encountered by disabled people and their organizations during the rise and evolution of disability advocacy in Canada. There are some varying opinions on the extent to which progress has been made on advancing a unified front toward more substantive participation in policy making (McColl & Boyce, 2003; Neufeldt, 2003). Disability advocacy is simultaneously progressing from its individual-focused, charitable and service provider-led beginnings, through the independent living movement, to a state of integral awareness of the established policy infrastructure and political power relations.

Collaboration among disability organizations appears to have facilitated the development of more extensive knowledge of formal government processes and of the avenues for influencing policy. However, Boyce et al. (2001) suggest that "organizations and their members need to further their knowledge of the policy arena and the different stages of policy making" (p. 168) through education and strategic development. It is this insinuation of less than optimal sophistication and maturation of the disability advocacy community in policy making that limits our ability to embrace citizen engagement as a primary mechanism for enhancing participation of people with disabilities in policy making in Canada. Additionally, "if individuals and organizations are to have an effective role in reviewing outcomes [through citizen engagement], they will need considerable analytical expertise" (Phillips, 2001, p. 28), which suggests that acquisition and co-ordination of specific and highly specialized skills is essential.

CONCLUSION

The concepts of public participation, consultation, citizen engagement and the nature of policy making have been discussed and critiqued, with particular reference to the potential for advancing disability issues in Canada. This chapter assessed citizen engagement as a mechanism for policy making and its potential benefits and limitations for individuals and organizations within the disability community. It concludes that the ongoing maturation of institutional structures and processes to operationalize such engagement, paralleled with the evolution of disability advocacy and diversity within the disability community, will enhance the potential for real collaboration in the future.

10

Who Are We? The Disability Community in Canada

MICHAEL J. PRINCE

INTRODUCTION

This chapter examines the meaning of disability community in the contemporary Canadian context. What initially may appear to be a simple question (who are we?) is complicated both conceptually and in practical terms. Four dimensions identify and illustrate the boundaries and composition of the disability community in Canada.

The chapter begins with an exploration of who the disability community is. The disability community is then examined as a sector of diverse organizations, as a new social movement, as a constitutional category of citizens under the *Canadian Charter of Rights and Freedoms*, and as a policy community of interest groups and advocacy coalitions. The organizational nature of the disability community, Canada's disability state and the capacity of the disability community are assessed.

Each of these analytical views captures some of the important features of the disability community in Canada today in addition to offering a particular perspective on disability. The exploration offers some insight into the organizational nature of the disability community and the existence of multiple discourses within the community. How these four dimensions interrelate is considered, including opportunities and challenges for co-operation and partnerships in the community, as well as for engagement with governments and other sectors.

BACKGROUND

From a formal organizational perspective, who actually is in the disability community? What is the breadth and composition of this community in Canada? These may seem basic questions, yet they can quickly become contested and intricate, raising a number of choices about the boundaries and membership of the community.

The Canadian Abilities Foundation lists over 5,300 organizations by, for, or of persons with disabilities in the voluntary sector in Canada (Canadian Abilities Foundation, 2004). Certainly, most people would agree that these are at the core of the community. This includes a variety of self-help groups, service providers and advocacy organizations. Beyond these, however, a host of questions arises. What of the informal social support networks of families, friends and helpful neighbours? What of private for-profit sector organizations that provide supports to persons with disabilities or fundraising assistance to disability-related societies, and professional, medical, research, and rehabilitation organizations? What about generic community service agencies or public policy think tanks that may serve persons with disabilities among others in their clientele? And are government officials and political institutions included or not?

The boundaries of the disability community, then, are not always clear or agreed upon. Nor do those boundaries remain fixed. The community has likely expanded a great deal over the last few decades and, recently, has struggled with the impact of public sector downsizing. There does come a point where the need to have actual consultations and partnerships takes over and decisions need to be made about distribution lists and invitations.

The Canadian literature rarely defines "the disability community" in an explicit manner in relation to the above questions. The tendency in documents is to (a) *exclude* government officials and agencies, legislatures, the courts, the professions, business firms, and the mass media; (b) *include* individuals and families, formal disability-specific organizations involved in self-help, service provision, and advocacy, and associations and coalitions representing these interests; and (c) *differentiate* this community from others within the voluntary sector in Canada, such as those for women, Aboriginal peoples, and seniors.

Consider, for example, the federal government's recent reports, *Advancing the Inclusion of Persons with Disabilities* (HRDC, 2002a; SDC, 2004a). The report makes repeated reference to "the disability community", from which several features can be noted. One is that all 3.6 million Canadians with disabilities constitute the disability community. A second is that the community comprises "a wide variety of disability organizations" in which persons with disabilities may be members. The reports mention provincial and national disability associations, veterans' organizations, and non-governmental organizations involved in international development. Interestingly, Aboriginal persons with disabilities and their representatives are distinguished, raising the question of the relationship of Aboriginal disability organizations with the larger disability community in Canada.

The overall image of the disability community, from these reports, is a system of organized interests and associations outside of the Canadian state, relatively segmented and specialized, although linked to other policy communities and social movements, organized labour, and business in working together to address disability issues.

TOWARD A BROADER UNDERSTANDING OF THE DISABILITY COMMUNITY

To understand better the history, social structures and processes of the disability community, the community has four dimensions, as shown in Table 10.1. I define community as a collectivity made up of people linked together through common beliefs, shared life conditions, locality, kinship, or shared interests and ideals (Rice & Prince, 2000, p. 214). Whatever the size or complexity of communities, an essential common denominator of a community is a pattern of relationships among people and the existence of experiences and needs shared, largely, by these individuals, families and groups. For many people, the notion of community also implies a level of resilience or capacity and self-determination set within a wider ecology of contexts and interdependencies.

The practical reason for presenting these four viewpoints is that each captures some important features of the contemporary

---

Table 10.1: Analytical views of the disability community.

- As a sector of diverse organizations with varying functions, perspectives and capacities.

- As a new social movement.

- As a constitutional category of citizens with rights-based identities.

- As a policy community of interest groups.

---

disability community in Canada. Moreover, each viewpoint in turn offers a particular perspective on disability: as a range of needs for daily living that require supports and services; as a basis for celebrating difference and diversity and thus creating positive images; as a ground for entitlements and substantive equality rights; and as a focus for policy dialogue, advocacy and political participation.

(a) As a sector of diverse organizations

The disability community entails far more than policy development and political advocacy activities. Indeed, most organizations in this community are concerned mainly with the provision of services and the acquisition of funds, staff, volunteers and other resources for running their operations. Most, as well, are locally based, non-profit agencies that receive funding and service contracts from governments (Bach, 2002). Thus, the disability community — as distinguished from the disability policy community — includes individuals, groups and organizations that are primarily or wholly engaged as caregivers, service providers or brokers, referral agents, consumers, and fund raisers. As a custom, they do not participate directly or regularly in public policy and political processes.

Rather than policy instigators, most of these organizations are policy takers, working on the edges of public policy processes. This seems especially the case for specific-disability service groups run on behalf of people with disabilities. Lobbying is usually not part of their mission. Any activism and social change is low-key and non-political, pursued through public education and role models (Boyce et al., 2001, p. 56).

In addition to mandate and mission, diversity in the disability community is apparent in many other ways (Canadian Centre on Disability Studies [CCDS], 2002). One profound difference,

MICHAEL J. PRINCE

implied in the above discussion, concerns the particular disability perspective embraced by specific organizations. An organization may be working in accordance with a perspective on disablement that gives more or less emphasis to biomedical factors, economic and labour market concerns, environmental barriers to integration, or a human rights and equality approach.

With respect to their capacity, disability organizations vary in the sources and amounts of their funding, numbers of paid staff and reliance on volunteers. They vary in terms of the size, continuity and nature of their membership base — whether they are an organization of individuals with disabilities, or of family members, or of professionals, or an organization of other organizations. Disability groups certainly vary with regard to their organizational history, general stability and internal complexity. With respect to scope, organizations are divided into those having a single disability focus and those with a multiple and cross-disability focus. With respect to scale, there are local, regional, provincial or territorial, national and international organizations.

(b) As a new social movement

Many observers identify the disability community as an example of a new social movement (DeJong, 1979; Drieger, 1989; Fagan & Lee, 1997). New social movements (NSMs) are a form of collective action, organized around diversity to promote social identities, that originated in the 1960s in a number of countries. (They are "new" in contrast to the older social movements initiated by trade unions and working class groups, organized to resist or restructure capitalism.) Besides people with disabilities, examples of NSMs are those representing women, environmentalists, and visible minorities. Based in felt grievances of shared discrimination, oppression and exclusion, they seek to challenge the traditional authority of professionals and other experts, and related language, roles and images of their group. In turn, they aim to enable disadvantaged individuals and groups to express their own voice in order to create new forms of public recognition and acceptance.

The disability community in Canada exhibits several characteristics of a NSM. These include:

- Claiming a self-defined identity in place of that previously dominant in society;
- Questioning traditional state practices and professional controls;
- Promoting an agenda of human rights and self-determination;

- Challenging a purely biomedical perspective on disability and promoting a socio-political model with a focus on the interaction between individuals and the larger environment; and
- Holding a strong interest in social reform and achieving greater influence in public services and programs generally.

The NSMs transcend local places and individual jurisdictions as well as social and economic classes. A NSM contains people from a diverse range of backgrounds, resulting in a decentralized network of organizations and a "pluralism of ideas and values" held by the members (Larana, Johnston & Gusfield, 1995).

(c) As a constitutional category of citizens

The placing of "physical and mental disability" in section 15 of the *Canadian Charter of Rights and Freedoms* in 1982 "has ensured that disablement and persons with disabilities are recognized politically" (Cameron & Valentine, 2001, p. 35). More than that, including disability in the *Charter* means that the most fundamental law of the land — the Constitution — recognizes people with disabilities as a protected class of persons with a guarantee of equality rights.

Disability is a socio-political status, and persons with disabilities are now a constitutional category by virtue of their explicit recognition in the *Charter*. To define and enforce these fundamental rights and freedoms, such as mobility and equality, litigation has become an important strategy of individuals with disabilities and organizations representing their interests. This has raised the profile of the Canadian judiciary in the disability field and the wider social policy domain.

Inclusion in the *Charter* has given weight to a pan-Canadian vision on disability issues, along with a general orientation, by many disability groups at least, to federal leadership and national standards in policy, and to the ideal of full citizenship as the ultimate goal for reforms. As Sherri Torjman (2001) has noted, "Ever since the heady days of Canada's new constitution and the introduction of a Charter of Rights and Freedoms which guaranteed the protection of disability rights, the disability community has regarded Ottawa as the champion of its issues" (p. 194)

The disability community is not indifferent to Canadian federalism. Many disability organizations have a federated structure with provincial chapters as well as a national office. For nearly 25 years now, disability associations, as a *Charter* group, have spoken out on constitutional reform ideas (Boyce et al., 2001; Cairns, 1995).

At the same time, disability organizations have directed attention to provincial and territorial governments (as well as urban and local governments) in removing barriers to participation for persons with disabilities in order to advance accessibility, equity, self-determination, and inclusion. The rights-based identity of people with disabilities is prominently linked to the *Charter*, but that identity is also substantially linked to the human rights codes and related laws of the federal government and, for so many areas of everyday life, of the provinces and territories.

Even with the constitutional entrenchment of the *Canadian Charter of Rights and Freedoms* in the early 1980s, provincial codes remain uniquely significant with their wider scope of application, extending beyond governmental activity to include private activities such as advertising, accommodation, business generally, contracts, employment, family law and transportation services. Thus, the *Charter* supplements, but will never supplant, the role of provincial and federal human rights laws in advancing the rights of persons with disabilities. The *Charter* has encouraged the use of rights talk in politics and policy making and the pursuit of equality litigation. As well, it has expanded the judicial review powers and, likely, the judicial activism proclivities of Canadian judges. *Charter* decisions on disability issues are contributing to the creation of national standards enforceable by the courts.

The Courts Challenges Program of Canada, in effect from the late 1970s to 1992 and then reinstated again in 1994, intends to clarify constitutional rights and freedoms, and to enable minority language groups and equality-seeking groups and individuals (particularly those mentioned in section 15 of the *Charter*) to pursue their legal and constitutional rights through the courts. With respect to equality rights, the Program funds only cases that involve a challenge to a federal law, policy or practice that raises equality arguments and are test cases dealing with a problem or raising an argument not already decided by the courts. Such test cases have the potential to end discrimination or improve the way the law works for disadvantaged Canadians. People with disabilities are eligible for funding, as individuals or as groups, as a *party* directly affected by a case or as an *intervener* who wishes to raise constitutional arguments in a case involving other parties. Since 1994, disability issues have been a prominent feature of the equality rights applications and the case funding decisions (Prince, 2001a, p. 184).

As a form of engagement by Canada's disability community, results of litigation for rights and against discrimination are mixed. In cases involving a range of institutions as diverse as a local school board, the federal correctional services, and provincial health care services, the Supreme Court of Canada has held that employers have a duty, under section 15, to make reasonable accommodations to the needs of a person with a mental or physical disability. The accommodations, however, are often narrowly interpreted and only slowly implemented by governments.

(d) As a policy community of interest groups and advocacy coalitions

The disability policy community is a segment of the larger disability community of diverse organizations. The disability policy community comprises representatives of groups and associations who interact with governments and wider public sector officials and organizations, shaping ideas and policy in this field and, more generally, across public policy with the aim of advancing inclusion and making equality (Stienstra & Wight-Felske, 2003).

All the interest groups regularly active in this field constitute the disability policy community. These groups represent, in a formal way, certain interests of their membership. They formulate and present their ideas, experiences and claims to one or more of governments, cabinet ministers, administrative officials, legislators, tribunals and courts. Like interest groups in general, disability organizations seek to exercise influence over public policy (strategies, plans, legislation, regulations, budgets, decisions) through such vehicles as consultation, mobilization, litigation, and deliberation, rather than to actually exercise public authority.

In a wider sense, the disability policy community includes individuals and groups with a potential involvement in the field, based on an indirect interest with disability issues. Participation by these groups is episodic, triggered perhaps by a certain issue in a given context. One meaning of building the capacity of the disability community, therefore, is to explore how to incorporate strategically more of these potential and peripheral participants into the core of the community.

Within the disability policy community in Canada are a series of associations. On behalf of a cluster of interest groups and service agencies, associations may represent a particular disability, a distinct client group, a specific provincial or regional area, or a functional activity such as legal advocacy. In addition, there are a number of umbrella associations, usually at the national level, that aim to represent comprehensively the relevant interests of that group.

167

The Organizational Nature of the Disability Community and Canada's Disability State

Looking at the disability community in these ways — as a sector of diverse organizations, as a new social movement, as a constitutional category of citizens, and as a policy community of interest groups and advocacy coalitions — shows that the community is both extensively organized and significantly differentiated by perspectives and structures. The disability policy field also contains various policy networks, the structural bridge between the disability community and the disability state.

Canada's disability state, if that term is used, refers to the legislative, executive, judicial, and administrative agencies that have a direct involvement in disability issues and with the disability community. Along with specific organizations and officials, the disability state includes the macro-institutions of parliamentary government, federalism, the inherent right of Aboriginal self-government, and the *Canadian Charter of Rights and Freedoms*.

Policy networks are specific organizational relations between (i) government and other state institutions and (ii) community agencies and actors. These networks form around particular issue areas, reform processes, and/or disabilities, jurisdictions, and policy instruments of importance to the community and the state. School testing, inclusive childcare, disability income benefits, accessible transportation, and labour market programs are illustrations of particular policy networks.

The idea of *community* implies a level of shared norms or common understanding among nearly all members. In the context of public policy, this shared understanding relates to the substance of policy (the proper role of governments, and the vision, principles and goals) and the process (structures, tactics and conduct) by which groups should engage with governments over these substantive issues. Experience in Canada strongly suggests that the disability community and governments have only had a national and intergovernmental policy focus for a decade. And even then, it is a partial and still contested vision. Both the community and the state contain various perspectives on disablement, some of which are in sharp tension with one another (Bickenbach, 1993). Not surprisingly then, the level of shared norms is still forming within this policy field.

The disability community also contains a multitude of organizations and several associations with specialized spheres of activity and responsibility. In principle, the benefits of differentiation for policy engagement are that it provides the organizational means for expressing a diversity of specific interests, and for providing specialized information on particular experiences across the country. By comparison, the disability community lacks a macro association that spans the entire community, co-ordinating the diversity of groups and broadly representing all the key interests. A potential drawback to this high level of organizational differentiation is that, on its own, it limits the capacity of the community to interact, to formulate strategies for the whole community, or to plan the actions of members in public policy processes (Coleman & Skogstad, 1990, pp. 16–21).

At the same time, the community is highly differentiated: "the state presents itself to the disabled citizen as a complex set of institutions" (Cameron and Valentine, 2001, p. 23). At the federal level of government alone, over 30 agencies, departments and commissions have disability-related programs and services (SDC, 2004a). Behind this complexity is an array of programs and diverse eligibility rules that raise concerns about equity, access, co-ordination, accountability and portability. Thus, to be more effective in disability policy engagement, the community and the state need to place more emphasis on integrative structures both within their respective sectors and between them.

Intra-community engagement involves disability organizations working in partnerships, and forming alliances and coalitions with other organizations in the disability community. It consists of such efforts as:

- Gathering information about disability support needs, issues and practices;
- Undertaking or sponsoring research, social audits, needs assessments, and community consultations;
- Meeting with affiliates and locals to share information, to obtain input, and to develop positions on policy issues and set priorities;
- Meeting and organizing with other disability organizations and associations to apply for joint funding or to advocate for a certain reform; and
- Forming and/or joining partnerships and coalitions among organizations within the disability community.

Transaction costs are associated with this series of activities, costs in time, budgets and staff in forging and managing such relations. For disability agencies, with very limited resources and a

169

mandate that is for service provision, these activities also represent considerable opportunity costs. Resources devoted to engagement undertakings are at the expense of being able to pursue other programming and service delivery work; hence, the need for collaboration among groups in the disability community. Examples of internal engagement are: holding community roundtables, community profiling, formulating a national strategy, developing a specific policy proposal, and producing election campaign statements.

Cross-sector engagement has to do with disability organizations and associations, working with organizations and associations in the larger voluntary sector and perhaps other sectors through coalitions and networking. Three types of coalitions exist — virtual, ad hoc, and permanent — and Table 10.2 outlines their features and functions.

In a given policy sector, any combination of these three types of coalition building might be present at a certain point or over a period of time. I would hypothesize that, in the past, ad hoc coalitions tended to be the most common type; that is now complemented by Web-based forms of coalitions and, to a degree, by permanent alliances forged between the disability community and, for example, the human rights movement. Based on mutual interest, the foundation of support for disability-related issues has broadened, and that support has somewhat been structured (Roeher Institute, 1997b, p. 168).

There can be little doubt that coalitions and networks are important resources for policy engagement, especially for marginalized groups such as people with disabilities. As communications capabilities have improved, coalition building and networking in the disability community have grown in number and effectiveness. Virtual coalition building seems especially important and necessary for persons with disabilities and disability organizations in large-scale countries like Australia, Canada, and the United States, as well as for advocates and agencies engaged in international work. The Internet in particular has emerged as a vital technology for reaching others and constructing identities of disability for the socially isolated as well as the geographically dispersed across vast distances (Meekosha, 2001).

Until the 1990s, there was little success in or inclination toward coalition building between disability groups and other social movements, such as Aboriginal or women's groups, in Canada. In part, it was because of a concern that such alliances might overshadow disability issues (Boyce, et al., 2001, pp. 62 and 130). Other factors were at play. DisAbled Women's Network (DAWN) Can-

Table 10.2: Coalition building by disability groups.

Type	Features	Functions
Virtual	• Communication networks • Loose affiliation • No formal structure	• Exchange information and ideas on shared interests • Learn from others • Build contacts/alliances
Ad Hoc	• Specific issue or purpose • Time-limited • Loose structure • Either within the disability sector or across sectors	• Rally support • Increase numbers • Share information • Present a broad and united front • Gain political attention
Permanent	• Broad area of concerns and issues • Ongoing activities • Formal structure with some staff to co-ordinate activities of mutual interest	• Raise numbers and profile • Generate and exchange information and ideas • Establish legitimacy and authority with political system • Build solidarity across groups

Source: Based on Boyce et al. (2001, pp. 135–36).

ada, a national feminist cross-disability organization, "was founded in response to the frustration women with disabilities felt because of the inaccessibility of the women's movement, and the indifference to women's issues from the disability community" (Roeher Institute, 1997, p. 166).

In cross-sector engagement, there may be competing advocacy coalitions in a given policy sector — two or more coalitions of various actors and groups who hold contending beliefs, priorities and strategies about disability policy. While the nature of policy networks varies by issue, time and place, the policy analysis literature suggests there tends to be two or more advocacy coalitions in a given policy field. An example is the clash between the Ad Hoc Coalition of Service Providers and the Ontario Advocacy Coalition over proposed provincial advocacy and guardianship legislation in the early 1990s. The two coalitions differed in many ways: their goals, membership base, funding, organizational structures, tactics, and perspectives on disability (Boyce et al., 2001). A lesson from this case is that coalition building may not mitigate political conflict, at least in the short run.

The Capacity of the Disability Community: What is It and Who Wants It?

The skill, legitimacy, potential, and effectiveness of the disability community are issues of strategic importance and abiding challenge (Canada, 1996, 2000a and 2004; CCDS, 2002; Drieger, 1989; Rice & Prince, 2000; Roeher Institute, 1997b). These and related issues are often encompassed by the concept of capacity, and the capacity of the community is seen as one of the central elements of inclusion for persons with disabilities in Canadian society. Indeed, a recent federal report measures the practice of capacity in terms of three measures, namely, human resources, financial resources, and structural and systems capacity. It concludes that the evidence against these measures points to some progress of late but also significant difficulties in the disability community's capacity (SDC, 2004b).

Strengthening capacity is a laudable objective of government, foundations and disability groups; but what exactly does it entail? Whose capacity in the community is to be enhanced, and to do what? And do governments, charitable donors and community groups always agree on what capacity building is about? The four-fold classification of the community presented here provides us with a way of addressing these questions, while recognizing significant differences within the community. Each perspective highlights particular aspects and meanings of capacity and of politics, indicating that capacity is, at root, a relational phenomenon with assorted features.

In thinking of the community as a sector of organizations, capacity relates to the ability of agencies, charities and service clubs, in what is sometimes called the traditional segment, to provide programs and supports to different categories of people with mental and physical disabilities. Capacity concerns aspects of organizational performance, such as the effective management of funds, staff and volunteers; the efficient and responsive delivery of programs; and a transparent and accountable system of governance. This entails an administrative politics of agency-client and agency-funding relations. An extended notion of capacity, from this perspective, and one increasingly proposed by advocates, is the ability and willingness of traditional service agencies to reach out and build partnerships with other groups in the community engaged in social action and community development. In this sense, capacity includes reviewing and redesigning services and programs so that they more fully respond to and include people with disabilities and their families in decision making.

Augmenting the capacity of the disability community as a new social movement would involve enhancing such activities as social critique and consciousness raising of people in the movement and wider society; celebrating and communicating in a positive manner the experiences and varied identities of persons with disabilities; and challenging the ableist attitudes, beliefs and actions in play in society and striving to institute progressive changes that tackle exclusion, cultural prejudice, and discrimination. The NSMs are, in an important sense, cultural movements, concerned with politicizing prevailing systems of values and norms (Young, 1990). Along with this cultural politics, the disability community as a NSM can be seen as engaged in the associational politics of forging networks and coalitions across different groups and sectors of society.

Increasing the role of the disability organizations in their status as a *Charter of Rights* group in the Constitution would imply an expanded ability in several areas: to access legal resources for litigation; to intervene in court cases; and to challenge apparent discriminatory laws, regulations, decisions and programs before tribunals, human rights commissions, and the judiciary. This approach involves politics and discourse of equality, human rights, and frequently adversarial and expensive legal processes. Although a critical tool for effecting social change and advancing inclusion, rights claiming through Charter politics is not, by itself, sufficient. It is also important to note that neither the federal nor the provincial and territorial governments much prefer this approach for addressing disability issues (Canada, 1998 and 2000b). Unfortunately, at times disability groups reluctantly resort to this form of legal politics out of frustration over the lack of progress through other channels.

If we think about the disability community as a network of interest groups and policy advocacy coalitions, capacity building is about contributing to policy discussions, program developments and reviews, effectively and in an opportune manner. Capacity also involves having the wherewithal of staff, time, information and research, and support by members to participate in consultations in addition to responding to public issues and governmental proposals, and initiating desired solutions and recommendations. Challenges exist in mobilizing the community nationally and keeping members united on difficult issues. Too often, even in cases where there is a consensus among an array of disability organizations and associations on a given issue, the consensus may partly be by default because some groups are unable to develop their own position. The federal government, through the Voluntary Sector Initiative, recognizes this problem and provides funding to certain national disability organizations and their affiliates to work on fostering capacity to participate in federal social policy processes (SDC, 2004a). Likewise, various provincial and territorial governments focus on creating new consultation spaces for disability groups.

Thus, with each perspective and dimension of the disability community is a specific and distinctive notion of capacity and related style of politics and discourse. This line of inquiry could extend to explore models of disability, identities of persons with disabilities, state-society relations, and the mix of virtual, ad hoc and permanent coalitions each perspective tends to emphasize. Overall, the politics of capacity building is about recognizing the multiple aspects of the phenomenon, the differing actors, conceptions, goals and preferences at work, and the interplay among them.

CONCLUSION

This chapter has argued that there is no one conception or organization form of the disability community. Disability entails differences. The disability community has been presented as terrain interconnected with, while in some respects different, from family, the market economy, and the state. It is a dynamic and differentiated collectivity, a series of public and personal spaces with their networks of activities, roles and power relations. The community is in and around us, and is who we are and aspire to be. The contemporary disability community in Canada comprises at least four distinct though related elements that overlap in various degrees and interact in myriad ways. The community clearly plays an important part in civil society as well as in the state as service providers, policy advocates, rights claimants and rights holders, and, as a social movement, as cultural change agents. In short, disability embodies diversity and expects democracy.

What links or connects this group of peoples and organizations, what makes disability a social category and political constituency is, to a large degree, widespread and recurrent experiences of discrimination, devaluation, stigma, exclusion and disadvantage (Doe, 2003). This common marginal status of citizenship, as members of the general Canadian community, is what makes disability a highly relevant category for analysis and action in all four socio-political spaces identified here (McColl & Boyce, 2003; Prince, 2001a).

This multifaceted nature of the disability community suggests that the so-called welfare state consensus has not collapsed but rather is being challenged and changed in complex and multidirectional ways. In the case of disability advocacy and rights organizations and coalitions, the state in Canada is under challenge and critique to alter practices, change beliefs and attitudes toward disablement, and extend rights and entitlements to income, supports and services, and employment opportunities. The community is calling for governments at all levels to play an enabling leadership role in managing and improving social conditions and life chances in Canada.

What makes the disability community inherently political is not only that it includes interest groups and advocacy coalitions, relations with governments, and court cases. At a fundamental level, groups of people, through various forms of collective deliberation and action, are raising issues, making decisions, recognizing and affirming differences, and seeking to shape or reshape beliefs, social practices and structural arrangements.

While we may read of some three million plus Canadians with disabilities (Canada, 1988, 2002b and 2004), some people may not readily self-identify as a person with a disability. And among those that do, many are not actually involved in disability organizations as members or active participants. Yet such references to the overall population may be, and indeed likely are, used to raise the public profile of this aspect of the human condition, as well as to augment the real and perceived significance of the activities by disability organizations and their leadership. Persons with disabilities who are not active in the community may become so on a given issue, mobilized or politicized in response to the action or inaction of a state or civil society agency.

And so the concept of "disability community" is a unifying concept, a phrase that encompasses an array of impairments and handicaps, needs, beliefs and goals, organizational mandates and structures, and activities and practices. Despite or perhaps because of this heterogeneity, the notion of disability community is useful as a systematizing concept and expression of certain experiences and values, just as are the concepts of the state, the private sector, and various other social groupings in Canadian society. If the notion of a community has merit, perhaps it is to see ourselves as part of something common, to gain a sense of purpose, and maybe even a way of sustaining hope and agency.

11

Social Change Partnerships: Advocates, Business and Government

AILEEN WIGHT FELSKE
AND OLGA KRASSIOUKOVA-ENNS

INTRODUCTION

Social change that strengthens civil society requires change at two levels:

- The creation of new social policies, and the legislation needed to express those policies; and
- The construction of new partnerships between government, business and volunteer organizations.

Advocacy groups for Canadians with disabilities are active at the level of consultation with municipal, territorial, provincial and federal governments, arguing for new or revised legal and policy structures drawn from Section 15(a) in the *Canadian Charter of Rights and Freedom*. At the community level, the challenge is to implement changes made possible by these initiatives. New models of service delivery and opportunities for people with disabilities are being created through a variety of partnerships between government, the business community, and voluntary organizations. An examination of what makes these partnerships successful and sustainable is important in the study of evolving social policy.

This chapter examines the various partnerships that have occurred among disability advocacy organizations, non-governmental organizations (NGOs), and federal and international governments. More specifically, the chapter includes

1. A review of the literature about partnerships between government and non-government organizations to identify the range of partnerships occurring;
2. A description of five examples of partnerships in which the CCDS has participated; and
3. A discussion of lessons learned.

BACKGROUND

Social science research in the political arena can be described as addressing the process of governing and the efforts of the electorate, individually and in groups, to influence government activities. Canadians with a disability have lobbied for 25 years using a human rights framework to combat individual and systemic discrimination and to create an inclusive Canadian society (Stienstra & Wight-Felske, 2003). The federal government has also adopted a human rights model and, using this approach, has conducted research that clearly documents disabled Canadians' experiences of social and economic exclusion (SDC, 2004a). At the same time, the Canadian public has indicated approval of new initiatives that are based on partnerships between the government, businesses and voluntary organizations.

Non-profit and voluntary organizations are seen as important change agents in improving the overall quality of life in Canada. In *Rethinking Government*, a report done by Communications Canada (2002), 67% of Canadians indicated that they have "a lot of confidence" in non-profit and voluntary organizations. Their confidence in private companies was reported at 46%, and at 28% for government initiatives. More than three-quarters of Canadians (77%) rate non-profit and voluntary organizations, compared to 44% for governments, as serving the public interest.

It is important, in meeting their inclusive society goals, that social change agents understand the range and nature of partnerships between governments, non-government organizations and business sectors. Torjman's review of partnerships between government and a wide range of voluntary organizations reports that increasingly these collaborations are characterized by multilateral partnerships; frequently these partnerships involve multiple levels of government or more than one government department, and the private and voluntary sectors. In a report for the Volunteer Sector Roundtable, the Caledon Institute of Social Policy (1998) saw two types of partnership in recent government activity:

> Collaborative arrangements ... made with organizations outside of the federal government... to share the costs, risks and benefits of particular initiatives, while at the same time increasing the involvement of the clients being served and enhancing the general level of goodwill with all parties (Treasury Board of Canada Secretariat, 1995, p. 1).

> [Relationships] ... in which government and other agents work co-operatively to achieve a ... goal at the community level ... [these relationships require] ... the sharing of resources, responsibilities, decision-making, risks and benefits, according to a mutually agreed-upon formal or informal arrangement (New Economy Development Group, 1996, p. 16)

Torjman states that the impetus driving these relationships is the assumption that "partnership represents, to all partners, a better strategy for a specific project or goal than each partner could achieve operating independently" (1998, p. 2). In other words, the partnership is considered to add value to the efforts of the individual partners, creating a result greater than what could be achieved individually.

In social policy, the devolution of social program delivery from government to private sectors reflects the political shift of neo-liberalism away from the welfare state. The role of partners in implementing the neo-liberal shift is critical. Researchers have examined these new partnerships using a variety of categories: the method used to create social change, the way power is shared, and the types of partners entering the partnership. A report by Ekos (1998) organizes partnerships into a typology based on the method of change:

- First, partnerships for social change, which: "provide(s) an important community service or tackle difficult problems such as family violence, unemployment or poverty" (pp. 6–8).

- Second, community investment partnerships where "business makes a substantive contribution to the community through active involvement with a non profit organization" (p. 8).

- Third, public education partnerships: "strategic alliances ... which seek to raise awareness around a social, economic or environmental concern" (p. 8).

The first two of his definitions speak to the direct partnerships that produce concrete observable change at the community level. However, while awareness may be raised, it is difficult to attribute changes to Ekos' third type of partnerships activity.

In an alternate model, Rodal and Mulder (1993) develop a typology of partnership based on the extent to which power is shared. They propose a model of partnerships that ranges from consultative partnerships to collaborative partnerships or "real" partnerships. While the primary purpose for government in a consultative partnership is to seek advice or obtain input, there is joint decision making, pooling of resources and sharing of ownership and risk in a collaborative partnership.

Klein (1992, cited in Torjman, 1998) also develops a typology of partnerships based on the type of partners that are involved (e.g., government, private sector, non-profit/community groups, and education institutions). When the Ekos categories of partnership and the Rodal and Mulder (1993) categories of power are considered together with the Klein categories of organizations, they offer a number of different dimensions along which to position partnerships: purpose, power-sharing, type of funding partner, the structure or mechanism of the partnership.

Partnerships with government in the creation of a civil society are not without their detractors. Pascal (1996) calls the term "government partnership" an oxymoron in light of the difficulty that governments frequently have in sharing power and decision making. He states that these relationships between voluntary sector and government are more accurately described as involving joint programming and consultations. Interviewees in the Pascal study warned about the potential for organizations to lose credibility as advocates when they entered into government partnerships. The volunteers of these advocacy-based NGOs can be drained by the level of bureaucratization needed to meet government accountability requirements. There is also the potential for organizations to abandon programs needed by their constituents in order to deliver programs that government deems important (Dow, 1997 cited in Pascal, 1996; Rekart, 1994). Torjman recognizes this tension when she states: "Governments are bound by legislation and are fully accountable for the use of public funds. ... [T]heir reporting lines tend to be structured, hierarchical and mandate-specific" (Torjman,

1998, p. 15). Despite the move toward alternative services delivery, governments may be hampered by internal norms and regulations. Governments are risk-averse, often influenced by public and political agendas, and lack openness to potential new avenues for the partnership. Finally, Torjman notes a lack of predictability of government agendas and funding as a barrier to partnership. An erratic commitment to the issue and unpredictable resources damages partnership potential.

Description of Five Partnerships Involving Canadians with Disabilities

All five of the examples of partnerships cited in this chapter relate to the economic marginalization of people with disabilities. Governments' response to the new economy of the neo-liberal society, *Improving Social Security in Canada* (1994, cited in Chappell, 2004a, p. 9) states that "the key to dealing with social insecurity can be summed up in a single phrase: helping people get and keep jobs." Globalization in the new economy has altered the face of work for Canadians, creating a bipolar workforce pool of low wage workers, with low education and few training skills, and a high wage workforce of professionals. Traditional employment models of industries are decreasing as economic competition through outsourcing undercuts their economic viability. New employment alternatives must compete in the North America market. Economic marginality has implications for social inclusion. Unstable economic conditions lead to social instability (e.g., marginal employment is associated with family breakdown) and also reduce the level of social protection available (Chappell, 2004). In Canada, analysts state that social policy and economic policies are merging. The incorporation of people into the formal labour market has been central both to policies to deal with poverty and exclusion, and to the development of social protection.

Canadians with a disability may lose the toehold they have achieved in the employment sector thus undermining the federal government initiatives toward an inclusive society. In many circumstances people with disabilities are only partly integrated into the labour market year (HRDC, 2000). Despite the federal government *Employment Equity Act* for its workforce and a commitment to job accommodations under the federal and provincial or territorial human rights codes, the earning power of disabled Canadians is still characterized as a "dual labour market". There are two classes of workers, secure employees on regular pay and "peripheral" workers, whose role in the economy is more marginal, and who are liable to displacement during economic cycles. Canadians with a disability are more likely to be in the peripheral class, marginal workers who move between casual and part-time work and joblessness.

The federal government recognizes this economic marginalization. In *Knowledge Matters: Skills and Learning for Canadians*, they comment on the economic risks of Canadians with a disability by stating: "Persons with disabilities ... face a number of barriers to labour market success, including lower levels of education, employer attitudes and behaviour, and a lack of workplace accommodations" (HRDC, 2002b, p. 2).

In a national survey (Statistics Canada, 2001d) on active living for Canadians with a disability, it recognizes the economic insecurity of families and individuals with a disability. The survey collected detailed information in a number of areas that are intertwined with social-economic security such as health, employment, education, housing, and "the need for and access to disability supports (e.g., specialized equipment and aids, specialized services, medications, assistance with completing everyday activities and out-of-pocket expenses related to disability)" (Statistics Canada, 2001d, Appendix A).

Following are some of the key findings:

- The unemployment rate for Canadians with disabilities was 16%, compared with 9% for those without disabilities.

- On average, people with disabilities earn 15% less than those without disabilities.

- Working-age adults with disabilities are more than twice as likely to be living on low incomes as adults without disabilities (26% of adults with disabilities were living below the low-income cut-off point, compared with 11% for those without disabilities).

- Among adults with disabilities, 17% of them were more than 25% below the low-income cut-off (depth of poverty), compared with 6% for those without disabilities.

- Parents, spouses and other caregivers may experience a reduced capacity to earn income as a result of their responsibilities; at the same time, they may face considerable expenses related to the family member's disabilities.

- People with disabilities face higher living costs associated with their disabilities (Statistics Canada, 2001d).

In 1993, Health Canada estimated the total value of productivity lost due to disability was $55.8 billion. Of this amount, $38.3 billion was lost due to long-term disability and $17.5 billion due to short-term disability (Health Canada, 1997). The main government response to unemployment is through economic policy, which addresses the issues by considering the workings of the economy as a whole. General measures to manage the economy have to be distinguished from "targeted" employment measures for a disadvantaged group. For example, employment subsidies and wage supplements are intended specifically to affect the labour market. Targeted measures are likely to be inefficient because they are used by a population likely to achieve re-employment even without the "incentive", or they create employment that only continues as long as the employer's fiscal supplements are available. Canadians facing long-term unemployment, or who have never entered the workforce are not aided by these active income security programs. Canadians with disabilities are tied to various forms of private or public passive income security, which, while offering a much needed health care insurance, inhibits the recipients' attempts to enter the employment field.

The CCDS, located in Winnipeg, Canada, is a consumer-directed, university-affiliated centre dedicated to research, education and the dissemination of knowledge on disability issues. Through its activities, the CCDS promotes the full and equal participation of people with a variety of disabilities in all aspects of society, on a local, national and international level (Enns & Neufeldt, 2003). It has been involved in five partnerships that exemplify the dimensions of partnership discussed in the previous section.

(a) Building bridges between the corporate sector and the disability community

The first project was a national initiative that analyzed the opportunities for and barriers to building bridges between the corporate sector and the disability community in two key areas: corporations' internal employment practices related to people with disabilities and their practices addressing disability in the broader community. Partnerships that made this research viable included the federal government, a range of private sector businesses and a project advisory committee from the disability community. The project funding was from Human Resources Development Canada.

(b) Best practices in the home-based employment of people with disabilities

The second project was a regional initiative aimed at examining home-based tele-work arrangements involving workers with disabilities. The partnerships in the project were workers with disability, consumer-based advocacy organizations, employers and unions, and financial institutions. Funding for this study was from the Royal Bank of Canada.

(c) Students with disabilities: transition from post-secondary education to work (phase 2 2003–2004)

The third initiative was another national study, examining the experiences of youths with a disability as they move out of post-secondary education into the area of employment. The project's partners included the federal government, the students with disability advocacy group National Educational Association for Disabled Students (NEADS), post-secondary institutions, and students. Project funding was from HRDC.

(d) Canada-Russia disability program 2003–2007

Funding for this fourth, international, initiative was provided by the Canadian International Development Agency. This is a program of action aimed to reform policies and practices in Russia affecting its most vulnerable populations, notably those with disabilities. It was intended to also have much wider application to "at risk" children, frail elderly people and working age adults experiencing sustained distress. Addressing issues faced by disabled people is particularly important because they typically are amongst the poorest of the poor in any society, are stigmatized (some more than others), and frequently experience discriminatory practices, often marked by inadequate or absent services and supports. The project is based on complex partnerships, not only within Russia and its regions, but with the Canadian partners. The importance of communication is highlighted by the long-term nature of the project, and the opportunities for both Canadians and Russians to make educational visits to their partner's countries. A tripartite model of engagement frames the various activities to be undertaken — involving the voluntary sector, government and institutions of higher learning.

183

(e) World Bank (WB) project

The partners in this project were the international organization itself, the advisory committee for the project, and a large team of investigators (many of whom had a disability), and the people involved in country-based projects. This research was not an isolated endeavour, but one that complements the recent creation of the Disability Advisor position at the World Bank. It contributes to the enhancement and effectiveness of poverty alleviation initiatives. Many, in the field and from national aid agencies around the world, anticipate that the leadership of the Bank in the area of disability and development will be similar to that shown by it in women/gender and development in previous decades.

Lessons Learned

The projects the CCDS has conducted have given the researchers experience in identifying challenges and pitfalls in establishing and maintaining partnerships.

(a) Choosing the right partners

Partnerships involve multilateral collaborations. In addition to the disability advocacy sector, the case studies described in this chapter involved multiple levels of government, multiple departments, the private business sector, educational institutions and members of the community. The lead organization that brokers these partnerships needs to understand the different management "ethos" of the partners, and the decision-making process of each one. Ensuring that all the "right" organizations are involved is a critical first step in the partnership process.

(b) Paying attention to the up-front work

The initial stages in a partnership may be difficult if partners, excited about the proposed opportunities and outcomes, push to implement before the various roles and obligations of each partner have been clarified. Putting significant time and resources into this pre-planning process, however, will create an atmosphere of trust and clear communication. At some level, all partners should feel that they need each other or that the issue or initiative cannot best be solved without the partners; that is, there are benefits to be gained from the loss of autonomy. In the beginning of the design stage of the Canada-Russia project, for example, partner organizations, including universities, disability organizations, and government, came together to determine areas of collaboration and

184

to develop a vision for integrated program work. The advantages of sharing expertise and an information base were immediately evident, including the opportunity to offer complementary disability training programs, whether informally, among professionals or through university curricula. Nonetheless, it was also clear that in order to be sustainable, the partnerships encompassed by the Canada-Russia Disability Program also needed to be nurtured and strengthened throughout the project.

(c) Negotiation and agreement upon goals and objectives

Ideally, goals and objectives should be clearly defined and agreed upon by the partners. The goals may be short-term and long-term, evolving over time. The negotiation of partnership goals may also include discussion around the partnership process, for example, how decisions will be made and how responsibilities will be assigned. In a longer-term initiative, setting short- and medium-term goals enables partners to feel a sense of progress and advancement. For example, in the study of students with disabilities, both the post-secondary institutions and NEADS played a role helping the CCDS find participants. The project advisory committee guided in the development of the questionnaire, and the CCDS ethics committee reviewed the study's methodology. Paid staff, many of whom were themselves disabled, then conducted the interviews.

(d) Implementing a structure

The case studies of partnerships in CCDS projects involved a multitude of different organizational arrangements, ranging from largely informal understandings to formal contracts or agreements. There may be several levels of partnerships, featuring different types of agreements, with the various organizations. Formal agreements provide partners with an opportunity to clarify goals, roles and responsibilities, and act as a road map over the project life-span. Agreements need to address the maintenance of the partnership in the longer term and the ongoing responsibilities of the partners to support the activities or products generated by the partnership. This can be important, as projects may have a lifespan that involves two or three different personnel. The projects history cannot be simply oral without the loss of valuable knowledge. Good contracts should also address the termination or extension of the partnership, as non-government organizations operate from a more fragile economic base and may encounter unplanned changes in status.

185

(e) Building trust

The process of building trust between partners builds on the interpersonal nature of the partnerships, the demonstrated accountability of the partners, and the clarity of communication. Projects such as the World Bank reflect the trust of a large international organization that the information gathered would be ethically gathered and useful. Although Disabled People International has a formal consulting role with the United Nations, the World Bank chose a more third-party approach to its project. Torjman's (1998) comment that government and non-government organizations are not natural allies has been confirmed in the partnerships that the CCDS has played a role. An understanding of the history behind advocacy groups and government consultations, as well as the differing philosophies of the competitive business world, has allowed the CCDS to act as a "third" party in these projects. Trust is built on clear communications and accountability. With third partner involvement, advocacy groups and government are able to work as partners in demonstration projects, without feeling compromised should other issues of lobby action with the government arise. This is illustrated in the student project with advocacy partner NEADS, which receives its funding from the federal government.

(f) Monitoring results

The investment of resources and shared responsibility requires issues of accountability to be addressed from the onset of partnerships. Advocacy organizations are accountable to their boards, volunteers and constituents. Government, often the funding source, has requirements around accountability and performance measurement. Accountability for funds is largely straightforward and handled through established accounting practices; however, the non-governmental organization may not have the background to easily meet this demand. Today's climate of accountability leads to evaluation and performance measurement for project outcomes. This may require the collection of data through the project or partnership. Steps should be taken to determine early in the process the types of information required, a process for data collection and the individuals/resources dedicated to the task. In the end, the strategy must meet the accountability requirements of all partners. The students with disabilities project, for example, received additional funding to follow up with participants on the identified issues.

CONCLUSION

Although people with disabilities of all kinds are the prime beneficiaries of the case studies, experience in Canada and elsewhere has demonstrated that addressing partnerships between governments, non-governmental organizations, private business sectors and advocacy groups in the creation of a more civil society benefits everyone, not only people with disabilities. For example, policies that increase employment access improve the country's economic welfare; buildings that are more accessible to wheelchair users benefit senior citizens, parents with strollers and others who walk with difficulty; or practices that respect the rights of disabled people become the standard of a modern, democratic and civil society. Partnerships that address viable models of increasing the economic security of people with disabilities have positive effects on the social security of all people.

12

Policy Shifts and Challenges: Coping Strategies of Disability Organizations

WILL BOYCE, KARI KROGH
AND EMILY BOYCE

INTRODUCTION

Community-based disability organizations in the early to mid-1990s encountered many fundamental challenges in Canada that required effective strategies to ensure that individual, organizational, and community needs were met. These challenges stemmed from structural and ideological changes in the socio-political environment, the economy, and the labour market, which were manifested through government and social welfare policies during this period. The core Canadian political-economic agenda in the 1990s shifted to an increased valuation of economic growth, corporatism, and deficit reduction, which was used to justify economic restructuring measures, such as massive cuts and bureaucratic changes to social assistance, employment insurance, disability pensions and supports, and community and health services. These cuts were justified and perpetuated by an overall ideological shift — at the social and political levels — from Keynesian welfarism (based on citizenship

188

rights to government and social supports) to neo-liberalism (based on individual responsibility for self-provision and the primacy of macro-economic needs over social needs) (Coburn, 2004).

The first challenge facing disability organizations thus involved increased consumer demand for services and advocacy as a result of the reduction in income, services, and benefits for individuals with disabilities in Canada (refer to Boyce, Boyce & Krogh, Chapter 16). Second, disability organizations themselves experienced drastic losses in government funding and support, resulting in reduced financial and resource capacities for serving the disability community. Third, organizations faced a decrease in member participation. This problem arose because of the inevitable intersection between the above cuts to individual benefits and cuts to community organizations that decreased opportunities for member involvement. As well, consumer-driven disability organizations are run by people with disabilities, and increased hardships for these individuals led to reduced human resource capacity for their organizations.

Understanding the responses of disability organizations to these challenges requires a holistic view of social movement strategies as a basis for asserting collective and individual rights. It is insufficient to consider only pragmatic tactical shifts in social movement organizations without also considering fundamental strategic shifts that may alter the overall purpose, or legitimacy, of the organization itself. To assist in this analysis, we first explore the fundamentals of social movement theory and how it applies to disability organizations in Canada.

Alan Scott (1990) defines a social movement as a "collective actor constituted by individuals who have common interests and ... a common identity. Social movements ... have mass mobilization as their prime source of social sanction ... and power as their goal. They are ... chiefly concerned to defend or change society, or the relative position of the group in society" (p. 6). Oliver (1990) has argued that disability organizations are part of a social movement since there are (a) marginalization from traditional politics; (b) a link of the personal with the political; (c) a critical evaluation of society; and (d) post-materialism.

There are two social movement theories that have particular applicability to disability organizations. Resource Mobilization theory proposes an economic analogy to explore the ability of specific social movements to acquire and use political, monetary and labour resources to facilitate organizational objectives (McCarthy & Zald, 1987; Zald & McCarthy, 2002). The resource mobilization approach examines the variety of resources required, linkages of organizations with external supporters, and the creation of change in the organization by this resource dependency. While this theory provides explanations of how an organization is set up and maintains levels of participation, it does not explain why the organization initially arises or its potential for long-term survival. In the context of disability organizations, Resource Mobilization theory can be used to explain the ability of such organizations to secure funds for self-development projects, as well as the political will for advocacy initiatives, and thus become intermediary change agents between the state and disabled persons.

New Social Movement theory has traditionally taken a different approach. Castells (1983) argued that contemporary social movements developed as a result of particular historical and cultural events that are anti-institutional and self-identifying in nature. He asserted that survival of a social movement organization depends on more than a rational mobilization of resources alone, since this inevitably leads to institutionalization and loss of purpose. Castells proposed that the future of such organizations depends on improved collective conditions, an autonomous community culture, and political self-management. Similarly, Touraine (1981) identified autonomy and self-identity as crucial for new social movements that are more concerned with reform, or with creating alternatives within the dominant society, than with increasing their own power. More recently, Scott (1990) suggests that a key feature of new social movements is the focus on: autonomy, at the personal level (for disability this means a focus on consciousness, self-expression and difference); challenging restrictions of freedom (disability focus on accessibility); and struggle at the collective level (disability focus on recognition and de-stigmatization). Shakespeare (1993) agrees that disability organizations have these features of new social movements, but also strive to use forms of organization that reflect cultural challenges to the dominant codes of management.

Canadian disability organizations met their challenges through the use of many different strategies aimed at improving personal and collective conditions, mobilizing organizational and political resources, and maintaining autonomy. This chapter describes and explores both these challenges and the corresponding organizational strategies in three sections. It is our hope that this account of organizational perseverance, innovation, and development in the context of an extremely regressive socio-political environment will provide strategic input and ideas for disability groups, and others, who encounter these same problems.

190

The study used a participatory action research approach to determine the situation of disability organizations in the mid- to late 1990s as policies of disability support were recalled or dramatically altered. The response to these changes on the part of organizations was explored from the perspective of those who were staff, board members and organizational members from the community. The study took place in three provinces in Canada: Ontario, Manitoba and British Columbia. Approximately 30 organizations (10 per province), primarily consumer-directed, agreed to participate in the project.

THE CHALLENGE OF
UNMET CONSUMER DEMANDS

Consumer demands on community disability organizations reached a peak in the mid-1990s. This demand resulted from strenuous financial, physical and emotional hardships experienced by individuals, in the context of high unemployment, major reforms to social welfare policy, and an increasingly regressive and intolerant socio-political environment. Many participants commented on this new socio-political climate:

> There's an expectation that everybody's equal ... that if you can sit upright, you better be earning your own keep, regardless of individuality ... a lot of people aren't having the support and they're becoming the scapegoats, the scapegoats for the economic situation as it becomes more negative. It's (considered) their own fault. (Ontario)

Thus, there was a rise in the need for direct services, as well as for individual advocacy and support in dealing with government bureaucracies. We now explore several strategies employed by disability organizations to ensure that consumers' needs were met in this time of increased hardship.

Strategies for Improving Personal and Collective Conditions

(a) Increase in direct services and casework

Organizations that had been engaged in large-scale community development initiatives, empowerment and integration projects, and in large-scale advocacy began to re-focus their energies on directly addressing consumers' practical needs:

> Our mandate has definitely shifted to the practical ... We went
> from a political law reform to a more practical level of the nuts
> and bolts of how an employer can hire a person with disabili-
> ties. (Ontario)

Increasing direct services was a more efficient and pragmatic
approach than continuing to concentrate on large-scale advocacy
initiatives, since it was clear that the government was not bending
to political pressure anyway.

(b) Workshops and personal education

A second strategy was to hold workshops intended to inform
and educate consumers about changes to individual benefits, such
as social assistance, CPP disability benefits, and employment insurance (EI). Reforms to these government programs were confusing
and frightening for many people with disabilities, and the demands
on organizations for support, advocacy, and information about these
changes were on the rise. One participant, whose organization
had previously focused on public advocacy, reported having shifted
to a practical, workshop-oriented approach in order to educate consumers about the changes affecting them:

> ... we're going to change tactics and do work ... within the con-
> sumer groups ... And to try and educate people to the issues
> that are going on around them. And some things that they can
> do about those issues. To try and empower people by showing
> them some examples of what can be done. (Ontario)

This workshop strategy facilitated the dissemination of information to individuals in large groups, which helped to reduce the time
spent by the organizations in providing individual counselling and
support. Consumers gained knowledge about the structural reforms
affecting their lives, and became better equipped personally to deal
with government departments and officials on issues affecting their
benefits. This, in turn, worked to the advantage of organizations
inasmuch as consumers were increasingly able to handle their own
issues and act as advocates for themselves.

(c) Becoming more consumer-driven

Several participants reported that becoming more consumer-
driven was a strategy for both responding to heightened consumer
demand for services and also a strategy to strengthen programs. A
participant from British Columbia felt that it was important to get
consumer input about specific services or projects the organization

should be providing. She reported that collecting consumer input and feedback could be done by setting up community focus groups:

> I think what we're looking at is [reaching] out to more people in our community who are disabled and find out what their needs are and how we might be able to help ... [O]ne of the things that I'm really working on doing is building sort of a series of focus groups reaching out to people in the community to come and talk with us on the issues ... so that we're really consumer-driven. (British Columbia)

Encouraging consumer input and feedback on programs and services was done efficiently and inexpensively. Organizations that provided housing and attendant care to consumers surveyed tenants on their overall opinions about the services, and conducted individual interviews to determine each consumer's needs and special requests. Focus groups and meetings also provided the necessary input for organizations wishing to design their programs and services according to the consensus of consumers in the community.

(d) *Decentralizing peer support, self-help and information services*

Several participants reported that their organizations were promoting a more decentralized operation of community services. Specifically, organizations began to motivate consumers to initiate peer support and self-help groups within their own localities or regions, while others tried to initiate information networks to keep their members and consumers informed. This was particularly helpful for people who were isolated either by distance or by withdrawal of services:

> The onus should be on consumers who do have that ability to help out every other consumer out there get up to speed.... I think we have a lot of people out in the boonies who are just struggling and they're lost and I think we need a kind of central resource pool where we can help each other. (Ontario)

This participant reported that being assertive, engaging in in-depth analysis, and just "laying it out on the table" was an effective method for motivating consumers to take responsibility for creating independent, localized support networks.

However, the ability of disability organizations to maintain their resource centres, hotlines, and general information services had become limited due to financial problems. Likewise, the ability of consumers to access these services became limited as a result of cuts to individual benefits and supports. Using email chain-letters and "phone-trees" to disseminate information and resources was suggested as another option:

> ... [I]t's like pyramid sales where one person gets it and sends it to five and those five send it to five, even if it's built as simplistically as that, it needs to be done ... [B]uild an effective network and then they (consumers) could funnel it down... (Ontario)

One participant suggested obtaining funding so that local libraries could set up accessible computer stations where people with disabilities could access the Internet. The benefits of this type of electronic network were that people with disabilities could access skills training modules, share information about the political climate, and access resources they normally would receive at disability organizations.

In all cases, participants argued that developing services that were decentralized and run by members themselves could ensure that some support would still be available to people with disabilities in the event that even more organizations were forced to close.

(e) The challenge of decreasing public resources

In the early to mid-1990s, disability organizations across Canada experienced a marked decrease in financial resources as a result of government funding cuts to organizations and regressive changes to government programs and departments that supported or funded disability groups. Several participants spoke about a noticeable change in the public's attitude toward the work done by their organizations and argued that this ideological shift reflected and perpetuated structural reforms affecting the disability community:

> There's a rethinking around ... a general feeling in society that the types of activities that community groups do in general, and disability groups in particular (do), it's something that people don't want to put resources into anymore, like the taxpayers, they think it's a waste of money. (Ontario)

Another participant, from Manitoba, spoke about a change in discourse and rhetoric used by the government when reporting or justifying cutbacks and reforms:

> Because the special interest terminology is what's being used, as soon as you have any interest that might be different from the

person in power, all of a sudden you're supposedly blowing your own horn at the expense of another member of the community. You want their piece of the pie and that's how you're portrayed as a special interest group once they label you. It's a strategy. And of course if you look at all the special interest groups, we make up all of society ... like it's a joke ... it does turn other sectors of society against you. (Manitoba)

Overall, participants felt that "special interest" terminology and rhetoric were being used to promote division, competition, and resentment — rather than a sense of solidarity — among the different social groups being affected by the cutbacks. The following section explores several key strategies employed by disability organizations to retain, increase, and generate funding in this new context.

Strategies to Mobilize Organizational and Political Resources

(a) Networking with politicians

Gaining political clout became necessary for many organizations seeking funding for projects and programs. To this end, many organizations acknowledged that they had taken certain measures to gain favour with funders that they may not have taken in the past. One organization reported using well-known community members to act as sponsors or patrons to their organizations. The organization made use of its patrons by including their names on their letterhead, in their newsletters, in their written proposals to funders, and by having them approach the government, or other funders, in person to set up meetings to negotiate project funding.

Networking with local and regional authorities became particularly important at this time, due to the downloading of funding responsibilities from the federal level to the provincial and regional levels. Participants specifically reported that raising the awareness of local Members of Parliament (MP) with regard to the services and goals of their organizations was of great benefit. In addition, some MPs informed disability organizations about new policies and areas of service that were most likely to be funded, which helped organizations decide which proposals and areas were worth working on. They could prepare, as organizations, for changes in the economic and political environment:

I think if an agency is going to survive, it needs to know exactly what it takes for a piece of policy to become law ... And that's

> where linking up with your local politician and going right down
> to the basics of understanding the Charter of Rights and Free-
> doms [is needed]. [We have] the right to understand government
> policy that is making these changes. (Ontario)

In sum, networking with politicians, either directly or through
patrons, was reported to be beneficial for organizations facing funding cuts.

(b) Policy participation

Beyond networking at the local level, policy participation and/
or resistance were cited often as strategies that organizations
needed to explore. Several participants reported forming coalitions
with other organizations and groups of consumers in order to pool
knowledge resources. In coalitions, the experienced and the inexpe-
rienced came together and participated in policy activities, and were
able to share and exchange their knowledge and expertise. Coalitions also heightened pressure on governments because of the sheer
number of people involved:

> We have to negotiate with the government and I think you can
> do that better if you've got strength in numbers, and I think the
> government tends to listen more if they've got more than just
> one agency coming to talk to them. (Manitoba)

Other organizations participated in policy work at the local
level. For example, an Ontario organization initiated a full partnership with a municipality, which gave it equal power in the creation
of local policies affecting people with disabilities. The formation of
advisory committees at the local level was undertaken by other disability organizations wishing to gain influence in the direction of
local policies.

In sum, the use of coalitions, partnerships, and advisory committees to participate in policy work was of benefit because it
brought large and diverse groups of consumers together, and
enabled the exchange of information and knowledge that is necessary to affect change at the policy level.

(c) Narrowing the project focus

Organizations applying for core or operational funding were
often required to be national in scope, which eliminated many disability groups that had been funded previously. These participants
reported that their organizations, now funded on a project-contract
basis, had insufficient funds to cover basic operating costs.

196

In order to survive, many organizations found it necessary to direct their resources and energies toward narrow projects, and to eliminate other services. Likewise, funding trends for projects (e.g., employment training) caused many groups to alter the program focus of their organizations:

> XYZ organization is prepared to give you $10,000 to do a research paper on mice. And so many organizations will grab it because there's ten grand there ... I see that organizations direct their energies toward where the money's coming from and so often it's coming from the government or a foundation or such thing, and you take the money, you do what is required to please the funder. (British Columbia)

Focusing solely on specific projects, gearing project foci toward funding priorities, and discontinuing services previously made possible by the existence of core funding, were unwelcome strategies for many organizations. Willingness to make these changes, however, did facilitate the survival of many disability groups.

(d) Changing mandates

Maintaining funding levels often required disability organizations to undergo partial or major changes in their mandates. Government funding became more contingent on the provision of direct services, specifically, employment initiatives. Other funding priorities included fee-for-service initiatives and business-oriented projects. Advocacy and empowerment programs, such as those funded through the Disabled Persons Participation Program prior to 1995, were no longer priorities for the federal government. In fact, many participants in this study reported that having advocacy in the organizational mandate was a surefire way to lose funding. One participant described this pressure:

> I think our Minister of Citizenship put it very bluntly: "You want funding, you side with us. You don't, then you lose your funding and your ability to do anything. (Ontario)

Other participants, who were forced to turn to private businesses for donations or sponsorship, and/or engage in lottery (bingos, casinos) fundraising activities, reported pressure to change their mandates from advocacy to "charity". One participant reported that their organization was planning to feign a charitable mandate in order to maintain tax deduction status on donations, without actually stopping its advocacy activities:

> ... [T]he thing we are looking at now is how can we change the official mandate of advocacy and how can we get the funding which is available for charitable organizations ... But it doesn't mean we going to change our mandate ... maybe officially but not actually. (Ontario)

Feigning changes in mandate in order to secure certain sources of funding is risky, and can result in full withdrawals of funding if discovered. Participants noted that it was possible to continue advocacy work and activism if done anonymously and discreetly.

(e) Public relation activities

Several participants reported that their organizations engaged in promotional activities to draw the attention of potential funders and donors. They reported that high unemployment and a general sense of financial insecurity among private citizens had led to a decrease in donations and a tendency to give only to high profile organizations:

> Everybody is facing cutbacks and then it's more of us out there chasing the same pie, in terms of the fund raising dollar, the donation dollar and so on. We're also faced with people's concerns about how secure their employment is and can they afford to give? When United Way raises how many million dollars, whatever it is, there's that ripple effect, where high profiling them can draw away from the small donations that people might make. They give it to the big high profile events. (British Columbia)

Self-promoting activities included advertising on community radio and television about the work, mandates, and donations-needs of their organizations. Manitoban participants spoke about contracting out to telemarketing companies as a cost-effective means of self-promotion and fundraising for disability organizations. The risk involved in this tactic, however, was that some canvassing companies claimed more than half of the funds raised, while others tended to misrepresent organizations to the public.

(f) The formation of partnerships

Many participants reported forming partnerships and linkages with other consumer disability groups, or on a multi-sectoral level with non-disability organizations. Through partnerships, organizations were able to economize on staff, volunteers and other resources for the implementation of specific projects and events.

This was considered a vital strategy for the survival of organizations in the context of scarce funding.

Partnership strategies allowed for information and resource sharing between disability organizations that may have been in competition in the past. Fundraising events done in partnerships were larger, attracted a greater number of consumers and donors, and ultimately generated extra funding for organizations. Multi-sector partnerships, between disability organizations and non-disability organizations, also facilitated new levels of funding and support, while working to bridge gaps between the disability community and the general public.

(g) The challenge of decreased capacity at the organizational level

Member participation in disability activism had declined as a result of the vast cuts to advocacy services, government non-responsiveness to lobbying tactics, and decreased morale among people with disabilities:

> A lot of us are pretty marginalized and vulnerable to begin with, so when these types of cuts happen, we're very prone to just disappearing, fading into the woodwork. (Ontario)

Cutbacks to individual benefits and to access-related programs made it physically difficult, and at times impossible, for members to continue participating in organizations:

> With the cuts at different levels, organization and individual, all the people that are involved ... people who have disabilities are dealing with their own personal livelihood, life issues. That's a pretty big stress and then on top of that, you're supposed to be keeping this organization afloat when its funding has been cut. (Ontario)

Many people felt at risk of having their benefits withdrawn if they were discovered to be participating — as volunteers, as active members, as participants in political activities, and even as participants in skills training programs offered by the government and/or community organizations:

> They (people with disabilities) have lost sight of the vision of an equal Ontario because of the climate. They're in fear of losing benefits. They feel they're walking on broken glass, on thin ice, whatever you want to say, that they are very vulnerable to the whims of the current government and in fact if they do become

vocal or speak out, that the axe is going to fall and they will lose another benefit. (Ontario)

Fears about being disqualified from receiving disability benefits were exacerbated by the fact that general systems of surveillance (CPP re-assessments, welfare fraud hotlines, increased monitoring by welfare case workers) were increasingly put in place during this time period. These forms of surveillance worked to decrease incentives to engaging in paid work, volunteerism, or simply being active in organizations — for many people with disabilities.

In combination, these problems became fundamental challenges to the idea of consumer-led organizations "of people with disability", which must be reliant on public support to allow self-help for those with disadvantaging conditions. The risk of reversion to professionally led organizations "for people with disability" and loss of autonomy and independence was severe. Solutions were found in several strategies that emphasized maintaining autonomy and increasing effectiveness.

Strategies to Maintain Presence and Voice

(a) Prioritize consumer voice in the organization

Prioritizing consumers' concerns and individual needs — at a heightened level — was cited by several participants as a strategy for encouraging volunteerism and member support of organizations:

> When you do expend more time and energy towards the client, customer or member, it's a good source for volunteers and private donations. (British Columbia)

However, often, organizations could not pay adequate attention to their members' needs because their staff were decreased and frequently overwhelmed with other responsibilities. A solution to this dilemma was suggested by a participant from Ontario. Her organization held large discussion meetings to make up for lapses in communication and to re-establish links with members and consumers. Holding these types of sessions on an infrequent basis was a solution for some organizations that could not afford to provide accessibility for regular meetings.

(b) Technological communication for meetings

In response to the decreased levels of member participation at meetings, several participants reported that their organizations were using technology as an inexpensive and accessible means to replace face-to-face discussions. One participant referred to a "multi-level communication strategy", in which many modes of communication are used together in order to accommodate a cross-disability need:

> You know, some people through e-mail, the Internet, some people by fax and some people just by phone, ... even by face to face ... a lot of them will be driven also by geographic location ... So we're gonna have to use a multi-geographically driven, multi-level communication driven, means of being in touch with one another, and also you know, keep in mind ... an access structure that goes through it. (Ontario)

Using technology at "multi-levels" was of most benefit to organizations with members with varying types of disabilities.

(c) Social activities as outreach method

Organizing social activities for members was reported by several participants to be an effective strategy for attracting new members and potential volunteers. According to one participant, adding a social dimension was necessary because the priorities of many consumers were, in fact, related to activities that countered isolation and stigma:

> ... [W]e have to add to it a bit of a social dimension ... political advocates are famous for not getting together to have a beer or getting together just to kinda socialize. And I think that nine out of ten disabled people I've talked to who, when you really get down to what their real needs are, they're looking for a boyfriend or a girlfriend or a place to meet or something fun. They wanna go sailing, they wanna, you know just the kinda stuff everybody wants to do. (Ontario)

Success in organizing social activities required that the location of the event was accessible and accommodating for everybody (especially those with visual or hearing problems). Pub nights, dinners, and dances required funds from either the organizations or members. However, many social events were organized with relatively little cost. Gatherings at the organizational office, just providing coffee for those who attended, was one example. Coffee houses in public places were also organized, by asking members to read their poetry, show their art, or tell stories.

Another participant argued that in order to attract people to organizations, it was necessary to strike a balance between work activities and social activities:

> We should be creating space for disabled people to do, you
> know, come together socially as well as to work for change ...
> You know, we have to play together if we're gonna work
> together. It can't all just be doom and gloom ... (Ontario)

(d) Connecting the personal and political

The political arena was a major area in which organizations —
mainly advocacy-based — attempted to increase member participation and support. Many organizations focused on consciousness
raising and empowerment strategies to encourage individuals to
get involved in advocacy and political activities. Creative and interactive techniques (often termed popular education), which allowed
people to become engaged in a process of consciousness raising,
were used. For example, art therapy and/or art groups were
designed to facilitate creative expression and integration of personal
and political issues:

> ... (the organization) encourages people with disabilities to do
> art, to express themselves that way. I think they actually exhibit
> some of the artwork there. Anything where people can feel in
> touch with their core, something nurturing, and something that's
> fun ... any way we can find to connect with our creative self,
> but that ultimately can lead to people taking action in their
> lives. (Ontario)

Popular theatre and interactive skits were also used as creative
techniques that inspired people to engage in discussion and take
political action:

> ... very well thought out skits that illustrate the things that you
> want to talk about. You do the skit and then you have discus-
> sions after the skit about what the skit was about. It's certainly
> effective in what I've heard of individuals going out, performing
> the skit and then taking the time, an hour or so after the skit
> has been done, to discuss what the hell it all meant. (Ontario)

Other strategies reported by participants to enhance political
awareness and motivate participation in political activism included
small and large group discussions, writing and art contests about
certain topics, group mural-making on selected issues, role playing
workshops, and direct education methods such as organizing speakers, panels, and conferences for consumers.

(e) Modelling Full Inclusion

Several participants reported that modelling the goal of "full inclusion in society" was a good strategy for organizations to increase member participation and volunteerism. Encouraging the participation of people with varying types of disabilities, and also participation by consumers of different ages, genders, classes, sexualities and races, was a positive demonstration that the ideology of social inclusion could be, and had to be, achieved in consumer organizations themselves:

> One of our big problems is we don't have a big volunteer base, but if you piggyback with another organization to do a fund raiser, you get more volunteers ... I think we need to bury some of the hatchets. When I first came ... I could not believe the turfing that takes place. Everybody is peeing on stumps to make their territory. We have hurt ourselves tremendously by that. Consumers are consumers are consumers. (Ontario)

Overall, attracting member support and participation in organizations, and securing ongoing commitment from volunteers, required an inclusive and safe environment guided by the values of anti-discrimination and cross-disability representation.

Strategies to Increase Effectiveness

(a) Screening, hiring and evaluating volunteers

Treating volunteers (either disabled or non-disabled) as if they were paid staff was an effective strategy used by a few organizations in the study. This involved screening and hiring volunteers as if they were applying for a job, allocating them to specific roles and responsibilities within the organization, and then reviewing their volunteer work as "skills training" that was beneficial to them. This process helped ensure the acquisition of committed volunteers, and enabled organizations to immediately pinpoint volunteers' strengths and skills. It also allowed the organization to maintain its own human resource management skill base when there were few actual employees. Some disability organizations attracted volunteers by offering them the opportunity to create their own paid work within the organization. Volunteers were recruited for specific roles, and given the responsibility to apply for project grants that could create their own wages. Participants reported that using a formal screening and hiring strategy was a successful outreach tool because it offered volunteers new levels of responsibility and respect:

> ... the deeper strategy is for getting people chances to learn camaraderie and belonging and being welcomed and being ... that's just as important as the dollars. It may not feed the kids at home, but ... what's important to them is being wanted ... needing to build the bond.... (MA)

Finally, disability organizations utilized work/study placement programs (through colleges, universities, high schools, and government initiatives) to secure skilled able-bodied volunteers for periods from four months to a year. These offered employment training to the volunteer, educated them about disability issues, and at the same time benefited the organizations. Some placement programs paid the student or trainee to work within the organizations, providing real savings for them to achieve needed tasks.

(b) Increasing staff skills

Participants spoke about finding new ways of getting an increased amount of work completed by fewer people. Hiring new staff members who already had the skills to carry out all the functions of a specific area of programming was mentioned by some participants as a way to maximize human resource capacity. For example, all fundraising could be done by a hired professional fundraiser; all the consumer advocacy work could be carried out by an experienced consumer advocate; all the accounting and budget work could be done by a hired accountant. However, hiring such specialized workers was also contingent on funding, which many organizations lacked.

Some organizations retrained their current staff instead of hiring new workers. One participant reported that her organization conducted retraining workshops three times a year, in order to keep staff updated on the status of the organization, the needs of the disability community, and what was expected of them.

Encouraging staff to self-educate, or work on their own skills development by taking courses and/or volunteering elsewhere, was reported by other participants as an efficient strategy. For example, one participant said she encouraged her staff to acquire skills such as learning to use the Internet, gardening, baking, sewing, cooking, and doing exercise programs. Such skills could be of personal benefit to the staff members as well as to the consumers who worked with them.

(c) Creating a better board of directors: skills, diversity and responsibility

Acquiring board members who were skilled in various capacities, had a diverse range of contacts and backgrounds, and were also willing to take on responsibility was a strategy used by several disability organizations. Recruiting skilled board members had become crucial in light of the economic and funding context since funding proposals, program reports, and other submissions had to be much more sophisticated to be accepted by the government and other funders. Several participants reported that they had recruited board members from diverse backgrounds, different communities, and a wide range of professions:

> ... [W]e wanted the community-based idea rather than a facility-based (board). So we do have a couple of parents sitting on the board ... We have a lawyer, we have somebody representing the school system ... [O]f course it's very important to have contact with the schools so that the school can help transition the individuals into a community-based program. (Manitoba)

Overall, it was necessary to recruit board members who could responsibly handle increasingly critical decisions concerning the organizational direction, staffing strategies and spending.

CONCLUSION

In the past decade, changes to disability-related programming and funding at the federal level in Canada resulted in less money to go around, increased competition between groups for funding, and pressures to change mandates or project foci to meet new funding requirements. In addition, organizations applying for, or relying on, provincial or local government funding sources also experienced barriers and cutbacks as a result of the new federal block social funding arrangement. As discussed in another chapter (refer to Boyce, Boyce & Krogh, Chapter 16), the elimination of the cost-sharing arrangement under the earlier program resulted in the elimination of national standards and a lack of incentive for provinces to put funds into "special interest groups". Finally, due to conservative agendas in many provinces, social welfare and community programs bore the brunt of cutbacks.

Lowered morale and personal stress over financial and survival matters played a large part in increasing consumer demands of disability organizations, and led to the inability of many people to extend their energies to issues at the organizational level. Issues of access, at both the financial and physical access levels, made it more difficult for people to attend meetings and stay actively involved in organizations. Finally, dependence on social welfare benefits was accompanied by powerful disincentives to engage in volunteer work, political activity, and training programs. Organizational autonomy was threatened, with a possible return to styles of "organizations for" people with disabilities, rather than consumer organizations.

In response, disability organizations attempted to continue to meet the personal and collective conditions of the disability community, despite increased consumer demands on their often depleted resources. Organizations increased their direct services and became more pragmatic in approach. They became more consumer-driven, held educational workshops on financial and policy issues, and developed decentralized networks for support and resources in the community. These strategies directly mediated the overwhelming demands being placed on organizations, despite cutbacks to organizational funding and lowered human resource capacities.

Participants reported many new strategies for maintaining, increasing, and leveraging funds for their organizations. Political networking and policy participation strategies sought to improve the financial situation by gaining credibility and influence at the government level. Changing mandates and narrowing the focus of projects were necessary strategies for many organizations faced with new funding trends in government and the private sector. Finally, self-promotional activities worked to encourage private donations, while partnership strategies allowed organizations to pool resources and ultimately enhance their capacities.

Disability organizations met the challenge of decreased human resource capacity by employing many creative and new strategies to increase member participation, encourage volunteerism, and motivate political participation. Technological communication was increasingly used to maintain contact with members and to ensure that meetings continued to be held. Prioritizing consumers' voices, concentrating on mandates of full inclusion, holding more social activities, and engaging in consciousness raising activities all worked as outreach strategies to encourage more volunteers, members, and advocates. Finally, organizations maximized human resources by promoting higher levels of skills among staff and board members, and by "hiring" work placement interns and committed volunteers.

These experiences of Canadian disability organizations in the last decade raise three issues of interest to social movement theory.

First, are the experiences and strategies of the disability field generalizable to other social movements? Second, does a Resource Mobilization perspective adequately account for needs of disability organizations both to be efficient and to support personal skill development of disabled persons? Third, does a New Social Movement perspective consider the practices of contemporary disability organizations to be reactive, and protective of their interests, or progressive in terms of social change?

Regarding generalizability, it is important to note that the organizations participating in this study were not chosen randomly, nor were they distributed evenly across the country. Nonetheless, attempts were made to include a broad range (type of disability, age, gender, ethnicity, SES) of organizations, as advised by a national disability organization. With this in mind, we find that the isolation of those with disabilities comprises particularly severe personal and political dimensions (due to physical limitations, lack of environmental access and accommodation, social stigma, and poverty due to lack of employment and disability costs). The effect of this simultaneous set of barriers is perhaps as great as, or greater than, that faced by other social movement sectors, such as the woman's movement and ethnic minorities. It certainly is greater than that faced by the environmental social movements or the labour movement, which do not face any capacity problems. At the same time, these barriers explain the relative fragility of disability organizations' successes, which are dependent on significant maintenance of both personal and political gains, even in comparison to retrenchments experienced by all social movements in the last decade. Thus, the strategies chosen by disability organizations to advance their position will necessarily be broader in scope and require greater comparative effort for equal gains as those used in other social movements.

An interesting distinction in the disability movement itself involves inter-generational differences between older and younger persons. Sandvin (2001) notes that younger disabled persons in Norway focus more on improving their own personal conditions and less on their identity as "disabled" or on maintaining the autonomy of disability organizations. This trend for youth may reflect an impact of school integration efforts, with both positive and negative dimensions, or it may merely reflect a more widely observed phenomenon of general youth disillusionment ("Gen-X") with economic opportunities and life plans.

Regarding Resource Mobilization theory, key debates focus on conflicts between varying goals and differing capacities of those in

WILL BOYCE, KARI KROGH AND EMILY BOYCE

social movements. For example, Zald and McCarthy (2002) ask whether goals and technologies of member mobilization conflict with goals and technologies of political protest. Clearly, from this study of disability organizations, both goals are dependent, to some degree, on having adequate resources. However, it is also interesting that many organizations in this time of restraint continued to focus on both political strategies and mobilization strategies — perhaps because these cannot easily be divided in disability. Political achievement requires skills, and skill development for disabled persons requires policy support. The continuum is indivisible.

A second tension in disability organizations revealed in this chapter is that between the capacities of leaders and followers. If it is to be a useful theoretical tool, a Resource Mobilization perspective must adequately account for disability organizations being both efficient and supportive of personal skill development for disabled persons. This tension is, again, perhaps revealed most acutely in times of restraint when programs are stripped to the essentials. Most disability organizations in this study did not sacrifice personal skill development for organizational efficiency, but tried to build personal capacity and organizational experience in a productive way, for example, by formalizing the expectations of volunteers and staff.

Finally, a New Social Movement perspective would ask whether disability organizations are culturally reactive or politically progressive (Buechler, 1995). It is important to conduct historical analysis that could document whether there have been recent changes in these organizations' political goals/strategies/risks that demand policy and resource shifts versus changes in cultural and social supports, including reduction of stigma in the public.

There were encouraging signs in this study that Canadian disability organizations have attempted to progress the political impact of their work by adoption of the "full inclusion" principle in their own spheres. In the past, disability organizations operated in silos of physical disability, sensory disability, developmental disability (often parent-mediated) and mental disability (often professionally mediated). These self-imposed silos arose largely from adoption of mainstream cultural stigma regarding differing abilities between these groups. There have been hierarchies of influence and power in these silos, with resultant benefits for some groups and disadvantage for others. The efforts by some disability organizations to "walk the talk" of full inclusion into society, by being inclusive in their own organizations, bodes well for progressiveness in the disability movement. This experience and example of social inclusion,

208

in itself, may be the most valuable, but unpredicted, consequence of a decade of strife for Canadian disability organizations.

To summarize, macro-level social, economic and political shifts have unique implications for people with disabilities and their organizations, and neo-liberal restructuring policies in the early to mid-1990s produced a particularly unique dilemma. As our study has shown, policy shifts negatively affected the resources, funding and material capacities of consumer organizations. At the same time, many people with disabilities experienced government restructuring measures in their personal and everyday lives, through dramatic reductions in benefits and personal income, as well as reduced access to publicly funded health, social, accommodation, and transportation services. They increasingly looked to consumer organizations to help replace some of these government services. However, individuals with disabilities are also organizations' human resources. Thus, a major dilemma is created as demand and need for organizations' services go up while, at the same time, organizations' capacity to provide service goes down due to fewer material and human resources. Unlike some other organizations and social movements, whose members do not so directly and physically feel the impacts of restructuring measures aimed at their personal lives, and whose human resources are not exclusively made up of people with impairments, disability social movements are at a particular disadvantage if they are to maintain their independence.

13

People with Disabilities and Political Participation

DEBORAH STIENSTRA
AND APRIL D'AUBIN

INTRODUCTION

Canada is portrayed both within its borders and across the world as a leader in electoral democracy. We say our citizens enjoy full democratic rights, including the right to participate in the electoral process. Yet this picture fails to capture the situation of people with disabilities in Canada for whom enjoyment of full citizenship rights is still emerging and the opportunities that exist to participate have been hard fought struggles. This chapter explores the barriers that have existed in the Canadian political system that have prevented the full and equal participation of persons with disabilities in formal and substantive political activities, including voting, involvement in political parties and running for public office. We argue that while some barriers to access at the level of formal politics, such as the right to vote and accessible voting locations, have been removed, substantial barriers remain that exclude people with disabilities from participating in the broader arenas of Canadian political life.

The chapter proceeds as follows:

1. To explore the background and history of electoral participation among people with disabilities;
2. To review strategies for political participation; and
3. To discuss barriers to political participation by people with disabilities.

BACKGROUND

The experiences of people with disabilities in claiming full citizenship reflect a broader framework of social inclusion and exclusion that some have used to explain the involvement (or lack thereof) of marginalized groups in the political system. Saloojee (2002) suggests, in trying to understand the political participation of newcomers and racialized communities in Canada, that the concepts of social inclusion and exclusion can be useful in explaining both formal political participation (involvement in voting and electoral mechanisms) and more substantive political participation (active engagement with political parties, part of policy community, ensuring a voice in decision making, advocating for electoral equality).

Social exclusion, then,

> ... relates intimately to processes which intentionally or unintentionally restrict people's participation in the political life and in the political activities of society ... social exclusion applied to political participation corresponds to diminished states of political participation and diminished access to valued political goods (representation, access to policy makers, etc). (Saloojee, 2002, p. 38)

Social inclusion is the reverse, that is, valued participation including political rights,

> ... barrier-free access to political parties[;] a sense of belonging and not being 'othered' and marginalized; a commitment on the part of political parties to ensure that all members of society have equal access to running for office; and providing all members of society with the resources to exercise democratic citizenship. (Saloojee, 2002, p. 45)

Social inclusion and exclusion are familiar concepts in the disability literature as well, although they have not been formally used to analyze political participation. The Roeher Institute (Cushing, 2003) reviewed the different approaches to social inclusion and exclusion in the literature, suggesting that these are useful concepts that could be further developed into measurable outcomes or indicators. They also developed the following working definition of social inclusion:

> People with disabilities want to be socially included in the sense that they, like others, want:
> - To participate as valued, appreciated equals in the social, economic, political and cultural life of the community (i.e., in valued social situations).
> - To be involved in mutually trusting, appreciative and respectful interpersonal relationships at the family, peer and community levels. (Crawford, 2003, p. 5)

Crawford further suggests that to make social inclusion a reality for people with disabilities, including, as he notes, in political processes, they need access to the situation, as well as the practical means or the supports necessary to participate as valued, appreciated equals (n.d., p. 9).

Over the past two decades, the organizations of people with disabilities have undertaken many strategic initiatives geared toward advancing their objective of full citizenship. These initiatives address the access to as well as the practical means for people with disabilities to participate in the electoral process, as well as access to it, including encouraging and informing people to become involved in the process of voting, having an influence on party platforms and getting people with disabilities elected to office.

A Historical Review

The 1981 *Obstacles Report* of the Special Parliamentary Committee on the Disabled and the Handicapped was the first, but not the last, political document to suggest access to the electoral process for persons with disabilities as an area for substantial change. It recommended a postal vote system, polls in locations that ensured accessibility for people with mobility disabilities, and removing the barriers to voting for people with mental disabilities.

The formation of the Special Parliamentary Committee on the Disabled and the Handicapped was an important event in the development of public policy affecting persons with disabilities. The parliamentarians travelled across Canada and heard directly from people with disabilities. People with disabilities, their organizations and their families were important key informants for the Committee. In addition, people with disabilities, such as Jim Derksen and

Pat Derrick, were included in the Committee's research staff. The Council of Canadians with Disabilities (CCD) negotiated with the Government of Canada to have its then National Coordinator, Jim Derksen, seconded to the Committee's research staff. The CCD wanted to have a disabled person on the Committee's staff who was familiar with the disability rights approach to public policy development. This was an approach that emphasized the elimination of barriers to participation rather than changing disabled people to make them fit into the existing environment. The Special Parliamentary Committee's recommendations on civil rights focused on eliminating environmental barriers to the participation of people with disabilities in Canada's democratic processes.

The Government of Canada did not immediately implement the recommendations related to access to the electoral process, arguing that amending the *Elections Act* was a lengthy and complicated process (Canada, 1983, pp. 4–6). The *Canadian Charter of Rights and Freedoms* gave additional impetus to ensuring access to the political process when it came into force in 1985. One part of the process of implementing the *Charter* was a review of federal laws for their compliance with the *Charter*.

In 1985 the House of Commons Subcommittee on Equality Rights released its report, *Equality for All*, recommending "that section 14(4)(f) of the *Canada Elections Act* be repealed so that the mentally disabled have the same right to be enumerated and to vote as all other Canadians" (Canada, 1985, p. 91). The Government of Canada responded:

> The Government agrees in principle that mentally disabled individuals should have the right to vote. It is giving careful study to a process to ensure mentally disabled individuals can exercise the right under a revised Canada Elections Act without abuse of the voting system or exploitation of their rights. (Canada, 1986a, p. 43)

Yet the provisions restricting people with mental disabilities from voting were not removed until the Canadian Disability Rights Council (CDRC), a legal advocacy organization of people with disabilities, took action. The CDRC was concerned that Section 14(4)(f) of the *Elections Act* constituted prima facie discrimination based upon Sections 3 and 15 of the *Charter of Rights and Freedoms*. In October 1988, the CDRC challenged Section 14(4)(f) in the Federal Court of Appeal. The Court found that the section in question violated Section 3 of the *Charter of Rights and Freedoms* and struck it down. People with disabilities celebrated this civil rights victory.

The accessibility of polling stations, identified in 1981 by the *Obstacles Report* as a critical measure to ensure access for people with disabilities to the electoral system, took even longer for action. Some leaders of the disability advocacy organizations decided to use human rights legislation to gain access to the polls.

John Lane and Jim Derksen described their attempts to make voting more accessible:

> We [Canadian Paraplegic Association-National] filed our complaint with the Manitoba regional office of the Canadian Human Rights Commission. The complaint concerned accessibility to election polls in the 1984 federal election. When the election was called in 1984, it was apparent to us pretty soon that quite a few polls were not going to be accessible. We had during at least two prior elections brought this up in the media and with Returning Office people. We saw access to the polls at election day as a basic human right. We brought it up before the Parliamentary Committee which Walter Dinsdale was involved with. We made formal presentations to the Committee on that, and it was even brought up in the Obstacles book. We had just about done everything through normal channels that we figured was appropriate, and it was pretty evident to us that zero progress was being made. For that reason when we saw the 1984 election come along and there were still a whole bunch of polls that were inaccessible to people in wheelchairs, we decided that by filing a human rights complaint we would remind them that they weren't doing what they said they would do. We thought that they would settle with us very quickly to avoid embarrassment. ... Elections Canada, as I say, fought it on a whole bunch of technicalities, and at the same time they incorporated a lot of what we were asking for in the proposed new Elections Act. It is rather bizarre. They have refused to seriously negotiate a conciliation. The complaint has been stalled a long time. (CCD, 1989, pp. 73–74)

On 17 February 1992, a Canadian Human Rights Tribunal rendered a decision in the human rights complaint discussed by Lane and Derksen. The Tribunal found not only that breaches of the *Canadian Human Rights Act* had been made in this situation, but that

> ... the right to equal treatment of physically-disabled voters in Canada includes the right of each person to the following:

    a. to level access to the offices of all Returning Officers and all advance polls;

    b. to level access to all other polling stations unless such requirements would preclude the establishment of a poll in an area.

    c. to be notified at least 26 days before election day in the event that a polling station in any area is not to be provided with level access;

    d. to be informed by the Returning Officer for the constituency, on request, the reason why any polling station which does not have level access, does not.

    e. to signs indicating where level access to a Polling Station is located, appropriate parking and signs indicating the location of parking for the disabled voter. (*Canadian Paraplegic Association v. Elections Canada et al.*, 1992, p. 61)

While people with disabilities were waiting for the decision of the Human Rights Tribunal on their complaint, other legislative and policy actions were taken to ensure access to the polling stations. In 1988 Parliament had before it a bill to improve access to the political process for people with disabilities, but it died on the order paper when an election was called. The Chief Electoral Officer decided to implement as policy the measures called for in the bill regardless of its adoption into law (Elections Canada, 1989).

For Canadians with disabilities, access to the formal political process was denied until the late 1980s. This created and maintained their exclusion from participating in Canada's political processes. The measures taken to ensure physical access to polling stations during voting as well as enfranchising people with mental disabilities were significant achievements in addressing that exclusion.

ENABLERS AND BARRIERS

Strategies to Enable Political Participation

The organizations of people with disabilities and their allies have developed at least three strategies to enable greater participation of people with disabilities as voters in the political process: counter campaigns; public education, working collectively and engaging the political parties.

(a) Counter campaigns

When we think of election campaigns, we tend to think of politicians taking the active role: going door-to-door, appearing on TV, making speeches, handing out buttons, putting up posters. People with disabilities and their self-representational organizations began to run their own counter campaigns during elections in order to educate politicians that disabled people were citizens who wanted their issues addressed during election campaigns and to raise general awareness about disability issues in society in general.

One strategy that was selected was becoming involved in elections in order to draw parties' and candidates' attention to disability issues. In 1984, people with disabilities turned the tables on federal candidates and parties with the Challenge Ballot. It sought support from federal election candidates for the following initiatives:

1. *Employment* — Contract compliance legislation requiring contractors of federal government services to state their plans for hiring disabled job seekers.
2. *Income Security* — National Comprehensive Disability Insurance to ensure basic income security regardless of disability cause.
3. *Special Parliamentary Committee* — Re-establishment of a Special Parliamentary Committee to monitor the implementation of Obstacles and Canadian Action Plan for the UN declared decade.
4. *Human Rights and Freedoms* — Establishment of a Rights and Freedoms Defense Fund to support Charter of Rights and Freedoms test cases.
5. *Disabled Refugees* — Commitment to accept 50 disabled refugees a year similar to other countries.
6. *Independent Living* — New federal/provincial funding programs to allow consumer control and purchase of essential personal services.
7. *Transportation* — Re-assert federal jurisdiction to provide fully accessible and economical inter-provincial bus services.

Each candidate running for election was asked to mark the ballot indicating whether he or she supported the public policy initiative suggested in the Ballot. Backgrounders were prepared on each of the priority issues contained in the Challenge Ballot and made available upon request. Candidates were informed that the results of the campaign would be made available to both peo-

216

ple with disabilities and the general public. The CCD used the results of the Challenge Ballot to advocate on priority issues throughout the life of the government that was formed. The organization created a newsletter, which tracked progress on priority issues and released periodic report cards. While the CCD has encouraged people to become involved, it has remained non-partisan. Information and analysis are shared, but candidates and parties are never endorsed.

Jim Derksen argues that the CCD led the way in mobilizing its members through this vehicle:

> We were able to make some real strides in terms of influencing government policies. Every time an election came along CCD canvassed the candidates who were running. CCD was one of the first groups of people in Canada to move forward on that activity. We identified the priority issues. We asked each candidate what was their position on our priority issues. We tabulated the results and analyzed them. We made the results known to our membership and the media. We did not take sides with one party or another. We made it worth their while to listen to our issues and to develop a position because they knew that the public would be told which of the parties and which of the candidates were in favor of our concerns. It was important to the public. It influenced votes and it gave us a power base. (Derksen, 2002a, p. 47)

(b) Public education

A number of disability organizations have encouraged people with disabilities to become involved in the electoral process using traditional forms of public education, such as special issues of newsletters or materials targeted to their own members. For example, in 1990, the Advocacy Resource Centre for the Handicapped (ARCH) produced an "Election Special" (Vol. 8, No. 5) of *Archtype*, its newsletter. ARCH wanted people with disabilities to know that their vote could have an impact on what party formed the government in the Province of Ontario.

Provincial disability advocacy organizations, including the Manitoba League of Persons with Disabilities (MLPD) and the Alberta Committee of Citizens with Disabilities (ACCD), have also developed public education materials to encourage the involvement of people with disabilities in the electoral process. The MLPD has produced the booklet "Manitobans with Disabilities and the Provincial Election", which highlighted six issues that consumers had identified as needing attention during the upcoming provincial

217

election: the *Public Schools Act*, housing options, regional health authorities, urban and rural transportation services, free government information and patients' rights. For the 1993 Federal Election campaign, the ACCD organized the Listen Up! Campaign, which was dedicated to having disability issues addressed in the Federal Election. The ACCD developed the following public education materials: posters, the candidate post card, which was designed so that people could share their views with candidates, an Election Kit for organizers, the "Did You Know" brochure, which provided information on disability issues, Listen Up! Buttons and a "What the candidates said" booklet.

The Canadian Association for Community Living (CACL) has also produced materials to encourage the families of people with disabilities and disabled people themselves to participate in elections. Like many other disability organizations, The CACL has actively encouraged Canadians in their network to become informed about national issues and to make an informed choice on voting day. The CACL circulated the *Charter for Community Living* to candidates running for office during the 1997 Federal Election (see Exhibit 13.1). The *Charter for Community Living* caused concern with at least one Elections Canada official. The *CACL Election '97 Update Newsletter* (Vol. 1, No. 3) reported that a returning officer discouraged local ACL members from circulating the *Charter for Community Living*.

Over the years, questionnaires to candidates seem to be losing their effectiveness. Political parties adapted to this strategy by having the party leader develop a response to the disability community, and candidates would reiterate the leader's statement. With the increased use of Web sites for putting out the party platforms, the methods of the 1980s and 1990s become less attractive. DisAbled Women's Network (DAWN) Ontario has led the way in embracing these new technologies. They effectively used their Web site to inform consumers about issues during the 2004 federal election. The DAWN Ontario Web site included a section devoted to Vote for Equality — A Voter Education and Awareness Campaign for Equality Rights. This Web site provided visitors with a one-stop shop, devoted to an equality rights examination of election issues. This Web site examined federal election issues through the lenses of gender, disability, poverty, and cities. It included an interactive feature where participants could take an Equality Rights Survey and then view the responses that were coming into this survey. This web site provided visitors with access to 18 different voter education campaigns. DAWN Ontario gives an important hint of

---

Exhibit 13.1: Charter for Community Living

The Charter for Community Living is an understanding between the community and its elected officials. Voters need to know that they can count on their elected officials to represent them once the voting is over. Politicians need to know the people and associations in the community to whom they can turn for consultation, information and assistance in addressing the needs of the community.

The Canadian Association for Community Living (CACL) is asking all the candidates running for election on __date__ for _____ Party of Canada in the riding, to agree to commit to the following actions if elected to the Federal Legislature on __date__ :

- to endorse the Association's Declaration of Saint John;

- to meet with individuals with disabilities, their families and representatives of the Association twice a year to discuss the progress and barriers to progress in the inclusion and integration of people with disabilities in the community; to promote the inclusion of people with disabilities in the development and amendment of government legislation and policy; and

- to raise and table an issue of concern to people with disabilities during the 1997/98 sitting of the Federal Legislature.

Signed   Dated

Thank you for taking the time and interest to complete the Charter for Community Living. ...

---

how self-representational advocacy organizations could be using Web sites in the future to encourage involvement in the electoral process.

(c) Collective Action

To strengthen the voice of people with disabilities, disability organizations have joined together, especially at election time, through joint statements and coalition building to make sure their issues are on the table. In 1993, the disability community came together and released a joint statement to candidates running in the 1993 federal election. The joint statement was supported by the CACL (and their provincial members from British Columbia, New Brunswick, Alberta and Manitoba), the CCD, the Canadian Association of Independent Living Centres (CAILC), the National Aboriginal Network, the Canadian Council of the Blind, and the

Canadian Association of the Deaf. The statement presented the principles the organizations were promoting to federal election candidates:

> There is a high degree of consensus in the disability community on the principles which should guide policy related to disability issues. These principles provide a framework for the reform of current income support and social service programs.
> * Right to full participation in all aspects of society;
> * Instead of charity, entitlement to adequate supports for living independently in the community;
> * Respect for and trust in the consumer with a disability;
> * Access to disability-related supports that are identified by the individual needs of the consumers;
> * Individual control and choice in all decisions affecting one's life;
> * Significant involvement by consumers with disabilities and their organizations in programs that directly affect their lives;
> * The protection of these principles through law and government policies;
> * Because the way in which government resources have been used is ineffective in addressing the needs of people with disabilities, we believe that reform of current income support programs must be a priority for the next government. (p. 4)

At the local level, people with disabilities from various organizations have also formed ad hoc coalitions for the purpose of participating in the electoral process. In Winnipeg, for example, various disability groups in the city jointly organized town hall meetings where candidates were invited to make their views known on disability issues. Individuals in these coalitions are free to publicly comment on the events that happen as a result of these collaborative actives. By forming loose, ad hoc community coalitions, people from all political perspectives can come together to make disability an issue during a federal election campaign while also remaining true to their own political convictions.

(d) Engaging political parties

People with disabilities have become increasingly involved in party politics, but the organizations of people with disabilities remain independent from partisan politics. Part of the goal of organizations has been to influence the platforms and programs of all parties. Yet there has been little success. The federal New Democratic Party's platform illustrates the greatest level of inclusion. This party has developed papers on disability issues and consulted with the disability community on their contents. In 1993, the NDP released *Our Commitment to Persons with Disabilities*. This policy document has not been a one-of-a-kind for the NDP. For example, in 2002, they issued a *Federal NDP Policy Paper on Disability Issues*. The NDP set their policy in a human rights framework and made commitments to strong national programs, national standards for disability supports, programs to address poverty among persons with disabilities, and strategies to make government more accountable to persons with disabilities. Many of the planks of the NDP platform echo statements made by disability advocacy organizations.

Analysis of the Liberal and Conservative 2004 election platforms suggests much less coherence between the disability community's advocacy and party platforms. The CCD argued that

> "Prime Minister Martin's announcement of $1 Billion 'over five years for a program to family caregivers including spouses, children and close relatives of seniors and persons with disabilities' misses the mark," said Marie White Chairperson of CCD. "While we agree caregivers need support, such an investment does nothing to remove the barriers we, as people with disabilities face, in our daily lives: our needs in the areas of transportation, training, education, employment, and income support remain." (CCD, 2004b, p. xxx)

Recently the federal Liberal Party recognized and removed one of their systemic barriers to people with disabilities. Liberal candidates had been questioned about their past experiences with mental illness. In January 2004, Prime Minister Paul Martin ordered the practice stopped and apologized to the Canadian Mental Health Association (Taber, 2004, p. A9). A review of the Conservative Party of Canada did not find any policy statements specifically on disability.

Disability organizations have recognized that concerns about disability also shape the campaigns run by parties. During the 2004 federal election campaign, people with disabilities challenged the federal parties to conduct accessible campaigns. Following are some examples of accessibility features that should be included in an accessible campaign:

- Print material also available in alternate media (Braille, tape, computer disk);
- ASL interpretation at public meetings;
- Campaign information written in plain language;

- Offices equipped with TTYs;
- Offices located in barrier free premises;
- Meetings and offices with designated disabled parking;
- Advertising of the availability of accessibility features;
- If parties provide voters with transportation to the polls, then accessible transportation should also be made available to voters with disabilities; and
- Accessible Web sites.

As people with disabilities join parties and begin to consider entering partisan politics, the issues of access increase in importance. It is a sign of greater inclusion in the political system that people with disabilities have shifted their advocacy attention to more substantive forms of political participation.

(e) Seeking public office

People with disabilities have sought and won public office. Some famous Canadian disabled politicians who come to mind are Lucien Bouchard, an amputee, who became disabled during his career, and Jean Chrétien, who was more or less "outed" as a person with disability during the 1993 federal election campaign (Graham, 1993). And, of course, Conservative Steven Fletcher was the first quadriplegic Member of Parliament. Despite these few notable exceptions, people with disabilities are largely invisible as public representatives.

People with disabilities, particularly people with severe or stigmatized disabilities, or disabilities that require significant accommodations, continue to be under-represented in Canadian politics. As well, some candidates and elected officials with disabilities remain hidden, passing as non-disabled people. This under-representation stems from negative public attitudes about people with disabilities, lack of knowledge about the costs and potential contributions of disabled people, and lack of resources for candidates with disabilities, including appropriate disability supports, money, and access to political opportunities. This section shares some of the experiences of election candidates with disabilities to reveal both the barriers that make it more difficult for persons with disabilities to attain public office and the remedies required to achieve substantive equality in Canada's electoral processes for persons with disabilities.

In 1990, Gary Malkowski, a deaf man, was elected to the Ontario legislature. Mr. Malkowski discovered many barriers both on the campaign trail and in the legislature:

First of all at the time of the campaign, the Election Finances Act did not allow for candidates' accessibility costs. There was an allowance for costs for disabled voters, but not for disabled candidates. Each candidate was allowed a budget of up to $45,000, depending on the number of voters in a riding. I had to cut the budget in half because I had to pay $20,000 for interpreters, which left insufficient funds compared to the expenditures by non-disabled candidates ... We had to fight with the Commission on Election Finances to put in place a new clause allowing accessibility costs outside of my campaign expenses and my campaign budget.

My campaign started late because it was difficult to get interpreters in place. It was summertime and the election was called at the last minute. A lot of interpreters were on vacation, at conferences, etc., which meant that I was really strapped for interpreters. We would have interpreters for two hours or half-a-day, whatever we could.

At first, people had questions about the fact that I was a deaf person and how I was going to be able to communicate by using the interpreter. But they were able to see that I could participate fully in the political process. During the canvassing we saw a lot of changes in attitude. For example, I went to the all-candidates meetings, I was on Rogers Cable TV debate. I think that really convinced constituents to reconsider their original attitudes ...

Actually, prior to setting up at Queen's Park, we found that sadly, there was not real accessibility. In fact, there are not TTYs here; the bells do not have flashing devices; there is no captioning on any of the TVs. We found that there were real difficulties in getting interpreters. The cost was not an issue. It was just a matter of working out details. Right now I am attending some meetings without interpreters and relying on someone to take notes. Sometimes the other MPPs share that work and take notes for me. I have had a lot of support from other Members, and the Government is trying very hard to get interpreters in place as soon as possible.

When the House opens next month, because of standing orders, an interpreter will not be allowed on the floor. It may take up to three days before we get the interpreter. We have to get approval from the Members to change the orders. (Malkowski, 1990, pp. 24–25)

As Malkowski's testimony reveals, there are numerous obstacles that hinder the full and equal participation of people with disabilities in Canadian politics.

Barriers to Political Participation

(a) Attitudes

Despite the potential for ableist backlashes and systemic barriers in the electoral process, people with disabilities in Canada continue to seek public office. For some, election takes repeated attempts. The late Percy Wickman, an Edmonton wheelchair user, was introduced to politics at the Northern Alberta Institute of Technology, successfully running for student council vice-president, using the slogan, "Wheel ahead with Wickman". After three unsuccessful runs for Edmonton City Council, Wickman was elected in 1977, where he served until 1986.

As Wickman noted in his autobiography *Wheels in the Fast Lane*, discriminatory attitudes about his candidacy as a person with a disability contributed to lost votes:

> It was becoming evident that this could be the big one as I was being picked by many to finally win a seat. Then the whispers started. "Why elect a disabled person, when there are so many healthy ones running?" "If successful, he will only represent the handicapped." Certainly some sympathy votes were picked up, particularly from those who sensed my determination and hunger for the job. But many, many votes were lost because of the unfounded fear that I could not do a proper job if elected. (Wickman, 1987, p. 71)

According to Wickman, by his third campaign as an incumbent, job performance, and not his disability, was the electorate's main concern:

> In my third and last successful bid for another term, my wheelchair did not have even a marginal influence on the outcome. The electorate judged me totally on my record and beliefs. Those who disagreed with me had no hesitation in telling me the way it was. Those who may have been previously swayed, one way or the other by my set of wheels were now looking at Wickman, the alderman and voting for the person just like any other candidate. I had proven that despite my disability, I could hold my own with the best of them. In a rather complacent campaign, I topped the polls in my home ward and narrowly missed the overall first spot in my final bid. (Wickman, 1987, pp. 72–73)

Following his stint in city politics, Wickman ran for and won a seat in the Alberta legislature as a Liberal in 1989.

Despite many years of law reform and awareness-raising on disability issues, the negative attitudes about disability experienced by Wickman continue to be experienced by candidates with disabilities. Ross Eadie candidly describes the discrimination he faced while running for Winnipeg City Council in 1998:

> My disability led to a few problems with voters and promoters. It first started off with a pamphlet which only showed my face with sunglasses on. A fairly large number of people called in to ask who does this Ross Eadie guy think he is?
>
> My campaign manager (now a good friend) explained to those who called that I was blind. We will never know if this sunglass issue cost us votes ... A woman called into the office saying she was not going to vote for me if it was going to cost her more tax dollars. I explained I used a computer with voice output to do most of my work and would require some assistance in getting to meetings outside of City Hall given a tight schedule. She said that was it, she wasn't going to vote for me because of paying for a computer. I explained to her that every City Councilor received a computer to carry out their jobs, and I would use my already-purchased voice synthesizer. She still said she would not vote for me because of the transportation. I did not bother to explain how past mayor (Susan Thompson) used city-paid transportation. I think she was determined not to vote for me.
>
> Another fellow didn't even listen to me at the door. He just went in the house and came out with money for the blind guy. I told him I could use the money for the campaign, but I really wanted his vote ... (Eadie, 2000. p. 27)

It is not only citizens who display discriminatory attitudes toward candidates with disabilities. Community leaders have also been influenced by stereotypes about disability. Some Manitoba election-night coverage served to reinforce stereotypes about the capabilities of persons with visual impairments. Eadie comments:

> In the end, I lost by a vote of 46 percent to 54 percent. At one point, I was ahead in the polls, and the former mayor of Winnipeg (Bill Norrie) was commenting on CBC television, saying I was an intelligent young man. But he said he did not know how I was going to keep up with all the reading. On the radio after the election I explained how the clerks department was very good at getting things onto computer disk. (Eadie, 2000, p. 28)

Eadie is now an elected school trustee in Winnipeg.

Due to the prevalence of disability stereotyping, candidates with disabilities need to address the impact of disability on their lives and ability in order to confront biases. Sam Savona, an NDP candidate in the 1997 federal election, made the following comments at an all-candidates meeting:

> I was born with cerebral palsy, which is a neurological disorder.
> As you can hear, I have a speech impairment and, as you can
> see, I'm a wheelchair user. I also have restricted use of my
> hands. Cerebral palsy does not affect my intellectual ability.
> These days, when my friends learn of my political plans, they do
> wonder about my mental health. (Feld, 1997, p. 14)

For disabled people, just as for non-disabled, having a sense of
humour and a willingness to be self-deprecating while on the hus-
tings can go a long way toward building links with the electorate.
While Savona lost the election, some parts of the electorate reacted
positively to his candidacy.

(b) Inadequate access to disability supports

Disability supports are essential if people with disabilities are
to pursue the activities that contribute to active citizenship: going
to school, working, having a family, enjoying recreation, giving
back to the community by volunteering and holding public office.
Just as some employees with disabilities require disability supports,
some candidates with disabilities need disability supports to function independently in the campaign environment. For example,
Ross Eadie hired a guide and driver to assist him in campaigning
door-to-door in his bid to become a Manitoba MLA. According
to Eadie, the Manitoba Government paid 100% of his election
expenses related to disability (Eadie, 2000, p. 29). The *Manitoba
Elections Finances Act* allows claims for disability supports. Candidates are reimbursed for the full amount of reasonable expenses
they incur related to their disability to enable them to campaign
during the election period (*The Elections Finance Act*, Chapter E32,
Para. 72(3) (a.1)).

The federal and British Columbia election laws allow accommodation costs for people with disabilities as "permitted personal expenses" of candidates to be claimed as part of a campaign
budget. The *Canada Elections Act* (Section 409(1)(c) and (d))
includes accommodation provisions for both candidates with disabilities and candidates who are caregivers to persons with disabilities, allowing both caregiving expenses and disability-related
expenses to be included as a personal expense of a candidate. In
Ontario, accessibility costs are excluded from the spending limits
for candidates.

However, some people with disabilities who have chosen public life as a career have encountered difficulties in having their disability supports needs met. Steven Fletcher, a quadriplegic, ran

successfully for President of the Progressive Conservative Party of Manitoba, a position that also required him to travel. In 2002, the Manitoba Public Insurance Corporation (MPIC) determined it would no longer cover the costs of Fletcher's attendant care expenses for travel outside Winnipeg associated with his PC Party responsibilities. Fletcher unsuccessfully challenged the MPIC ruling at the Automobile Injury Compensation Appeal Commission (AICAC) and at the Manitoba Court of Appeal.

The experience of Gary Malkowski, a former Ontario MPP, also illustrates the need for disability supports as a candidate:

> I tried at one point to canvass electors without interpreters. It was a very awkward situation. It turned people off for sure. Once, I brought the interpreter in, there was a complete change in attitude. The people I spoke to felt very comfortable and they were able to communicate with me. That was very helpful. (Malkowski, 1990, p. 24)

Difficulties such as those faced by Gary Malkowski and Steven Fletcher illustrate the barriers faced by people who use disability supports. It is more difficult for these Canadians to follow their career path to elected office. A very practical problem remains: how does someone who uses disability supports negotiate campaigning in the face of costly support needs? It is an issue that non-disabled campaigners do not face. The cost of disability supports can be a significant disincentive to running for public office for many people with disabilities.

(c) Lack of role models

People with disabilities who are contemplating running for public office have few role models to inspire them to pursue their dream. Even elected officials, such as former Prime Minister Jean Chrétien, or the former Premier of Quebec Lucien Bouchard, both of whom live with an impairment, may not identify themselves as a disabled person. This is particularly true for people with disabilities who are not part of the organized disability rights movement. People with disabilities unaffiliated with disabled people's groups may have more limited access to the newsletters and autobiographies that tell the stories of politicians with disabilities. Sam Savona was inspired by the success of his deaf friend Gary Malkowski. Savona's involvement in the 1997 election campaign encouraged a student with cerebral palsy to let her name stand for the presidency of her student council (Feld, 1997, p. 14).

When political parties reach out to people with disabilities, this helps to overcome the disincentive caused by the lack of role models and the limited history of people with disabilities seeking public office. Sam Savona began to think about running for office when an NDP federal party worker approached the NDP Disability Caucus to see who was interested in running in the upcoming election. Following that overture, Savona relentlessly pursued candidacy.

Gary Malkowski (1997) was able to find a helpful person inside a party that was willing to mentor him. He describes his experiences in the following manner:

> Prior to being an elected member of the Ontario Provincial Parliament (and then a defeated candidate in the next election) I had no experience in any parties.... I was able to make a friend with a Member of the Provincial Parliament who provided me with support in making connections with the Provincial Party office and the Riding Association which supported me, a disabled/deaf candidate to run for a provincial seat. I ran as a candidate for the provincial York East NDP riding ... (pp. 1–2)

Having a disability caucus within a political party can help to raise the profile of disability issues and, possibly, encourage candidates. Parties may also want to create special funds to promote the candidacy of disabled candidates, or create broader diversity funds to assist with a range of under-represented groups, modeled after the special funds for women candidates in several parties.

(d) Inaccessible places and spaces

The built environment continues to present barriers to people with disabilities. Candidates with various disabilities find that many buildings do not conform to universal design standards; thus they must develop innovative strategies for getting their message out to the public. Sam Savona concentrated his efforts in large apartment buildings that had elevator service and at subway stations. While this may be a workable approach in Toronto or another large metropolitan area, candidates with disabilities in rural areas would have to develop other tactics. One First Nations woman with a visual impairment who ran for chief of her band council was assisted by family and supporters to travel in her community while campaigning.

Inclusion for people with disabilities in representing Canadians in public office will require much work in ensuring accessible spaces, providing appropriate disability supports, ensuring role models, and changing public attitudes to accept that people with disabilities can and should be legitimate public representatives.

CONCLUSION

People with disabilities do still not have the opportunity to participate in Canada's political systems on the basis of inclusion as valued and appreciated equals; and as a result, the vision of full citizenship remains unrealized. Over the past two decades, largely as a result of the unrelenting efforts of the organizations of people with disabilities, there have been some changes that create more inclusion, especially in formal political participation.

Barriers to accessing formal political processes, including voting in elections, still exist, as the CCD continues to report complaints about access in every federal election. Yet many barriers to voting for people with disabilities have been removed. People with intellectual or mental disabilities have gained the right to vote. Accessible polling locations and alternative ways of voting have become the rule. These are markers of increased inclusion of people with disabilities in formal political participation.

Ongoing work is required, and undertaken primarily by disability organizations, in providing the necessary supports for people with disabilities to participate in formal politics. Public education campaigns, including those using new information technologies, assist greatly in ensuring that people with disabilities are able to be informed and engaged voters.

Much work is needed, however, to ensure inclusion for people with disabilities in substantive political participation, including participating in political parties and becoming public representatives. There are many barriers to access for people with disabilities in various areas of political life, such as accessible campaigns in which people with disabilities can participate as volunteers, party workers or candidates. On top of these barriers to access, there remains significant exclusion of people with disabilities, especially those with visible disabilities, in participating in these areas. Some areas that need to be addressed include changing attitudes about the value and need for people with disabilities to participate in these areas, as well as creating spaces and place where people with disabilities can participate as valued, appreciated equals in Canadian political life. When this type of inclusion occurs, the political landscape of Canada will change.

14

Electoral Participation among Disabled People in Canada

MARY ANN McCOLL

INTRODUCTION

To conclude this section on the participation of people with disabilities in the policy process, it is important to look at electoral participation — one of the most basic forms of civic participation in a democracy (Shields, Schriner & Schriner, 1998). Living with a disability highlights issues of personal control and identity, and therefore has the potential to be highly deterministic in the way individuals view their role in shaping society and the institutions that govern it (Schur, 1998). In fact, Shields, Schriner and Schriner (1998) suggest that the electoral participation of potentially vulnerable groups in society (such as people with disabilities) should serve as a test of our beliefs about democracy and the ability of an individual or group to influence their own destiny in society. The disability rights movement is based on a view of disabled people as citizens, and the assumption of equality of people with disabilities under the law (McColl & Bickenbach, 1998; Schur, 1998). Equity for people with disabilities requires that society take disability issues into consideration, and for that to happen, disabled people need to function as citizens, exercising their right to vote and to contribute to the democratic process. Furthermore, the success of the disability rights movement requires that people with disabilities, to some extent at least, function as an interest group, voting in predictable ways on issues that affect them.

This chapter explores the following:

1. How disabled people in Canada participate in the electoral process;
2. How they differ from the balance of the electorate on specific issues; and
3. What factors affect their electoral participation.

To fulfill these objectives, data are advanced from the 1997 Canadian Election Survey. Although a similar survey has been conducted at two subsequent elections (2000 and 2004), neither instance included the disability filter question. Therefore, the only possibility of identifying a disabled sample was to single out those who had been excluded from work due to a disability. The 1997 data although older offer a more representative disabled sample and were therefore preferable (refer to sampling methodology discussed in McColl, Chapter 3).

Electoral participation in the developed world has been decreasing over the past three decades. In Canada, it reached an all-time low in 2000 of 61% (CRIC, 2001). This trend has been reflected in most Western democracies, most notably the United States and the United Kingdom. A number of explanations for voter attrition have been advanced, but the most salient appear to be the following:

- Values and attitudes toward institutions and authority have changed;
- Electorate is increasingly cynical about the role of government and the importance of leadership;
- People are increasingly distanced from the political process; and
- A decline in civic education renders voters ignorant of their civic responsibilities.

PATTERNS OF ELECTORAL PARTICIPATION

International research has shown that voter profiles are relatively predictable the world over. People are more likely to vote if they are male, older, better educated and more prosperous. In addition, people who vote are more likely than those who do not to be married and in a stable living situation. When we look at the demographics of disability, these trends would lead us to expect lower voter participation among disabled people.

Surveys have shown that our expectation would be upheld: voting and voter registration tends to be 10–20% lower among disabled than non-disabled citizens (Schur & Kruse, 2000; Shields, Schriner & Schriner, 1998). Furthermore, voter participation among disabled people runs contrary to the trend in the general population. Whereas older non-disabled citizens are more likely to vote than younger people, among people with disabilities, voting drops off with age. The disposition toward voting has been shown to be unaffected by the severity of disability, but it has been shown to be related to other indicators of social participation (Schur & Kruse, 2000). Those disabled citizens who were employed or who participated in voluntary organizations voted at the same rate as their non-disabled employed counterparts (Rosenstone & Hansen, 1993; Schur & Kruse, 2000). More important than the disability itself in predicting voter participation was the ability to drive and the ability to participate in other community activities. These findings together suggest that it is a general mobility factor that largely determines the extent to which disabled citizens vote.

When asked about real and perceived barriers to electoral participation, a sample of Americans with disabilities noted that transportation to the polling station, access to the polling station, and access to the polling booth were substantial determinants of participation (Schur & Kruse, 2000). Among those who had actually voted in recent elections, fewer than 10% were inhibited from participating as a result of these barriers. Among those who had not voted in recent elections, a three- to five-fold increase was seen in the expectation of these barriers to electoral participation.

How Disabled People in Canada Participate in the Electoral Process

In Canada, 7.7% of the sample of the 1997 Canada Election Survey identified themselves on a filter question on the telephone survey as having "a long-term disability or handicap". A further 1.2% either refused to answer or did not know. The remaining 91.1% constitute the non-disabled comparison sample used in this chapter. Those who said they had a disability further specified that the principal cause of their disability related to mobility (41.2%), other causes, such as mental health problems, pain and cognitive problems (32.1%), agility (11.1%), sight (8.8%) and hearing (7.0%). The average age for the disabled sample was 54.4 (± 16.9) — significantly older than the average age for the non-disabled sample — 43.0 (± 15.3) (p < .05).

Participants were contacted twice — during the 36-day campaign period for the federal election in the spring of 1997, and within eight weeks following the election. The results presented include data from both points in time. Prior to the election, there was a significant difference between disabled and non-disabled Canadians in terms of their intention to vote. Whereas 82.2% of disabled voters definitely intended to vote, only 76.2% of non-disabled voters were so certain (p = .039). An even larger margin of almost 8% separated disabled from non-disabled in terms of actual voting. While 81.7% of non-disabled respondents actually voted, 89.9% of disabled citizens voted (p = .022). These numbers are considerably in excess of general polling estimates cited earlier at around 60%. One can only assume that participation in an election survey raised the consciousness of respondents and prompted them to vote in higher numbers.

Despite favourable electoral participation, it does not appear that people with disabilities are particularly satisfied with the democratic process. The issues shown in Table 14.1 show considerable disaffection in the portion of the electorate with disabilities. They report that they have little say in how the country is run, and that federal policies in recent years have been more likely to make their lives worse rather than better. Both of these perceptions are significantly stronger than in the general population. The disabled sample appears to feel marginalized and disenfranchised compared to their non-disabled counterparts.

How Disabled People in Canada Differ from the Non-disabled Electorate on Specific Issues

Table 14.2 shows the results of seven questions where participants were asked about the importance of particular election issues to them personally. The values in the table represent the proportion of the sample that said the issue was very important to them. The table shows that a consistently higher number of disabled participants than non-disabled rated items as very important. For all seven issues, at least half of the disabled sample rated them as very important.

The most important issues for the sample of disabled voters were fighting crime, keeping election promises and protecting

Table 14.1: Satisfaction with democracy and policy.

	Disabled	Non-disabled	p
Unsatisfied with the way democracy works in Canada	50.7	40.8	.002
People like me don't have a say in how the country is run	39.3	33.3	.004
Federal policies in recent years have made my life:			.027
Better	9.0	5.9	
No difference	64.1	69.9	
Worse	26.9	24.2	
Provincial policies have made my life:			.545
Better	9.2	11.1	
No difference	59.5	57.5	
Worse	31.3	31.3	

Table 14.2: Responses to specific election issues by disabled and non-disabled Canadians.

	Disabled	Non-disabled	p
Fighting crime	77.6	68.8	.003
Keeping election promises	76.0	74.7	.498
Protecting social programs	71.8	60.8	.000
Serving the interests of Quebec	63.3	56.3	.330
Preserving national unity	59.1	54.7	.021
Reducing the deficit	57.1	60.6	.272
Cutting taxes	48.2	41.7	.048

social programs. While keeping election promises was about equally important to both constituencies, fighting crime and protecting social programs were significantly more important for disabled participants. Two other issues that were rated as very important by about half of the disabled sample were also significantly more important to disabled than non-disabled voters: preserving national unity and cutting taxes.

What Factors Affect Disabled People in Canada in Terms of Their Electoral Participation

Finally, the post-election survey asked non-voters what had influenced their decision not to vote. The results by disability classification are shown below in Table 14.3. The results for the disabled subset of the sample are significantly different from the non-disabled (p = .036).

The top two reasons that disabled people did not vote were "other" and sick. Almost 40% of those who did not vote invoked one of these two reasons. We may speculate that the "other" category could have included reasons referring to accessibility of the venue or polling booth, but these details are not specified on the public access data set. Almost five times as many disabled as non-disabled citizens failed to vote due to illness. However, only about one-quarter as many disabled as non-disabled voters stated that they did not vote due to cynicism, and about a third as many because of being too busy.

Table 14.3: Reasons for not voting in previous election

	Disabled	Non-disabled	p
Other	19.4	14.6	.036
Sick	19.4	4.0	
Work	16.1	12.0	
Don't know who to vote for	16.1	11.8	
Cynicism	6.5	24.0	
Too busy	6.5	14.6	
Absent	6.5	8.6	

CONCLUSION

In summary, this brief re-analysis of the Canadian Election Survey for the 1997 federal election allowed us to identify a subset of people with disabilities from the national sample, and to compare their experiences of the election with those of their non-disabled counterparts. Contrary to expectations derived from the literature, the survey showed that disabled people were significantly more likely than non-disabled to express an intention to vote, and to actually subsequently vote. Whereas American studies suggest that disabled people participate in elections at rates 10–20% lower than non-disabled voters, this survey showed an excess of 8% among disabled voters. Voting rates are high generally in this survey, probably because of the sensitizing effect of the survey — 82% of non-disabled and 90% of disabled respondents, respectively.

The rate of participation among disabled voters suggests that barriers to electoral participation are consistent with findings of actual barriers found in the literature. About 2–8% of voters in Schur and Kruse's (2000) study encountered transportation problems or other physical barriers in attempting to access either the polling station or booth. The only evidence we have in this study is the 19% who stated an "other" reason for not voting, which one might speculate refers to accessibility issues, along with other miscellaneous reasons.

One of the main reasons non-disabled people decline to vote is cynicism about the electoral process, about the candidates, and about the value of a single vote (CRIC, 2001). Our results show that disabled people were significantly less likely than non-disabled to label their reason for not voting as cynicism. However, they did express some disaffection when asked about the value of the democratic process. They were significantly more likely to state that they felt democracy was ineffective, that people like themselves could not make a difference, and that federal policies in recent years had left them worse off. According to Schriner and Shields (1998), these attitudes are common among disadvantaged groups in society. The slow pace of reform leaves disadvantaged groups feeling that more privileged groups consistently benefit from government policy, and that it is impossible to change things to benefit those in society with less power. These attitudes in turn form part of a vicious cycle, leading to wider gaps between "haves" and "have-nots", and ever-lower levels of electoral participation.

Interestingly, people with disabilities were no more likely than non-disabled to feel that they had been either advantaged or disadvantaged by provincial policies. Thus, people from the disabled group appear to be making distinctions between federal and provincial services. As discussed earlier, the main provincial services for people with disabilities include health care, education and training, assistive devices and income supplements. The most visible federal policies include the CPP disability benefits and the disability tax credit, both of which have come under considerable criticism in recent decades. If these are, in fact, the policies that voters associate with the federal government, it may explain the perception that disability services have been eroded at the federal level.

Ironically, the federal government has been relatively supportive of people with disabilities in recent years, and it is generally held that disability issues are favoured at the federal level (Torjman, 2001; Cameron & Valentine, 2001). For example, the Office for Disability Issues (ODI) has engaged stakeholders in discussions and produced reports about disability and inclusion; Statistics Canada has participated actively in the development of WHO's 2001 ICF; a number of *Charter* decisions have found in favour of equity for disabled people; and the Supreme Court has upheld the guilty verdict regarding Robert Latimer and the murder of his disabled daughter. However, these are all what Schur (1998) would refer to as abstract issues — related to discrimination, stigma, citizenship and equality. They do not carry with them immediate tangible benefits that participants can point to and say that they are better or worse off. Schur (1998) also makes a distinction between activists and non-activists in her discussion of political participation. She refers to the politicization of some disabled individuals and groups, often consistent with longer duration of experience with disability. The assumption is that more experience with disability alerts some individuals to the importance of these symbolic issues, in addition to the tangible issues affecting day-to-day life.

With regard to the election issues of importance to people with disabilities, the two that most distinguished the disabled from non-disabled samples were fighting crime and protecting social programs. Both of these issues suggest that people with disabilities live with a high degree of awareness of their vulnerability in both a private and a public way. They are aware that they are potentially vulnerable in their private lives to victimization at the hands of criminals, and that they are vulnerable in a more public way to changes in the social safety net that would leave them without needed services. The other two issues where disabled people were significantly different in their evaluation of personal importance were national unity and cutting taxes. As mentioned above, the disability tax credit has been under review for some time for its inadequacy to compensate for the excess costs of living with a disability. The national unity finding is harder to explain — it may be a subject for further research to better understand how vulnerable or disadvantaged groups relate to constitutional issues.

A number of authors have suggested that there is a role for disability organizations in enhancing the democratic participation of their members, and actualizing the disability vote on important issues. Services like voter education may be valuable, since disabled voters were 5% more likely than non-disabled to say they did not know whom to vote for. Evaluation of polling stations for accessibility and informing members about accessibility provisions at the various stations might be another possible role. Disability organizations might also help on election days to "get the vote out" by providing transportation or escorts to the polls. Finally, disability organizations have a role to play in educating candidates about disability issues and communicating to them the power of the disability sector to influence election outcomes. According to Scotch (1989), the disability movement has become a forceful presence in social welfare politics, and Schriner and Shields (1998) refer to its potential to effect change by calling it "the sleeping giant of American politics" (p. 33). Here in Canada, 17% of voting age people are disabled. With electoral participation rates as low as 60–70%, as they have been in recent years, a fully mobilized disabled constituency could potentially represent a quarter of the voting public — a formidable democratic force indeed.

Section IV

Specific Policy Issues

This section, the largest of the book, consists of nine chapters and offers perspectives on specific policy issues:

- Economic policy — income replacement, financial support, vocational participation, education and training;
- Health and social policy — access to health services, personal care and substitute decision-making; and
- Community policy — transportation and cultural policy.

According to Cameron and Valentine (2001), economic policy spans both federal and provincial jurisdictions, with vocational programs, disability issues, and Aboriginal programs governed at the federal level and welfare provisions, health care, education and training, workers' compensation and social insurance at the provincial level.

Human rights, tax credits, disability pensions and employment insurance cross federal/provincial jurisdictional boundaries. Transportation is a good example of a

policy area that covers three jurisdictions: federal, provincial, and regional/municipal.

ECONOMIC POLICY

Chapter 15

In the first chapter of this section, Jongbloed provides a historical review of income and employment policy relating to people with disabilities in Canada. She reviews and critiques the underlying ideology for economic policy relating to disability, and notes some of the basic tensions that persist in the system between collectivism and individualism, between welfare state and capitalism, between charity-, investment- and rights-based approaches to economic policy.

Chapter 16

Boyce and colleagues provide a critical review of income and employment supports over the period from 1990 forward. They point to cuts, shifts and squeezes in the sector as the source of increasing economic disadvantage for disabled people. They consider both the individual and the organizational levels, and note how the two levels are inextricably intertwined and dependent on government support.

Chapter 17

In Chapter 17, Lawand and Kloosterman offer a summary of the major federal program that provides income and employment services to Canadians with disabilities — the Canada Pension Plan Disability Program. They focus on recent history, from 1990 forward, and discuss new initiatives in retraining, work incentives, allowable earnings and return to work. They focus on the individual as the recipient of benefits, and note the need for new ways of thinking about the goal of return to work, given what appears to be a hard ceiling on employment outcomes.

Chapter 18

Timmons' chapter analyzes initiatives related to inclusion in education and training. Many provinces have policies that encourage inclusion of children with disabilities in regular classrooms. The provision of employment-related training and supports is complex.

Over the past six years, various federal government documents have emphasized the importance of disability-related supports and services, but action has not occurred.

HEALTH & SOCIAL POLICY

Chapter 19

Literature that describes the barriers experienced by people with disabilities in gaining access to health services is largely American. Three aspects of access are examined: physical barriers, attitudinal barriers, and expertise barriers. McColl reports the findings of a Canadian study that identified structural determinants and barriers to access to health services. Federal and provincial laws and policies that enable access for people with disabilities are identified, as are omissions in policy that impede access to health services.

Chapter 20

Yoshida, Willi, Parker and Locker provide a perspective on personal care. They analyze the social and political forces that enabled the development of the Ontario Self-Managed Attendant Service Direct Funding Pilot between 1974 and 1994. Elements that facilitated the emergence of this project were the readiness of the disability community, the presence of advocates outside the community and changes in provincial government philosophy. Strong vision, leadership and broad-based support also helped ensure its success. These authors focus on Ontario; however, other provinces have similar programs. For example, the Choices in Independent Living (CSIL) Project in British Columbia provides individuals with disabilities with funds to employ and train anyone (except a family member with whom they live) as a personal assistant. This enables them to exercise choice and control.

Chapter 21

On the same theme of choice and control, Kerzner provides a thorough discussion of substitute decision-making within an empowerment framework. She puts forward the ideological and legal basis for determining capacity to make independent decisions, and describes typical methods of assessment. She advances the argument that capacity, like innocence, should be presumed unless proven otherwise. This is not always the case when assumptions are made about capacity of people with disabilities.

COMMUNITY POLICY

Chapter 22

Laws against discrimination do not prevent individual acts that may harm another's dignity. Frazee views various social movements such as the feminist movement, gay pride and the disability rights movement as collective claims for recognition. She emphasizes the importance of the disability movement in challenging dominant norms of beauty, health and autonomy.

Chapter 23

This chapter chronicles the advances in and barriers to accessible transportation in Canada. The year 1981 was not only the International Year of Disabled Persons, but also the year in which the *Obstacles Report* was published. The federal government has broad authority in the area of transportation, and many improvements were made to transportation policies under federal jurisdiction between 1980 and 2001. Disability advocacy organizations and individuals with disabilities played very important roles in these improvements.

15

Disability Income and Employment Policies in Canada: Historical Development

LYN JONGBLOED

INTRODUCTION

Ideas about disability have changed considerably over time. In the first 70 years of the 20th century, individual medical and vocational limitations were seen as the main obstacles preventing individuals with disabilities from participating fully in society. The focus was on providing support services to these people and on improving their ability to engage in full employment. Those unable to work received some financial compensation. In the 1970s, a socio-political definition challenged the individualistic conceptualization of disability by stating that disability stems not from individual limitations but from the failure of the social environment to adjust to the needs of people with disabilities (Hahn, 1985). Efforts were made to enhance the participation of people with disabilities in their communities by altering the physical, social and institutional environments.

This chapter examines how changing views of disability have been reflected in the development of federal income and employment policies in Canada. It also examines the development of disability income and employment policies in relation to the broader paradigms of national social policy development. Specifically, the chapter covers the following:

1. Provides a historical review of the social policy context in Canada;
2. Reviews the history of federal employment and income policy as it pertains to people with disabilities; and
3. Discusses and critiques the underlying ideology of income and employment policies in Canada.

BACKGROUND

Canada's colonial links to Britain and Europe fostered beliefs about the importance of collectivism, respect for authority and acceptance of the need for state intervention. These values are reflected in the country's policies and social structures (Lipset, 1989). Disability policy development was part of the evolution of these collectivist social policies. As Canada industrialized, provincial governments introduced legislation to ensure that workers who were injured on the job were compensated. Toward the end of the First World War, the federal government introduced compensation payments for veterans with disabilities. These two groups of people were viewed as "more deserving" of government intervention than other groups because their work had contributed to the country.

The *Unemployment Insurance Act* of 1940 was the first federal welfare state program introduced in Canada. Under this Act, unemployment insurance was to be funded by premiums paid by employers and employees, backed by the Consolidated Revenue Fund. The next stages of welfare state development were concerned with opening up social programs to all Canadians. The *Hospital Insurance and Diagnostic Services Act* of 1957 and the *Medical Care Act* of 1967 provided universal access to hospital services and physician care, respectively.

The federal government also developed individual contributory social insurance schemes. In 1965 it introduced the Canada/Quebec Pension Plan (R.S.C. 1985, c. C-8), a contributory pension scheme that provided a national system of social insurance to the paid labour force — specifically, for people in retirement, widows and widowers, orphans, persons with disabilities, and children of disabled contributors. The objectives of the federal Canada Assistance

Plan of 1966 were the creation of a consistent national welfare apparatus and the extension of assistance to anyone who might need it, with need being the only criterion (Hum & Simpson, 1993). The above mentioned programs related to employment, income and health services were helpful to people with disabilities because they were more likely to use these programs than was the general public.

Canada's welfare state is a bourgeois welfare state: an outcome of acceptance by the middle class of the importance of distributing the country's wealth more evenly. Programs have been established not only to meet the needs of poor people, but also to ensure that all Canadians have access to education and health-care services. Welfare states can be classified according to their emphasis on capitalist development versus provision of social entitlements to their citizens. Graycar and Jamrozik (1989) identified three divisions in welfare states' programming: expenditures in favour of low-income groups (e.g., unemployment benefits, old age pensions); universal provisions (e.g., public education, public health care, public transportation); and expenditures in favour of high-income groups (e.g., assistance to industry, concessions to business, tax-free dividends). As a market-oriented welfare state, Canada is not very sympathetic to people with income security problems (National Council on Welfare, 1989). However, there was greater willingness in providing income support services that favour low-income groups between 1945 and 1975 than there is now. Since 1975, this willingness has been diminishing, and this affects people with disabilities because a high percentage of these individuals depend on expenditures, such as income support and public housing, that favour low-income groups (Torjman, 1988). There has been ongoing emphasis on funding universal services used by the majority of the population (e.g., health care, education) and an increased interest in assisting producers of goods and services that favour high-income groups. While redistribution to high-income groups is seldom questioned, there is a belief that budget deficits result from spending on welfare programs for low-cost sectors. In reality, these deficits stem primarily from large expenditures on entitlement programs such as education and health (Crichton & Jongbloed, 1998).

By 1980, Canada had begun questioning whether the welfare state was the best form of social organization (Pleiger, 1990). Goals began to shift from those of a welfare state to those of a welfare society, which proposed that financial redistribution alone would not create a true collectivist society, and that all citizens should be accepted for what they could contribute. The aims of the welfare

245

society were reflected in the 1982 *Charter of Rights and Freedoms*, which identified four groups as particularly disadvantaged: women, native people, visible minorities (i.e., groups who are visibly non-Caucasian), and people with disabilities.

Historical Review

The questions of what it means to have a disability and what society owes people with disabilities have been answered in different ways at different times. Accordingly, policies developed at particular points in time emphasize particular aspect of disability and goals.

Medical and economic models

The medical and economic models of disability co-existed between 1910 and 1970, and they shaped the formation of income and employment policies during those years. The medical model views a person with a disability as functionally limited and as having special medical needs that deserves a charitable response in the form of provision of health services (Bickenbach, 1993). The economic model of disability is predicated on an individual's inability to participate in the paid labour force (Bickenbach, 1993). It assumes that an individual's ability to work is determined primarily by his or her functional capacities, and there is little focus on altering job expectations to accommodate the individual (Hahn, 1993). People with disabilities are seen either as past contributors to the economic system and, thus, deserving of assistance, or as outsiders of the economic system who merit only charity (Stone, 1984). The main concern of the economic model is to distribute and reduce the costs associated with limited productivity. In this model, disability is not located solely in the individual; it is a function of the individual within a social context (Bickenbach, 1993).

Hospitals and disability pensions for war veterans were established during the First World War. Rehabilitation programs were aimed at returning people to the labour market. At about the same time, training assistance was developed to meet the needs of injured workers. Provincial workers' compensation schemes, introduced between 1914 and 1950, were social insurance systems wherein coverage was usually compulsory (Ison, 1989). A personal deficit was presumed to be the reason for the individual's unemployment, and the primary goal of rehabilitation was to return the individual to work as soon as possible. For example, the Workers' Compensation Board of British Columbia aims first to return the worker to the same job with the same employer. If this is not possible, the aim becomes return to a modified job with the same employer, then return to a different job utilizing transferable skills with the same employer or a modified job with a different employer, and so on (http://www.worksafe.com). Although the primary rationale of workers' compensation is economic efficiency, the medical model also influences workers' compensation policies in that earning capacity is usually estimated in terms of the nature and degree of the injury, and employability is therefore assessed as a medical, not an economic, phenomenon (Stone, 1984).

Welfare state policies introduced in the 1960s included the 1961 *Vocational Rehabilitation of Disabled Persons Act*, which was aimed at returning people with disabilities with no other resources to the workplace. It enabled the provinces to recover 50% of vocational training costs related to individuals with disabilities. The 1965 Canada Pension Plan (CPP) was a result of a federal-provincial agreement to provide a national system of social insurance. It took the form of a retirement pension for those in paid employment, as well a disability pension. Disability benefits are paid to those who contributed to the CPP, provided that their disabilities are severe, permanent and prevent regular employment.

The Canada Assistance Plan expanded the scope of federal involvement in social policy. It encouraged integration of assistance programs across provinces and extended cost sharing to a wide range of social services, including programs for people with disabilities. It also resulted in the standardization of social assistance plans across the provinces. Social assistance legislation reflects a response to medical and economic needs by providing minimal financial support to those unable to work.

When use of motor vehicles increased, governments passed legislation requiring drivers to take out insurance for themselves and third parties at risk. At first these insurance policies were arranged between the drivers and private insurance companies. Later, some provincial governments, including British Columbia, decided to become the insurers themselves.

The Insurance Corporation of British Columbia (ICBC) separates the determination of the extent of injury from compensation for loss. Adjustors contract external health professionals to access the extent to which a particular injury affects an individual's ability to function independently in a diversity of settings. Another department has the mandate of facilitating return to work.

Private disability insurance also developed in the middle of the 20th century. Such insurance may be taken out by individuals, groups of self-employed people, or by employers who offer this as a benefit. Private disability insurance companies proactively focus on the individual's return to work. Frequently, long-term disability will pay 65–70% of a person's salary for two years if the worker may be able to return to an alternative job more suited to their capabilities. If there is no possibility of return to work, payment will continue for longer.

In the mid-1980s it was recognized that the country was experiencing major transitions in the areas of technology, and trade and that the labour force would require help to adjust. The federal income support program of unemployment insurance and social assistance were changed and redefined as transitional support for workers between jobs; with the exception of social assistance programs for persons with severe disabilities. Retraining programs and work incentive programs were introduced to help people get off social assistance. However, the federal government withdrew from labour market training between 1997 and 2000, and at that time, the provinces assumed new responsibilities for employment (Canada, 1996).

In 2002, the federal government instituted a program entitled Employability Assistance for Persons with Disabilities, which was then replaced by the Multilateral Framework for Labour Market Agreements for Persons with Disabilities. The goal of this program is to improve the employment of persons with disabilities by enhancing their employability and increasing job opportunities. The federal government contributes funds to provincial programs and services to enable labour force participation of Canadians with disabilities.

Social Development Canada's Opportunities Fund for people with disabilities is aimed at helping people with little attachment to the labour force become self-employed. It works in partnership with disability organizations, the private sector and provincial governments.

Socio-political model

In the 1970s organizations concerned with human rights began forming across the country. Groups representing people with disabilities argued that improvement in the status of persons with disabilities required alteration in the external environment rather than changes in individual functioning (Driedger, 1990). These demands were made in the context of other societal changes, namely (a) the International Year of Disabled Persons in 1981, and (b) the introduction of the *Charter of Rights and Freedoms* in 1982. The Charter designated individuals with disabilities as one of four disadvantaged groups. This timing enhanced the responsiveness of the federal government to the demands of disability rights advocates.

The politicization of disability during the 1970s and 1980s resulted in the creation of the socio-political model of disability, which, in contrast to the individual focus of the medical and economic definitions, emphasized modification of the social environment (Hahn, 1993). Activists emphasized the goals of respect and equality and aimed to destigmatize particular groups through empowerment rather than legal remedies (Bickenbach, 1993).

Obstacles, a report by the Special Parliamentary Committee on the Disabled, called for amendments in legislation related to human rights, transportation, physical access, housing, employment, and income (Canada, 1981). Considerable progress was made in the areas of housing, access, and transportation between 1983 and 1991 (Young, 1992). Though income and employment are important determinants of health and inclusion, there has been little progress in income and employment policies for people with disabilities over the last two decades. Many people with disabilities live in poverty. The major causes of poverty are unemployment and underemployment. Approximately 70% of non-disabled persons ages 15 to 64 were in the workforce in 1991, compared with 40% of persons with disabilities in this age group (Fawcett, 1998).

The representation of people with disabilities in the labour force can be increased by such measures as affirmative action and contract compliance. However, the response of the federal government in these areas has not been strong. The 1986 *Employment Equity Act* was designed to promote the implementation of programs that would help ensure that women, native people, persons with disabilities, and visible minorities could achieve equitable representation and participation in the Canadian workforce. It applies to federally regulated companies with 100 or more employees, which operate mainly in the fields of banking, transportation and communications. Employers are required to identify workplace barriers and to develop and implement equity plans for women, Aboriginal people, members of visible minorities and people with disabilities. They were obligated to report annually to the responsible minister regarding the representation of the four groups within the workplace. The Act contains no mandatory enforcement procedures; the only penalty is for failure to report employment equity plans. The vision was that employers would be encouraged to implement employment equity because the reports could be scrutinized and used to submit systemic discrimination complaints under the *Canadian Human Rights Act*. In 1986, a Federal Contractors Program for employment equity requires contractors with 100 or more employees and with contracts worth $200,000 or more with the federal government to commit to implementing employment equity initiatives. However, employment equity legislation applies to less than 10% of the Canadian workforce.

The *Employment Equity Act* of 1996 included the federal public service. In 2001 the Public Service Commission, charged with recruiting qualified people to public service jobs, developed an innovative approach to marketing qualified individuals with disabilities by having them meet directly with managers. The Rapid Access Coordinator locates qualified candidates with disabilities and prepares them to meet directly with managers (http://canparaplegic.org/national/level2).

The *Canadian Human Rights Act* (amended in 1998) prohibits discrimination in employment practices on the basis of disability. It stresses the obligation of employers to provide accommodations but limits the employer's duty to accommodate if the accommodation needs of the individual would impose undue hardship.

Critique of Income and Employment Policies

Disability policies related to income and employment are fragmented, for two reasons: first, programs developed incrementally to deal with separate demands; and second, disability policies are part of general welfare state policies, which are also fragmented.

Between 1910 and 1975 there was incremental development of federal, provincial, and private sector policies to meet the needs of particular groups of the population. However, this led to the income of a person with a disability who is not working being determined by three conditions: (a) whether the person became disabled at work or in a car accident; (b) whether the person had contributed to the CPP before the disability; or (c) whether the person is a war veteran. The workers' compensation boards base compensation levels on a proportion of the workers' insurable earning before the accident and the extent and duration of the injury (Rioux, Muszynski & Crawford, 1992). An individual not at fault but seriously injured in a motor vehicle accident in British Columbia would be given generous income support, physical rehabilitation, physical maintenance, home renovations, an adapted transport van, and vocational rehabilitation. However, many people with disabilities do not fall within this category and therefore are not eligible for such benefits. Instead, they receive provincial social assistance, a program of last resort, characterized by low-income payments and needs-testing. These benefits are generally set lower than that can be earned in the workforce to encourage people to seek and retain employment; however, benefits are *so* low that many recipients live in poverty.

These eligibility criteria have different implications for people with different types of disabilities. Those injured in car accidents or at work and those with private disability insurance will generally be given considerable assistance to return to work; and if that is not possible, they will likely have generous income support. However, a person with a developmental disability or a mental illness will likely be more disadvantaged financially. The financial situation of an individual with a disease such as multiple sclerosis (MS) will depend on whether the individual qualifies for a CPP disability pension or had private disability insurance when she discovered she had MS.

The current disability system does not acknowledge that all people with disabilities need adequate income support regardless of the cause of their disability. There are several barriers to the development of equitable income policies for people with disabilities. First, it is not a priority of the federal government. Second, reform in this area requires agreement among the federal, provincial, and territorial governments, and such consensus is not easily achieved. Third, the legal profession and the private insurance industry benefit financially from the current system and oppose the move to a comprehensive scheme. Both groups have strong input into the political process, and the federal government is reluctant to antagonize them (Muszynski, 1989). Groups representing people with disabilities are less powerful and less well organized.

Since 1980 groups representing people with disabilities have emphasized the rights of these individuals to employment and adequate income. Federal and provincial governments have attempted to change attitudes of employers and remove environmental barriers to the employment of those with disabilities by focusing on anti-discrimination legislation and individual rights (e.g., the *Employment Equity Act* and the *Canadian Human Rights Act*). Thus, an individual who has been denied accommodation can file a complaint under the *Human Rights Act*. However, people with disabilities face non-accommodating environments, inadequate income support, lack of opportunities and little political influence, all of which stems from an unfair distribution of societal resources, not from discrimination (Bickenbach et al., 1999). The focus on attitudes and individual rights ignores the barriers to employment erected by economic structures and power relationships. People with disabilities have little power in the current economic structures; power lies with the owners of capital. The majority of jobs are in private companies, and the owners/managers of these companies are free to choose who will fill these jobs. People with disabilities do not possess the right to a job (Russell, 2002).

High poverty and unemployment rates among people with disabilities persist. Louise Arbour, UN High Commissioner for Human Rights, claims there is a long history of reluctance to give effect to economic, social and cultural rights in Canada. She recounts the story of the 1948 Universal Declaration of Human Rights and notes the reluctance of Lester Pearson, Secretary of State at the time, to endorse the Declaration. The reason for this was misgivings among the political elite about the inclusion of socio-economic rights in the Declaration. There have been important advances in the recognition of social and economic rights in Canada over the decades, but Arbour (2005) states that there is still a reluctance to give effect to economic, social and cultural rights. The 1982 *Canadian Charter of Rights and Freedoms* created the possibility for articulating the rights-based component into public policy decisions. Section 7 of the *Charter* guarantees "the right to life, liberty and security of the person", which is originated from the UN Declaration of Human Rights, "freedom from want". However, 22 years of *Charter* litigation reveal that both litigants and the courts are reluctant to deal directly with the "claims emerging from the right to be free from want". Civil and political rights have been championed by Canadian courts when the federal government uses repressive criminal legal power. But there is considerable hesitation regarding social, economic and cultural rights and protecting weaker parts of the population on grounds other than discrimination (Arbour, 2005).

CONCLUSION

Disability is associated with medical and economic challenges and with discrimination issues. The medical model of disability focuses on medical needs. The economic model stresses participation in the form of economic integration; and the thrust of the socio-political model is the attainment of rights and equality (Bickenbach, 1993). There is, however, no coherent set of goals underlying federal or provincial employment and income programs. The development of disability policies related to income and employment in Canada were part of the evolution of collectivist social policies, which were aimed at distributing the country's wealth more evenly. During the 20th century, incremental development of particular programs to deal with specific demands (e.g., the needs of injured workers) led to an array of fragmented policies and programs (e.g., the CPP and Canada Assistance Plan), which are part of general welfare state policies that are also fragmented (Crichton & Jongbloed, 1998). The cause of a person's disability not only directly affects the amount the person gets but also the type of assistance with regard to returning to work or finding new work he or she receives. Furthermore, individuals with some form of insurance, such as motor vehicle, workers' compensation, or private disability insurance, receive more help than those without.

In the 1980s disability groups advocated for co-ordinated, equitable income and employment policies that would treat individuals according to need rather than cause of injury. These efforts were unsuccessful partly because the federal and provincial governments could not reach an agreement and partly because lawyers and insurance companies benefit from the current system and oppose policy reform (Muszynski, 1989). It is unlikely that these policies will be reformed in the near future.

In the 1970s people with disabilities proposed a socio-political definition of disability that emphasized their rights to employment, adequate income, transportation and access, and placed the responsibility for meeting these needs on the social environment. Federal and provincial governments have attempted to change attitudes and improve job opportunities for people with disabilities by enacting legislation (e.g., *Employment Equity* and *Canadian Human Rights*) that reduce discrimination and establish individual rights. However, there has been little progress in the areas of income and employment. The focus on individual rights ignores structural barriers exit in areas such as private ownership or social economy (Russell, 2002) and the maldistribution of power and resources (Bickenbach et al., 1999). Canadian society is willing to protect vulnerable parts of the population from discrimination, but reluctant to give effect to economic rights.

16

Income Support and Employment Policy Reforms in the Early 1990s: Implications for People with Disabilities and Their Organizations

EMILY BOYCE, WILL BOYCE
AND KARI KROGH

INTRODUCTION

Community-based disability organizations provide many essential supports and services to people with disabilities. At the same time, it is people with disabilities who drive these organizations through their paid work and volunteer activities. In the early to mid-1990s, policy reforms in the areas of employment and income support negatively affected many individuals with disabilities, and this impact extended to organizations dependent on their participation. Simultaneously, federal policy reforms decreased the capacity of many community-based disability organizations to meet the emergent support and advocacy needs of community members affected by income cuts and employment restrictions. Policy changes affecting both individuals with disabilities and their organizations reflected broader ideological and structural shifts in the Canadian political economy at this time, from Keynesian welfarism (based on the notion of citizenship rights to government and social supports) to neoliberalism (based on the notion of individual responsibility for self-provision and the primacy of macro-economic needs over social needs) (Coburn, 2004).

This chapter describes and analyses key policy reforms during the early to mid-1990s that worked to the disadvantage of people with disabilities, both directly and as a result of challenges arising for disability organizations. Changes to employment insurance, employment training, CPP Disability benefits and supports, and provincial social assistance are examined for their impacts on the livelihoods, capacities and choices of people with disabilities, both as individuals and as participants in community-based organizations. Shifts in federal policy affecting disability organizations' funding and programming are described and discussed for the challenges they posed to the ability of organizations to meet consumer needs, and to remain community-based and consumer driven.

POLICY AFFECTING INDIVIDUALS
WITH DISABILITIES

(a) Employment Insurance

People with disabilities who can work have traditionally relied on employment as their income source, and those who are unable to work have tended to rely on disability benefits and social support programs. However, structural disadvantage in the labour market often leads to a significant number of individuals being unable to secure employment despite their desire to do so. The 1991 Health and Activity Limitation Survey (HALS), for example, found that 11% of people with disabilities who were not in the labour force demonstrated both a willingness and an ability to work in the paid labour force (Fawcett, 1996). Barriers to labour force participation included personal limitations, material inaccessibility of many workplaces, the lack of structural supports in communities and workplaces to enable labour force participation, and discrimination on the part of employers (Fawcett, 1996).

Between 1991 and 1995, the percentage of people with disabilities who were employed decreased, and this rate was consistently lower than that of people without disabilities. In 1991, 48% of people with disabilities were employed, compared to 73% of all adults without disabilities (Canada, 1998). In 1993, the number of people with disabilities who were employed all year was a mere 39%, compared to 75% of people without disabilities; and in 1995, these numbers fell to 31% for people with disabilities and 75% for able-bodied individuals (CCSD, 2002). The 1993/1995 statistics are based on people aged 35–49 who are high school graduates. Thus, these statistics are not directly comparable to the 1991 statistics on "all adults".

In the context of the early to mid-1990s, economic recession and lower overall employment rates in Canada led to increased disadvantage in the labour force for people with disabilities. Correspondingly, the need for unemployment insurance rose. However, the federal Unemployment Insurance (UI) program was restructured in ways that tightened eligibility requirements and reduced payouts, leaving many people who were previously eligible for insurance with lower or no benefits. In 1990, 88% of all unemployed workers were eligible for benefits. By 1997, under the new Employment Insurance (EI) program, only 43% of all unemployed workers were eligible (NCW, 1997). The total number of EI beneficiaries was 1.4 million in 1992, and it declined steadily over the following years, hitting a low of 0.9 million in 1997 (Lin, 1998). Additionally, between 1992 and 1999, total EI transfer payments to individuals showed a steady decrease. In 1992, benefit payouts totaled $19 billion; by 1995, this had dropped to $13 billion (Lin, 1998); and by 1999, benefit payouts had fallen to just over $10 billion (Statistics Canada, 2001b) — almost a 50% decrease in just seven years.

Changes to EI in the 1990s worked to the systematic disadvantage of people with disabilities. In 1993, applicants were automatically disqualified for benefits if they voluntarily left their jobs, or were fired, or refused suitable employment. This amendment reflected the belief that such persons were somehow "undeserving" of employment insurance. In some instances, these were people with disabilities who were forced to leave places of employment "voluntarily" due to changes in their physical capabilities, structurally inaccessible work environments, harassment or discrimination.

Other amendments to the program included the toughening of entrance requirements (i.e., being accepted to receive EI benefits) and reductions in amount or duration of benefit entitlements. By 1996, eligibility for EI and the amount and duration of benefits had become totally contingent on the number of hours worked and the amount of money earned prior to making a claim for benefits. People who worked in part-time, temporary and/or low-paid jobs — out of necessity or because of discrimination in the labour market — were disproportionately disadvantaged by these amendments. Likewise, repeat claimants were less likely to receive benefits. Many people with recurring disabilities or medical problems and have to make repeat claims were disqualified from the EI program.

In sum, the early to mid-1990s saw fewer jobs available in the labour market, with stricter eligibility requirements and cutbacks to EI entitlements. These resulted in people with disabilities having fewer opportunities to earn income of their own and decreased access to income replacement programs previously available under EI. Ineligibility for EI also led to the disqualification of many people with disabilities from employment and skills training programs, which were previously available to them under the old UI program. This issue will be discussed further in a later section on organizational-level policy.

(b) Canada Pension Plan (CPP) Disability Benefits

The CPP Disability benefits also underwent regressive reforms and cutbacks in the same period. The federal government greatly reduced its overall expenditures on CPP Disability benefits through minimizing pension rate increases and stricter eligibility requirements.

Between 1995 and 2000, total expenditures on adult disability benefits through the CPP declined from $2.9 billion to $2.5 billion; likewise, the number of adults receiving benefits decreased from 300,000 to 283,508 in the same period (Torjman, 2002). Persons receiving CPP Disability benefits also received little real increase in their benefits in the past decade. In 1989, the maximum monthly rate for benefits (calculated in 2002 dollar value) was $940.43. In 2002, this had risen to $956.05 — a mere increase of about 15 constant dollars in 13 years (HRDC, 2002b). These maximum rates are based on a flat rate component plus an earnings-related component. In reality, the average benefit is about $200.00 lower, because many people earn less than the maximum earnings-related contribution. The average monthly rate across Canada, which also has not undergone substantial change in the past decade, was $719.93 in 2002 (HRDC, 2002c). These rates seem inadequate when other factors are taken into account — such as low employment rates, the costs of living, extra costs of having a disability, cuts to health and community services, and cuts to social assistance and other disability supports.

Beyond fiscal cutbacks, eligibility requirements for CPP Disability benefits also became more stringent. Prior to 1997, workers who had paid into the CPP for two of the last three years, or five of the last ten years, would qualify for the disability benefit. Amendments to the CPP in 1997 changed the contributory period to four of the last six years — a requirement much tougher to meet for those with chronic health conditions.

Although the *CPP Act* continued to define disability as a condition that is "severe and prolonged" for "long continued and of indefinite duration", making a person "incapable regularly of pursuing any substantially gainful occupation" (R.S., 1985, c. C-8, s. 42(2)), the new contributory requirements clearly conflicted with this definition and worked to disqualify people from benefits. First, people's disabilities could be deemed insufficiently severe and prolonged *specifically because* they have been able to work in four of the past six years. Second, many people who did have prolonged and severe disabilities would not qualify for benefits because they had been unable, as a result of their disabilities, to fulfill the contributory requirements in four of the past six years. In sum, people with recurrent or episodic problems would neither qualify under the definition of disability, nor have met the full contributory requirements.

New adjudication guidelines adopted in 1995 also contributed to the decline in the number of people eligible for CPP Disability benefits. These guidelines used the medical model to determine disability; socio-economic factors as indicators to determine who was in need of benefits were eliminated. The 1995 changes excluded many people whose conditions were not necessarily "medically verifiable", but who may have been able to prove their disability by using their past work history and socio-economic status as indicators. The socio-economic factors worked to include people with episodic conditions, stress-related conditions, mental disorders and environmental sensitivities (Torjman, 2002). In addition to tougher eligibility requirements, new measures for the review of already approved cases were implemented in 1993. People with disabilities were re-assessed over time to see if they still met eligibility requirements for CPP Disability benefits. Between 1993 and 1995, 12,055 people with disabilities underwent re-assessment, and 4,911 beneficiaries were subsequently cut off from benefits. In the last fiscal year of this period, about 23% of people who were re-assessed were deemed ineligible for continued CPP Disability benefits (Torjman, 2002).

On the whole, CPP Disability benefits became less accessible and less adequate as a source of income security in the 1990s. Unable to secure benefits through the CPP, many people with disabilities turned to provincial social assistance and other forms of support.

(c) Provincial social assistance programs

As CPP Disability benefits and EI became more difficult to access, more people were forced to turn to provincial social assistance programs to survive. However, provincial social assistance programs also underwent regressive reforms and had substantial cutbacks to funding, which eliminated many people from the welfare rolls and intensified poverty among those who received social assistance.

These provincial reforms began when the federal government froze monetary transfers to provinces through the Canada Assistance Plan (CAP) between 1990 and 1995, despite rising unemployment rates and increased demands on provincial welfare systems. This meant that provinces ended up putting more money into social assistance than the federal government, despite the cost-sharing arrangement specified in CAP policy. In 1995, the situation worsened as the federal government announced massive cuts to social spending. By 1998, total annual federal transfers to provinces for health care, education, and welfare and social services had decreased by 14% — a drop of almost $4.2 billion in funding per year to provinces (NCW, 1997). In addition, a new controversial "block funding" mechanism called the Canada Health and Social Transfer (CHST) was implemented by the federal government. Under CHST arrangements, block funds are doled out to provinces, and provinces are authorized to spend the funds as they wish on health care, education and social assistance programs. In the welfare arena, this meant the elimination of a common needs-test that was used as a national standard for welfare eligibility, and provinces were allowed to disqualify certain groups of people from receiving welfare.

Between 1995 and 2001, the total number of people on welfare in Canada decreased by 37.8%, with approximately 1.2 million people leaving the welfare rolls (NCW, 2002). Although increasing employment rates played a partial role in this, a more important impetus were provincial cutbacks to social assistance levels, new and stricter eligibility requirements, and the introduction of programs such as workfare, drug testing, and welfare fraud hotlines to cut down on the number of people "abusing" the system. These measures all added to a climate of intolerance, suspicion, and resentment of those receiving social assistance, while intensifying poverty among those in the welfare system.

For people with disabilities on social assistance, these reforms were devastating.

EMILY BOYCE, WILL BOYCE and KARI KROGH

In 1991, 19% of people with disabilities relied on provincial social assistance as a primary income source (Canada, 1998). Although there has been no further national data collection on this issue, it is likely that the number of people with disabilities requiring social assistance increased throughout the early to mid-1990s as a result of unemployment and reforms to CPP Disability benefits and EI. However, the likelihood of them being approved for welfare benefits, and the actual amount of benefits paid out to those on social assistance, decreased dramatically.

The National Council of Welfare statistics, as shown in Table 16.1, reveal that people with disabilities relying on social assistance in Canada did not fare well financially in the regressive climate of the 1990s. They saw the amount of their benefits decrease dramatically through the years, both in absolute terms and relative to the poverty line. For those who did not meet the definition of "disabled" under provincial welfare programs (and were thus only eligible for general benefits as "employable" persons), their financial situation was even worse. In all cases, people relying on welfare as a primary income source lived far below the poverty line, as determined by Statistics Canada's low-income cut-offs, and this poverty intensified with cuts to their benefits.

Table 16.1: Social assistance for persons with disabilities — Average yearly benefits in relation to poverty line in Ontario, Manitoba and British Columbia (2002 Dollars).

	1991	% Poverty Line	2001	% Poverty Line
Disability Benefits				
Ontario	$13,000	75%	$11,446	62%
British Columbia	$10,122	58%	$ 9,522	52%
Manitoba	$ 8,316	49%	$ 7,438	41%
General/"Employable" Benefits				
Ontario	$ 9,220	54%	$ 6,623	36%
British Columbia	$ 7,133	40%	$ 6,251	34%
Manitoba	$ 7,866	46%	$ 5,352	29%

Source: NCW, 2002.

Apart from the inadequate levels of income support, note the difference between disability benefit levels and general employable benefit levels and how disastrous it was to be re-classified as "employable".

In sum, reforms to provincial social assistance programs in the 1990s resulted in fewer people being eligible for welfare and a dramatic decrease in benefits over the years. For people with disabilities, these reforms had a magnified impact. As a social group already predisposed to systemic disadvantage in the labour market, and as a group targeted by EI and CPP policy reforms at the federal level, it became necessary for many to turn to provincial social assistance in order to get by. Simultaneous reforms to these programs worked to the further disadvantage of people with disabilities.

POLICY AFFECTING COMMUNITY-BASED DISABILITY ORGANIZATIONS

Due to these individual-level policy changes, demands on organizations of persons with disabilities increased dramatically in the early to mid-1990s. There was a rise in the need for direct services, as well as increased consumer demands for individual advocacy and support in dealing with government bureaucracies (Boyce et. al., 2000). However, disability organizations experienced a marked decrease in financial resources as a result of government funding cuts to organizations and regressive changes to government programs and departments that supported or funded disability groups. This section explores policy changes that impacted the ability of disability organizations to ensure consumers' needs were met in the time of increased hardship.

The changing social and ideological climate described earlier perpetuated and justified the funding cuts to disability organizations. Increased competition for government funding occurred within the disability community, as well as between disability organizations and other community groups.

On a structural level, a critical reason for the increased competition was the elimination of disability-specific programs and funding sources at the federal level, as well as the assimilation of disability-specific programs into broader government departments. For example, several key changes to disability funding occurred with the creation of Human Resources Development Canada (HRDC) in 1993. First, the Secretary of State (SOS) was dismantled and replaced, in part, by HRDC. The SOS had been responsible for the status of people with disabilities since 1983, and the Disabled Persons Participation Program (DPPP) was under the SOS mandate. Since 1985 the DPPP had doled out approximately $3.2 million a year to disability organizations and community programs aimed at enabling the integration and full participation of people with disabilities in the community. Under HRDC, the citizenship and social development focus of the SOS in general, and the DPPP in particular, changed to an employment focus. By 1995, the DPPP had been cut completely.

Second, the National Welfare Grants program was also put under the HRDC mandate in 1993. This program had previously been operated by the Department of National Health and Welfare, and it funded national disability organizations. In 1995, the federal government announced that funding through the National Welfare Grants program would be phased out completely over a three-year period. In 1998, the Social Development Partnerships Program (SDPP) was established under the mandate of HRDC to replace or "streamline" the DPPP and National Welfare Grants Program. Non-national community-based organizations are therefore unlikely to benefit from this program.

Third, HRDC was given authority over the EI program, whereas the previous UI program had fallen under the mandate of the Canada Employment and Immigration Centre. Under the UI program, $45 million a year had been designated for the Canada Jobs Strategy, which funded employment training and job support initiatives for people with disabilities. Many of these programs were administered by community-based disability organizations. With the introduction of EI, the Canada Jobs Strategy was replaced by the Human Resources Investment Fund (HRIF), with approximately the same budget. However, HRIF programming was much more "mainstream" and was to be administered by the provinces with little involvement of disability organizations. In addition, only people eligible for EI could access HRIF programs, whereas people with disabilities could access Canada Jobs Strategy programs regardless of whether they were receiving unemployment insurance. As described earlier, fewer and fewer people with disabilities could meet the new eligibility requirements under the EI program, and so many people were disqualified from employment training programs they previously had access to under the Canada Jobs Strategy.

Finally, a new HRDC-directed program, the Opportunities Fund (OF), was announced by the federal government in its 1997 Budget, with $30 million a year directed toward assisting people with disabilities in preparing for and obtaining employment. This program, in effect, was meant to replace training programs previously available to all people with disabilities under the Canada Jobs Strategy. The OF was developed in response to the Andy Scott Task Force recommendation that the federal government fill the gap in employment and labour market programming for people with disabilities that was created by reforms to EI and HRIF legislation (Canada, 1996). It was also meant to facilitate greater involvement on the part of disability organizations, in that organizations could apply for project funding in employment training areas.

However, this program did not prove particularly fruitful for many disability organizations. First and foremost, the budget for the OF ($30 million per year) was much less than that of the Canada Jobs Strategy ($45 million per year). Second, the actual involvement of community disability organizations was low, according to respondents in an evaluation administered by HRDC. Respondents from local communities reported that there was considerable reliance on large organizations and very little outreach at the local level. Finally, the OF — with its strict employment focus and emphasis on measurable and direct results — added to an atmosphere in which disability groups felt pressured to gear their mandates exclusively toward employment initiatives if they were to gain funding from the government. Other problems included the fact that people with disabilities could qualify for training through the OF only if they were *ineligible* for EI. This meant that EI recipients had access to HRIF programming, but not to OF programs that actually involved community disability organizations on some level. In addition, disability groups funded through the Opportunities Fund were only allowed to offer services to those who qualified for OF training, and thus had to exclude certain consumers based on government regulations.

In sum, changes to disability-related programming and funding at the federal level resulted in less money to go around, increased competition between community-based disability organizations for funding, and pressures to change mandates or project foci to meet new funding requirements. In addition, organizations applying for, or relying on, provincial or local government funding sources also experienced barriers and cutbacks as a result of the new CHST block funding arrangement. As discussed in the first section of this chapter, the cancellation of the cost-sharing arrangement under the earlier CAP program resulted in the elimination of national standards and a lack of incentive for provinces to put funds into "special interest groups". Due to conservative agendas in many provinces, social welfare and community programs bore the brunt of cutbacks under the CHST. The following section explores the impact of these changes on the ability of disability organizations to remain community-based.

DUAL IMPACTS OF POLICY REFORMS ON INDIVIDUALS AND THEIR ORGANIZATIONS

In the early 1990s, people with disabilities encountered major disincentives to getting involved in disability organizations, both as volunteers and members. Many individuals feared losing their benefits through CPP Disability and provincial welfare programs if they volunteered or participated in their organizations (see Chapter 12). The requirements for receiving disability benefits through the CPP included a proven inability to work and a formal status as "permanently unemployable". Effective August 1995, additional measures were implemented through CPP Disability to eliminate work disincentives, though it is unclear as yet the degree to which work incentives were created. For example, engaging in volunteer activities no longer triggered *automatic* re-assessment, but it was still taken into account during regular re-assessments and initial applications to the CPP. More positive amendments included a three-month trial work period in which recipients continued receiving benefits upon return to the workforce, and a fast-track re-application process was implemented for those who entered but then left the labour force because of recurring problems.

Likewise, in the early 1990s, social assistance programs in many provinces had "unemployability" as a requirement for eligibility. Many people therefore felt at risk of having their benefits withdrawn if they were discovered to be participating — as volunteers, as active members, as participants in political activities, and even as participants in skills training programs offered by the government and/or community organizations (see Chapter 12). Changes to the social assistance programs in some provinces have occurred since the 1990s however. In 1996, British Colombia introduce a new social assistance program (BC Benefits, which included the *Disability Benefits Program Act*) that removed the concept of "unemployability" and, in fact, all employment-related factors from the definition of "person with a disability". In 1998, Ontario introduced the *Social Assistance Reform Act*, including the *Ontario Disability Support Program Act* (*ODSPA*), which also eliminated "permanent unemployability" as a major category of disability. However, eligibility for benefits remains to require one of the following three impairments: (a) inability to attend to one's personal care, (b) inability to function in the community, or (c) inability to function in the workplace. The eligibility requirement is arguably disincentive to work or to community involvement. In Manitoba, eligibility continues to be based on either inability to earn sufficient income or inability to take care of oneself by reason of disability.

Overall, fears about being disqualified from receiving disability benefits could be exacerbated by the fact that systems of surveillance (CPP re-assessments, welfare fraud hotlines, increased monitoring by welfare case workers) were increasingly put in place during this time. These forms of surveillance worked to intensify disincentives to engaging in paid work, volunteerism, or simply being active in organizations for many people with disabilities.

CONCLUSION

This chapter has shown how economic recession, unemployment, and reforms to federal and provincial social welfare policy had negative financial impacts on people with disabilities. Consequently, people with disabilities were far more likely to live in poverty than people without disabilities. In 1991, 21.9% of all adults with disabilities lived below the poverty line, compared to 12.6% of people without disabilities (Fawcett, 1996). The degree of poverty experienced by people with disabilities intensified during the early to mid-1990s, both in urban and non-urban areas of Canada. In 1995, the poverty rate for people with disabilities living in urban areas across Canada was 36.1%, compared to 23.1% of people without disabilities (Lee, 2000).

For people with disabilities, inadequate incomes and financial strain are magnified due to the extra costs associated with having a disability. In 1991, for example, 33% of adults with disabilities reported having significant costs associated with disability that were not reimbursed by any public or private plan (Canada, 1998). Although there is a lack of data tracing these numbers forward in the past decade, surveys of the general population have shown that Canadians are spending more and more on medical products, drugs, and health care services: between 1993 and 2001, total personal health expenditures rose by 37%, from over $18 million to over $29 million (Statistics Canada, 2001c). Given the general rise in private citizens' responsibility to pay for health-related costs, it is

265

likely that individuals with disability-related costs are feeling the financial effects on a magnified level.

Beyond the impact of policy changes on individuals, it is important to emphasize the result of policy changes at the organizational level. Canadian society is known for its volunteerism and emphasis on community systems to provide care and services to those who are disadvantaged. A major advance in this respect is the understanding that disabled persons themselves must participate in these efforts if they are to be relevant, effective and sustainable (Boyce, 1999). Community-based disability organizations have been key players in effectively promoting employment and income support policy in Canada (Boyce et al., 2001). However, their ability to do so has been compromised over the past decade in a number of ways. First, Canadian disability organizations have experienced increased consumer demand for services and advocacy as a result of the reduction in income, services, and benefits for individuals with disabilities. Second, disability organizations themselves experienced drastic losses in government funding and support, resulting in reduced financial resource capacities for serving the disability community. Third, these organizations faced a marked decrease in member participation. This problem arose because of the inevitable intersection between the financial cuts to individual benefits and the budget cuts to community organizations that decreased opportunities for member involvement. Essentially, increased hardships for individuals led to reduced human resource capacity for their organizations. Finally, near total dependence on benefits through mainstream CPP, EI and provincial social assistance programs was accompanied by powerful disincentives to engage in volunteer work, political activity, and training programs. In the context of such limitations, the organizational autonomy of a consumer-based social movement can be threatened with a possible return to styles of "organizations for", rather than "organizations of", people with disabilities.

17

The Canada Pension Plan Disability Program: Building a Solid Foundation

NANCY LAWAND AND RITA KLOOSTERMAN

INTRODUCTION

This chapter will focus on efforts by the Canada Pension Plan (CPP) Disability program over the last decade to support and assist its beneficiaries to return to work. Since the 1990s, CPP Disability's policy framework and instruments have moved beyond passive income support to actively supporting and encouraging clients to work to the level they are able.

A description of the CPP and the disability program will be followed by a profile of the current CPP disability population. A series of return-to-work measures introduced over the last 10 years will be outlined, with some discussion of outcomes.

The chapter will conclude by looking at some policy challenges and at where efforts to address them will be focused in coming years.

BACKGROUND

The Canada Pension Plan (CPP) was introduced in 1966 as a social insurance program with the objective of providing some measure of income protection to Canadian workers and their families against loss of earnings resulting from retirement, severe and prolonged disability or death. The CPP is funded through the mandatory contributions of Canadian workers, employers and the self-employed. The federal government and the provinces and territories are joint stewards of the CPP. Policy changes to the CPP that have an impact on benefits or the financing of the Plan require the approval of Parliament and of at least two-thirds of the provinces representing two-thirds of the Canadian population. The Plan is administered by Social Development Canada (SDC). The program operates across Canada, except Quebec, which operates a similar program — the Quebec Pension Plan (QPP).

The CPP Disability is a component of the CPP that was designed to provide some protection to working Canadians, including the self-employed, against the loss of earnings due to a long-term disability from any cause. A monthly benefit is provided to individuals who have made sufficient contributions to the CPP and who have a severe and prolonged disability that prevents them from working regularly at any job. (Note: Beneficiaries must have a severe and prolonged mental or physical disability as defined by CPP legislation. "Severe" means that the condition prevents the person from working regularly at any type of paid work, and "prolonged" means the condition is long-term or likely to result in death.) A monthly benefit is also available to beneficiaries' children who are under age 18 or between the ages 18 to 25 and attending school full time. A second important role is to help beneficiaries return to work if and when they are able to do so.

Since its inception in 1966, the CPP Disability program has become the single largest public long-term disability insurance program in Canada. It is one component of the disability income system, which also includes workers' compensation (for injury or illness on the job through the WCBs), provincial/territorial income support programs (income and asset-tested), private disability insurance, auto-accident insurance and veterans' pensions. CPP Disability pays benefits to all who are eligible, regardless of income or benefits received from other programs.

In 2003–2004, $3 billion was paid to about 290,000 adults and some 92,000 of their children. During the same period, over 60,700 applications for CPP Disability benefits were received by

SDC. In addition, close to 5,800 appeals were heard by the Review Tribunal and the Pension Appeals Board, the two successive levels of arm's-length appeals bodies to which CPP Disability applicants can appeal if their original application and request for reconsideration (internal administrative review of the original decision) are denied.

PROFILE OF CPP DISABILITY BENEFICIARIES

CPP Disability beneficiaries have severe and prolonged medical conditions that prevent them from working. This is a very stringent test of disability and results in a client population that, for the most part, will not easily be able to leave the benefit and return to regular employment. The beneficiary population is dynamic and has evolved considerably in just over a decade. Between 1992 and 2003, the proportion of female CPP Disability beneficiaries increased from 37% to almost 50% (see Figure 17.1). This reflects in part the growing number of women participating in the workforce, as well as the fact that there are more women of working age with disabilities in Canada than men — 53% compared to 47% — as

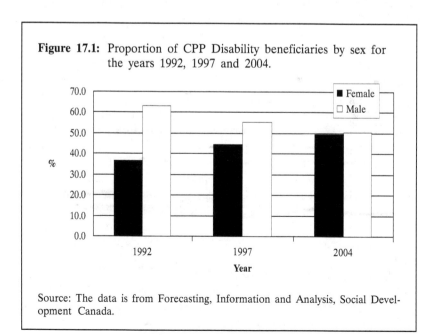

Figure 17.1: Proportion of CPP Disability beneficiaries by sex for the years 1992, 1997 and 2004.

Source: The data is from Forecasting, Information and Analysis, Social Development Canada.

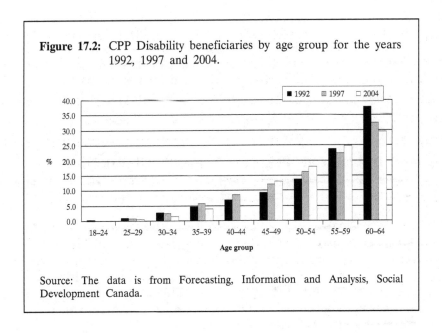

Figure 17.2: CPP Disability beneficiaries by age group for the years 1992, 1997 and 2004.

Source: The data is from Forecasting, Information and Analysis, Social Development Canada.

indicated in the 2001 Participation and Activity Limitation Survey (HRDC, 2003).

As shown in Figure 17.2, the age group structure is also shifting; there are fewer recipients in the 60–64 age group but beneficiaries who are between 45–59 years old are continuing to increase.

The main medical condition of CPP Disability beneficiaries has also shifted over time from a significant concentration in musculoskeletal conditions to an almost equal mix of mental disorders and musculoskeletal conditions. Indeed, those with mental disorders account for one out of four beneficiaries, a doubling of this group since 1992. During the same period there has been a significant decrease in beneficiaries with circulatory system conditions and a steady increase in those with nervous system conditions.

Information on the level of education only started to be collected in administrative data in 2000; however, it does show some very interesting trends, especially in comparison to the Canadian population as a whole. Female beneficiaries tend to be better educated than male beneficiaries; nevertheless, recent CPP Disability beneficiaries continue to be less likely to have post-secondary education than the general Canadian population.

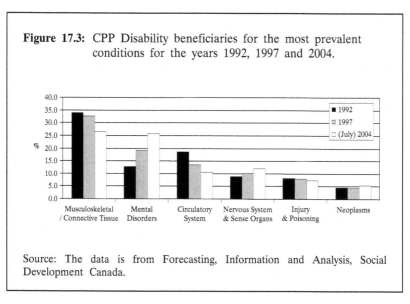

Figure 17.3: CPP Disability beneficiaries for the most prevalent conditions for the years 1992, 1997 and 2004.

Source: The data is from Forecasting, Information and Analysis, Social Development Canada.

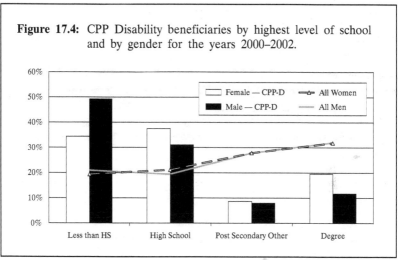

Figure 17.4: CPP Disability beneficiaries by highest level of school and by gender for the years 2000–2002.

Figure 17.5 indicates that CPP Disability beneficiaries are disproportionately represented in semi-skilled trades and unskilled work.

As the profile of beneficiaries changes over time, their potential to return to work also changes. For example, as a greater proportion of beneficiaries have higher education levels and are

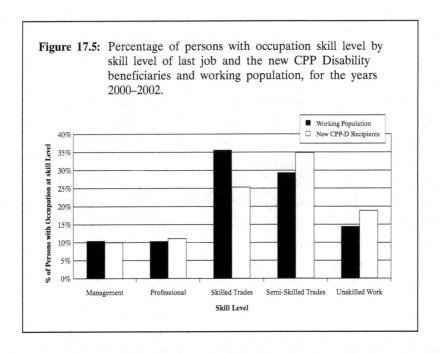

Figure 17.5: Percentage of persons with occupation skill level by skill level of last job and the new CPP Disability beneficiaries and working population, for the years 2000–2002.

younger, there is a greater likelihood they could succeed in returning to work. It becomes increasingly important to develop policies and interventions that are tailored to the needs and aspirations of these clients, notwithstanding the fact that only a very small proportion of CPP Disability clients could be expected to return to work.

RETURN-TO-WORK MEASURES

For many years, there was little interest either from clients or the disability community in active return-to-work measures for CPP Disability beneficiaries. The expectation of the disability community that people with severe disabilities could not work started to change in the late 1980s. The social and economic benefits of assisting disabled persons in making the transition from dependence on income support to the paid workforce were increasingly recognized. Ultimately, it was viewed that this group should be encouraged to be in the labour force to the extent they are able. At this time, there was also a perception of systemic disincentives in the CPP Disability program that prevented clients from making a successful return to work.

While most CPP Disability beneficiaries will likely not return to employment because of the seriousness of their medical conditions, a significant minority will have the opportunity and desire to participate in some form of work activity because it gives them a connection to the community, feelings of self-worth and an improved income. In order to address the employment needs of people with disabilities, the CPP Disability program introduced a series of return-to-work measures, both in policy and legislation, in the 1990s and early 2000s. These measures were developed to help reduce the fear of trying employment and to build trust between clients and the CPP Disability program. Both are essential if clients are to take the "risk" of returning to work.

Early Initiatives

(a) Vocational rehabilitation

A major initiative was the establishment of a vocational rehabilitation component as a regular part of the CPP Disability program. Historically, rehabilitation efforts within the CPP had been minimal or non-existent; it was widely perceived that CPP Disability benefits, once granted, would continue until retirement or death. However, new technology, medical treatments and skills training, as well as interest from clients and the disability community, made it feasible to provide support for selected clients with severe disabilities to become part of and remain in the workforce. In 1991 a pilot project to assess the feasibility of establishing vocational rehabilitation as a regular component of the CPP Disability program was launched.

In 1996, the pilot was evaluated and found to have been successful in assisting clients to return to work, as well as generating savings in foregone benefits payments. Consequently, CPP Disability started to offer vocational rehabilitation services on a permanent basis in 1998. Vocational rehabilitation services are designed to help clients reintegrate successfully into the labour market — either with their former employers or with employers in new fields to which they can adapt their skills and abilities. These services, based on individualized return-to-work rehabilitation plans, are provided to clients who are medically stable and motivated to return to work; they include vocational assessment, planning, skills development and job search assistance.

273

(b) Work incentives

In 1995, work incentives were introduced to address concerns that the CPP Disability program discouraged clients from trying to return to work or attending school by immediately suspending or cancelling their benefits. These policies were established to reflect the realities faced by persons with severe disabilities trying to re-enter the labour force — a process that often required more than one attempt. Clients were allowed a three-month work trial. During the work trial, they could work at a substantially gainful level and still collect CPP Disability benefits. (Note: This means the ability to perform employment that is productive and profitable, as measured in part by a dollar amount which is set annually, and against which a person's earnings are compared. Earnings alone do not determine whether the regular capacity to pursue work exists. Elements of functional capacity and productivity must also be assessed.) If the person can demonstrate the ability to sustain regular work, then benefits are discontinued. Clients could participate in volunteer work or attend school on a part-time or full-time basis without having their file automatically reviewed. Clients who did return to work but found that they could not cope because of the same disability could access a streamlined short-form application.

Recent Measures

In recent years, additional steps have been taken to actively support and encourage CPP Disability clients in their attempts to return to work and provide some of the necessary preconditions for beneficiaries to make the decision to try employment. These initiatives were developed in part to reduce beneficiaries' fear of losing their benefit permanently if they returned to work.

Allowable Earnings

In 2001, an "allowable earnings" policy was approved to specify the amount clients could earn before having to inform SDC ($4,100 in 2005). Prior to this change in policy, clients were expected to inform SDC as soon as they earned any income.

With the allowable earnings policy in place, clients need not report earnings until they reach the annual threshold. The department then reviews their circumstances, offering support to encourage further work activity if appropriate. If the income is earned primarily from sporadic work, and there is no capacity for regular employment, the client's benefits will not be affected even as the threshold is exceeded. This allowable earnings policy is sometimes misunderstood to represent the threshold at which CPP Disability benefits will be stopped. This is not the case, however. A client must be able to earn considerably more than this amount on an annual basis to be considered capable of substantially gainful employment.

An annual CPP Disability client newsletter called *Staying in Touch* was introduced in 2001. The newsletter informs all CPP Disability beneficiaries of relevant issues, such as work incentives, tax measures and any changes made to the program. Regular communications with clients and providing flexible return-to-work measures have been essential features of the CPP return-to-work strategy.

(a) Automatic reinstatement

The government has also introduced the automatic reinstatement of CPP Disability benefits. This provision was established in recognition that fear of losing the security of a monthly CPP Disability benefit is a significant disincentive for individuals with severe disabilities who are thinking about trying employment. Automatic reinstatement allows CPP Disability clients who leave benefits for work to have their benefits reinstated if they are unable to continue working because of their disability. This new entitlement is available for two years from the time the benefit is ceased. A simple confirmation from the client and his/her doctor will serve to restart CPP Disability benefits. The amendment to the CPP is in force starting 31 January 2005.

The introduction of automatic reinstatement in the CPP provides a considerably higher level of support for clients returning to work than previously available. Now, CPP Disability beneficiaries who wish to try employment will have a reliable safety net that significantly reduce their fear of having their benefits stopped. It is expected that more clients will be encouraged to try to return to work as a result of this change to the legislation. This provision is of particular benefit to clients with episodic or cyclical conditions, as there are no limits on the number of times a client can try to return to work and subsequently request a reinstatement of benefits.

While the automatic reinstatement of non-contributory disability benefits is common, automatic reinstatement is an unusual feature of a contributory program. In effect, it suspends the contributory requirements of the program for this particular group of people for a fixed period of time. As a result, there are two groups who can qualify for a CPP Disability benefit: those who meet the contributory and other eligibility criteria, and those who, having been on the benefit, try return to work but fail in the first two years.

(b) Return-to-work continuum

Furthermore, CPP Disability is looking at other ways to offer more services to a wider range of its clients, who have diverse needs and may not require the intensive interventions provided by vocational rehabilitation services. Some beneficiaries will have an improvement in their medical condition or their ability to adapt to their limitations; they will return to work and no longer require income support. Others, without any change in their medical condition, will adapt to their limitations and want to participate in a minimum level of work. Still others, particularly those with severe illnesses of a cyclical nature, may alternate between periods of work activity and periods when they cannot work — periods when income support is required.

To improve its support to CPP Disability clients wishing to re-enter the workforce, a new continuum of return-to-work services has been implemented. These services range from timely advice and information to clients who are able to re-enter the labour force on their own, to assessment and intensive vocational rehabilitation services for those with the potential to return to work but who require additional supports. Using a case-management approach, SDC will partner with other programs and services to help clients with the full range of available resources.

(c) CPP Disability beneficiaries who returned to work

In a given year, less than 1% of beneficiaries leave the CPP Disability rolls because of a return to work. In 2003–2004, for example, 1,240 CPP Disability beneficiaries reported a return to work and had their benefits stopped. In the same year, 120 CPP Disability clients completed vocational rehabilitation and their benefits ceased.

The fact that these numbers are very small is not surprising given the clientele of CPP Disability. In addition, the process for getting onto CPP Disability benefits can sometimes be lengthy if appeals are involved. Those who have invested a significant amount of time and energy to get onto CPP Disability are unlikely to start trying to go back to work shortly after their benefits begin.

A study done a few years ago showed some interesting characteristics shared among those who do return to work. Data from 6,270 CPP Disability beneficiaries whose files were reviewed between January 1997 and July 2000 because they reported a return to work were analyzed. Those most likely to return to work during that period tended to be younger — 72% were under the age of 50, with the average age being 47. A significant majority (80%) had been CPP Disability beneficiaries for less than five years. This suggests that the longer people are on benefits, the less likely they are to attempt to return to work. This is in keeping with much of the literature on the work patterns of persons with disabilities. Those who returned to work also tended to have higher levels of education — about 40% had a university or college degree. Clients with a mental disorder, a musculoskeletal condition or neoplasm (cancer) were the most likely to return to work.

Compared to the CPP Disability population as a whole, those who returned to work were younger and more likely to be single; those with mental disorders and cancers returned to work in greater proportion than their representation in the beneficiary population. Of all clients ceased due to a return to work between January 1997 and July 2000, almost 83% had not returned to disability benefits by 2002.

In a recent evaluation of the CPP Disability vocational rehabilitation program, participants showed some similarities to those who returned to work on their own. The evaluation looked at 230 CPP Disability vocational rehabilitation clients who started the program in 1998. The average age of participants was 40.3 years at the commencement of their vocational rehabilitation, and 35.7 years when they started receiving CPP Disability benefits. Almost two-thirds of participants had a high school diploma. The main medical conditions of participants were mental disorders, musculoskeletal disorders, diseases of the nervous system or sense organs and medical conditions associated with injuries and poisoning (HRDC, 2003).

The findings in both studies are consistent with some of those found in other studies of disability benefit recipients who returned to work. Work done in the United States on Social Security Disability Insurance recipients showed that those who were younger, more educated, single, male and received lower benefits had higher probabilities of returning to work than other claimants (Hennessey & Muller, 1995; Muller, 1992). A more recent study using data from the New Beneficiary Follow-up Survey found that those most likely to work were younger and had higher levels of education.

Also, the likelihood of working was the same across the range of medical conditions (Schechter, 1997). Another interesting finding from this survey was that most of the beneficiaries who worked did so for reasons of financial need, and they did not attribute their decision to an improvement in their health.

The CPP Disability vocational rehabilitation evaluation also analyzed some of the outcomes of the participants to determine whether the program was fulfilling its objective of providing reasonable, cost-effective vocational rehabilitation measures to its clients in facilitating a return to substantially gainful employment. The results of the evaluation show that people who complete vocational rehabilitation are 56% more likely to stop requiring CPP Disability benefits compared to a group of clients who did not complete vocational rehabilitation, either because they dropped out before the end of the program, or they never took vocational rehabilitation but were assessed as likely to return to work, or they had reported employment earnings. Among all who stopped receiving CPP Disability benefits, those who completed vocational rehabilitation were 15% more likely to move into employment and 11% more likely to move into substantial gainful employment in comparison to those who did not complete vocational rehabilitation. This includes those who dropped out before the end of the program and those who never took vocational rehabilitation but were assessed as likely to return to work as well as those who had reported employment earnings (HRDC, 2003).

Evaluating the outcomes of some return-to-work measures is not feasible because of data limitations or the fact that not enough time has passed in order to do a proper assessment. This is certainly the case for automatic reinstatement. In addition, better instruments are needed to measure the outcomes on CPP Disability beneficiaries. For example, it has not been possible to identify the clients taking advantage of allowable earnings. A comprehensive evaluation encompassing all of CPP Disability's return-to-work measures will be conducted in 2007–2008. By then the new automatic reinstatement provision will have been in force for a couple of years and the return-to-work continuum fully developed. A closer look at the CPP Disability beneficiaries who take advantage of the return-to-work measures will also be undertaken to identify the beneficiaries that are likely to return to work and why, and what contributes to their success.

POLICY CHALLENGES

The CPP Disability program faces a number of challenges in helping beneficiaries return to work if and when they are able to do so. The key challenge is how best to encourage more beneficiaries to take advantage of the existing work incentives. The experience of less than 1% of disability beneficiaries leaving the benefit rolls for employment is stubbornly consistent across several OECD countries with different disability income systems and return-to-work programs (OECD, 2003, p. 58). Many countries are grappling with the problem of encouraging larger numbers of disability beneficiaries to try employment.

CPP Disability clients have been returning to work on their own, but not always successfully. The ability to work despite having a severe medical condition is a phenomenon that policy-makers need to understand better in order to design more effective incentives. It is important to be able to identify which beneficiaries are likely to return to work and why, so that policies and supports can target those beneficiaries and help increase the number of clients who successfully return to work.

(a) Need for better data on outcomes

A significant barrier to better policy research is insufficient data and evidence to indicate whether return-to-work measures in place are having an effect on individual clients. For example, the allowable earnings policy only requires CPP Disability clients to inform SDC of their earnings above a certain level ($4,100 in 2005). There is no clear picture of how many beneficiaries are currently working at a minimum level. In addition, the Department has little information on long-term outcomes for clients who take advantage of the various work incentives within the CPP Disability program. Do they come back onto benefits? Which incentives helped them to be successful? Privacy considerations make it difficult to track clients' outcomes after they leave benefits, which in turn reduces the ability to adjust return-to-work policies accordingly. It is anticipated that it will be easier to track outcomes as clients start availing themselves of automatic reinstatement.

(b) Redefining success

We also recognize that there is a need to redefine success, as it cannot always be measured by a return to regular employment. Even if some beneficiaries cannot earn enough to leave the benefit, it can still be a positive outcome. This is especially true if beneficiaries experience an improved quality of life through more active involvement in the community by volunteering, attending school or increased social interactions. Perhaps the time is right to look beyond the usual success indicator — the number of CPP disability beneficiaries who leave benefits — and recognize social participation as valuable both in itself, for individuals who do not have the capacity to work, and as a stage on the path to full-time work for those where employment may be a viable long-term objective. This is a future direction that SDC will be exploring.

(c) Do work disincentives still exist?

Another challenge is the possible disincentive caused by the fact that clients lose all of their CPP Disability benefits at once if they have demonstrated that they are able to work regularly. This is in essence a 100% effective marginal tax rate. Although the CPP Disability program's work incentives may encourage CPP Disability beneficiaries to work part time, the 100% effective marginal tax rate may discourage people from working beyond the amount that would result in their CPP Disability benefits being discontinued. People need to earn a significant amount to ensure that full-time regular work is more attractive than part-time/occasional work and collecting CPP Disability. By quickly reinstating them onto benefits, automatic reinstatement provides a safety net for former beneficiaries who find they cannot continue working because of a recurrence of their disability. It is hoped that this new provision will help alleviate the fear associated with leaving a secure though small monthly benefit.

(d) Interaction with other disability income programs

The interaction between CPP Disability and other disability income programs presents another challenge in supporting clients to return to work. A CPP Disability client could be receiving a benefit from the WCB, a provincial/territorial income support program, or a private disability insurance plan. These programs have their own rules and policies with regard to returning to work and do not necessarily co-ordinate their efforts where joint clients are concerned. This challenge is being addressed by developing closer partnerships with the other disability income providers, especially provincial/territorial income support programs for persons with disabilities.

(e) What works best for whom?

One of the biggest challenges is to develop the right set of work incentives and employment supports for the CPP Disability population. As discussed above, this population has unique characteristics and requires a unique set of supports. The CPP Disability population is older, has less formal education and comes from lower skilled occupations than the Canadian working-age population. Most have had a prolonged absence from the workforce (two years or more) and are likely to have severed the relationship with their employer. Many are unable to return to their former type of employment due to medical considerations, and they require re-training or re-orientation of their work possibilities.

More analysis is needed to determine whether the current set of measures is suitable for all CPP Disability clients. It is likely that those with mental disorders need different supports than those with chronic/cyclical physical disabilities, and those with lower skills require different supports than those with more transferable skills. What are the best return-to-work tools for the different sub-groups of CPP Disability beneficiaries? In addition, knowing what works and what does not work is essential in developing appropriate return-to-work measures for persons with disabilities. A recent Parliamentary Committee report on CPP Disability recommended that the federal government create the necessary conditions to permit SDC to implement pilot projects to test a variety of approaches with the various disability income providers to determine what works best in overcoming return-to-work barriers (Canada, 2003c). SDC is in the process of exploring this possibility.

FUTURE DIRECTIONS

To address the policy challenges mentioned above, SDC is undertaking a number of activities. First, it will continue to monitor the results of new initiatives. Part of this work will involve coming up with the appropriate tools to measure outcomes for clients who try to return to work and determine the work incentives they have taken advantage of. Now that automatic reinstatement has come into effect, data will be systematically collected on beneficiaries who return to work and leave benefits for employment to help determine what supports were helpful and to evaluate longer-term outcomes. The CPP Disability program will continue to research and develop additional return-to-work measures. An online self-assessment screening tool for CPP Disability beneficiaries is currently being developed. It is designed to assist them in understanding their level of preparedness or readiness to return to regular employment following a prolonged absence from the workforce.

Another focus of SDC's efforts will be on examining how research on disability prevention and early intervention can be incorporated into CPP Disability's return-to-work measures. Research demonstrates that early intervention can reduce the severity of certain disabilities and significantly improve employability for most. This results in improved quality of life for persons with disabilities, savings to income support programs, increased tax and other revenue, reduced health costs, and protection/retention of human capital. More research and demonstration are needed to determine when and how to effectively intervene with working-age adults while they are employed (or self-employed) but are developing a significant disability, so that their diminishing or reduced capacity to work will not lead to permanent job loss and dependence on disability benefits.

As stated earlier, a number of areas will require ongoing monitoring and analysis. For example, are beneficiaries modifying their behaviour to remain on benefits? Are they maintaining their earnings below $4,100 because they are afraid that reporting earnings above this amount will result in their benefits being ceased? Evidence from other countries that shows earning thresholds can result in individuals limiting themselves to part-time work (OECD, 2003; Seebohm & Scott, 2004). The issue of possible behavioural effects of CPP Disability's return-to-work measures needs to be explored through research. In addition, further analysis is needed to uncover what works best for which group of clients. The research and analysis will help the Department to develop more flexible return-to-work measures and make work a possibility to an even larger portion of the CPP Disability population.

CONCLUSION

It is a significant challenge for CPP Disability beneficiaries to return to work. They have severe and long-term disabilities that limit their ability to work regularly. In addition, they also face a number of barriers to employment, including an erosion of skills due to an extended absence from the workforce, finding employment that accommodates their disability, and obtaining the necessary supports to make employment a viable option.

About 1,400 beneficiaries leave benefits per year. Although the numbers are not unexpected, they also do not tell the whole story about the effect of policies and legislation which have been aimed at encouraging CPP Disability clients to return to work. In some cases not enough time has passed to know the outcomes of the initiatives (such as automatic reinstatement). It also takes time to overcome the legacy of mistrust and apprehension that beneficiaries have of dealing with income support programs. Fear of financial and emotional risks associated with the benefit system can be strong deterrents to seeking employment.

The return-to-work measures put into place by CPP Disability have attempted to build a solid foundation of trust and communication. Progress is being made, but it will take time before the message filters through to current and new CPP Disability beneficiaries that doing some work is allowed (and even encouraged), and it will not result in the immediate ceasing of benefits and that a safety net is available for those who do not successfully transition from benefits to employment.

Although the work capacity of CPP Disability beneficiaries is limited, it is hoped that the more recent return-to-work measures will double or triple the number who leave benefits for employment. At the same time, it will be important to build social participation into the list of positive outcomes. With the right level of support, work is an option for many CPP Disability beneficiaries and it will enable them to fully realize their potential, play a more active part in society, and become increasingly independent.

18

Education and Training: A Focus on Inclusion Initiatives

VIANNE TIMMONS

INTRODUCTION

This chapter focuses on initiatives to support the inclusion of children and adults with disabilities in education and training. Inclusion is defined as all people in a given community having the opportunity to learn, play and work together, regardless of their handicaps or difficulties.

The chapter first examines the inclusion of young children with disabilities, then inclusive education practices with school aged children and, finally, presents information related to support for training for employment.

In Canada, early childhood education and care fall under provincial/territorial jurisdiction, not federal. Since each province and territory has its own policies and practices that pertain to the education of children with disabilities, there are significant challenges in identifying the initiatives concerning the inclusion of children young children and school aged children.

INCLUSION INITIATIVES FOR THREE AGE GROUPS

Inclusion of Young Children

The federal government oversees programs in early childhood for Aboriginal communities, the military, and new Canadians (Childcare Resource and Research Unit, 2001).

We do know that the rate of disability among young children is lower than the rate of disability in adults. This discrepancy has to do with diagnosis, identification challenges, and the acquisition of disabilities after birth (Canada, 2000a).

Childcare practices vary from licensed daycares, home care, and nannies to family supports. In the briefing notes in *Early Childhood Education and Care in Canada 2001: Summary*, it is noted that "research indicates that the quality of much of Canada's available regulated child care is less than exemplary. In any case, the majority of young children are cared for in private unregulated arrangements while their parents are at work" (Childcare Resource and Research Unit, 2001, p. 1).

For children with disabilities early intervention programs are critical. Irwin, Lero and Brophy (2004) state that

> [h]igh quality programs are important for all children. And children with special needs most certainly benefit much more in programs that not only provide opportunities for social interaction with others, but also afford them opportunities to develop their skills and abilities in stable well-run programs that are attentive to their needs and their parents' concerns. (p. 3)

They list the critical elements that are needed to promote high quality inclusion practices in community-based child care programs:

* Directors' and early childhood educators' knowledge of and training in inclusion;
* Their attitudes;
* Their access to a range of resources and supports;
* Their leadership; and
* Policies that support inclusive practices.

Timmons (2005) identified the importance of family involvement in any educational programs. Despite active family involvement is critical for the child's success, families of children with special needs in Canada face extraordinary pressures in supporting their children. *Young Children with Disabilities in Canada — An Overview* (Canada, 2002a) reports the following:

- One in five young children with disabilities lives in a lone-parent family.
- Among preschoolers with disabilities in two-parent families, less than half have both parents in the paid labour force.
- Almost a quarter of children with disabilities live in low-income families.
- Children with disabilities rely on parents to take on multiple roles of therapist, teacher, playmate and advocate, in addition to providing physical care.
- Parents of children with special needs report high levels of stress.

For families with young children with special needs, it is critical that they have access to high quality child care programs which are inclusive settings to ensure maximum development for their children.

The federal government has committed to developing a national child care policy in its 2004 Budget. This commitment should see a new era in child care programs and services in Canada.

Education of Children with Disabilities

Recent research by Willms (2002) found that heterogeneous-grouped children experienced higher educational gains than homogeneous-grouped learners. There is support in the education sector for inclusive education, and many provinces have policies that support inclusive practices; however, it is not consistent across the country.

There remains in Canada a tension between special education and inclusive education (Crawford, 2004a,b). Although many jurisdictions have policies that seem to favour inclusive practices, the special education infrastructure appears unchange and the disconnect between policy and practice remains.

Crawford (2004b) notes a shift to more inclusive practices in recent years, as evident by the increase in the number of children with disabilities being educated in the regular classroom. However, many children in Canada are still educated in segregated settings, and each province has a very different picture of inclusive education practices.

The impact of inclusionary practice was evident in a presentation by the Canadian Education Statistics Council at a Canadian Ministers of Education meeting on 1 March 2004. This presentation

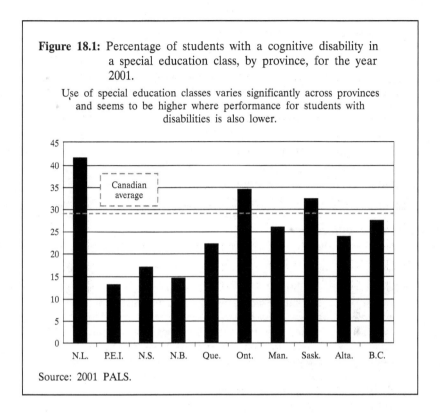

Figure 18.1: Percentage of students with a cognitive disability in a special education class, by province, for the year 2001.

Use of special education classes varies significantly across provinces and seems to be higher where performance for students with disabilities is also lower.

Source: 2001 PALS.

provided a national overview of education of children with special needs in Canada.

The provinces espouse inclusive education as the preferred option; but as can be seen from the graph shown in Figure 18.1), this is not always in practice. Crawford (2004b) writes that

> ... although Ontario's policy, [legislation] and infrastructure [are] quite extensive, the Human Rights Commission (2003a) reported that 'stakeholders continue to express concerns ... [and] report that special education practices and procedures in school settings at the local level are not consistent with the Ministry of Education's own directives....' (p. 23)

Within provinces there are often inequalities. Crawford (2004b) points out that from district to district and even school to school there may be different resources, policies, and/or practices for children with special needs.

Timmons (2003) identifies leadership at the school level as central to the promotion of inclusive practices:

> A school climate that promotes inclusive practices will not develop without leadership; the kind of leadership that sets up an enabling environment with mentorship and collaborative opportunities for staff. (p. 31)

There is little training for administrators in promoting and supporting inclusive education initiatives as the majority of graduate programs for administrative leadership do not have course content in this area. It is a challenge for an administrator to find information and knowledge on how to move his/her school toward an inclusive environment.

Crawford (2004b) summarizes the Canadian scene:

> While Canadians face many challenges to gaining information and knowledge about how students with disabilities are faring in primary and secondary educational arrangements, there is an increasing shift to regular classroom placements for children with disabilities, although a small yet fairly consistent proportion of students with disabilities are mainly in special program placements. Despite progress in moving towards more inclusive education arrangements, it is difficult to move that agenda forward in the special education policy and program framework that continues to prevail widely in Canada. (p. 38)

There is no panacea to this problem. It will take a co-ordinated effort by the Ministers of Education across Canada to develop a framework that promotes a consistent approach to inclusive education. Although there seems to be a varied approach in Canada, inclusive education practices here are far more advanced than in many other countries. For example, Ireland and the United Kingdom have a comprehensive system of segregated schools, and the move toward accountability and published school achievement scores have derailed the inclusive education movement. Canada has an opportunity to emerge as a leader in inclusive education as it has emerged as a world leader in human rights.

In the Aboriginal communities in Canada there are additional problems that compound the challenges of inclusive education. A high turnover of staff, English as a second language issues, cultural differences, professional development opportunities, and lack of specialized support in rural and remote northern communities add many more dimensions to the inclusive education movement (O'Donoghue, 2001). The separate education funding program through Indian and Northern Affairs gives autonomy to many band schools. It is a challenge to gather information on the policies and practices of inclusive education in these communities due to the autonomy they have.

Canada is a country with a vast land mass and diversity of races and cultures. The country is truly multi-cultural, with only 19% of Canadians reporting Canadian as their ethnic origin. Seventy-seven percent of Canadians live in cities, and 3% of Canadians are Aboriginal. The combination of cultures and languages creates challenges in the educational system (Timmons, 2003), and yet Canada's challenges are also its strengths. Canada is a country of diversity with an excellent educational system that can present itself as a leader in the inclusive education movement.

Employment and Services for Adults

Having a disability in Canada increases the chances that a person will live in poverty and experience unemployment. This is a challenging area to describe as

> ... it is complex in that the constellation of programs around disability must come into focus at the federal and provincial/territorial levels: counselling, information, education, training, income security, disability supports, human rights measures, measures for employers and a range of other measures. (Crawford, 2004a, p. i)

The provincial/territorial ministers responsible for social services released a document in October 1998 called *In Unison*. The document called for policies and practices that would enable the full participation of people with disabilities in Canadian society, and there were objectives that focused on employment:

* Reduce reliance on income support programs;
* Promote access to training programs available to all Canadians;
* Increase availability of work-related supports;
* Encourage employers to make appropriate job/workplace accommodations; and
* Promote work and volunteer opportunities for persons with disabilities.

Following the *In Unison* document was the *Social Union Framework Agreement* (SUFA) of 1999, which in many ways mirrors the intent of the document. The SUFA highlights the principles of equality, fairness, rights and dignity of women and men, and their diverse needs (Crawford, 2004a).

In a document on benefits and services for persons with disabilities (Fawcett et al., 2004), it is noted that 57% of adult Canadians with disabilities require some type of aid related to their disability, and approximately 70% need support for daily living. Among those who required aid devices, approximately two-thirds have their needs met. Support for daily living is notably inadequate as 70% of adults who receive help identify it as free or volunteer, with the free support provided primarily by family and/or friends. The more severe the disability, the higher potential there is to have needs unmet.

One challenge that was highlighted in the above report was the lack of knowledge about where to get information on programs that provide support. Twenty-five percent of adults with disabilities who stated they did not have their needs met also stated that they did not know how to get information on supports available for their needs. In this report the following conclusions were made:

- The report found that those most likely to live with unmet needs are:
  □ people with severe disabilities;
  □ those with low incomes;
  □ those of working age; and
  □ those who require high-cost items (e.g., electric wheelchairs, scooters, and lifts).

- The likelihood of having your needs met also relates to the nature of the disability. With respect to numbers, close to half of those with unmet needs require an aid/device to assist with mobility (this is largely due to the high prevalence of this disability type), but the rate of unmet needs is highest amongst those with speech and learning disabilities.

- Overall, two-thirds of adults who require some type of aid/ device have their needs fully met; one-quarter have their needs partially met; and close to 1 in 10 have none of their needs met.

- The rate of unmet needs is higher among those with severe disabilities, especially those living below low-income cut-off levels (LICO).

- There are large areas of unmet needs for those on welfare (e.g., 56% for aids and 45% for assistance with daily activities). Those who are employed are the least likely to report unmet need for aids, devices and support with daily activity.

- Cost concerns are the main reason for unmet needs, and cost affects persons with severe disabilities the most.

- While cost is the greatest barrier listed with respect to the acquisition of required supports and services, a substantial proportion of individuals note that a lack of information about where to obtain supports and services plays a major role in their unmet needs. Seventeen percent of individuals report that they did not know where to obtain aids/devices.

- The report also finds the requirement for support with activities of daily living is very high. Currently, these supports are being provided primarily through informal sources such as families and friends. This suggests that the formal infrastructure for such supports, such as organizations and agencies, can adequately service only a small fraction of those in need (Fawcett et al., 2004).

The report, *Advancing the Inclusion of Persons with Disabilities* commissioned by Social Development Canada (SDC), stated:

> By the year 2020, Canada may have a shortage of nearly one million workers. The country must take measures now to make sure all working-age adults have the right skills and opportunities to participate fully in the economy and in society.
>
> Skill development and learning are among the government's highest priorities for Canadians, especially for persons with disabilities and Aboriginal people. Research shows us that persons with disabilities still encounter a number of barriers to full participation in learning and work. Women with disabilities and Aboriginal persons with disabilities face even greater challenges that others. (HRDC, 2002a, p. 31)

Crawford (2004a) calls for the government to engage partners in a concerted effort for promoting policies and practices that remove barriers to participation in employment and society. He goes further by challenging the government to have people with disabilities integrated in "policy development, program design, monitoring and evaluation as they have particular insight into how best of intentions can go awry when translated into public policy and program terms" (p. 121).

CONCLUSION

Inclusion initiatives related to very young children and school-aged children, as well as supports for training and employment of adults, have been discussed. The Council of Canadians with Disabilities (2003b) is calling for a Disability Related Support Plan for Canada. They applaud government reports such as *In Unison*; however, they lament the fact that there is no action plan associated with these reports. They argue this support plan is essential because Canadians with disabilities experience isolation and ongoing dependence.

The supports that they are calling for, they state, must be provided for "individuals across the lifespan — children, youth, adults and seniors". In 2004 the Federal-Provincial-Territorial Ministers responsible for Social Services in Canada released a report called *Supports and Services for Adults and Children with Disabilities in Canada: An Analysis of Needs and Gaps*, where they vowed to work together to ensure that people with disabilities can participate in all aspects of Canada society. The intent is there, as it has been for many years. The challenge is that there seems to be a paralysis with regard to action. Hopefully, the next decade will have less rhetoric and more action. Despite the commitments made, people with disabilities continue to be marginalized in our communities.

19

Structural Determinants of Access to Health Care for People with Disabilities

INTRODUCTION

Our own research and that of others (Hanson et al., 2003; Iezzoni et al., 2002; McColl et al., in press) shows that while people with disabilities are relatively high users of health services, they also have significantly more unmet health needs than comparable members of the general population. Even after controlling for the effects of health and chronic disease, disability still represents a significant source of unmet health needs. American statistics at both the national and local levels confirm that people with disabilities are high-end users of health services, including both institutional and community services (Batavia & DeJong, 2001; Bockenek, 1997; DeJong, 1997; Meyers et al., 1989). Bockenek (1997), Hanson and colleagues (2003) cite national survey data in the United States as evidence of difficulties experienced by people with disabilities in attaining appropriate and accessible health services.

This chapter aims to

1. Provide background on the issue of access to health services for people with disabilities;
2. Identify policies that affect access issues for people with disabilities in Canada;
3. Identify barriers and gaps in policy that inhibit access to health care; and
4. Analyze existing policies for improving access to healthcare for people with disabilities.

BACKGROUND

The literature points to a number of inequities in the delivery of health services to people with disabilities, and particularly to difficulties for people with disabilities in accessing health care (Anderson & Kitchin, 2000; DeJong, 1997; Rosenbach, 1995; Rummery, Ellis & Davis, 1999; Turner-Stokes et al., 2000). Groch (1991) found that while many public institutions, such as hospitals, used the rhetoric of "responding to the needs of disabled citizens", few were actually committed to ensuring the rights of those citizens.

There are a number of possible reasons why people with disabilities may experience unmet needs and have problems gaining access to adequate levels of health care. The recent joint report of CMA/CNA suggests that the reasons for decreased access to health services are: the increased prevalence of chronic diseases, shortages of health professionals and general underfunding of the health care system. However, people with disabilities encounter a number of other very specific barriers that impede their access to health services: physical barriers, transportation problems, financial barriers, organizational and administrative considerations, provider knowledge gaps and attitudinal problems in attempting to access information of health and preventive services (Bowers et al., 2003; Iezzoni et al., 2000).

The most straightforward definition of access refers to the presence or absence of *physical barriers*. This is arguably also the easiest to remedy; yet, it remains a significant problem for people with disabilities when accessing health care. Stairs, cramped quarters and narrow doorways are all examples of physical barriers to just getting in the door of a doctor's office. These barriers send a further message that the practice may not be accessible to people with disabilities in subtler ways. Turner-Stokes and colleagues (2000) found problems of physical accessibility even within a general hospital, and they concluded that there was a need for greater awareness of disability within the health care system. Little wonder then that access problems are experienced in the broader community health care environment. In a survey of medical offices in Texas, Grabois, Nosek and Rossi (1999) found that 18% were not compliant with requirements of the *Americans with Disabilities Act*. Forty percent required patients to bring their own attendant with them if they needed assistance in transferring or moving; 19% examined their patients in their wheelchairs, rather than on an examining table; and 61% had office equipment that they knew to be inaccessible. Recent Canadian data show that while 74% of doctors said their offices were accessible, only 40% of their patients with spinal cord injuries agreed (Shankardass & Bugaresti, 2004). Twenty-seven percent said they were not satisfied with access to their doctor's office, and 33% were not satisfied with health care accessibility in general. Only half of the doctors' offices surveyed were compliant with the CMA guidelines for universal access (Jones & Tamari, 1997).

Although not strictly within the purview of the health care system, *transportation problems* are cited in virtually every study as one of the most significant barriers experienced by people with disabilities in attempting to access health care (Bockenek, 1997; Starfield, 1997). Undoubtedly, this refers not only to transportation itself, but to a variety of logistical considerations that make a simple trip to the doctor an ordeal for someone who is not independent in getting around in the community. Transportation issues are beyond the scope of this work; however, they must be mentioned, given how pervasive they appear in the literature.

Another reason that access to health care may be a problem for people with disabilities is the assertion by several researchers that there are *financial disincentives* in the system for doctors to take on patients with disabilities. Maguire and associates (1998) study "carving out" of high-risk patients from practice rosters in the United States, and they list 41 conditions, among them many disabling conditions, where there is evidence of systematic carving out of complex patients from caseloads or rosters. Veltman et al. (2001) and Chesson and Sutherland (1992) offer evidence of doctors in the United Kingdom refusing to take on patients with disabilities because of the service demands they typically represent. Seventeen percent of Veltman's disabled sample had trouble finding a family doctor, and 9% felt that they had been refused service because of their disability. Twenty-two percent of doctors in the survey conducted by Grabois, Nosek & Rossi (1999) admitted that they preferred to refer disabled patients to another doctor rather than take them into their practice. According to Iezzoni et al. (2002), people with disabilities require more of the doctor's time than non-disabled patients for a number of reasons:

- history taking is often lengthier and more complex because of the overlying impact of the disability on presenting the health complaint;

- people with disabilities often need more time and assistance with transferring and dressing in order to be examined;

- positioning for examination may require more logistical considerations; and

- if there is any degree of cognitive impairment, communications may generally be more time-consuming and demanding. Regardless of the compensation system, high-intensity patients make it difficult for doctors to achieve efficiency targets and maximize economic benefits in practice.

Whether capitation, managed care or fee for service, research has shown that people with disabilities can be systematically disadvantaged when seeking health care (Beatty et al., 2003; Iezzoni et al., 2002; Safran et al., 2002).

With regard to *organizational considerations* for patients with disabilities, these may include such things as the presence of trained staff to provide personal assistance to disabled patients in the waiting room, in the office and in the examining rooms. Full and equal access may require doctors to make home visits, to offer telephone advice, or to undertake other accommodations for which they are arguably not compensated, and that they would not extend to their non-disabled patients.

Another obstacle to accessible health care for people with disabilities is the level of *knowledge* possessed by most practitioners about disability in general, and about specific disabling conditions and their natural history, complications and secondary conditions (DeJong, 1997). Sanchez (2000) found that knowledge and expertise regarding the health care issues of people with disabilities was far from acceptable among providers of health services. Knowledge about common health problems that are associated with particular disabilities was very poor. To complicate matters, there appeared to be a denial of lacking expertise, to the extent that some professionals claimed expertise that they did not possess. Iezzoni et al. (2002) note that technical quality of care was significantly worse for patients with disabilities than it was for non-disabled patients in a large population-based sample. While it is unreasonable to expect that a doctor with one spinal cord injured patient will be an expert on spinal cord injury, it is also unacceptable to suggest that such patient should settle for a compromised standard of care. The answer is not simply to expect more of particular health professionals, who are currently stretched to the limit to provide service in a constrained environment. Rather, the solution probably lies in exploring alternative models of service delivery that overcome these problems. Lishner et al. (1996) suggest several models that might be explored: outreach, mobile service, telemedicine, case management, networking and shared care. In addition, interdisciplinary models of health care alluded in earlier chapters may also provide some effective options.

Finally, perhaps the subtlest barrier, and yet arguably the most pervasive, is *attitudes* toward disability and health. Sanchez and colleagues (2000) observed that even in the current era of heightened awareness of the need for accessible services, attitudes of providers toward people with disabilities remained a significant deterrent to good quality care. Problems of insensitivity and ignorance were compounded by the perception among providers that they were already doing all that was necessary. Unfortunately, negative attitudes among physicians have been shown to mirror those of society in general, creating real obstacles for people with disabilities (Antonak & Livneh, 2000). Negative attitudes among physicians have several notable consequences on health service delivery to this population, and they have been shown to

- affect the opinions of the public, hospital managers, other health professionals and medical students on health-related issues (Paris, 1993; Tervo et al., 2002);

- influence the allocation of funds to research and health care improvements that would benefit people with disabilities (Claxton, 1994; Paris, 1993); and

- have significant ramifications for responsiveness to treatment and reintegration into society for persons with a disability (Mercer at al., 2003; Paris, 1993).

In addition to these negative impacts, unrecognized prejudices can also influence physician judgments and interventions, which have profound effects on the treatment process (Duckworth, 1988). According to Sanchez and colleagues (2000), the issue of physician attitudes is further complicated by a prevailing perception that attitudes are already all that they should be.

A number of authors noted that people with disabilities reported they felt significantly disadvantaged in their interactions with health service providers because of negative attitudes about disability. Iezzoni et al. (2002) found that interpersonal aspects of care were significantly worse among people with disabilities, who reported feeling rushed and dismissed, resulting in a lack of confidence in the process of care. Veltman et al. (2001) surveyed people with various disabling conditions about their experiences with the health care system. They found that 27% felt rushed, 17% felt their doctor didn't listen, 10% felt devalued by service providers, and 19% felt the service they received was inadequate. They also found that those with deteriorating conditions were most likely to be dissatisfied.

Negative attitudes toward disability can take on a number of different forms. The simplest is the view that a person's disability is a negative trait (Tervo et al., 2002). Slightly subtler, but equally troublesome for a disabled patient, is the view that the disability is "abnormal". Veltman et al. points to an interesting paradox that is often expressed by people with disabilities when recounting their experience of talking to health service providers. Whereas 20% of their sample felt that doctors were insensitive to the impact of their disability, another 20% felt that doctors were *over*sensitive to the disability. That is, they felt that the doctors tended to attribute everything to the disability and perhaps not explore new complaints as thoroughly they should be. Iezzoni et al. (2002) attribute discordant expectations between physicians and disabled individuals to how extensively the disability affects various aspects of life, the individual's perception of his or her health, and even the relationship between disability and life expectancy.

In summary, the literature on access to health services for people with disabilities arises mainly out of the American experience, and it is only partially applicable to the Canadian situation because of differences in payment and delivery of health care in Canada. In the remainder of this chapter, we examine structural determinants and barriers to access to health services; we also explore policy alternatives and implications at the federal, provincial, regional and professional levels.

POLICIES ON ACCESS TO HEALTH CARE FOR DISABLED CANADIANS

In order to provide a detailed examination of policies relating to access to health care for people with disabilities, we have undertaken an extensive review of policy-related documents that met the following inclusion criteria:

- They had either direct or indirect implications for policy governing access to health services;

- They could be classified as either health policy or disability policy;

- They were either actual legislation or regulations, or commissioned reports, or program directives and policies, or sanctioned guidelines;

- They were enacted or written between 1990 and 2005, with the exception of several documents from the 1970s and 1980s that are still influential, in particular, the federal and provincial health and human rights legislation; and

- They corresponded to one of the jurisdictions under consideration: federal, provincial, and regional/municipal.

The documents included in the analysis are listed in Table 19.1. Although we recognize that there may be provincial and regional differences in policy and its application, the project has focused on one jurisdiction at each level. This analysis uses Ontario as the example of provincial policy and southeastern Ontario/ Kingston as our regional example. This document review benefited from the input of an expert panel composed of representatives of federal and provincial governments, consumer representation, and health policy experts.

Barriers and Gaps in Existing Policy

(a) Federal

With regard to the federal level of jurisdiction, the most basic assurances of equality of access to health services are provided by the 1982 *Charter of Rights and Freedoms* and the 1985 *Canadian Human Rights Act*. Two sections of the *Charter* are pertinent here: Section 7, which assures everyone the right to life, liberty and security; and Section 15, in which people with disabilities are explicitly named as one of the five groups afforded assurances of freedom

Table 19.1: Documents and sources considered in policy analysis.

	Documents and Sources
Federal	Romanow Report (2002) Kirby Reports (2002) Advancing the Inclusion of Persons with Disabilities (2004) Future Directions (1999) In Unison (1998) Canadian Human Rights Act (1985) Canada Health Act (1984) Canadian Charter of Rights & Freedoms (1982) The College of Family Physicians of Canada (CFPC) Canadian Medical Association (CMA)
Provincial	Accessibility for Ontarians with Disabilities Act (2004) Ontarians with Disabilities Act (2001) Ontario Building Code (1997) Regulated Health Professionals Act (1991) Health Care Accessibility Act (1990) Health Insurance Act (1990) Ontario Drug Benefit Act (1990) Ontario Human Rights Code (1990) The College of Physicians and Surgeons of Ontario (CPSO) Ontario Medical Association (OMA) Education Future Physicians for Ontario (EFPO) Council of Ontario Faculties of Medicine (COFM) Ontario Provincial Coordinating Committee on Community and Academic Health Science Centre Relations (OPCCCAR) Ontario College of Family Physician (OCFP)
Regional/Local	Primary Health Care: Models and Initiatives (2004), Southeastern Ontario District Health Council Kingston, Frontenac, Lennox & Addington Health Unit Accessibility Plan (2003, 2004), City of Kingston

from discrimination. The *Human Rights Act* similarly states that "all individuals should have an opportunity equal with other individuals to make for themselves the lives that they are able and wish to have, and to have their needs accommodated" (The preamble). Also included is a piece of case law that arose as a *Charter* challenge and was expected to have dramatic implications for access to health (and other public sector) services by people with disabilities; yet, in the intervening seven years, it has apparently had little impact.

One additional piece of federal legislation shaping access to health services for people with disabilities is the 1984 *Canada Health Act*. In this Act, the conditions for federal transfer payments for health are set out, among which are comprehensiveness, accessibility, transferability and universality. The definition of "reasonable accessibility" in the *Canada Health Act* requires equal access for everyone, provided that services are available. The accessibility criterion was designed to refer primarily to economic barriers to access, and, to a lesser extent, to physical, attitudinal and expertise barriers.

A number of federal government reports also shape policies of access to health services for people with disabilities. Since the mid-1990s, the Office for Disability Issues in the federal department of Social Development has conducted federal-provincial-territorial consultations and released a number of reports that set out a vision and direction for disability policy in Canada. The first report, *In Unison* (Canada, 1998), did not mention health services explicitly but referred to a constellation of disability supports, including those offered by the health care system. The second report, *Future Directions* (HRDC, 1999a), referred explicitly to prevention and health promotion, and outlined areas for development to improve the health of people with disabilities. The most recent report, *Advancing the Inclusion of Persons with Disabilities* (SDC, 2004a), reported on progress on the disability agenda as well as the performance of the government's disability-related programs and services. It listed the six measures that included disability supports, skills development and learning, employment, income, capacity of the disability community, and health and well-being.

Two major recent reports (Kirby, 2002; Romanow, 2002) on the present state and future prospects of the health care system in Canada coincidentally focused on its sustainability. The Romanow report dealt in detail with access but, in referring to the situation of people with disabilities, delegated consideration to provincial and regional health authorities.

(b) Provincial

At the provincial level, not surprisingly, the policy-relevant documents are dominated by legislation. In Ontario, legislation exists that governs health care and services to people with disabilities. First and foremost, the 1990 *Ontario Health Insurance Act* sets out the terms under which individuals are insured for hospital and medical expenses, and doctors are compensated for the provision of those services. There is also legislation governing a number of other health-related issues, such as the regulation of health professionals (including family physicians), drug benefits and human rights (e.g., 1990 *Ontario Drug Benefit Act*, 1991 *Regulated Health Professionals Act*; 1990 *Human Rights Code*).

In 2001, Ontario proclaimed the *Ontarians with Disabilities Act, 2001* (ODA) (tabled by the Ontario Ministry of Citizenship & Immigration). The Act promotes accessibility for people with disabilities and requires all recipients of public funds to prepare accessibility plans, including school boards, colleges and universities, municipalities, public transportation organizations, and hospitals. Doctors' offices, however, are exempted from consideration under the ODA because they are often housed in private buildings. In spring 2005, the *Accessibility for Ontarians with Disabilities Act, 2005* (AODA) augments the then existing ODA. The new Act extends accessibility requirements to private sector service providers; thus, it will include primary care facilities. While the new AODA overcomes many gaps of the ODA, it has a 20-year implementation time frame; thus, it is unlikely that needed changes will be carried out in the very near future. For this reason, the physical accessibility of primary care continues to be an issue in Ontario. On the other hand, there is no such legislation addressing accessibility in place in other provinces.

In addition, all provinces have been actively involved in recent years in primary care reform, redesign and renewal. Planning documents and reports are included that outline elements, principles, and directions for the development of an accessible, affordable, sustainable system of primary care.

We acknowledged that a considerable number of other provincial legislation is not covered in this policy scan, and they might have an indirect impact on the provision of health services. Following are some examples from Ontario:

- *Compulsory Automobile Insurance Act* in 1990
- *Privacy Act* in 1985
- *Workplace Safety and Insurance Act* in 1997

- *Health Care Consent Act* in 1996
- *Substitute Decisions Act* in 1992

At both national and provincial levels, we also sought documents or policies pertaining to health services and disability from the colleges of doctors and professional organizations, specifically:

- The College of Family Physicians of Canada (CFPC)
- Canadian Medical Association (CMA)
- The College of Physicians and Surgeons of Ontario (CPSO)
- Ontario Medical Association (OMA)
- Educating Future Physicians for Ontario (EFPO)
- Council of Ontario Faculties of Medicine (COFM)

These organizations had relatively little to say about considerations offered to patients with disabilities. The *Canadian Medical Association Journal* published guidelines for office accessibility (Jones & Tamari, 1997), but to date the Association has taken no initiative to adopt or promote these. None of the other professional organizations or licensing bodies had any guidelines or policies.

(c) *Regional/Municipal*

At the regional/municipal level, we considered the Southeastern Ontario District Health Council (SEO-DHC) and the Kingston, Frontenac Lennox and Addington (KFLA) Health Unit. Neither had explicit policy relating to access for people with disabilities. In Ontario, the District Health Councils have no authority over the provision of health services, and they act primarily as advisory and planning bodies. In March 2004, the SEO-DHC released a report of a survey of primary care models and initiatives in the area; however, it made no specific reference to services to people with disabilities. There were no guidelines regarding accessibility for people with disabilities in the criteria for recommendation of new programs being considered by the DHC.

Similarly, there were no special considerations for people with disabilities in accessing preventive services through the Health Unit, such as sexual counselling, family planning, immunization, and domestic health and safety. There was no mention of people with disabilities or their particular issues around fertility, preventive health behaviours, or any other health unit programs.

MARY ANN McCOLL

Policy That Is Enabling

Following an in-depth examination of the policy-relevant documents outlined above, it is clear that there is policy that enables access among people with disabilities as well as policy that inhibits or prevents access at each level of jurisdiction.

In the category of enabling policies are a number of pieces of legislation ensuring equal access and freedom from discrimination for people with disabilities, specifically, the *Canadian Human Rights Act*, the provincial *Human Rights Code*, and the *Charter of Rights and Freedoms*. These laws are intended to militate against systematic disadvantage of particular individuals or groups in all aspects of Canadian society. The *Charter* explicitly mentions people with disabilities among those whose rights must be protected, and the *Canadian Human Rights Act* insists that people with disabilities experience not only equality, but also accommodation of their particular needs. In addition, two test cases (*Eldridge* and *Quesnel*) are cited in which access to health services was challenged by people with disabilities on the basis of human rights. In both, the plaintiffs were successful in requiring the provider to make the necessary accommodations; however, neither has had the precedent-setting effects that were initially anticipated.

Another piece of federal legislation that must be considered enabling is the *Canada Health Act*, which ensures universality and accessibility of health services to all Canadians. According to the universality provision in the *Canada Health Act*, 100% of eligible claimants must be covered by the publicly administered insurer. The universality provision is particularly impressive when one considers the alternative. If disabled people were required to purchase private health insurance, as they are in some countries, they would face with prohibitive premiums because they are considered high-risk patients; most likely, they would be denied insurance for anything related to the disability since it is a pre-existing condition.

All of the statutes mentioned above establish a culture and a set of expectations about access in Canadian society in general, and in the health care system in particular. These same expectations are expressed in the federal documents: *In Unison* (1998), *Future Directions* (1999) and *Advancing the Inclusion of Persons with Disabilities* (2004), all published by the Office for Disability Issues in the federal department of Social Development. These documents outline a framework for disability services and express the commitment to provide appropriate levels of service.

304

Policy That Is Disabling

On the negative side, there are a number of explicit barriers, gaps or omissions in policy that impede access to health services for people with disabilities. At the federal level, the accessibility provision in the *Canada Health Act* is somewhat disappointing in access issues that relate to people with disabilities. Admittedly, the Act is intended to ensure that financial barriers do not impede access to health care; but in so doing, it neglects other types of barriers that particularly affect people with disabilities. It states that "reasonable access" must be provided for medically necessary services. However, it defines reasonable access in terms of "where and as available". It makes no provision for the distribution of physician human resource, physician practice patterns, or other systemic issues around availability that disproportionately affect people with disabilities. Whereas systemic access problems result in delays and inconvenience for many, they literally result in preventing access among disabled people.

Also at the federal level, the Romanow and Kirby reports (both released in 2002) focus on access to the health care system. Regrettably, neither deals adequately with disability, and there is no consideration given to the particular disadvantages that people with disabilities face in relating to the health care system. Given that people with disabilities are disproportionately high users of the health care system, this seems an unfortunate omission indeed.

At the provincial level, Ontario has two pieces of legislation that deal explicitly with accessibility — the 2001 *Ontarians with Disabilities Act* and the 2005 *Accessibility for Ontarians with Disabilities Act*. Both are intended to create an infrastructure in the province to promote barrier-free design and to raise awareness of accessibility, and they should have appeared in the previous section on enabling legislation. In fact, both fail to address primary care directly. The 2001 Act required that all publicly funded services (including hospitals, schools boards, colleges and universities, municipalities and public transportation organizations) prepare annual accessibility plans. However, doctors' offices were exempt from consideration. Although they receive public funds, the premises themselves are in private hands and thus are not required to comply with the Act. The 2005 AODA covers both public and private building and services, and it will rectify this loophole; however, the Act is scheduled to be implemented in five-year intervals over 20 years, and it is unclear where doctors' offices will fall in the schedule.

Another gap in provincial policy relates to compensation models for physicians. Regardless of the model of compensation (fee-for-service or capitation), no consideration is given for patients with extraordinary needs, such as people with disabilities. For example, an office visit may take longer with someone who has difficulty transferring onto the examining table or removing items of clothing, and yet no consideration is given for this in current compensation models. In addition, the fee schedules tend not adequately cover the real costs of home visits, and there is no coverage for telephone consultations, despite both are services that accommodate some of the extraordinary difficulties people with disabilities might have with physical access. Similarly, for doctors who are reimbursed on a capitation schedule, no adjustment is made for disability in the capitation rates. Capitation schedules take account only of age and gender, making someone whose care is more complex than his or her contemporaries an unattractive patient. Together, these provisions act as disincentives to providing service to people with disabilities in a manner consistent with fully accessible care.

Furthermore, the family physician acts as the conduit to many of the disability-related benefits and services required by people with disabilities. Several examples include assessments for parking permits, tax exemptions, insurance claims, equipment prescriptions and support services. Many of these assessments and administrative visits are not covered at all by provincial insurance, and must be paid for out-of-pocket. To the extent that these ancillary services are more likely to be needed by people with disabilities, these types of costs represent a financial barrier to access. No relief is offered by the 1990 *Health Care Accessibility Act*, which refers only to insured services.

As regards the regional or municipal levels of jurisdiction, this is the level at which provincial building codes are typically enforced by building permits, business licences, or occupancy permits. However, building codes only apply to new buildings, or to renovations, alterations or repairs of existing buildings; and furthermore, historic or heritage buildings are exempt. Even if the building code was enforced to the letter, it represents only a minimum standard of accessibility. It does not specifically refer to health professionals, nor does it conform to contemporary standards of universal design.

The municipality surveyed (Kingston, Ontario) had no specific provision for ensuring access for people with disabilities to medical offices. In fact, it had no specific policy except when it applied to their own public buildings. Although a new accessibility plan has recently been released by the City of Kingston, health services are not among the services listed in the report. Perhaps because health services are publicly funded, it is assumed that they are required to be accessible; however, as we have shown, this in not the case for doctors' offices.

The regional level is typically also the level at which health services are planned. Even in Ontario, where the district health councils are not involved in the delivery of services, they are still important players in the planning of health services and health facilities in the region. In our survey, the local DHC had no guidelines or provisions to ensure access for people with disabilities in their planning processes.

Finally, at the professional level, the governance structures that oversee medical practice had nothing to say about expectations with regard to access or service for people with disabilities. They had no education standards about disability, no continuing education programs on disability, no expectations for physical accessibility of practices, and no mention of disability in their disciplinary procedures. Furthermore, there appeared to be no incentives in the system for family physicians to make their practices more accessible. There are currently no programs offering assistance or rewards for compliance with universal design standards or attempts to improve accessibility.

Four Types of Barriers

Going back to our definition of the three aspects of access, it is possible to classify the gaps and barriers in policy according to physical barriers, attitudinal barriers and expertise barriers. Table 19.2, on the following page, summarizes the foregoing discussion in terms of the types of policy barriers and gaps that our analysis identified. A fourth category was included to capture systemic issues that exceeded the boundaries of any of the other three categories.

(a) Physical accessibility

The first of the four barriers considered is the fact that some publicly funded health services are offered in non-accessible premises. For example, community offices of doctors and other health professionals are exempt from existing accessibility legislation if they are not housed in public buildings. Thus, even though they are compensated by public resources, health professionals in private practice are not subject to accessibility requirements imposed on

Table 19.2: List of policy-related barriers to access to health care for people with disabilities.

	Barrier/Gap
Physical	• Physician offices not necessarily in public buildings, therefore not subject to accessibility by-laws; offices often in rented premises, where landlord is not aware of disability or human rights issues • No resources or programs available for renovation, improvements, acquisition of accessible equipment • Building codes represent only minimal standards for accessibility • Transportation and parking a problem
Attitude	• Stereotypes about disability interfere with positive interactions • Conflation of illness and disability; application of medical model to disability • Tendency to over- or under-attribute other health problems to disability
Expertise	• Minimal coverage in medical curricula about disability • Lack of availability of continuing medical education opportunities re: disability • Need for a critical number of patients per year in order to be current/credible in a particular disability area
Systemic	• Maldistribution of health human resources throughout the provinces; extreme shortages in rural and northern areas; particularly disadvantages people who are more demanding to serve, such as people with disabilities; general shortage of family doctors • Practice reimbursement options differentially affect quality and access to service

public services. Furthermore, there appear to be no resources or programs to assist practitioners to make their premises accessible, nor are there incentives in any of the structures governing private practice to motivate them to enhance the accessibility of their facilities. None of the provincial insurance plans, provincial medical bargaining units, national professional associations, or the provincial regulatory bodies have any standards of accessibility, expectations of their members, or programs to enhance accessibility. In other words, there are no structural requirements for accessibility of private health professionals' offices, leaving only a sense of duty to serve disabled patients and to maintain accessible premises.

While the literature suggests that people with disabilities do have expectations with regard to accessibility of health services, to date there has been little systematic expression of those expectations or communication with professional organizations, government bodies or the public at large. Canadian standards and guidelines already exist for accessibility of medical practices (Jones & Tamari, 1997); however, little effort has been made to promote or ensure these to date.

(b) Attitudinal barriers

By far the subtlest of the four barriers discussed is the issue of attitudes toward disability. As in the literature summarized earlier, there are a number of different, even conflicting, attitudes that people with disabilities report as interfering with their access to equitable and appropriate health services. These usually consist of some combination of incorrect assumptions (SDC, 2004b):

* about the origin of the disability;
* about the effects or consequences of the disability; and
* about expectations of people with disabilities.

When and if they occur, these inaccuracies may result in over- or under-estimates of important issues about disability and health. Either way, they result in care that is less than optimal.

One of the most troubling misunderstandings pertaining to disability is the idea that it is an illness. Particularly within the health care system, people with disabilities report that they encounter a conflation of illness and disability, resulting in the pathologization of the disability itself (Australian Institute of Health and Welfare, 2004). This leads to patronizing, disempowering attitudes that, while intended benevolently, can be highly destructive.

Two themes that currently exist in the health care system are likely responsible for perpetuating negative attitudes toward disability. The first was an ethos about physical strength and stoicism that they maintained still pervades the medical profession (Byron & Dieppe, 2000; Mercer et al., 2003). The second was a general inflexibility within the health care system to accommodate patients' needs, as opposed to the needs of the system, organizations, institutions and providers. Byron and Dieppe (2000) noted also that the medical orientation toward the biological sciences may be incompatible with the problems experienced by people with disabilities, many of which have more to do with cultural and environmental factors than with biology.

(c) Expertise barrier

Whereas national statistics tell us that about 10% of adult Canadians (aged 15 to 64) live with a disability, many of those have temporary or mild disabilities that do not potentially compromise their standard of primary care (Statistics Canada, 2001a). A considerably smaller proportion (6% of adults aged 15 and over) have severe physical disabilities, arising from chronic conditions like arthritis, multiple sclerosis, spinal cord injury, or a variety of other major disabling conditions (Statistics Canada, 2001a). These disabilities result in mobility and daily living limitations that may compromise peoples' ability to access health care. Further, this small group may be highly heterogeneous in terms of underlying diagnoses and functional problems. The truth is that most health professionals cannot possibly be experts in the natural history, usual complications, latest treatments, controversial issues and available programs for every disabling condition presented.

There is fairly conclusive evidence in the literature that a significant relationship exists between the volume of a particular problem seen over a 12-month period in a medical practice and the health outcomes achieved by the patients involved. A recent systematic review of 272 studies found few literature disputing this finding (Halm, Lee & Chassin, 2002). The relationship between volume and outcome held at both the individual physician and the organizational level (i.e., hospital or practice). Critical volumes ranged from 10 and all the way up to several hundred, depending on the prevalence and complexity of specific procedures. Although this conclusion usually applies to specific procedures such as surgeries, it supports the notion that it is difficult to provide the best possible care when a condition is rare or infrequently seen. Even if all people with disabilities were considered as a single category, most family practices would arguably not achieve a critical volume.

(d) Systemic barriers

The literature shows conflicting evidence about the extent to which people with disabilities are served better or worse under different practice options and payment schemes, such as fee-for-service, salary and capitation. Although much of the literature in this research is American, it may help to inform our situation.

As shown by Starfield and colleagues (1998), capitation settings afford greater accessibility and availability to patients and are more family-centred. Iezzoni and associates (2002) found that people with disabilities were more likely to see specialists within managed care settings, and that specialists were more likely to be accessible to people with disabilities. Safran, Tarlov and Rogers (1994) found capitation practices to be high on co-ordination, but low on comprehensive service. Overall, Beatty and colleagues (2003) concluded that access to care was better for people with disabilities in managed care than in fee-for-service.

Kroll, Beatty and Bingham (2003), however, noted that satisfaction with care was lowest in managed care for people with disabilities. In a sample of individuals with spinal cord injuries, multiple sclerosis and cerebral palsy, managed care practices demonstrated a lack of disability-specific knowledge and provider competence. Maguire and associates (1998) noted a tendency in capitation practices; that is, because of the way compensation is calculated, practitioners, consciously or subconsciously, engage in "carving out". In other words, access to these practitioners was restricted to patients who would not be too demanding on their practice. DeJong (1997) categorically stated that people with disabilities were disadvantaged in capitation payment systems, which often include disincentives to refer patients to specialists and to serve high-users of service. He advocated specifically for the need to adjust capitation schedules to take account of the needs of high-users. Beatty and colleagues (2003) also found lower use of specialists among managed care organizations for people with disabilities, and that included referrals to rehabilitation specialists.

With regard to fee-for-service practices, Safran, Tarlov and Rogers (1994) found organizational access (ability to reach a doctor, book an appointment, etc.) to be higher than in other types of practices, along with good continuity and accountability. Beatty and associates (2003) also found that fee-for-service practices were more likely to provide access to specialists and to prescription medications. There were more primary care visits, more visits to specialists and diagnostic services, and fewer hospital referrals and repeat prescriptions for fee-for-service versus capitation practices (Gosden et al., 2001).

Finally, salaried-model practitioners have been found to offer more direct patient-care hours than fee-for-service, to work more off-hours, and have higher levels of patient satisfaction and access

(Gosden et al., 2003; 2001). However, continuity of care was found to be better in fee-for-service settings than salaried (Gosden et al., 2001). There were no significant differences in quality of care between the fee-for-service and salaried models (Gosden et al., 2003).

In summary, the literature from other jurisdictions shows that there is no consensus about the model of practice that best serves the needs of people with disabilities. Instead, what is suggested by this literature research and the preceding discussion about expertise is that the best solution is a system that offers a variety of models, providing people with disabilities the same kinds of choices that non-disabled Canadians enjoy.

CONCLUSION

This chapter has examined the policy context for access to health services in Canada. We have looked at three levels of jurisdiction (federal, provincial and regional/municipal), and a broad cross-section of policy, from legislation to program guidelines to position statements. We have shown that while a basic policy framework exists to ensure equality for people with disabilities and access to health services for all Canadians, no specific policy exists to ensure access to health services for people with disabilities. Four types of barriers are revealed by a detailed examination of policy. Physical barriers exist because some community health services are situated in private buildings that fall out of accessibility legislation. Attitudinal barriers exist due to misunderstandings about the relationship of illness and disability. Expertise barriers exist because of the heterogeneity of disability and the depth and breadth of specific knowledge required to provide expert disability health service. Systemic barriers exist as a result in the way health services are funded and distributed.

In Canada, we place great stock in the accessibility of our health care system. It has become, in fact, a feature of our national identity. The largest single sector of any provincial budget is health care, consuming in about 30% of public resources. And yet, some of the most vulnerable of our citizens are compromised in terms of access to health care. There has been some reluctance in the disability advocacy movement to place health care on its agenda. It seemed philosophically incongruous to advocate for more attention from the health care sector while at the same time attempting to distance itself from the medical model. However, this philosophical stance may have inadvertently compromised the health of individuals and groups. Perhaps a more moderate conceptualization of disability can more effectively deal with the "real-life" problems of living with a disability, some of which are undeniably related to health.

20

The Emergence of Self-Managed Attendant Services in Ontario: An Independent Living Model for Canadians Requiring Attendant Services

KAREN YOSHIDA, VIC WILLI,
IAN PARKER AND DAVID LOCKER

INTRODUCTION

For many people living with disabilities, personal assistance or attendant services are essential for their quality of life (Nosek, 1993). In fact, many people living with disabilities would be in institutions if attendant services did not exist. Over the past 30 years, adults with physical disabilities who use attendant services have shown their ability to live independently and take responsibility for

1 We acknowledge the support of the Social Science Humanities Research Council & Human Resources Development Canada in the form of a grant (#817-95-0006) awarded to Dr. Karen Yoshida as principal investigator of the project entitled, "A Case Study Analysis of the Ontario Self-Managed Attendant Services Direct Funding Attendant Service Pilot: Independent Living in Action". This project was funded within a Strategic Grant competition entitled, "Integration of Persons with Disabilities". We also acknowledge information and insights from our many key informants of the study.

all aspects of their daily lives (Working Group of the Direct Funding Pilot, 1993). However, these services had shortcomings in that they were not portable, there were no choice of attendants (e.g., some women had to accept male attendants) and the hours of service were not flexible. This lack of flexibility often meant social restrictions (e.g., no help at work). Many wanted to take more control of their support services by receiving the funds directly, managing and employing their own attendant workers.

The concept of living independently in the community has been central to the discussion of funding for attendant services in the United States and Canada (Driedger, 1989; Shapiro, 1994). Two "early" principles have remained fundamental to the independent living movement: first, people with disabilities know best their needs; second, living in the community requires appropriate supports and services to meet those needs (Zukas, 1979). The concept of independence, from an independent living perspective, also rejects traditional medical definitions of the term — that independence only means someone is "physically capable" to do the activities of daily life. Choice, flexibility and control in services (e.g., attendant services) are central to the independent living movement in Canada (CAILC, 2004); together, they constitute an important form of "independence".

The Ontario Self-Managed Attendant Service Direct Funding Pilot (SMAS-DFP) was a two-year project that began in 1994. It was a response to the demands of Ontario consumers (in Ontario, "consumer" is used to denote the recipient of attendant services) to have choice, flexibility, control and full responsibility as individual employers over their attendant services. The project tested the self-managed direct funding (SMDF) model with a group of 100 people. It was successful, and an expanded government program was implemented in Ontario, Canada in 1998. The unique aspect to both the pilot and, later, the program has been the central role that people with disabilities played in designing, administering and operationalizing the pilot and the full government program. To our knowledge, there is no other government program in the world that is fully administered by people with disabilities.

This chapter first identifies the key social and political forces between 1974 and 1994 that facilitated the emergence, development and achievement of the SMAS-DFP. Key definitions are provided, and the methodology of the study that examined these social and political forces is described. The chapter then presents the study findings, including four pre-existing conditions that created a social and political climate for the SMAS-DFP and five critical factors that moved the pilot forward. Major achievements of the pilot project are highlighted.

BACKGROUND
Key Definitions

The following definitions are essential to understanding the differing forms of service provision in the attendant service field (CILT & Roeher Institute, 1997c):

- Attendant Services consist of self-directed services for people with physical disabilities to assist them with routine activities of daily living. Assistance is provided by another person, and it may include both housekeeping and personal services. The term "attendant services" is used instead of personal assistance or attendant care. In Ontario, the term "attendant care" has been rejected as the word "care" has a medical connotation that is not in keeping with an independent living perspective, and is associated with helplessness, sickness and the inability to manage personal needs (Roeher Institute, 1997a).

- "Consumers" means disabled people who are dependent upon attendant services for their independence.

- Individualized funding is an arrangement for allocating funds to individuals according to their disability-related needs. Individualized funding may flow to individuals through direct funding or to a third party through managed care. Individualized funding is determined on the basis of an individual's needs (Roeher Institute, 1997a; CILT & Roeher Institute, 1997c).

- Self-management refers to people with disabilities who are legally responsible for making their own arrangements for attendant services. Their attendants are their employees.

- Managed care refers mainly to a non-profit organization (i.e., third party) in the community that is run by a volunteer board of directors but receives money from the government with a mandate to manage and provide attendant services. In managed care, a consumer's money goes to an organization, and a consumer contracts with that organization for his/her services. In Ontario, these services have been provided in two settings: (a) support service living units, and (b) outreach attendant services (attendants travel to a home or apartment).

- Support service living units (SSLUs) are leased living quarters, sometimes with a "shared living" component, where attendant services are included in the lease.

- Direct funding means that attendant services funding is funnelled directly to consumers who develop their own service plan based on experiential knowledge of their needs and negotiate the plan and budget with a panel of peers. Upon acceptance as eligible, they are responsible for all aspects of managing their own services (e.g., hiring, training) and must do a financial report quarterly based on generally accepted accounting principles. They register as an employer with Revenue Canada (now Canada Revenue Agency).

Philosophical Orientation

This chapter reports the results of a participatory research approach (Oliver, 1990; Woodill, 1992). Two of the research collaborators are people living with disabilities, and they both were key members of the attendant service user community (i.e., in the design and implementation) pushing for direct funding. They provided key directions for the research project so that it was conducted with an equitable partnership approach (Yoshida et al., 1998).

Case Study Approach

We used a qualitative case study methodology to achieve our objectives. A case study approach is appropriate when the focus is on a contemporary event within a real-life context (Yin, 1994). In our study, there were two sources of data — documents and key informant interviews. The documents collected and analyzed include key, specific SMAS-DF movement materials (e.g., Attendant Care Action Coalition), key general movement materials (e.g., independent living movement, normalization and consumer movement), relevant national and provincial government documents, and conference proceedings. The key informants that were interviewed all had a direct or an indirect role in the emergence of this movement. We used critical ethnography (Denzin, 1994) to analyze these data. Critical ethnography seeks to understand the underlying elements or issues of an event. For the study, we wanted to know the "critical" factors that supported the emergence of the SMAS-DFP at this time.

ANALYTICAL FRAMEWORK FOR SMAS-DFP

Figure 20.1 illustrates the analytical framework for the SMAS-DFP. Based upon our analysis of the data, we believe that the emergence of the Ontario SMAS-DFP came about at that time due to pre-existing conditions and critical factors associated with the process of achieving the SMAS-DFP.

Following were the pre-existing conditions that created a social and political climate for the SMAS-DFP:

(a) Existing social movements and their ideological foci;
(b) Precedents to self-managed direct funding in Ontario;
(c) Prior experiences in the development and governance of attendant services; and
(d) Changes in Ontario provincial health policy and government structure.

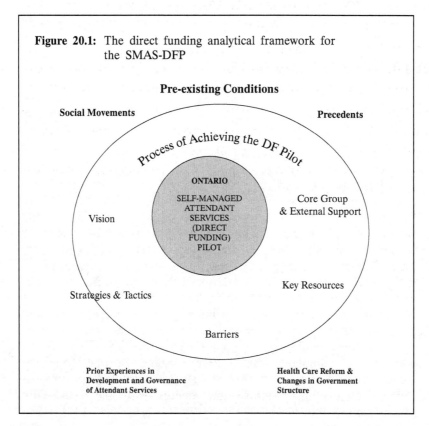

Figure 20.1: The direct funding analytical framework for the SMAS-DFP

Pre-existing Conditions

Social Movements

Precedents

Process of Achieving the DF Pilot

ONTARIO
SELF-MANAGED
ATTENDANT
SERVICES
(DIRECT
FUNDING)
PILOT

Vision

Core Group
& External Support

Strategies & Tactics

Key Resources

Barriers

Prior Experiences in
Development and Governance
of Attendant Services

Health Care Reform &
Changes in Government
Structure

These conditions allowed the SMAS-DFP to move forward with four critical factors that the attendant service user community developed and utilized to promote the pilot:

(a) A strong and clearly stated vision;
(b) Core group, external support, and resources;
(c) Strategies and tactics; and
(d) Dealing effectively with barriers.

The framework's overlapping circles reflect the interaction between the existing conditions and these factors. These relationships will be more clearly articulated in the following sections.

Pre-existing Conditions

(a) Pre-existing social movements and the cumulative vision

The emergence of the Ontario SMAS-DFP benefited from an evolving social environment in Ontario and Canada, which valued the rights of individuals to have control over their lives, to live "independently" in the community, and the equality of opportunity for all citizens. This social climate and vision of independent living evolved from the influence of four other social movements — the movements for de-institutionalization, normalization/community integration, consumerism, and civil rights (DeJong, 1979; Shapiro, 1994). De-institutionalization and normalization have espoused the value of the individual and the right of the person to live outside of an institution in the community with appropriate supports. These social movements were primarily focused on people living with "mental" and intellectual disabilities. While consumerism has focused on the rights of consumers of goods and services, the civil rights movement extended the notion of equal rights and opportunities to all citizens within a society.

The independent living movements in both the United States (DeJong, 1979) and Canada (Driedger, 1989) were influenced by these social movements and have elaborated on the collective vision of individual rights and freedoms. The philosophy and vision of the Canadian independent living movement show strong civil and human rights principles (CAILC, 2004). These principles stress the need for individuals with a disability to take responsibility for their lives and to see themselves as citizens with rights and responsibilities. A guiding principle of the independent living movement is that

319

disability has less to do with functional limitations and more to do with environmental barriers.

(b) Precedents to self-managed direct funding in Ontario

The notion of individualized and direct funding payments for attendant services has been around for more than 20 years (Snow, 1993). The works of Adolf Ratzka of Stockholm, Sweden are most notable in this area. He started the Stockholm Cooperative for Independent Living (STIL) in 1984 (Ratzka, 1993). This organization functioned as a co-operative, and the members were — and still are — able to receive payments directly to choose their own personal assistants. This Swedish initiative was an important catalyst for people with disabilities in Canada, as they began to examine mechanisms for personal support in the form of brokerage or individualized funding.

In 1987, a national symposium on brokerage and individualized funding was held in Ottawa. One focus of this national conference was the need to clarify the use of the term "service brokerage" as professionals tended to use the term with respect to case management and co-ordination. In addition, federal/provincial governments were reviewing the Canada Assistance Plan and the Vocational Rehabilitation Disability Program with respect to increasing support and developing new ways of facilitating community living and employment for people with disabilities (Strachan & Tomlinson, 1987). This symposium created a Canadian context for further discussions on service brokerage and individualized funding.

People with disabilities could draw precedents from existing programs in Ontario and Canada that also made direct payments; for example, vocational rehabilitation and workers' compensation occasionally allowed the person with a disability to purchase services of an attendant directly (Snow, 1993). While these programs were based on very specific criteria, such as entitlement, they are examples in which people could receive money directly from the government to purchase goods and/or services. Other precedents to SMDF could also be found in orders-in-council. Orders-in-council were exceptional provincial government arrangements. They can be utilized to provide funding to a third party agency allowing a few individuals the opportunity to hire their own attendants. Orders-in-council to allow SMDF were implemented beginning in the late 1970s and carried on to the early 1980s.

Another precedent of direct funding that more closely resembled the direct funding model was the Ontario Special Services at

Home Program, which began in 1982. According to a senior government official, this program began after the closure of five institutions for children living with disabilities between 1979 and 1984 as part of the de-institutionalization/normalization movement.

(c) Prior experience with the development and governance of attendant services

Another important pre-existing condition was that people with disabilities and their advocates in Ontario had extensive prior experiences, individually and collectively, in the development and governance of attendant services in the form of SSLUs. The SSLUs were privately leased apartment units with 24-hour on-site attendant services but available within regular, integrated apartment units. The impetus for the creation of these units was strongly advanced as a result of the 1973 conference organized by the Ontario Federation for the Physically Handicapped. At this conference, there were representatives from Toronto and Ottawa, where two of the four demonstration projects would be held. A representative from the provincial government's Ministry of Community and Social Services suggested that the services be without cost to consumers. The Toronto mayor at the time, David Crombie, authorized a City of Toronto task force to examine various aspects of life (e.g., housing, transportation, etc.) for people living with disabilities (City of Toronto, 1973). This task force, with Cheshire Homes Foundation, developed an alternative to institutionalization in the form of four demonstration and support services housing projects — SSLUs.

The success of these demonstration projects, which began in 1974, led to a working group of Cheshire Foundation representatives, service providers, consumers, and government officials from the Ministry of Community and Social Services to establish policies for the SSLUs in 1983 (Ontario, 1983). This partnership experience between the attendant service user community and the Ontario government provided the foundation for future interactions and collaborative work.

(d) Health care reform and changes in provincial government structure

Another important pre-condition was the health care reform that started in the late 1960s and 1970 and ended in 1995 within the province of Ontario. The change in health care reform and the subsequent change in government structure of health care were important to the achievement of the SMAS-DFP. During the Progressive Conservative leadership (1960s–1970s), there was a focus on long-term care needs of seniors and persons with disabilities regarding living in the community. This interest continued during the Liberal government (1985–1990) as they were examining new ways of viewing health. The Liberals' position paper on long-term care, *Redirection of Long-Term Care and Support Services in Ontario* (Ontario, 1991), expressed the need to bring health and social services-related support programs together. The foundation of this reform was provided by the following principles: the right of the individual to self-determination; to promote racial equity and cultural diversity; to promote the importance of family and community; and to promote equitable access to appropriate services. Given this policy framework, the potential for a SMAS-DF type pilot was now viable (Ontario, 1991). This potential was also realized in the form of an explicit verbal commitment in 1990 by the Liberal government to initiating a Direct Funding Pilot.

In 1990, under the Liberal government, the two ministries of Health and Community and Social Services amalgamated the Long-Term Care and Support Services into a single division called the Community Health and Support Service Division. In September 1990, the New Democratic Party won the provincial election. This new government's long-term care report, *Partnerships in Long-Term Care* (Ontario, 1993) was more forceful on the issue of individual rights as "consumer empowerment" and the need for control of services. Most importantly, the issue of a SMAS-DF Pilot was explicitly stated in this document (Ontario, 1993).

The Progressive Conservative Party became the government in 1995. Their view on long-term care was similar to the NDP government's, and there was no specific Progressive Conservative position paper on long-term care. This evolving health care reform and the supporting policy frameworks and documents would be an important anchor upon which the attendant service user community would be able to lobby for direct funding in the face of changes in government leadership.

Critical Factors

Based on our framework, there were five important factors that influenced the process of achieving the pilot. These were vision, core group/external support, key resources, strategies/tactics, and barriers/resolutions.

(a) Vision

As discussed previously, Ontario-based SSLUs were set up first as demonstration projects, with the first units established in 1974. Usually, these services are delivered by agencies that hire and train attendants, and these agencies are controlled by non-users. In many cases, this arrangement works well and the consumers are happy with the arrangement. However, some consumers have found that limits their life choices as they have little or no control over who will come into their apartment, how much attendant time might be available to them on short notice, and the service itself is not portable. Non-portable service means that the consumer can only receive attendant services in the SSLUs. Despite these systems were originally designed with a great deal of input and lobbying from consumers (Ontario, 1983), consumers that used attendants were asking for more responsibility and "risk" in return for greater choice, flexibility and control of their services.

In the early 1980s, due to these limitations, a number of consumers convinced government that they had the right to have individualized attendant services that were different from the SSLU program. Some people whose needs went beyond the number of hours allocated in the program turned to orders-in-council for individualized funding contracts with individuals but administered through a third party (ACAC, 1986).

The orders-in-council became a catalyst for the ongoing movement toward direct funding as an option for Ontario consumers. In 1986, the government started the Outreach Attendant Care Program, which was an option not tied to dedicated housing units but rather a catchment area. Due to the high demand for SMDF orders-in-council, many of these recipients became concerned (although unsubstantiated) that the government was planning to transfer them to the new outreach program (CILT & Roeher Institute, 1997). However, the outreach program did have some advantages. For example, orders-in-council were subjected to yearly reviews, meaning there was no guarantee of monies (ACAC, 1993).

Some order-in-council users, together with consumers who wanted an alternative to Outreach or SSLUs, organized themselves and formed the Attendant Care Action Coalition (ACAC) to lobby for the continuation of the order-in-council mechanism. At that time, ACAC was a predominantly southern Ontario-based coalition, with consumers from Toronto and London and areas between.

In 1988, the Ministry of Community and Social Services responded by contracting a consultant, John Lord, to write a report that would review attendant service programs, produce recommendations for program expansion, and seek a solution to the order-in-council mechanism. The findings from the Lord report, *Independence and Control: Today's Dream, Tomorrow' Reality* (Centre for Research and Education in Human Services, 1988), showed the need to provide a direct funding option.

The ACAC wanted to develop a service delivery model that had as its foundation the independent living principles of choice, flexibility and control on the part of the consumer. The model would value the people who were the attendants and their relationship with the consumer. The ACAC/CILT put forward a document (ACAC, 1993) that was part of the vision for the development of the direct funding model in Ontario. The following principles were central to the vision for direct funding.

- Self-directed attendant services are an essential support to some citizens to enable their full participation in society.

- The enhancement of full participation of the citizen with a physical disability in society must be an important part of the design and the operation of the self-directed attendant services.

- Recognizing that there is a variety of individual capabilities, citizens with physical disabilities have the right to exercise the highest level of choice and control over services, including the administration of resources.

- Recognizing individual lifestyles, citizens with physical disabilities have the right to exercise choice and control over all aspects of self-directed attendant services.

- Self-directed attendant services are a reasonable accommodation that allows the citizen with a physical disability to meet basic human needs and rights; therefore, they should be provided free of cost to the person with a physical disability.

- Self-directed attendant services are different from other services, such as health care and welfare, in that the consumer is the centre of expertise for his/her own services.

- Individuals who perform attendant services are engaged in valued and essential activities and should be paid accordingly.

- The level of resources for the self-directed attendant services must be sufficient to support full participation in society, as determined by the citizen with a physical disability.

- Recognizing the citizen's right to freedom of movement, attendant services to individual persons must be free from ties to specific physical locations and must be fully portable.

These principles guided the vision of SMAS-DFP and provided other consumer and community groups the blueprint for lobbying the government.

The ACAC's vision was supported by the Liberal government's John Lord's 1988 report. To solidify the success, in 1990, the ACAC, together with London Cheshire Homes and the Centre for Independent Living in Toronto (CILT) Inc., organized a provincial conference on direct funding called "Woodeden 90 — Flying On My Own" in London, Ontario. This was the first-ever provincial (Ontario) attendant services consumer conference. The conference brought together consumers and their attendants, researchers, independent living resource centres' members, government officials, service providers and even the Minister of Community and Social Services, the Honourable Charles Beer. The conference allowed government officials to see the strong support and hear directly from consumers about the need for direct funding. Following the conference, the ACAC held a press conference stating that the government would announce a pilot using the Disability Network Television show during this time. This show was a partnership between the Centre for Independent Living in Toronto and the Canadian Broadcasting Corporation. The minister later announced that the government would pilot a project for direct individualized funding for 500 people. A month later an election was called, and the Liberals lost the election and were replaced by the New Democratic Party (NDP) in the fall of 1990.

(b) Core group/external support and key resources

After the Woodeden conference, the CILT staff and Board of Directors made an official commitment to support all activities surrounding the direct funding initiative. The CILT, an established independent living resource centre, was perfectly situated to act as support and later as the lead organization in the direct funding initiative. This was important, as the ACAC was a loosely knit group that did not have the resources to maintain and sustain lobbying efforts. The CILT provided ACAC with vital organizational and resource support (e.g., getting grants, doing mass mailings, or holding meetings without seeking help from a supportive community agency), so that the ACAC could mobilize and organize their efforts. Thus, the ACAC became ACAC/CILT.

With the election of the New Democratic Party, the ACAC/ CILT was faced with having to re-educate and lobby a new government. The CILT's resource base was vital during this time. The CILT had developed a database from the Woodeden conference list, and this allowed for recruitment of and communication with members for renewed lobbying efforts. The ACAC could now mail direct funding information to over 400 individuals and organizations in Ontario. The CILT began to communicate with other centres across the country, asking for advice and support. For example, many discussions were held between the ACAC and the Winnipeg Independent Living Resource Centre where consumers there had extensive experience of lobbying for and administering the supports and resources for a government-run direct funding program.

Between 1990 to 1993, the CILT, the ACAC, the seven members of the Ontario Network of Independent Living Centres (ONILC), and the Canadian Association of Independent Living Centres (CAILC) formed an alliance that eventually developed a proposal for a direct funding pilot. The ONILC was established in 1993 because the executive director of the CILT needed partners to support the direct funding pilot. During the 1990s, there were four independent living resource centres in Ontario. This alliance submitted their proposal to the Ontario Minister of Health, Francis Lankin, in February of 1992. The proposal outlined a 24-month pilot program that would be administered by the CILT and run by the ONILC. This proposal was endorsed by the Consumer Coalition on Long-Term Care Reform, which was established in April 1992. The Coalition consisted of consumer groups such as Persons United for Self-Help (PUSH), Advocacy Resource Centre for the Handicapped (ARCH) and the Association of Community Living. The Coalition was formed to give input into the government's long-term care reform. The ACAC/CILT sought their endorsement as it was a valuable asset at the negotiation table to show that direct funding had a broad cross-disability base of support.

Beside the support from ACAC members, the independent living resource centres, and other disability-related organizations, a few attendant service providers also supported this proposed new model of service delivery. Most notable of this group was Cheshire Homes, London, which provided local consumers with both outreach and SSLU attendants. The Executive Director, Judi Fisher, was instrumental in setting up both Woodeden conferences

(1990 and 1993) along with Jackie Rogers, a long-time Cheshire Homes Foundation member and consultant. They, together with other key people in the London area, used their time and government contacts to help the direct funding initiative. There were other key individuals from within and outside of government who also supported the project. Most notable were individuals from the Ontario Ministry of Health Policy Branch — Long-Term Care Division and the Operations Branch. Their tireless support was vital, and the project would have failed without it. Government bureaucrats within the Ministry of Long-Term Care understood the basic concepts of attendant services and direct funding. Other key government officials either worked within the field or had relatives who were living with long-term disabilities, and the issues of control, choice and being able to live a life of dignity were important to them. These officials were able to champion the cause to senior levels of management within the Ministry. Officials there, again, had personal experience with the existing system, so they understood the direct funding concept and its benefits. A senior service provider was also instrumental in facilitating the directing funding option. This individual used his/her contacts to let the ACAC/CILT know when to ask for a meeting or when to set up a conference, and who to invite. These individuals were pivotal to achieving the direct funding pilot.

(c) Strategies and Tactics

The ACAC/CILT and their external supporters (i.e., government bureaucrats and community advocates) developed a number of strategies to maintain a "visible" profile and to educate government officials on the vision and goals of direct funding. The main strategy was to distribute detailed fact sheets aimed at government officials. These fact sheets stressed civil liberties, the consumer's right to portable, self-managed services that would allow freedom of movement throughout the province and other similar positive messages.

Over the next six months, this lobbying continued in a number of effective ways. One tactic was that the ACAC/CILT devised a mock application for direct funding and sent copies of it out to almost 400 members of the now-growing database of ACAC members. More than 100 applications were returned to the CILT, which were then passed on to the Long-Term Care Division of the Ontario Ministry of Health.

KAREN YOSHIDA, VIC WILLI, IAN PARKER AND DAVID LOCKER

The ACAC/CILT stayed away from demonstrating against the government, and avoided any type of negative advocacy. All of ACAC/CILT's activities promoted the message that directly funded attendant services would allow consumers to contribute to the community and carry out their social responsibilities. In addition, both the ACAC and the CILT presented at the Ontario Standing Committee on Social Development. Specifically, submissions were presented by both Mr. Ian Parker and Mr. Vic Willi to the Standing Committee regarding Bill 43, *The Regulated Health Professions Act*, on 8 August 1991. The main reason for attending was to defend the concept of self-directed attendant services as non-medical. This also raised the profile of the direct funding initiative.

In carrying out these activities, the ACAC/CILT constantly found itself relying on the previous experience of consumers. Consumers involved in the consultations had many years of daily experience (some as many as 25 years) with attendant services' development and governance. Because of this extensive knowledge base, workable solutions were found for the "What if ..." type of questions that were often posed by government and community partners. For example, one question asked early on by government partners and the minister's staff was related to what would happen if persons receiving direct funding were to "spend the money on beer". The ACAC/CILT was able to point out to their government colleagues that there would be a serious consequence to the individual if they chose to spend their direct funding monies in this way. In another example where an individual recipient may not have the money to pay attendants and, therefore, would have reduced service such as not having his/her food cooked, not getting assistance in and out of bed, or not receiving help using the washroom, the ACAC/CILT was again able to refer to the various government programs, such as vocational rehabilitation services and workers' compensation, that used various forms of direct funding without any similar issues (Snow, 1993).

The CILT also pointed out that individuals in society are generally allowed to make mistakes, take risks and even make stupid decisions, so why shouldn't a few disabled persons have the right to benefit from that experience? The emphasis of CILT's message, however, remained focus on responsibility and citizen rights.

One of the most powerful tactics used by the ACAC/CILT was to cite various direct funding programs happening in other Canadian provinces. These provinces had dealt with similar issues that the Ontario government partners were now raising. The ACAC/CILT was able to connect with government officials in other provinces because of their collaborating relationship with the independent living resource centres (ILRC) across Canada. For example, the late Al Simpson of the Winnipeg ILRC connected the ACAC/CILT to the key government official of the Manitoba direct funding program. In turn, the ACAC introduced one of their key government partners to speak with this individual, which started a province-to-province discussion on shared government issues. This was a key turning point as provincial governments rarely "talk" to each other. It was important, for validation purposes, for a provincial jurisdiction to know that a proposed initiative was actually being done in another jurisdiction.

These discussions with the Ontario government were significant also because some of the issues surrounding direct payments to individuals could have powerful consequences. One such issue was the question of "income" versus "services", which had implications at a federal government level. In order for Revenue Canada at the federal level to allow cash payments to an individual to be considered something other than "income", the provincial Ministries of Finance have to ask Revenue Canada for a special ruling. The payments to an individual on direct funding are usually explained by the provincial government as "payments in lieu of service" to which the individual would otherwise be entitled. Dealing with Revenue Canada was clearly beyond the ACAC/CILT's ability, but they were able to alert the Ontario government contacts to the fact that this had to be done and had been done successfully by Manitoba. In the Ontario case, Revenue Canada determined that direct funding payments to individuals would be considered similar to social assistance; thus, the payments should not be reported as "income" but payments in respect of medical expenses.

One other major strategy was the preparation of a comprehensive position paper called *Direct Individualized Funding for Attendant Services: Proposed Model*. A summary letter was prepared by the alliance, consisting of ACAC, CILT and CAILC, in 1992. As a result, the Ontario government set up a steering committee consisting of government policy people, political staff, and users of attendant services from the various consumer organizations involved (consumer partners). The Steering Committee worked on the government policy paper for the direct funding pilot. In October of 1992, a modest grant from the Ontario Ministry of Health was given to CILT to hire the ACAC spokesperson as a consumer-consultant to work full time on the initiative.

Between 1992 and 1994, the SMAS-DF Steering Committee met frequently to work through the policy paper and the setting up

329

of the SMAS-DF pilot. One of the major government requirements that had to be adhered to was the 180-hour per month cap on service. The cap at that time was three hours per day or 90 hours per month (four hours with Ministry approval). The SSLUs provided more than that with no cap. The Steering Committee was asking for six hours per day. Although this limit was felt to be restrictive in certain cases (e.g., for ventilator users), it was a non-negotiable issue for the government at that time. Many drafts of the proposal were developed and circulated before a final proposal was accepted in August 1993. In 1994, a second Woodeden conference was held near London, Ontario. At this conference, the Minister of Health, Ruth Grier, announced that the SMAS-DF pilot would begin in July 1994.

(d) Barriers and resolutions

As with any new vision, the proposal for a new model of service delivery was greeted with skepticism. Part of the reason for this initial caution was that the traditional models of service delivery for consumers were based on medical/rehabilitation principles that assume recipients of attendant services are "sick people" in need of "care". Therefore, these recipients would not be responsible for making decisions and/or being in control.

The need to defend the ACAC's original principles of self-directed attendant services and self-management arose on a number of occasions. For example, the Ontario Medical Association (OMA) and the Ontario Nurses Association (ONA) nearly succeeded in stopping some key activities of attendant services, which would have forced the role of the attendant to become more medical in nature.

During the development of the *Regulated Health Professions Act* (RHPA), which is an Act to regulate the practice of a number of health professions, the authors of the draft regulations were clearly not aware of the existence or even the concepts of attendant services/self-direction as they had included in their draft regulations certain activities such as requiring assistance to go to the washroom. Implicit in the drafted Act was also the assumption that suctioning and catheterization were medical acts to be performed by nurses. Proposed by the OMA, this draft legislation would make it illegal for attendants to perform such routine activities and subject to a $25,000 fine.

Recognizing the negative impact the draft legislation would have on self-directed attendant services, the CILT/ACAC and ARCH worked with the OMA (and later the ONA), and an exemption was written into the legislation for activities directly related to self-directed attendant services. The CILT/ACAC and the ARCH did this in part by disconnecting attendant services from traditional "health care" delivery.

Another barrier to the SMAS-DF related to organized labour. In prior years, there had been consumers who complained about problems with unionized workers, for example, refusing to lift or transfer them. Organized labour, however, was concerned with the rights of the employee: employees working without a contract; not having wage parity; having no direct supervisor with whom to lodge concerns; overall working environment safety; and abuse of employees by the disabled employers. In meetings with labour representatives, the CILT/ACAC was able to address these concerns. They reasoned that consumers are defined as "vulnerable employers", who would be putting themselves at risk if they abused the worker(s) they were dependent on for their day-to-day existence. A mutually respectful, trusting and balanced relationship between the employer and the employee was vital for attendant services to work. The ACAC/CILT believed that this relationship has always been at the heart of attendant services. As well, the ACAC/CILT stressed the well-being of attendants, ensuring that they were well treated and well paid.

The SMAS-DF Pilot moved ahead without a final resolution on these issues with organized labour. However, organized labour redirected their attention to the larger issues of long-term care reform and the provincial social contract happening at that time. It was agreed that labour's issues would be examined during the pilot. The ACAC/CILT continued to keep labour contacts informed of its progress.

Another barrier was the resistance to change on the part of service providers and consumers. Some attendant service providers feared that the new model might result in the loss of current and future clients. To address their concern, the ACAC/CILT first demonstrated that a large number of people were on waiting lists to receive attendant services. It then clarified the self-managed option was not considered to be an answer to all attendant service needs. The self-management model was an additional option that was meant to complement the existing services. Furthermore, the SMAS-DF policy would not allow individuals to remain in an SSLU while receiving direct funding, allowing access to SSLUs for people who are on attendant service waiting lists.

Major Achievements of the Pilot

There are two key areas that stand out as unique achievements of directly funded, self-managed attendant services programs anywhere in the world. First, the program is wholly administered by consumer-controlled organizations (e.g., an ILRC in partnership with other ILRCs in the province). Second, consumer management and administration extends down to the level of the self-manager.

From the outset, consumer control was a prime goal, and it would need to be central throughout the systems and processes used that governed and administered the pilot on a daily basis. However, funds go from government to individuals would not be practical. The SMAS-DF Steering Committee felt that the CILT would likely be a stable funding distributor, and its partnership with the ONILC could provide strong resource supports to participants across Ontario. The CILT was contracted as the central administration, which involved the sending of funds to participants, managing the individual agreements with each person, and reviewing financial reports.

This is the first example that we are aware of where a consumer-controlled and operated organization has been given the responsibility to manage all the day-to-day administrative functions for a directly funded and self-managed attendant services program. This model allows for consistency of independent living principles throughout the operation of the pilot by establishing the credibility of consumer control in the overall process from top to bottom and allowing participants to deal with their peers in their own system.

The concept of peer (consumer) validation (ACAC, 1993) was developed to reflect independent living (IL) principles within the application/selection process. The concept of the peer validation process has philosophically underpinned the direct funding pilot application and selection: the applicant is first an active agent in becoming informed of the process and developing a proposal (the application) with the assistance of direct funding resource people; the applicant then presents and negotiates their application to a peer selection panel. This concept is new compared to the usual methods where professionals or other non-disabled persons control access to human services.

A peer approach was put into effect in the pilot in two main ways: (i) focus on an informed consumer, and (ii) peer selection panels. Consumers interested in managing their own attendant services were encouraged to become directly informed about the expectations, criteria and responsibilities of the application/selection

332

process. This approach reflects the IL principle that consumers are the ones who really need the information if they are to make informed choices and decisions about their own services and lives. Other systems focus on educating the professional or other intermediary about the above details. In many respects, these systems create dependency of recipients on these "experts". Since knowledge is power, the pilot's system of informing and targeting consumers directly led to their empowerment in this whole process.

Consumers were expected to start the process and complete their own individual applications with support from an ILRC resource person. The expectations of this process and the consumer's role in it are different to the many systems in which someone else fills out the application on the client's behalf, asking the client certain questions while offering her/his "expert" advice about what is best for the client.

The pilot system demanded a great deal of ambition on the part of the applicants. In return, the applicants generally got to know thoroughly their strengths based on past experiences, education, life/family roles and needs reflected in their own work. This knowledge was extremely useful for the requirements that they would face if they were to manage their own attendants and act as independent employers.

The IL philosophy also was reflected in the establishment of peer selection panels, which took advantage of the consumer's life experience and knowledge. Panels typically consisted of three people: a consumer, such as an experienced user of attendant services from the applicant's region; a representative of the ILRC (often a consumer himself or herself) in the applicant's region; and a representative from the central administration (CILT) (again, often a user of attendant services or a staff person educated and managed by a consumer administrator).

In the selection process, applicants attended an interview with the panel at a site outside of the individual's home, such as in the community and, often, at an ILRC. Applicants were required to present their application, explain and negotiate the hours and budget proposed, and come to an agreement with the panel. They were also asked questions concerning skills needed to self-manage. While some applicants felt the process was intensive, most applicants viewed it as an opportunity to put forth their own individual plans and strengths.

In early 1997, an external review of the pilot project for Self-Managed Attendant Services in Ontario was completed by the Roeher Institute. The evaluation of the pilot project was done over a two-year period (1995–1996) with all 100 participants chosen for the Pilot. According to the evaluation report, the pilot achieved a number of outcomes (CILT & Roeher Institute, 1997):

(a) It established a consumer-driven partnership with CILT as the pilot administration and ONILC as a resource support network.

(b) The pilot achieved a diversity of participants with respect to the region of the province, rural/urban settings, and living arrangements of participants.

(c) Self-managers stated that the pilot made a difference in terms of increased self-determination in all aspects of their lives, reducing their sense of vulnerability, greater independence, a stronger sense of self-esteem, more fulfilling personal relationships and greater social participation.

(d) A number of self-managers reported greater chances for paid employment and career advancement as a result of the pilot.

(e) The pilot created effective employer-employee relationships by enhancing the accountability of both employer and employee, which encouraged greater levels of mutual respect. As well, attendants who had worked in other service systems reported much higher degrees of job satisfaction in working directly for people with disabilities.

(f) Overall, the pilot provided appropriate supportive resources to consumers wishing to participate in the self-management pilot, such as manuals and clear administrative and reporting procedures.

(g) The pilot was responsive to individual needs, such as supporting the hiring of attendants where services were not previously available.

(h) Based on the findings from this pilot, direct funding for attendant services appears to be a cost-effective alternative to Outreach and SSLUs.

Labour's issues were addressed during the development of the self-manager training and in the Roeher Institute evaluation of the pilot. The final results of the evaluation suggest that labour's concerns were positively dealt with. These issues continue to be attended to on an ongoing basis in the direct funding program.

The success of this pilot was instrumental in the government's announcement in July 1998 to make this a permanent program of the Ontario Ministry of Health. The program was expanded to provide funding to an additional 600 people over the next few years.

The program currently has 691 participants, ranging in age from 17 to 93. The majority of the participants are between 45 and 64 years of age (46.5%), with the second largest group between the age of 25 and 44 (35%). Sixty percent of the participants are females. The program also has participants with a diversity of health conditions. The largest group of participants lives with multiple sclerosis (245), and the second largest group lives with spinal cord injuries (19%). The remaining participants either live with other neuro-muscular conditions (e.g., cerebral palsy, polio, spinal muscular dystrophy, stroke and spinal bifida) or arthritis. Attrition to the program for the year 2003/2004 was 4% due to death or withdrawal. There are 300 applications pending for the program, which attests to the appeal of the program.

CONCLUSION

This chapter examined many elements that facilitated the emergence and development of the SMAS-DFP. These were internal factors related to the physical disability community, as well as external factors, such as advocates outside of the community and changes in government philosophy on health reform and structure. All of these factors came together over time, allowing the SMAS-DFP to become a reality.

This vision was created and moved forward by a core group of people recognized for their leadership in the community. Supporters of the SMAS-DFP came from inside as well as outside of the core community/membership. These supporters provided key resources to be used toward the goal of the SMAS-DFP. The vision, leadership, broad-based support and resources were all important to deal with the multiple barriers to the realization of the SMAS-DFP, and the proponents of the SMAS-DFP were able to develop specific approaches and tactics to deal with barriers.

21

Mental Capacity through a Disability Law Lens

LANA KERZNER

INTRODUCTION

When individuals are not mentally capable to decide things for themselves they rely on others to do so for them, by necessity and law. Others may make important decisions about such fundamental aspects of their lives as where they will live, what they will eat, the health care that they will receive and how their money will be spent. In this context their independence is threatened and often ultimately stripped away. Because the removal of an individ-

I express my sincerest appreciation to Phyllis Gordon, executive director of ARCH, for her contribution to the ideas in this chapter and reviews of drafts, as well as to C. Tess Sheldon, Amy Wah and Cara Wilkie for their research assistance. While the subject of mental capacity laws and their underlying principles are of equal importance to persons with disabilities throughout Canada, the chapter draws disproportionately on Ontario laws because of my greater knowledge of them as a practising lawyer in Ontario.

Lana Kerzner is staff lawyer at ARCH Disability Law Centre in Toronto, Ontario.

ual's right to make choices offends basic human dignity and citizenship, it should be done only when justified and with procedural safeguards in place.

The issue of mental capacity and substitute decision-making leaves most people in a state of unease, never quite able to strike the appropriate balance between the conflicting values of independence and the desire to protect those perceived to be vulnerable. The concept of mental capacity features prominently in the work of a number of professions — most notably, lawyers, health care providers and ethicists — each attempting to define and work with it. Yet, the answers to most questions remain unclear and unsatisfactory. What is really meant by "mental capacity"? What is the rationale for removing one's right to decide and where should the line be drawn? What is the most appropriate method of assessing mental capacity and who should be charged with undertaking this task? How does the law treat mental capacity issues?

A critical evaluation of the impact of mental capacity laws reveals that persons with disabilities often are treated differently than other members of society. At the same time, it is in the lives of persons with disabilities that mental capacity issues most often come to the fore. To provide a basis for understanding the impact of mental capacity laws on persons with disabilities, this chapter will explore the following:

1. What is meant by mental capacity;
2. Mental capacity in the legal context;
3. The importance of mental capacity laws to and their differential impact on persons with disabilities; and
4. Supported decision-making in the context of mental capacity laws.

BACKGROUND

The issue of mental capacity is of particular significance to persons with disabilities. Some specific disabilities are known to have an effect on mental capacity or are commonly associated with diminished levels of capacity. These include intellectual disabilities, disabilities that result from acquired brain injuries, dementia and psychiatric disabilities. This does not mean that every individual who has one of these or a variety of other disabilities experiences a diminished level of capacity. Rather, it highlights the reality that any treatment of mental capacity issues will necessarily be of importance to a portion of the population of persons who have disabilities.

In addition, even people with disabilities who do not have diminished levels of capacity are often inaccurately perceived to be not mentally capable (Downie & Caulfield, 1999). It has been stated that "[t]he tendency to conflate mental illness with lack of capacity, which occurs to an even greater extent when involuntary commitment is involved, has deep historical roots ..." (Weisstub, 1990, p. 116). Similarly, people whose disabilities affect their speech so that their oral communication is difficult to understand, or they are unable to speak altogether, are routinely and mistakenly assumed not to be mentally capable. People with whom they interact (for example, health care professionals) often, without making any inquiries, look to others to speak for and make decisions on behalf of the person with the disability.

The paternalistic attitudes that society historically has harboured toward persons with disabilities lead to a false justification for inappropriately controlling the lives of persons with disabilities who are mentally capable. The Supreme Court of Canada, in *Eldridge v. British Columbia (Attorney General)* stated:

> It is an unfortunate truth that the history of disabled persons in Canada is largely one of exclusion and marginalization ... As a result, disabled persons have not generally been afforded the 'equal concern, respect and consideration' that s.15(1) of the *Charter* demands. Instead they have been subjected to paternalistic attitudes of pity and charity.... (*Eldridge v. British Columbia (Attorney General)*, 1997, p. 668)

Some laws that apply specifically to persons with disabilities authorize the removal of autonomy from adults who have not been found to be mentally incapable (*Developmental Services Act*, 1990, s. 7(b)). Still other laws allow for others to make decisions for persons with disabilities without any proof that the person with the disability is not mentally capable (*Ontario Disability Support Program Act, 1997*, 1997, s. 12(1); *Ontario Disability Support Program Act, 1997*, O. Reg. 222/98, s. 49). Such laws apparently are considered to be acceptable when applied to persons with disabilities but would never be seen as appropriate for the rest of society. These laws and their differential impact on persons with disabilities are described in more detail below.

No aspect of the life of a person with a disability is immune from being affected by determinations by others of their level of mental capacity. This results from the current state of Canadian laws that require, as a precondition of engaging in most activities, that an individual possess a requisite level of mental capacity. The ability to make decisions about health care, banking and paying bills, where individuals will live, who they will marry and their receipt of government benefits will all be impacted by judgments about their level of mental capacity. A judgment that an individual is mentally incapable in some or all of these contexts removes his or her independence and allows others to decide for them.

MENTAL CAPACITY IN THE LEGAL CONTEXT

What Is Mental Capacity?

The Supreme Court of Canada has stated that "... *[C]hoice presupposes that a person has the mental competence to make it*" (*E. (Mrs.) v. Eve*, 1986, p. 435). The corollary of this is that when individuals are determined to be mentally incapable their legal right to make decisions for themselves is removed.

Nevertheless, there is no one uniform test or definition for mental capacity in Canadian law (*Banton v. Banton*, 1998, p. 189). While there are many laws and articles that address mental capacity, no discernible definition emerges. The notion of mental capacity has been in constant use, but there is a lack of analysis of its contents or definition (Somerville, 1994). It is both surprising and patronizing that laws can have such a fundamental impact on people's lives and remain so elusive.

The uncertainty extends even to the appropriate terminology to describe this concept. Various terms have been used in different laws, at different times and in different jurisdictions. These include "lunacy", "incompetence" and "incapacity" (Doron, 1998, p. 96). "Mental capacity" is a term that is frequently used in the legal context today and, that being the case, it will be used throughout this chapter.

In Ontario in the last 20 years, two significant reports on mental capacity contain thorough analyses of these issues. These culminated in the *Final Report of the Advisory Committee on Substitute Decision Making for Mentally Incapable Persons* (Fram, 1987) and an Enquiry on Mental Competency — Final Report (Weisstub, 1990). These reports together remain important sources on the issue and form part of the history of Canadian thought on mental capacity.

As a starting point to understanding this concept, one can take Professor Weisstub's definition of "mental decision making capacity": "... the capacity to make an informed choice with respect to a specific decision" (Weisstub, 1990, p. 31). This, however, is neither concrete nor detailed enough to guide our actions.

Further, it has been stated that "[t]here are as many different operational definitions of mental (in)capacity as there are jurisdictions" (Capacity Assessment Office, 2005, p. II.1). To gain a full understanding of laws relating to mental capacity in Canada, reference to federal and provincial legislation and case law must be made.

Our laws do not address the question of mental capacity from a global standpoint. Rather, the issue of mental capacity is addressed in specific circumstances. As a result, the concept of partial capacity has evolved. The notion of partial capacity recognizes the reality that individuals may possess the requisite mental capacity to make some decisions but not others. Equally important is the recognition that an individual's level of capacity can fluctuate over time (Goddard, 2005). This means that there may be times in a person's life where he or she is mentally capable to make certain types of decisions and other times where this is not so. For example, an individual who becomes unconscious during a seizure will not be mentally capable to make decisions; however, when he or she regains consciousness, he or she will likely regain mental capacity as well.

There are many different tests for mental capacity depending on the legal context and the type of decision to be made. It has been stated that this is so because of the different public policy purposes each test is intended to serve (Doron, 1998). There are, for example, laws relating to the mental capacity to consent to health care, make a will, marry, manage property, make personal care decisions, give a power of attorney and retain a lawyer. Griesdorf sets out a summary chart of some of the tests for capacity (2004).

As the test for mental capacity differs depending on the relevant transaction, so too does the required level of mental capacity. The ability to make various types of decisions requires separate decision-making capabilities and assessments. In *Calvert (Litigation Guardian of) v. Calvert*, Mr. Justice Benotto stated that "[a] person can be capable of making a basic decision and not capable of making a complex decision" (*Calvert (Litigation Guardian of) v. Calvert*, 1997, p. 293), and he concluded that while Mrs. Calvert "... may have lacked the ability to instruct counsel, that did not mean that she could not make the basic personal decision to separate and divorce" (*Calvert (Litigation Guardian of) v. Calvert*, 1997, p. 294). Similarly, taking charge of one's own financial matters may require a higher level of understanding than a decision to appoint someone to make financial decisions on their behalf by making a power of attorney.

To illustrate the importance of context, consider an individual who has an intellectual disability. With respect to where she lives, she may have very strong preferences and well thought out reasons for her choice. She may wish to live in a particular residence because her friends live there and she likes the neighbouring park and the proximity to her family. She may choose this in preference to living with her parents because she desires the companionship of her contemporaries. In contrast, in the context of sophisticated health care decisions she may not be mentally capable to make a decision about risky major surgery. This decision would require an understanding of her current health status and the complexities of the procedure, as well as the particular risks, benefits and consequences.

The fact that an individual has a disability should have no bearing in and of itself on a determination of whether that person is mentally capable. A determination of whether an individual is mentally capable is based on that person's decision-making process. Clearly, whether that person uses a wheelchair, uses augmentative or alternative modes of communication or is blind has no bearing on their ability to make decisions. This applies equally to disabilities that can result in mental impairments, such as psychiatric disabilities and dementia. Individuals who have these types of disabilities are incapable only if there is a causal connection between the mental impairment and their ability to make a particular decision. In this regard, the following has been said:

> [A]ccording to Dr. George, many schizophrenics are able to operate at a very high level of intellectual competence and are only deficient in the mental processes in a particular area or areas of their thoughts. With respect to the respondent, Dr. George has satisfied me that she is mentally competent to appreciate the legal aspects of the divorce process, to weigh its probable consequences upon her and to make a reasoned judgment on what action she should take with respect thereto. (*Bugden v. Bugden*, 1974, p. 243)

Despite the different tests for mental capacity, there are similarities between many of them. An illustration of this is found by comparing the language in the tests for mental capacity used in Ontario's *Substitute Decisions Act, 1992* and *Health Care Consent Act, 1996* (*Health Care Consent Act, 1996*, 1996, s. 4(1); *Substitute*

LANA KERZNER

Decisions Act, 1992, 1992, ss. 6, 45). These incorporate two basic requirements: the ability to understand relevant information and the ability to appreciate reasonably foreseeable consequences. More specifically, it has been stated that "[t]o be 'mentally capable' means that a person must have the ability to understand information relevant to making a decision and the ability to appreciate the reasonably foreseeable consequences of a decision or lack of decision" (Monticone, 2004, p. 7.7). It is important to remember that this definition is used simply as guidance for understanding the concept of mental capacity. In many contexts the definition of capacity differs, may be more or less extensive and may be less clear (Griesdorf, 2004). Reference to the law that relates specifically to the relevant situation must always be made.

It is also important to understand that the above legal test for mental capacity is a cognitive test. This is not the only type of legal test (Capacity Assessment Office, 2005). Indeed, it has been argued that for persons with disabilities the traditional focus on the tests of rationality and capacity should be replaced by a "status and recognition" approach, which

> ... shifts the lens and asks what it means for one person to respect the self-determination of others. In other words, rather than restricting our consideration to whether a "patient" is capable of consenting to a medical procedure or whether a "bank client" can enter a contract, we ask whether and how a physician or a banker is fully respecting and promoting the self-determination of the other person ... respecting self-determination is not about ensuring that the person passes a capacity test before you engage with them as a person. It's about finding out who the person is, his or her history and hopes.... (Roeher Institute, 2001a, p. 43)

How Is Mental Capacity Assessed?

Since there are several contexts in which there is a requirement to be mentally capable, the assessments take place in different situations and may be undertaken by different categories of individuals. For example, the lawyer the client is seeking to retain may be charged with the task of deciding whether the client is mentally capable to instruct, the health practitioner offering a particular treatment may be charged with the task of assessing capacity to consent to that treatment and the parties to a contract may form assessments about the capacity to enter into the contract.

While the law may articulate general tests for mental capacity, it offers little guidance for how assessments are to be undertaken. Capacity assessments are not an exact science (*Knox v. Burton*, 2004, p. 290). It does not appear as though, at least in the legal context, there are objective, uniform criteria that are applied in all situations. Nevertheless, many sources describe the test of mental capacity as one that assesses cognitive, decision-making ability (*Banton v. Banton*, 1998; Doron, 1998). This type of assessment is based not on the content of the decision ultimately made, but rather on the process the individual employed in arriving at that decision. The inquiry focuses on the ability to understand relevant information and to appreciate reasonably foreseeable consequences.

The fact that an individual makes a decision that others perceive as foolish, socially deviant, or risky does not indicate that the decision was incompetently made. As Mr. Justice Quinn stated: "The right to be foolish is an incident of living in a free and democratic society" (*Koch (Re)*, 1997, p. 512). He added that "[t]he right knowingly to be foolish is not unimportant; the right to voluntarily assume risks is to be respected. The State has no business meddling with either. The dignity of the individual is at stake" (*Koch (Re)*, 1997, p. 521).

In the context of persons who have disabilities, the importance of respecting their competently made decisions cannot be overstated. It all too often happens that neighbours, relatives and friends want to remove an individual's right to live as they choose when their lifestyle does not accord with "social norms". Because the person has a disability there is a tendency to view him or her as in need of protection and to cite a behaviour with which one does not agree as evidence of incapacity. A neighbour who observes a university student living in a messy, cluttered home and existing on a less than nourishing diet of pop, potato chips and ice cream would not likely be alarmed by this behaviour, let alone consider taking any action. However, if the person who lives across the street from that neighbour exhibits the same lifestyle but is a person with a disability, the neighbour might be more likely to begin taking steps to have the person's right to make decisions removed. This often occurs notwithstanding the fact that there is no evidence of incapacity.

As stated above, in many legal contexts, the assessment of a person's mental capacity focuses on his or her ability to understand information relevant for making the decision and the ability to appreciate the consequences of a decision or lack thereof. Typically, the following two distinct cognitive abilities are assessed:

1. One assesses whether the person has a working knowledge of the facts relevant to the decision, such as his or her health, financial or personal care status. He or she must also have sufficient intellectual and cognitive ability to process and assimilate information about the choices that he or she may make (Capacity Assessment Office, 2005).

2. One assesses the ability to appreciate the consequences of a decision or lack of a decision. This aspect to the test focuses on the reasoning process behind the person's decisions and explores the particular personal weights that the person attaches to one outcome or another (Capacity Assessment Office, 2005).

An important discussion of this legal test for mental capacity can be found in the Supreme Court of Canada's decision in *Starson v. Swayze*.

In assessing the factual accuracy of the individual's understanding, it is not an assessment of the person's prior knowledge. The question is the extent to which the person can retain, interpret and manipulate information once it is provided to him or her. For example, a person faced with a decision of whether to take a medication with serious risks is unlikely at the outset to know enough about that particular treatment to decide whether she wants to proceed. In order to assess her capacity to make this decision, she must first be provided with all relevant information about the medication. It is only then that an assessment can be made as to whether she understands it.

Because each prong of the assessment requires different abilities, it is possible that an individual will not satisfy the test for capacity because he or she cannot satisfy each prong. Consider a request that an individual receives for a donation as part of a campaign for the local hospital. She may be able to understand that the hospital is where she goes for medical care and that the hospital is in need of money. She may also know how much money she has. However, she may not be able to appreciate that as a consequence of making a donation to the hospital she will deplete her food budget and may not have sufficient money to feed herself.

Implementation of the Legal Test of Capacity

Most often determinations of capacity are made by professionals, including health care providers and lawyers. Assessments of capacity are generally supposed to be on the basis of the process the individual went through in arriving at his or her decision. However, often the assessor's conclusions about mental capacity inappropriately reflect their opinion about the actual decision that has been made, rather than the process undergone to arrive at that decision (Somerville, 1994). The practical reality is that the outcome of assessments may inappropriately reflect the personal views and biases of the assessor (Gordon & Verdun-Jones, 1992).

Experience shows that when the assessor disagrees with the decision made, he or she is likely to conclude that the person is not mentally capable (Downie & Caulfield, 1999). Professor Somerville points to a study in which it was found that "... the more it [the person's decision] differed from what the psychiatrist thought he or she would decide in the same circumstances, the more likely it was that the person would be adjudged incompetent" (Somerville, 1994, p. 184). The assessor thus often arrives at a false determination that an individual is mentally incapable.

It is an unfortunate reality that there is a general lack of appreciation in the public, including among the professionals who conduct the assessments, about how persons with disabilities view their lives and their circumstances. This may simply be a function of an inability to understand an individual's perspective if one has never experienced it oneself. Helen Henderson, a disability columnist at the *Toronto Star*, vividly expressed the reality that a decision one anticipates one would make if one's life were different is often changed by the perspective one gains when the life they imagined becomes a reality: "If it were me 40 years ago contemplating a life of multiple sclerosis, I might have said I'd rather shoot myself. Now, I know the part of life I value most started after the diagnosis" (Henderson, 2005, p. L4).

Consider an individual with a disability who uses attendant services to assist her with daily activities such as transferring from her wheelchair, eating and bathing. She has been receiving services from the same person for a number of years and has not had to pay for the service as it is funded by the government. When the government program changes she can no longer receive services from that individual for free. Her options are to change to another person or to pay personally for services from her original attendant. She has a very limited income; thus, in order to pay her original attendant, she can no longer afford to pay for accessible transportation. This would severely limit her activities, as she would only be able to go to destinations to which she can travel independently in her wheelchair. Nonetheless, she chooses to continue to receive services from her original attendant rather than change to the new one, whose services she would receive for free.

To someone who has not lived her experience, her decision might be viewed as inappropriate because it is not seen as a rational economic response to change to a paid-for attendant. She might thus be assessed as not mentally capable. However, exploring the rationale for her decision would reveal a carefully reasoned explanation. The new attendant will not be familiar with her needs and routines. In addition, the new attendant will not be able to come at times that are convenient for her. Such a switch will likely result in even more upheaval in her life. She will have to devote time each day to training and learning to work with a new attendant. To accommodate the new attendant's schedule, she must change the times she eats, bathes and sleeps. Her work hours will have to be altered, she will no longer be able to attend her regular social activities, which conflict with her new meal times, and she will have to wake up each morning much earlier than she wishes.

It is easy to see how in these circumstances an assessor could arrive at the wrong conclusion about mental capacity because she is not familiar with the kinds of considerations a person with a disability must weigh in arriving at a decision. The assessor may disagree with the ultimate decision made as she cannot understand why a person would make that decision. This may result in an inaccurate determination that the person is incapable.

From Paternalism to Autonomy

Over time various justifications have been articulated for the removal of an individual's right to make decisions when he or she is determined to be mentally incapable of doing so. It has been stated that "[p]aternalistic intervention to assist the incompetent has historically been justified as an exception to the dominant principles favouring individual autonomy" (Weisstub, 1990, p. 51). The era of paternalistic thought dates back centuries. In 14th century England, the Crown, as *parens patriae*, was responsible for the protection and care of the "mentally incompetent". This jurisdiction subsequently was vested in Canadian courts as well. The *parens patriae* jurisdiction was founded on the attitude that there is a need to act for the protection of those who are believed not to be able to care for themselves. It is to be exercised in a manner that is said to promote the "best interest" of the protected person (*E. (Mrs.) v. Eve*, 1986, p. 426; Weisstub, 1990, p. 51). The underlying assumption

346

was that the individual's personal and economic affairs could be better managed by others (Doron, 1998, p. 102).

The emergence of the human rights movement following the Second World War and the subsequent enactment of the *Canadian Charter of Rights and Freedoms ["Charter"]* in 1982 raised the importance of the values of liberty, autonomy and freedom from unnecessary intervention. There has been an increasing recognition by the Supreme Court of Canada and legal writers (Gordon & Verdun-Jones, 1992) that respect should be given to the human rights and autonomy interests of all persons, including persons with disabilities. In the context of mental capacity, the Supreme Court recently stated that "Unwarranted findings of incapacity severely infringe upon a person's right to self-determination" (*Starson v. Swayze*, 2003, p. 759). The Court also recently advanced the value to be placed in autonomous decision making in relation to mentally incapable persons in *Nova Scotia (Minister of Health) v. J.J.*

Weisstub's 1990 report on mental competency observes that the *Charter* confirms the priority to be given to individual rights (Weisstub, 1990). The Fram report too emphasized this by stating that

> ... [t]he Canadian Charter of Rights and Freedoms, as a constitutional document, is part of the fundamental law of Canada. As a result, consideration of the values given expression in the Charter must inform any review of the law relating to substitute decision making. (Fram, 1987, p. 41)

Specifically in relation to the *parens patriae* jurisdiction, the Supreme Court has gradually moved toward placing importance in the value of autonomy when determining what is in an individual's best interest. In *E. (Mrs.) v. Eve* the Supreme Court stated that the jurisdiction is to be exercised only for the benefit of the person with the disability and not that of others. In so doing, the Court eschewed the commonly held assumption that families and professionals always know what is in the best interests of persons with disabilities (*E. (Mrs.) v. Eve*, 1986).

Presumption of Capacity

Most writers on the topic of mental capacity assert that all adults are presumed to be mentally capable (Gordon & Verdun-Jones, 1992; Verma, 1995; Weisstub, 1990). The presumption of capacity exists in many different legal contexts. For example, there are specific laws that presume capacity to enter a contract (*Substi-*

tute Decisions Act, 1992, 1992, s. 2(1)), capacity to accept or reject medical treatment (*Health Care Consent Act, 1996*, 1996, s. 4(2)), capacity to give evidence (Ontario *Evidence Act, 1990*), and capacity to make a will (*Vout v. Hay*, 1995).

Where a presumption of capacity operates, individuals are granted the right to make decisions that affect their own lives. This does not mean that everyone is always mentally capable of making decisions, but that all interactions with persons with disabilities should presume mental capacity unless there is proof to the contrary, just as this is the case with persons who do not have disabilities. This presumption is crucial to protecting an individual's ability to control his or her own life, essentially, their autonomy. When individuals are not allowed to make choices for themselves, they no longer have control over what will happen in their lives, and their autonomy is diminished.

An analogy can be drawn between individuals whose liberty is removed by being found to be incapable and individuals whose liberty is removed by being found guilty of having committed a crime and, perhaps, serving time in jail. In the criminal context, every person charged with an offence has the constitutional right to be presumed innocent until proven guilty. This is a right enshrined in subsection 11(d) of the *Charter*. If individuals whose liberty is at stake having been charged with a criminal offence are presumed innocent until proven guilty, those whose liberty is at stake by being determined to be mentally incapable should benefit from a similar presumption: the presumption of being mentally capable (Downie & Caulfield, 1999). Mr. Justice Quinn in *Koch (Re)* illustrated vividly the relative lack of procedural safeguards in findings of incapacity (in the context of Ontario's substitute decision-making laws), as compared to findings of guilt in the criminal context (*Koch (Re)*, 1997). The importance of the presumption of mental capacity and fair process is especially so in light of Professor Weisstub's observation that "[t]he determination of incompetency is even in some cases a stronger degradation of the human being than it is to be declared 'criminal' " (Weisstub, 1990, p. 30).

Charter Values and Current Laws

The current value placed on autonomous decision-making is reflected in principles that have been articulated in *Charter* jurisprudence and by writers on mental capacity. The challenge is to transform those values into reality. This involves respecting and giving legal recognition to models of decision-making that have been created so that persons with disabilities have the right to make choices as independently as possible. Weisstub has stated that "... the enactment in 1982 of the *Charter* confirms the priority to be given to individual rights ..." (Weisstub, 1990, p. 48). Examining mental capacity laws from the perspective of *Charter* values highlights the extent to which various laws advance independence for persons with disabilities.

Disability advocates have successfully argued over the past several years that *Charter* rights must include values of dignity, autonomy, inclusion and citizenship (Chadha & Sheldon, 2004; *Nova Scotia (Workers' Compensation Board) v. Martin; Nova Scotia (Workers' Compensation Board) v. Laseur*, 2003). Section 7 of the *Charter* guarantees the right to life, liberty and security of the person, and section 15 of the *Charter* guarantees the right to equality. These sections read as follows:

> **s. 7** Everyone has the right to life, liberty and security of the person and the right not to be deprived thereof except in accordance with the principles of fundamental justice.
>
> **s. 15**(1) Every individual is equal before and under the law and has the right to the equal protection and equal benefit of the law without discrimination and, in particular, without discrimination based on race, national or ethnic origin, colour, religion, sex, age or mental or physical disability.

It is important to note that these rights are not accorded absolute protection as they are subject to sections 1 and 33 of the *Charter*.

All laws, including those related to mental capacity, are to be applied and interpreted in a way that is consistent with the *Charter*. Personal autonomy to make inherently private choices goes to the very core of the liberty interest protected under section 7 of the *Charter*. Further, section 15, the equality provision, mandates the promotion of a society in which all persons enjoy equal recognition at law. In this context, the Supreme Court of Canada has stated that "[h]uman dignity ... is enhanced when laws recognize the full place of all individuals and groups within Canadian society" (*Law v. Canada (Minister of Employment and Immigration)*, 1999, p. 530). The Court stated that the *Charter*'s guarantee of equality "... is concerned with the realization of personal autonomy and self-determination. Human dignity means that an individual or group feels self-respect and self-worth" (*Law v. Canada (Minister of Employment and Immigration)*, 1999, p. 530).

In the current fabric of Canada's democratic society and with the existence of the *Charter* and recent judicial decisions, the values of equality, liberty and autonomy are essential considerations to any removal of decision-making rights on the basis of mental incapacity. The Supreme Court of Canada in *Nova Scotia (Minister of Health) v. J.J.* has now explicitly recognized the intrusiveness of a finding of incapacity and the resulting limitation on an individual's autonomous decision making and liberty (*Nova Scotia (Minister of Health) v. J.J.*, 2005).

Commentators cite experience that supports the view that benign paternalism is no longer tenable (Gordon & Verdun-Jones, 1992). In particular, "[r]esearch has shown that protective intervention in the lives of mentally or physically disabled persons can cause a higher incidence of deterioration and death than would result without interventions, particularly if such intervention leads to institutionalization in a nursing home or mental hospital" (Jost, quoted in Weisstub, 1990, p. 53).

Mental Capacity as a Mechanism for Differential Treatment

Many of us expect and plan our lives on the basis that we have the right to live as we choose. For example, we may choose whether to take medicines with unpleasant side effects or to disregard our doctor's advice, and we may choose whether to live downtown or in the suburbs. In contrast, if we have been found mentally incapable, we cannot make these personal choices. Decisions are imposed on us by others. Our right to be treated equally and to full inclusion in society is removed. Drawing the line between capacity and incapacity may reflect society's desire to include or exclude persons from full participation in the community.

In today's society, persons with disabilities are subject to stereotypes characterizing them as in need of care and charity (Chadha & Sheldon, 2004). They are thus particularly susceptible to being assessed as incapable. The practical result of these historic and deeply embedded prejudicial attitudes is that some laws that are geared specifically and only to persons with disabilities authorize the removal of the individual's right to make decisions. They may justify their existence under the guise of unstated but seemingly presumed incapacity and/or the mere existence of disability reflecting their stereotypic underpinnings.

Ontario's *Developmental Services Act*, for example, contains a provision that allows a person to apply for admission to a facility

350

or for assistance or services on behalf of a person whom he or she believes has a developmental disability (*Developmental Services Act,* 1990, s. 7(b)). This is the case regardless of whether the person who has the developmental disability is mentally capable. This means that someone other than the person with the disability is allowed to make choices about that person's life, even when the individual may be fully capable of making his or her own choices. It appears that this law equates having a developmental disability with mental incapacity. It embodies a view that individuals who have developmental disabilities are incapable in all circumstances, and it flies in the face of our laws, which recognize that mental capacity is task specific and may change over time.

Another example can be found in the *Ontario Disability Support Program Act, 1997.* This statute provides income support for persons with disabilities. It allows the Ministry of Community and Social Services to appoint a person to act for the person with the disability if the Ministry is satisfied that the person is using or is likely to use his or her income support in a way that is not for the benefit of himself or herself or those with whom he or she resides (*Ontario Disability Support Program Act, 1997,* 1997, s. 12(1); *Ontario Disability Support Program Act, 1997,* O. Reg. 222/98, s. 49). Income support can then be paid to the person appointed instead of the person with the disability (*Ontario Disability Support Program Act, 1997,* 1997, s. 12(2)). The effect of these provisions allows the government to decide when complete control for managing benefits should be removed from the person with the disability. There is no requirement at all in law that there be any inquiry into or finding that the person is mentally incapable of managing his or her property. In fact, it appears that under the *Ontario Disability Support Program Act, 1997* recipients of benefits are treated as though they are mentally incapable when Ministry staff believe they are making unwise financial decisions. The individual's right to choice as to how to manage his or her money, and thus his or her autonomy, is removed even in the presence of full mental capacity.

The above two laws demonstrate that the earlier paternalistic approach is still embedded in our legal system. They are in contrast generally to statutes that do not specifically address disability issues where people have a complete and unlimited right to manage their property unless there is a finding of incapacity.

In addition to specific laws such as the *Developmental Services Act* and the *Ontario Disability Support Program Act, 1997,* some legal processes have a differential impact on persons with disabilities. For example, in the litigation context, laws exist that provide for a mechanism to enable persons who are mentally incapable to have their rights advanced in court through the appointment of a "litigation guardian" (*Rules of Civil Procedure*, 1990, Rule 7). A litigation guardian is usually a person whose duty it is to attend to the interests of the mentally incapable person in court proceedings. The litigation guardian gives instructions to the lawyer and takes the necessary steps in the proceedings on behalf of the person who is incapable.

However, there are litigation contexts in which there is no established process for enabling people who are incapable to advance their rights. This is particularly so in the context of many administrative tribunals, such as the Ontario Rental Housing Tribunal and the Human Rights Tribunal of Ontario. In the absence of an established mechanism for a person who is mentally incapable of benefiting from the assistance of another individual, the person is prevented from advancing his or her legal rights in the same manner as others.

Consider, for example, an individual who lives in an apartment that is in disrepair. A remedy for this might be found in tenancy laws that allow a complaint to be dealt with by a specialized tribunal. If the tenant is mentally capable, he or she could go to the tribunal to initiate the complaint. However, the tenant who is mentally incapable may experience difficulties in launching the same complaint if there does not exist a process to allow him or her to be represented by a litigation guardian.

The case involving the tenant who is mentally incapable will likely become bogged down in arguments about proper process and who should be entitled to act on his or her behalf. There is a risk that such a process will not be established or that the case will be unfairly delayed as the adjudicator attempts to arrive at a resolution. In the worst case scenario, the person who is mentally incapable will not be able to advance his or her rights altogether. This individual will continue to live in unsatisfactory conditions, whereas a similarly situated person who possesses mental capacity will likely be able to compel the property owner to have the matter resolved before the tribunal.

Supported Decision-Making

What is empowerment? It is the process by which we can achieve control over decisions that affect our lives. It means gaining independence through mutual support and cooperation, encouragement and understanding. It is the passing of power from one person to another. The process of learning to shift power to a person with a handicap and his or her family is also one of empowerment. (Roeher Institute, 1989, p. 7)

For many persons with disabilities, personal relationships of support are central to their achievement of equality and well-being. A number of types of such supports are a current reality in Canada (Roeher Institute, 2001a). They aim to empower people with disabilities; that is, to preserve their autonomy and dignity as much as possible in the face of limited capacity. It has been stated that mutual support among family and friends of people who have a disability can "... be a foundation for designing systems that give real decision-making power to those who lack it" (Roeher Institute, 1989, p. 4). To this end, the models acknowledge and include family, friends and other support people. Typically people come together to support the person with the disability to make decisions and in many other aspects of their lives. Various terms have been used to describe these relationships, including Supported Decision-Making Networks, Circles of Support, Support Clusters and Microboards.

The value of support systems in assisting people whose levels of mental capacity may be in question has been widely recognized by people outside of the disability community as well (Doron, 1998; Fram, 1987; Munson, 2002; *Koch (Re)*, 1997). The Fram committee emphasized the importance of supportive services to promoting autonomy and expressed the view that those who can make their own decisions with support should not lose their right to do so (Fram, 1987). Individuals should be considered mentally capable in law as long as they can live safely with the assistance of supports such as family and friends (Munson, 2002). Mr. Justice Quinn explicitly recognized the role of supports when he stated that "... mental capacity exists if the appellant is able to carry out her decisions with the help of others" (*Koch (Re)*, 1997, p. 521).

Despite the fact that critics have called for legal recognition of such supports (Gordon & Verdun-Jones, 1992; Roeher Institute, 2001a), their legal status, to the extent that it exists at all, is not comprehensive and uniform across Canada (Roeher Institute, 2001a). While some provinces, including Ontario, do not have legislation that explicitly legally recognizes supported decision-making, other provinces have adopted legal alternatives to provide such support in varying ways (Doron, 1998; Roeher Institute, 2001a).

Accordingly, it appears as though there is a limited but growing appreciation in Canada that it is important that laws relating to mental capacity respect these models and other similar approaches to decision making. Ultimately, this is the most respectful approach to recognizing the dignity and autonomy of persons with disabilities. Legal approaches to mental capacity that ignore their needs and wishes patronize them; their expertise regarding their own needs gives way to society's often ill-informed opinions about mental capacity and persons with disabilities. Recognizing appropriate supports minimizes unnecessary interference with liberty and is most respectful to persons with disabilities.

In fashioning laws that respect the autonomy and equity of persons with disabilities, regard should be paid to the legal measures developed around the world. Professor Herr has described laws of various countries, including Sweden, Germany and Israel, that have undergone reforms to recognize the autonomy of persons with disabilities (Herr, 2003). They introduce less restrictive alternatives for decision making and recognize supported decision- making. Professor Herr states that "[t]here is a global search for personal support solutions that are empowering rather than disenfranchising" (Herr, 2003, p. 430). He further states that "[s]elf-advocates and scholars demand ... reforms that will replace the paternalism of the past with authentic partnerships for the future" (Herr, 2003, p. 447).

In the ongoing development of mental capacity laws, it is important to canvass the views of persons with disabilities as to how best to maintain their ability to live independent lives and make choices for themselves. Ultimately individuals with disabilities will be empowered. At the same time, society's expenditure of time and resources in unnecessary and unwanted intrusions in people's lives will be minimized.

CONCLUSION

There is a general consensus that adults should be presumed to be mentally capable to engage in all activities unless there is proof to the contrary. Courts and writers in the legal, health and ethics professions strive to give content to the meaning of mental capacity, drawing on their combined expertise. At the heart of this challenge is the reality that any definition determines where the line will be drawn between the right to autonomous decision-making and the loss thereof.

There is no single test in law for mental capacity. Rather there exist a number of tests; individuals are determined to be mentally capable or incapable to engage in specific activities or to make specific decisions. Nonetheless, many of the tests are similar in that they focus on the cognitive abilities of understanding information and appreciating foreseeable consequences of decisions. Individuals with limited cognitive abilities may be able to engage in some activities, such as marrying or hiring a lawyer, but not others, such as purchasing a house or making decisions about medical treatment.

The lives of persons with disabilities are frequently touched by mental capacity laws. It is a reality that a portion of persons with disabilities experience limitations in cognition while many more without such limitations are nonetheless subject to stereotypes that label them as incapable. The community as a whole is thus particularly vulnerable to losing their right to participate equally in Canadian society by determinations of mental incapacity. If one has a disability, the odds are that he or she will be more likely to be considered mentally incapable.

The Supreme Court of Canada and the *Canadian Charter of Rights and Freedoms* have moved us from the age of paternalism to the promotion of individual autonomy. The values of dignity, autonomy, inclusion and citizenship are now part of Canada's current legal framework. It is hoped that the evolution of mental capacity laws will follow this direction and, in doing so, will recognize current and future decision-making models embraced by the disability community to promote independent decision-making and inclusion.

APPENDIX

Legislation

Adult Protection Act, R.S.N.S. 1989, c. 2.
Canadian Charter of Rights and Freedoms, Part I of the *Constitution Act, 1982*, being Schedule B to the *Canada Act 1982* (U.K.), 1982, c. 11.
Developmental Services Act, R.S.O. 1990, c. D-11.
Evidence Act, R.S.O. 1990, c. E-23.
Health Care Consent Act, 1996, S.O. 1996, c. 2, Sch. A.
Ontario Disability Support Program Act, 1997, S.O. 1997, c. 25, Sch. B.
Ontario Disability Support Program Act, 1997, O. Reg. 222/98.
Rules of Civil Procedure, R.R.O. 1990, Reg. 194.
Substitute Decisions Act, 1992, S.O. 1992, c. 30.

Jurisprudence

Banton v. Banton (1998), 164 D.L.R. (4th) 176 (Ont. Gen. Div.).
Bugden v. Bugden (1974), 52 D.L.R. (3d) 241 (N.S.S.C. (T.D.)).
Calvert (Litigation Guardian of) v. Calvert, (1997), 32 O.R. (3d) 281 (Gen. Div.), aff'd (1998), 37 O.R. (3d) 221 (C.A.).

LANA KERZNER

E. (Mrs.) v. Eve, [1986] 2 S.C.R. 388.

Eldridge v. British Columbia (Attorney General), [1997] 3 S.C.R. 624.

Knox v. Burton (2004), 6 E.T.R. (3d) 285 (Sup. Ct.), aff'd (2005), 14 E.T.R. (3d) 27 (Ont. C.A.).

Koch (Re) (1997), 33 O.R. (3d) 485 (Gen. Div.).

Law v. Canada (Minister of Employment and Immigration), [1999] 1 S.C.R. 497.

Nova Scotia (Minister of Health) v. J.J., [2005] 1 S.C.R. 177, 2005 SCC 12.

Nova Scotia (Workers' Compensation Board) v. Martin; Nova Scotia (Workers' Compensation Board) v. Laseur, [2003] 2 S.C.R. 504, 2003 SCC 54.

R. v. Swain, [1991] 1 S.C.R. 933.

Starson v. Swayze, [2003] 1 S.C.R. 722, 2003 SCC 32.

Vout v. Hay, [1995] 2 S.C.R. 876.

22

Exile from the China Shop: Cultural Injunction and Disability Policy

CATHERINE FRAZEE

Culture ... is not so much a set of things — novels and paintings
or television programs or comics — as a process, a set of practices. Primarily, culture is concerned with the production and
exchange of meanings — the "giving and taking of meaning'
between the members of a society or group. Thus culture
depends on its participants interpreting meaningfully what is
around them, and making sense of the world, in broadly similar
ways. (Hall, 1997, p. 2)

EXILE

Our rights to be free from harms and deprivations are sanctioned
by law — locally, nationally and internationally. Yet, as Michael
Ignatieff (2000) has noted, there is nothing natural about our recognition of the rights of every human being. The notion that
human rights are universal, and that they must prevail across culture and history, "has had to make its way into our hearts against a
much more intuitively obvious notion: that the only people we
should care about are the people like us" (p. 40).

Justice will only thrive in conditions that "draw upon a deep sense of human indivisibility, a recognition of us in them and them in us" (Ignatieff, 2000, p. 39). But while human rights doctrines and instruments express this sentiment magnificently, the evidence all around us is of a profound disconnect between human rights and human consciousness. For all of our efforts, the entrenchment of rights has been matched by the entrenchment of poverty, violence and despair. Our victories in the quest for justice have, for the most part, benefited individuals, not the larger body politic. Those of us with robust supports and hardy constitutions have managed to make our way, if tentatively, at least somewhat visibly, to this nation's universities, textbooks, courtrooms and other corridors of power. As a disabled woman, I, and others "like me" have managed to ride the wave of the rights revolution, but how many members of my own community have been caught up in its undertow?

Is our current architecture of human rights protection adequate to the task of sustaining and supporting a just society for disabled citizens? For me this is not an abstract question. Indeed, it crystallized rather sharply a number of years ago when I was at the height of my powers as a human rights champion, mid-way through a three-year appointment as Chief Commissioner of Ontario's Human Rights Commission:

> While on an otherwise unremarkable shopping expedition at a downtown Toronto mall, I spotted an item in a store window that seemed worthy of consideration for my niece's upcoming birthday. The store being over-crowded with merchandise and therefore inhospitable to my power wheelchair, and I having no particular inclination on that afternoon for an impromptu access and accommodation workshop, I asked my friend to go in and investigate while I waited outside.
>
> The process took a little time, as it turned out there were several items in the general category that my friend needed to compare and consider. After a minute or two, as I somewhat absent-mindedly gazed in the store window, I became aware of the rapid approach of a small, thin, sharp-eyed man who could only be the store manager. Presuming that he was embarrassed by the inhospitality of his premises, I moved toward the door wearing my most reassuring smile and hastily composing the too-familiar benediction that would put him at ease. I admire the spunk of my comrades who would have permitted this fellow to rearrange every display case in his store to conform to my particular dimensions and not feel obliged to purchase a suitcase of trinkets in return, but I cannot match their spunk.

So, summoning all of the grace of a well-heeled cripple, I reached for his eyes and firmly but politely tossed out the words "Please don't worry...". In the space of an instant that defies measure, I imagined his arms flailing to grasp this olive branch. In the space of that same instant, I awoke from my imagining to discover his arms truly flailing, in broad, heaving broom-like sweeps. Flailing toward — no, against — in fact, **at** — me.

It took a moment for me to understand that I was being shoo'd away.

In that frozen moment, I learned that simple statutory prohibitions against discriminatory conduct are no shield from the ambush to dignity that smolders inside culture. In the 14 years of activist struggle and analysis that now stand between me and the expressed aversions of that sharp-eyed stranger, I have learned that survival within a culture that relegates "people like me" to a status of aesthetic outcast calls for more nuanced defences than the blunt protections of anti-discrimination legislation.

There was no doubt — there is no doubt — that I could have wrestled this brute to the floor with the muscle of my provincial human rights code. I could, a few months and a Human Rights Tribunal decision later, swagger back into his store, secure in the knowledge that I had every right to be there. But of course I did not. Call me a coward, but I have never returned to the scene of that ambush. Not for all the trinkets in that store, nor for all the satisfactions of a sweet anti-discrimination victory, would I — could I — again expose myself to that man's contempt.

The store manager had invoked — for all intents and purposes, successfully — an aesthetic injunction, an assertion that people like me should remain outside of his visual field, should not be seen in or in proximity to his domain. It was not that he had prohibited me from entering his store — that was a harm that could have been easily remedied. In this extreme — but most assuredly not isolated — distortion of human recognition, he mirrored back to me all of the fears, prejudice, and hostility of an ableist world, and in so doing, had slashed into my most integral sense of being.

Iris Marion Young (1990) writes compellingly about the ways in which our dominant aesthetic culture constructs entire social groups as ugly or degenerate. She argues that oppression persists in our society in no small measure through aesthetic judgments, unconscious and unexamined aversions and the jokes, images and stereotypes pervading the mass media. In this, her work complements that of feminist legal scholar Catharine MacKinnon, who makes the following observation:

> ... Words and images are how people are placed in hierarchies, how social stratification is made to seem inevitable and right, how feelings of inferiority and superiority are engendered, and how indifference to violence against those on the bottom is rationalized and normalized. Social supremacy is made, inside and between people, through making meanings. (1993, p. 31)

The subordination of persons or groups relegated to the status of other takes many forms — the shrug, the "shoo", the catcall, the curse, the stare, the eyes that refuse to meet ours — the insistent reminder of one's place as "one of them, not like me". The layer upon layer of presumption, judgment, stereotype, erasure. The universalizing of one particular experience and perspective held up as neutral and normal, as in the preposterous suggestion that reliance upon certain technologies — automobiles, subways, cell phones, email — are positive markers, whereas reliance upon other technologies — wheelchairs, prostheses — are markers of a diminished human and social status.

Most devastating are the aesthetic injunctions. Sometimes these are formally entrenched in public policy — as in the City of Chicago Ordinance enacted in 1911 and finally repealed in 1973:

> No person who is diseased, maimed, mutilated, or in any way deformed so as to be an unsightly or disgusting object or improper person to be allowed in or on the public ways or other public places in this city, shall therein or thereon expose himself to public view, under a penalty of not less than one dollar nor more than fifty dollars for each offense. (Chicago Municipal Code 33–34 (1966))

Often, these judgments are entrenched in the public imaginary. Consider, for example, the figure of Robert Latimer. Embedded in our consciousness are images of a man of the land, rough and rugged like the landscape he inhabited, the land he worked with his strong hands and his straight back. Mostly, we saw him in winter, his steamy breath reminding us of the harsh realities of survival in an uncompromising environment — a Canadian paragon of Darwinian survival. Compare this image to the figure of Tracy. She was always pictured indoors, although we know that she went to school each day in the same elements that Robert so easily and surely stood in. Tracy's figure appears as nature's exile, impossibly delicate, fragile, and not long for this world, with or without her father's intervention.

Resistance

Disabled people know the consequences that flow from violating our culture's aesthetic taboos. We have internalized this knowledge, at times with dire results. And we have politicized this knowledge, at times with a vengeance. Against every expression of cultural imperialism — the judgments that we are ugly, or sick, or idle, or perverse, or weak, or degenerate — disabled people increasingly invoke the tools of culture. These are the tools of narrative, story-sharing and conversation; tools of naming, language, history, tradition, humour, image and performance; tools that reflect and interpret the way we live our lives. These are tools of solidarity, identity and celebration: affinity, against aversion.

Since the 1980s, a canon of artistic works produced by disabled artists has grown and become more organized and political (Barnes & Mercer, 2001). Disabled artists have taken up positions of cultural critique and contribution, introducing new subject matter and media to the cultural field (i.e., forms, modes, content and styles that emerge from the disability experience). This disability arts and culture movement marks the growing political power of disabled people to assume control of artistic media in order both to counter cultural stereotypes and misrepresentation and to present alternative framings of disability as a valued human condition. Disabled artists in Canada and internationally are therefore producing artistic works that challenge and reshape our culture's dominant understanding of the disability experience. As Michael Bach has written:

> Without major shifts in our cultural landscapes, our life circumstances will continue to be shaped by icons of oppression that distort the public imaginary, that crowd marketplaces and public spaces.... Re-inventing ourselves, speaking back and speaking out, is the work and process of culture. It is work that takes place in the arts, in philosophy, in pedagogy, in political struggle — work bound together by an aspiration to reform the dominant culture. This project is possible only in a new poetics of language, image, movement, and media, controlled and guided by the experiences, voices, histories, talents, ideas and ideals of oppressed people. (2004, p. 2)

The assertion that "Black is Beautiful", as Young notes, pierces through racist consciousness, "deeply unsettling the received

CATHERINE FRAZEE

body aesthetic ... of racism" (Young, 1990, p. 160). Similarly, the celebration of Gay Pride parodies the dominant culture's exclusive claim to "healthy sexuality and respectable family life" (Young, 1990, p. 161). Post-colonial struggles of Aboriginal and other peoples have shifted the focus unflinchingly toward the colonizing power's devastation of land, resources, and identities. So, too, the taunt "Piss on Pity" situates the disabled upstart in ways that destabilize an ableist grasp upon the moral high ground of assumed benevolence.

When disabled people lay claim to culture, we assert ourselves as the "people like us", rejecting the dominant narrative that tells us we are the deviant "other". The more we disrupt the cultural applecart, the more the dominant culture is forced to "discover itself" (Young, 1990, p. 166), as if for the first time, as **particular** — that is, as white, Anglo-European, male, straight and non-disabled. As disabled people claim our own rich, complex, positive identities, we "seize the power of naming difference itself" (Young, 1990, p. 171).

As we speak back against dominant norms — norms of virtue, beauty, health, relationship, intelligence, love, fidelity, responsibility, and autonomy — we assert our own definitions and experiences. We raise our consciousness and dispute the values that underpin majoritarian culture. What do *we* consider virtuous? How do *we* perceive and express beauty? What health determinants matter *to us*? What are *our* responsibilities to ourselves and each other? In what diverse ways do *we* express intelligence, love, autonomy? These are radical, *cultural* means of pluralizing norms, of *particularizing* meaning that has been falsely held out as neutral or universal.

CULTURE AND THE POLICY AGENDA

How then do processes of cultural rehabilitation and resistance play out in policy arenas? The broader significance of the culturally transformative work of disability activism becomes apparent when we consider the role of culture in shaping social practices, social institutions and social policy. In taking up questions about the production and exchange of meanings related to disability, we set ourselves the task of examining, reflecting upon and confronting cultural forces that shout down and shut down the voices of disabled citizens.

Framing policy research and scholarship within discourses of culture is both novel and ambitious, demanding new language, new

362

methods and new conceptual orientations. It is work for which there is no ready groove within mainstream research and policy agendas, work that does not find an easy fit in conventional responses to the "problem" of disability. In this context, the landscape for disability research and activism in the domain of culture is still emerging. However, the following are seen as priority areas for policy attention as disabled artists in Canada and internationally struggle toward the establishment of a strong and influential cultural voice. Broadly speaking, this work unfolds in four parallel and overlapping streams.

Breaking *into* Culture

Robust mobilization of disability activism through the arts in Canada is contingent upon the kinds of funding and exhibition/ performance opportunities available, the criteria by which supports and opportunities are awarded and the nature of artistic projects typically favoured. In the eyes of many (notably including gatekeepers in arts funding, arts infrastructure, arts media and arts discourse), disability and art intersect only in therapeutic contexts. The far more politicized tasks of creating and affirming cultural identity and deconstructing the politics of both art and disability invariably leave disabled artists outside the parameters of traditional supports in both disability and mainstream arts sectors.

Two examples will help to illustrate the dimensions of this problem.

• Negotiating funding opportunities for groundbreaking disability artworks is invariably fraught with difficulty; such work is generally excluded from grant monies earmarked for disability-related programming because it is neither "rehabilitative" nor "measurably applicable" to the "real" lives of people with disabilities. Moreover, central funding organizations for disability research tend to look upon artistic modalities as outside the more rigorous and practical approaches of science, ethics, law and medicine. Consider, for example, the experience of David Mitchell and Sharon Snyder, writers and producers of the groundbreaking American documentary account of the disability arts movement, *Crip Culture Talks Back*. In their pursuit of financial support for this project, the filmmakers discovered that disability organizations with grant monies turned them down because the project lacked a rehabilitative focus. Major American disability research granting agencies turned them down because art isn't rigorous by scholarly measures; mainstream arts organizations like PBS turned them down because the project lacked "the powerful stuff of first person melodrama" that audiences demand from their disability stories. In the end, *Crip Culture Talks Back* was funded by the Mayo Clinic. Canadians can't allow our up-and-coming cultural contributors to fall through these kinds of cracks.

• Much rights advocacy has focused, with modest success, upon making arts venues accessible for disabled patrons. Implicit, however, in dominant discourses on arts accessibility is the notion that disabled people's place in the art world is as *consumers*, rather than *producers* of artistic works. Despite legal obligations to ensure that artistic venues are accessible to disabled persons, standards of compliance are invariably oriented toward disabled patrons, rather than disabled performers and exhibiting artists. For example, as theatres gradually concede the necessity for accessible seating and public washrooms, there continues to be little or no recognition of the necessity for accessible stages and dressing rooms.

Within this context, and working closely with the Canadian disability arts community, policy-makers must seek to appropriately recognize and cultivate the cultural contributions of this sector, as disabled artists seek to gain access to audiences, environments and creative opportunities.

Breaking *from* Culture

The great social movements that have converged in the equality seeking discourse of the late 20th and early 21st centuries have distinctively pursued agendas of social rehabilitation and resistance in significant measure through collective, identity-based claims for cultural recognition. Similarly, disability scholarship recognizes a quest for collective identity in the emergence of an arts movement within the broader disability rights arena. Disability arts and culture therefore represent an important juncture in the emancipatory journey of disabled people — as disabled citizens take control of words, images and ideas that have historically worked against them.

Within this context, how does the creative work of artists within the disability arts and culture movement challenge, complicate or confront the dominant lexicon of disability representation? Two examples drawn from a larger study on the state of the art in

Canadian Disability Arts and Culture (Abbas et al., 2004) will help illustrate the policy dimensions of *breaking from culture*:

• Popular culture has tended to present a narrow, inaccurate view of disability that either frames disability as tragic defect, or frames disabled people as curiosities to be gawked at or feared. Art is both a product of culture and a key mechanism by which the politics of a culturally sanctioned norm are enforced. The voices, experiences, and struggles of disabled people are either strikingly absent, or grossly and stereotypically misrepresented in mainstream art and culture. Voices speaking back against stereotypic images of disability must continually confront a dominant narrative of disability — a task that requires not simply introducing disability to non-disabled audiences, but introducing disability with honesty and authenticity. In extending critical attention to the fast-growing canon of disability arts, the larger arts and culture sector in Canada must examine and explore representations of disability that break free from colonized, sentimental and/or stereotype-driven framings. Emphasis must be placed upon experimentation with and evaluation of a range of curatorial and critical strategies with a view toward both supporting and legitimizing the contributions of disabled artists presently under-represented in galleries, on television, in films, in theatres and on performance stages of all kinds.

• Questions of the interaction between audience and performer and the extent to which disability arts and culture influence attitudes toward disabled people remain at this time relatively unexplored. A major strength of disability arts and culture lies in countering the dominant discourse of disability. Not coincidentally, audience accounts express strongly that to witness a performance in this genre is to be challenged and made uncomfortable as much as it is to be affirmed and uplifted. What this suggests is that "changing attitudes" is not a simple enlightenment arising from new and better information. Consciousness-raising about a group of people so negatively situated with respect to mainstream culture can be troubling and difficult work. disability arts and culture is here at its most politically potent. As the disability arts movement grows and matures, audiences must also become increasingly sophisticated in understanding the complexities of what is being enacted. Because cultural work is reciprocal in nature, research initia-

CATHERINE FRAZEE

tives and cultural funders must focus attention upon both sides of this relationship.

Dialogues *with* Culture

In what Susan Bordo refers to as our "Nike universe of values", epitomized by the slogan "Just do it", our dominant cultural imperative is "[S]top whining, lace up your sneakers and forge ahead, blasting your way through social limitations, personal tribulations, and even the laws of nature" (Bordo, 1998). While disabled Canadians have made some gains in advancing an equality perspective and influencing our nation's social policy agenda, a prevailing ethic of hyper-individualism will, if unchecked, continue to undermine the equality claims of citizens whose *"productive"* capacities fall below the standard of a fully autonomous and productively self-sufficient "Ideal Citizen" (Ticoll, 1996). It is for this reason that policy-makers must seek to challenge, in cultural domains and fora, values and convictions that render disabled people invisible and subordinate.

Cultural forms afford the opportunity for disabled people "to contest ... the marginalization of their lives; bringing people together in ways that enable them to recognize each other, and to challenge their exclusion from society. In that sense, [culture] is an essential route to collective empowerment" (Abbas et al., 2004, p. 4). It is also, demonstrably, an effective strategy for informing and educating the non-disabled world about its own biases and prejudice.

Accordingly, whether the content area is autonomy or abuse, biotechnology or disability supports, policy development and dissemination can be infused with processes that give voice to the lived experience of disabled citizens. Research undertaken in the emergent tradition of arts-informed research — that is, "research that brings together the systematic and rigorous qualities of social science inquiry with the creative and imaginative qualities of the arts" (Cole & Knowles, 2001, pp. 10–11) — allows for the investigation of cultural forms and phenomena while at the same time *contributing* to culture. Research outputs are therefore both intellectual and aesthetic, entering into dialogues with their respective audiences in new languages of image, metaphor and gesture. Cultural products created by disabled artists, in dialogue with policy-makers — an exhibition of visual arts giving witness to the experience of abuse, an anthology of poetry and narrative writing exploring themes of autonomy and self-determination, a theatrical presentation dramatizing the tensions and human implications of prenatal screening and selective abortion, or a photo essay on homelessness and disability —will add depth and vitality to social policy work related to disability.

Reflections *on* Culture

Dorothy Smith and others have written about social and cultural regimes — systems of structuring relations that give coherence to our social arrangements and practices. According to Smith, regimes provide the order within which we know ourselves and others, and the order within which we make sense of our privileges and deprivations. Smith observes that the very coherence of a social order generates contradictions. Such anomalies, she reminds us, "attack the very character of our régimes ... endanger[ing] its coherence" (Smith, 1992, p. 210).

Social policy initiatives related to disability must be premised upon an interrogation of how normalcy functions as a regime and how disability is generated as its anomaly. In every possible sphere, good disability policy requires illumination and critical examination of purportedly *"neutral"* and *"objective"* judgments of value made by those who "enjoy close alignment with [conventional] notions of normality" (Fitzgerald, 1999, p. 271).

Reflecting on culture therefore requires the following:

- Resist pressures to privatize or individualize the dilemmas of disability and seek accounts and responses that are fully contextualized.

- Counteract the ideological forces that isolate and exclude disabled people from positive social and cultural recognition.

- Uproot and disrupt destructive stereotypes that erode the self-perceptions of disabled citizens, characterizing them as tragic victims and social burdens.

- Link patterns of social neglect and cultural invisibility to experiences of deprivation and marginality.

Listed below a few examples of questions that might emerge from such framings:

- How do current bioethical debates on topics ranging from sterilization and selective abortion to medical care allocations and assisted suicide create and support a *culture of control* under-

CATHERINE FRAZEE

pinning modern Western medicine and philosophy? How does a disability perspective on these issues illuminate the necessity to liberate discourses of choice, autonomy, dignity, risk and self-determination from the distortions and appropriations of an ableist culture?

• With regard to policy discussions related to human reproduction, health care and end-of-life choices and decisions, how does the introduction of a disability perspective challenge assumptions embedded in the language in which such debates typically unfold?

• How have cultural representations of disability in mass media, popular cinema, music and literature been played out in contemporary social policy? What stresses and harms flow from cultural images, and how are these taken up by disabled citizens in their negotiation of social place and identity?

• How can social policy measures assist in confronting "aesthetic imperialism" — the ways in which our dominant culture constructs an entire social group as degenerate, untouchable or ugly (Young, 1990, p. 125)?

• How does contemporary Canadian jurisprudence frame discourses of "dignity" or "suffering" in relation to disabled and non-disabled people? How do quality of life assessments undertaken in medical, legal, legislative, academic and "everyday" contexts develop and sustain norms and values related to disabled people?

CONCLUSION

Disabled equality-seekers are "duking it out" on public stages and in public spaces. The result, at best, is a displacement of privilege and power, emerging from a declaration of strong and confident minority culture. Will the end result be simply a substitution of *us* for *them* and *them* for *us*? I believe not. In the chaos that results, when privilege and power shift, there are opportunities for the formation of new identities — both for *us* and for *them* — which are not fixed but plural. In her exploration of an expansive formulation of *rights* and *recognition* in a multicultural context, Morag Patrick has the following observation:

368

Here we are dealing with the problems that arise when a social group experiences the absence of social rather than legal recognition. The liberal focus on rights should not obscure our view of the political significance of feeling esteemed within a sociocultural environment. (2002, p. 36)

Embedded within our culture — a culture that prides itself upon principles of non-discrimination and constitutional equality — are countervailing ideologies premised upon a flawed conviction that disability disadvantage is both natural and inevitable. Canadian policy-makers must be well equipped to undertake multidisciplinary dialogues about the cultural values and regimes that shape Canadian law and social policy. Policy researchers and commentators can contribute vital intellectual capital to this task, taking up projects of historical research, discourse analysis, critical observation and the development of alternative legal and ethical framings.

23

Making Federally Regulated Transportation Systems Accessible to Persons with Disabilities

APRIL D'AUBIN

INTRODUCTION

Soon after the publication of the 1981 *Obstacles Report*, attention was given to transportation issues — not only because they were seen to be an essential part of access, but also because the federal government had broad authority in this area. This chapter examines issues related to federally regulated transportation systems for people with disabilities in Canada. It first describes the history of federal transportation policy and emphasizes the contribution of disability organizations to the development of accessible transportation systems. Stakeholders in the area of accessible transportation are then defined and various modes of transportation described. The public policy framework is outlined, and key events that influenced Canada's public policy environment are examined, including a rising interest in human rights. Important events that tipped Canada's public policy environment away from improved access in the federally regulated transportation are described.

Despite the importance of transportation in everyone's life, meeting the transportation needs of people with disabilities has been a limited priority for Canadian transportation stakeholders, except for people with disabilities. In 2005, despite almost 30 years of advocacy on accessibility issues, disability advocacy organizations said that accessibility in the federally regulated transportation system was eroding, particularly in the air and rail modes.

For people with disabilities, especially those involved in self-representational advocacy organizations, the advancement of accessible transportation has been a high priority. Indeed, inaccessible transportation options and the desire to remove barriers in the transportation system had mobilized disability advocacy organizations at the local level in the 1970s. Advances in accessible transportation have largely been the result of the advocacy efforts of people with disabilities. Since the 1970s, these organizations have been keeping the pressure on both the federal government and transportation providers (Baker, 2005).

Jerome E. Bickenbach, in his article "Disability Human Rights, Law, and Policy", notes that there are four approaches to rights for persons with disabilities: "1. enforceable antidiscrimination legislation, 2. constitutional guarantees of equality, 3. specific entitlement programs, 4. voluntary human rights manifestos" (2001, p. 568). In the area of transportation, Canada has relied heavily on voluntary codes of practice to provide access to the federally regulated transportation system for persons with disabilities. This chapter will show that a voluntary approach to access is an inadequate method for ensuring access to the federally regulated transportation system for persons with disabilities.

Henry Enns and Aldred Neufeldt, in *In Pursuit of Equal Participation: Canada and Disability At Home and Abroad*, point out that the roles disability advocacy organizations have played in policy development in Canada are not well known outside of the disability community. They state, "On reading various accounts that include only minor references to disability advocacy organizations, one gets the impression that governments have been at the leading edge of introducing innovations in approach to disability issues" (Enns & Neufeldt, 2003, p. 3). To acknowledge and demonstrate the importance of their role in disability policy development, this chapter will place a particular emphasis on the contribution of disability advocacy organizations to the field of accessible transportation. Like Enns and Neufeldt, in *In Pursuit of Equal Participation*, I start with a "bias towards the perspective of disability advocacy organizations", and like Enns and Neufeldt, I also endeavor to accurately reflect the roles of other stakeholders (Enns & Neufeldt, 2003, p. 4).

In *In Pursuit of Equal Participation*, Neufeldt discusses the phenomenon of "tipping" events, which push public policy toward a particular approach to disability issues (Neufeldt, 2003, p. 223). In this chapter, events and issues that have tipped Canada toward or away from increased accessibility are identified, and the continuing obstacles and emerging barriers to the mobility of persons with disabilities are examined.

BACKGROUND

David Baker (2005) explains that even in pre-Elizabethan times transportation was viewed as a public good and in need of regulation so that it could be used by all for the good of the nation. Early English courts required transportation service providers to treat everyone equally (Baker, 2005, p. 20). Several centuries later, Canadians with disabilities are still seeking equality in the country's federally regulated transportation system.

Transportation Barriers

The Canadian federally regulated transportation system developed largely without any consideration of the needs of people with disabilities. Due to design assumptions that did not consider the needs of the whole population, the federally regulated transportation system has been rife with barriers that prevent the full and equal participation of people with disabilities. People with disabilities who use wheelchairs, walkers or scooters find airports, terminals, stations, buses, trains, airplanes and ferries continue to have stairs, very narrow aisles or corridors, and other barriers that do not accommodate mobility aides. Washrooms are not constructed with sufficient space for a mobility aid, and easy-use fixtures are not always in place. There is insufficient space allocated for service animals on many carriers. Information is not communicated in alternate media for people with sensory impairments. Plain language explanations of procedures and practices continue to be rare. Staff and transportation service providers have ableist attitudes toward disability. (The foregoing was meant to be an example of some barriers and should not be considered an exhaustive list of barriers.)

One of the obstacles to accessible transportation policy has been the tendency to view people with disabilities as the problem and fail to understand the real problem: the barriers to full and equal participation existing in the federally regulated transportation system. Take for example the concept of "transportation disability". The report *Disability and Transportation in Canada: Demographics, Needs and Opportunities Summary Report* provides the following definition of transportation disabilities:

> Individuals who, because of their health problem or condition, are unable to use transportation services, or use transportation services with more difficulty than those in the general population. (Hickling Corporation, 1992, p. 4)

The report goes on to say that the definition also relates to "the specific difficulties they [people with disabilities] encounter" (Hickling Corporation, 1992, p. 4). The medical model approach to all disability issues is a problem that people with disabilities and their advocacy organizations have been addressing for many years.

In the late 1970s, people with disabilities began to challenge the inaccessibility of the transportation system, and, slowly, their arguments began to be heard by decision-makers. People with disabilities and their advocacy organizations asserted that they had unique expertise on barrier removal, and they should be consulted by government and service providers and included in processes where services and public policies were being developed. Over the years, people with disabilities have been recognized as stakeholders in the transportation sector.

People with disabilities have been advocating that systems, like transportation, should be designed according to the principles of universal design. With universal design, systems and environments are developed in a manner that also considers the needs of the widest range of people in the population. Universal design promotes products and environments usable by all people, to the greatest extent possible, without the need for adaptation or specialized design (The Center for Universal Design, 1997).

People with disabilities make up a significant proportion of the Canadian population — 12.4%. The Participation and Activity Limitation Survey (PALS) shows that the three most frequently reported types of disability for Canadians aged 25 to 54 are pain, mobility, and agility. With the aging of the population, barrier removal in the federally regulated transportation is becoming an issue for more and more Canadians (Human Resources Development Canada, 2003).

The Stakeholders

In the area of accessible transportation, there are many different stakeholders. Following are some of the relevant stakeholders who play a role in the development of public policy on accessible transportation:

- People with disabilities who face barriers in the federally regulated transportation system and the self-representational advocacy organizations of persons with disabilities;
- Minister of Transport and officials in Transport Canada;
- Canadian Transportation Agency — a regulatory agency — and its staff;
- Passenger carriers (air, rail, ferries, inter-provincial buses) and their advocacy associations (Canadian Bus Association, Canadian Urban Transit Association, Transportation Association of Canada, Air Transport Association of Canada, Canadian Ferry Operators Association of Canada);
- Manufacturers of passenger carriers; and
- Transportation unions.

To varying degrees, each of these actors plays a role in advancing or hampering the accessibility of the federally regulated transportation system. With respect to the development of accessible transportation policies, three stakeholders have been particularly important:

1. People with disabilities and the self-representational organizations of persons with disabilities,
2. The Government of Canada and its various officials and agencies, and
3. Transportation carriers.

People with disabilities and their organizations have played a key role in the advancement of accessibility in the federally regulated transportation system. Some examples of the work that has been done are as follows: Many individuals with disabilities have been filing complaints with the regulatory agencies responsible for the system. For example, Henry Vlug laid complaints in the regulatory system to remove barriers faced by deaf travellers (Canadian Transportation Agency [CTA], 1998b). In 1991, pressure from the Canadian Paraplegic Association led to an inquiry into the accessibility of the motor coach industry. In 1995, pressure from the Canadian Council of the Blind led to research on the communication barriers encountered by persons with visual impairments in the transportation system. The Council of Canadians with Disabilities has lodged complaints with the regulatory agency. People with disabilities have shared their expertise about access with the Minister of Transport and Transport Canada, and with the Transportation Development Centre in its research and demonstration projects.

Transport Canada is the federal government department tasked with developing and administering policies, regulations and services for the federally regulated transportation system. Transport Canada has developed transportation policy statements relating to accessibility, and it has also operated a funding program to promote accessibility. The Minister of Transport has the ultimate responsibility for directing the activities of the Department. Transport Canada has undertaken activities in the areas of policy development, research and development initiatives, and funding programs that have contributed to increased access in the federally regulated transportation system.

Some significant bodies that play a role in increased access:

- **Ministerial Advisory Committees** — committees appointed by the Minister of Transport to provide advice on accessible transportation issues.

- **Transportation Development Centre (TDC)** — the TDC has been mandated by Transport Canada to undertake research and development activities in support of the Canadian transportation system. The TDC has delivered an accessibility program that has assisted in the development of various technical innovations, such as aircraft boarding devices and accessible buses.

Accessibility of Various Modes of Transportation

(a) Air

In Canada, there is a hub and spoke system in operation. Generally speaking, large centres act as the hubs and are serviced by larger aircraft, and regional carriers using small aircraft service smaller centres. Smaller aircraft are less accessible than the larger aircraft. For example, the storage facilities on some small aircraft cannot accommodate a power wheelchair. Smaller aircraft are increasingly being used in Canada. As a result, in some instances, carriers are replacing accessible services with inaccessible services. At one time, airports were operated by Transport Canada; they are now operated by local airport authorities.

(b) Rail

VIA Rail, a Crown corporation, provides passenger rail services in the eight continental Canadian provinces. Its major stations have been equipped with lifts. With VIA I, each train is equipped with one accessible car. Accessibility declined in the VIA system with the incorporation of the Renaissance cars. (See later section, "Case Example of an Accessibility Struggle", for more on the Renaissance cars.)

(c) Marine

Ferries operating in coastal waters and harbours are under federal jurisdiction. In Atlantic Canada, Marine Atlantic Inc. operates a ferry service, with BC Ferries operating ferries on the west coast.

(d) Inter-provincial bus

Inter-provincial motor coach service is available throughout Canada. With advance booking, people with disabilities have access to inter-provincial bus transport.

The inter-provincial bus industry, working in collaboration with people with disabilities and their organizations and Transport Canada, developed a voluntary code of practice, which came into effect 1 October 1998. This occurred after the federal Minister of Transport threatened to regulate the industry for access, if it did not achieve a voluntary mechanism. The code of practice is not a regulation. "It is a set of guidelines for offering accessible inter-city bus transportation to persons with disabilities through the provision of accessible buses and terminals and the provision of services by trained staff" (Transport Canada, 1998, p. 1). Transport Canada operates a complaint mechanism that addresses barriers encountered by persons with disabilities travelling by inter-provincial bus.

THE PUBLIC POLICY FRAMEWORK

Jurisdictional responsibility for the various modes of transportation has been established by law, court decision and agreements between levels of government. The 1867 *British North America Act* (BNA Act) assigned responsibility for international shipping and railways to the federal government. It also gave the federal government jurisdiction over inter-provincial transportation. The Act, however, did not address possible future advances in transportation technology. In 1952, a decision by the Supreme Court of Canada placed air transportation in federal jurisdiction. While inter-provincial bus transportation is in federal jurisdiction, regulatory authority was delegated to provincial motor transport boards in 1954 (Health and Welfare Canada, 1980). The BNA Act gave the provinces jurisdiction over "local and private" matters; thus, taxis, private automobiles and urban mass transit are under provincial jurisdiction.

When Newfoundland joined Canada in 1949, the Terms of Union established that the federal government would assume responsibility for the railways in Newfoundland. In 1962, the Roadcruiser bus service replaced passenger rail in Newfoundland. The federal government maintained jurisdiction over Roadcruiser.

Some Federal Acts Affecting Accessible Transportation

(a) Canadian Charter of Rights and Freedoms

Section 15 of the *Charter* guarantees equality rights to persons with disabilities. The Court Challenges Program funds eligible test cases that seek to strike down federal laws, programs and policies that offend Section 15.

(b) Canadian Human Rights Act

Canadian Human Rights Act prohibited discrimination against people with disabilities. People with disabilities who experience barriers to their mobility in the federally regulated transportation system have been encouraged by the Canadian Human Rights Commission to first make a complaint to the Canadian Transportation Agency.

(c) Canada Transportation Act and the Canadian Transportation Agency

The *Canada Transportation Act* addresses the economic operation of the transportation industry and establishes the regulatory framework for this industry.

The 1996 *Canada Transportation Act* regulates the rail, water, air and surface transportation in Canada. The Act established the Canadian Transportation Agency (CTA), which has regulatory responsibility for access.

Key Events in Improved Access in Federally Regulated Transportation

(a) A rising interest in human rights

In Canada, there has been an increasing interest in social inclusion. Canada's official bilingualism policy demonstrated how polices and practices could be altered to make Canadian society more inclusive. At the provincial level, the McRuer Commission looked into civil rights in Ontario (Legislative Assembly of Ontario), and the Quebec National Assembly drafted a law to protect the rights of persons with disabilities. The 1978 *Canadian Human Rights Act* included protections for persons with disabilities, as did the *Canadian Charter of Rights and Freedoms*. However, the *Canadian Human Rights Act* only protected people with disabilities from discrimination in the labour market. After much advocacy by the disability community, the Act was amended to include protection from discrimination for persons with disabilities in the provision of goods, services, facilities and accommodations (Crichton & Jongbloed, 1998, p. 28).

In 1986, for the Mobility in the Global Village conference, Gordon Fairweather, Chief Commissioner of the Canadian Human Rights Commission, made the following connections between human rights and accessible transportation for persons with disabilities:

> The words "human rights" conjure up images of women, colored people, disputes about employment patterns and education, debates concerning anti-discrimination laws and the Charter of Rights and Freedoms. But for millions of Canadians, "human rights" has a much more direct application: it involves the ability to move freely within the community. These are the Canadians with transportation handicaps, many of whom live within a short distance of a transit service that they cannot use. One activist summed up the feelings of those who have been denied the most basic mobility rights: "An entire social movement arose over the question of where certain people must sit when they ride the bus. I can't even get on the bus." (Fairweather, 1986, p. 1)

People with disabilities recognized the transformative possibilities of human rights law and theory and began to apply human rights arguments to disability issues (Bickenbach, 2001). Human rights arguments were applied to the transportation issue. At the Mobility in the Global Village conference, disability advocate Ron Kanary stated:

> Persons with disabilities speak as citizens in terms of rights. We formulate our issues on these lines ... Access to Canadian transportation services is a right that has been guaranteed to disabled citizens in Canadian legislation, policy statements and regulatory bodies. (Kanary, 1986, p. 280)

(b) Individual complaints

Grassroots individuals with disabilities have played a significant role in barrier removal in federally regulated transportation by filing complaints with the various regulatory bodies that have been in place in Canada. Some significant cases will be highlighted in this section.

THE CLARRIS KELLY CASE

In 1978, Clarris Kelly, a law student who used a wheelchair, wanted to travel by train unaccompanied by another person who would be responsible for assisting her. Kelly believed that she was self-reliant and did not require an assistant during her train trip. At that time, decisions about the carriage of a person with a disability were at the discretion of VIA Rail personnel at the point of service. In the Kelly case, a VIA Rail staff person determined that Kelly was not self-reliant. In October of 1978, Kelly filed a complaint with the Canadian Transportation Commission (CTC). The CTC ruled that VIA Rail's practice of requiring that another person take responsibility for a wheelchair-using passenger was "prejudicial to the public interest" and "an affront to the dignity" of persons with disabilities.

The CTC ruling established four important principles: self-determination; one person, one fare; equality of access; and dignity of access. David Baker, who has called the Clarris Kelly case the *Magna Carta* of transportation access in Canada, describes the impact of the CTC's decision in the following manner:

> In the end the Committee made four major orders:
> 1. Disabled people were given the right of <u>self-determination,</u> [emphasis present in original] i.e. to decide whether or not they required an attendant.
> 2. The principle of "<u>one person one fare</u>" was adopted, i.e., the attendant was perceived alternatively as an extension of the disabled person or of the service provided by the railway, but in either event, would be permitted to travel on the disabled person's ticket.
> 3. Despite a plan by the railway to install mechanical lifting devices in all major rail stations over time, the railway was

required to immediately provide manual boarding assistance
at its 13 largest stations, i.e. equality of access;
4. While aware of the additional risks faced by people with
disabilities when traveling, the Committee found them not
to be so substantial as to justify denial of carriage (i.e., the
dignity of risk). Also, the railway was not permitted to
extract waivers of liability from such passengers. Allowing
waivers would have reduced the incentive for improved
safety procedures reflecting the special needs of disabled
passengers. (Baker, 1986, p. 2)

Disability rights organizations in Canada have made it a priority to extend the principles established in the Kelly case to other
modes and to other aspects of Canadian life.

THE ADELIA CASE

In the Adelia case, Air Canada refused to transport Ruth
Adelia because she was not travelling with an attendant. In *Adelia
v. Air Canada*, the CTC ruled that people with disabilities have the
right to decide whether or not they need an attendant when travelling by air (*The Globe and Mail*, 1986).

Individual complaints have made a great contribution to
improving access in the federally regulated transportation system.
While this is true, there are nevertheless some disadvantages to
an individual-driven complaint system. The individualized complaint system puts the responsibility on grassroots people with disabilities to force change. This model takes a toll on persons with
disabilities. The Canadian Hearing Society provides the following
observation:

A number of passengers have filed human rights complaints with
the Canadian Transportation Agency and the Canadian Human
Rights Commission, but this is a slow and ineffective process.
Currently, individual complaints have to reach the Supreme
Court of Canada before change occurs. Even with landmark
cases, individuals must bear the sole responsibility to fight for
their rights if transportation service providers or Transport Canada does not provide access. This is costly in time, money and
human dignity. (CHS, 2000, p. 3)

The individual driven complaint system is not unique to the
area of transportation. Individual complaints have also been a key
component of Canada's human rights system.

(c) Federal funding to promote accessible transportation

The federal government has allocated funds for the development of transportation at the local level. In 1978, the federal government began to provide funding under the Transportation of Disabled Persons Program (TDPP) to improve accessible transportation in Canada. Transport Canada described the program's objective in the following manner: the program focused on policy development, funding, research and demonstration and knowledge transfer (Transport Canada, 1990).

The TDPP was under the direction of the Minister of Transport and the Deputy Minister; however, it considered the priorities recommended by people with disabilities and the transportation industry (Transport Canada, 1990). For example, the TDPP would receive the priorities from the Transportation of Disabled Persons Implementation Committee (TDPIC), an advisory committee participated by people with disabilities. The TDPP objectives were

> to fund, promote, and coordinate initiatives intended to benefit elderly and disabled persons in improving access to transportation services under federal jurisdiction, as well as to promote the development of a safe and efficient national transportation system while meeting government objectives. (Transportation Development Center, 1998, p. 15)

In 1991, the federal government launched a five-year National Strategy for the Integration of Persons with Disabilities that contributed $158 million to 10 federal government departments for the purpose of improving the status of persons with disabilities. The Strategy directed $24.6 million toward improving accessible transportation in Canada.

(d) Ministerial advisory committees on accessible transportation

In May of 1979, Transport Canada formed the Advisory Committee on the Needs of the Handicapped (ACTH) to provide advice on accessibility issues. People with disabilities were key to this committee. Various stakeholder activities were promoting increased consultation with people with disabilities. The Transportation Development Center stated, "The pioneering work by TDC led to the recognition in Transport Canada that consultation and consumer input were needed to help guide their accessible transportation initiative" (TDC, 1998, p. 16). The self-representational organizations of people with disabilities had also been calling for people with disabilities to be included in consultative and advisory bodies. The establishment of this committee sent an important signal that the Government of Canada was listening to the demands of people with disabilities to be included in a meaningful manner in the development of public policies on disability issues. In 1985, the federal government created the Transportation of Disabled Persons Implementation Committee (TDPIC), which was mandated to advise the Minister of Transport on the implementation of the national transportation policy. Currently, the Minister of Transport has an Advisory Committee on Accessible Transportation (ACAT), which is made up of representatives from national disability organizations and transportation service providers. The Committee provides advice to the Minister, although one of the weaknesses of the advisory committee model is that the advice provided is often disregarded.

(e) Federal transportation policy

The Minister of Transport established a policy on transportation of disabled persons in 1984. Ron Kanary of the Coalition of Provincial Organizations of the Handicapped (COPOH, known as the Council of Canadians with Disabilities [CCD] since 1994), in his keynote presentation at the 1985 COPOH Conference, addressed the policy. The goal of the policy was to remove barriers to federally regulated transportation. People with disabilities were involved in the development of the national policy on transportation of disabled persons.

In 1991, the Minister of Transport issued a new policy statement on accessible transportation: *Access for All — Transport Canada's Policy on Accessible Transportation.* This document made the following policy commitment:

> Accessible transportation is a right, not a privilege. All Canadians should be able to use Canada's transportation system without impediment. Transport Canada supports fully integrated, barrier-free transportation that accommodates the needs of persons with disabilities. (Transport Canada, 1991, p. 2)

Access for All set out the following principles:

- **The Right of Access** — The Government of Canada is responsible for ensuring that safe, reliable and accessible transportation services and facilities are available to able-bodied and disabled persons alike. When travelling, persons with disabilities are entitled to be treated with the same dignity, consistency and consideration afforded to other travellers and to receive services customarily available to the general public. This entitlement extends to information and directions that can be understood by travellers with cognitive or sensory disabilities.

- **Terms and Conditions** — Passengers with disabilities should not be subject to unreasonable terms and conditions of carriage, nor face additional charges or higher fares related to transportation services provided for them.

- **Seniors' Needs** — The travel requirements of senior travellers must be considered in ensuring accessible transportation. It has been shown that improvements designed to benefit seniors frequently benefit all travellers.

- **Independent Travel** — All disabled travellers should be assumed to be self-reliant with respect to any services required unless they, or their chosen representatives, state otherwise.

- **Integration** — Transportation services for elderly and disabled travellers should be provided in conjunction with regular services wherever possible. The integrated approach has been shown to provide broader social and economic benefits than parallel services.

- **Attaining Accessibility** — Accessibility is a term that must be constantly redefined. Although minimum standards of accessibility can be defined, maximum standards cannot. As each goal is achieved, new goals must be set if we are to succeed in making Canada's transportation system accessible to all (Transport Canada, 1991, pp. 6–7).

Government policy statements do not have the force of law. While they are important symbols of a government's commitment, they provide no real remedies when a person with a disability encounters a barrier in the transportation system.

(f) Public meetings and conferences

CRCD CONFERENCE

In March 1978, the Canadian Rehabilitation Council for the Disabled (CRCD), Health and Welfare Canada and Transport Canada co-sponsored a national symposium on transportation. In 1978, the CRCD viewed itself as an advocacy group on disability issues. The CRCD held the conference, hoping that the information brought to light would influence Federal and Provincial governments toward improving transportation services for people with disabilities (CRCD, 1978, Preface). In the "Conference Orientation", Dr. D.P. Dezil stated:

This gathering is unique in the development of transportation systems for the handicapped in Canada. To the best of my knowledge it is the first time that such a group has come together from all parts of Canada representing senior government officials as well as a cross-section of managers, administrators, specialists and entrepreneurs with actual 'hands on' experience in the planning and operation of systems for the transportation [of the] handicapped.

The aim of this seminar will be first to review the present state of handicapped transportation in Canada, second to focus on directions for the future and finally to make these views known to legislators, their officials and the general public.

It is particularly fitting that this symposium has convened at this time. We are at a crossroads in the development of transportation services for the handicapped and a number of important issues need to be resolved if we are to establish a sound and coherent direction for the future. These issues cover a wide spectrum, ranging from fundamental questions linked to social philosophy, through technological considerations regarding the efficiency and effectiveness of various transportation systems, to matters of strategy — how best can the necessary changes be implemented? (CRCD, 1978, p. 1)

There were 10 recommendations developed at the conference. These recommendations urged the federal and provincial governments and transportation providers to address the transportation issues of persons with disabilities as transportation issues rather than as medical or social issues, and that funding programs and legislation be developed with the aim of improving accessible transportation for persons with disabilities. The CRCD also thought that it should take the lead on this issue. The tenth recommendation stated:

The CRCD should take the lead as an advocacy group in promoting[,] through its national and provincial organizations and through other agencies, an increased public awareness of the needs of handicapped travellers, as well as an awareness on the part of governments at all levels of the need for legislation, programs, coordination and research to improve the provision of transportation services. (CRCD, 1978, p. 163)

Positions such as this created tensions with the emerging disability rights movement, where people with disabilities spoke for themselves on issues such as accessible transportation. Enns and Neufeldt note that "CRCD would fade from view, its hopes for coordinating the broad group of organizations concerned with motor impairment dashed" (Enns & Neufeldt, 2003, p. 54).

COPOH [CCD] CONFERENCE

In 1979, the Coalition of Provincial Organizations of the Handicapped (COPOH) brought people with disabilities together for an open national forum on transportation. This conference also served to focus attention on disability issues. It made the point that people with disabilities were the legitimate spokespersons on disability issues.

CANADIAN TRANSPORTATION COMMISSION HEARINGS ON ACCESSIBLE TRANSPORTATION

In November of 1979, the Canadian Transportation Commission held an open meeting on the transportation issues of persons with disabilities. The Commission heard from people with disabilities and their organizations, VIA Rail, Air Canada, and government departments. Jim Derksen, who was the national co-ordinator of the CCD in 1979, reflects back on this event:

> In the Seventies, influenced by the civil rights movement in the United States and the women's movement, people with disabilities started to organize. We began to see our problems may not be our disabilities. We began to work on the issues that concerned us. One of our first issues was transportation. In 1979, the Council of Canadians with Disabilities (CCD) held a transportation conference in Ottawa on the right of persons with disabilities to use public transportation. In order to get people to Ottawa, we had people travelling in the freight car of a train because the passenger cars were not accessible; we had people manhandled up the stairs of airplanes because there were no accessible means to board wheelchair users. We convinced the Canadian Transport Commission to have a public hearing on transportation and people with disabilities. At that hearing we told all the stories about how difficult it was to get to Ottawa. We got a lot of media attention. We got a lot of political attention. We were saying this is not about charity. This is about us being able to use the same sort of public transport that has been developed for citizens. These public transport systems have been developed in such a way that they do not serve us. We need to redesign them. We were carving out values of inclusion, integration and equality rights. (Derksen, 2002b)

René R. Gadacz provided the following assessment of the impact of these events in *Re-Thinking Disability*:

In 1979, COPOH's second forum on Accessibility of Transportation (Ottawa) that coincided with the Canadian Transportation Commission's public hearings resulted in a National Policy on Transportation of Disabled Persons (Department of Transportation) and greater accessibility of such carriers as Air Canada and VIA Rail. (Gadacz, 1994, p. 154)

Other stakeholders in the transportation sector were beginning to hear the message on accessible transportation delivered by the disability community. The 1980s was a time of considerable progress in the area of accessible transportation.

(g) International Year of Disabled Persons and the Special Parliamentary Committee on the Disabled and the Handicapped

The United Nations designated 1981 as the International Year of Disabled Persons (IYDP). Canadians embraced IYDP, and activities were initiated at the local, provincial and federal levels. For example, at the local level, community groups were busy building ramps into churches and community clubs; at the provincial level, co-ordinating committees were developed to help fund local projects; and at the federal level, the House of Commons struck a Special Committee on the Disabled and the Handicapped, which was mandated to report on the needs of Canadians with disabilities.

The Special Committee, which included representatives from all parties, travelled across Canada and heard from Canadians with disabilities about the barriers in their lives that prevented them from participating fully and equally in Canadian society. Consumers told the Committee about being refused air flights because they were viewed as a safety risk, about being asked to sign waivers by carriers wanted to be absolved from the responsibility of providing safe transportation to people with disabilities, about being required to travel with an attendant and then having to pay for the attendant's fare. In February 1981, the Committee tabled in the House of Commons 130 recommendations in a report called *Obstacles*. The *Obstacles Report* was a watershed event in disability history in Canada. In this report, Parliamentarians echoed what they had heard from citizens with disabilities, and many of the recommendations supported the participation of self-representational advocacy organizations in the planning and development of disability services, programs, and policies (see recommendation No. 83). The *Obstacles Report*'s recommendations 83 through 92 addressed transportation issues:

No. 83 — That the Federal Government direct the Minister of Transport to develop, in consultation with disabled persons and their organizations, and to publish a National Transportation Policy on Transportation for Disabled Persons and to provide reasonable access to all transportation modes under federal jurisdiction. ...

No. 84 — That, pending the adoption of the a National Transportation Policy for Disabled Persons, the Federal Government, through the Department of Transport develop and implement a plan which will ensure that major transportation terminals (including air, rail and ferry) under its jurisdiction be reasonably accessible ... That the Federal Government, through the Department of Transport, publish a schedule outlining its plan and schedule for achieving reasonable access to transportation terminals.

No. 85 — That the Federal Government ensure that all passenger transport equipment purchased or retrofitted with Federal funding, be reasonably accessible to disabled persons.

No. 86 — That the Federal Government request the Canadian Transport Commission to require the Roadcruiser bus service in Newfoundland to provide a mechanical facility or a service for lifting people in wheelchairs on and off the vehicle.

No. 87 — That the Federal Government directs the Department of National Revenue to exempt the purchase of accessible intercity buses from the Federal Sales tax to encourage the development of an accessible intercity bus service across Canada.

No. 88 — That the Federal Government, through the Minister of Transport require that air carriers adopt a policy of accepting the disabled traveller's estimate of his/her self-reliance, without medical certificates or waivers of disability. That where necessary, boarding assistance be provided by carriers. That where an attendant is required to care for the personal needs of a disabled traveller, that attendant will travel free. That where more than one seat is required for the transport of a disabled person for various reasons arising from his/her disability, only one fare will be charged for that traveller.

No 89 — That the Federal Government request the Canadian Transport Commission (CTC) to require air carriers to have available at airports a few wheelchairs and batteries to be loaned to disabled passengers in case of loss or severe damage, and to require air carriers to reimburse, at replacement cost rather than purchase price, owners of lost or severely damaged wheelchairs.

No 90 — That, where the Federal Government has jurisdiction over parking ... a uniform national policy be developed ...

No. 91 — That the Federal Government negotiate with the Provinces a cost-sharing agreement to establish a fund similar to the Student Loan Program to assist disabled drivers in the retrofitting of personal vehicles. ...

No 92 — That, in the event that any future initiatives of expansion of the Urban Transportation Assistance Program (UTAP) is undertaken, the Federal Government instruct the Minister of Transport to direct a specified portion of the funds to the transportation needs of disabled persons. (Canada, 1981)

It is not unusual for a government report to be released containing positive recommendations — library shelves are full of them. After some initial excitement, these reports languish on the shelves gathering dust. The disability advocacy community did not allow the *Obstacles Report* to gather dust, hammering on the 130 recommendations for five years.

The *Obstacles Report* held currency for many stakeholders — even ministers in subsequent governments. Take, for example, the following statement sent by Minister of Transport Don Mazankowski to the open national forum on transportation issues sponsored by COPOH:

I hope you will agree that positive steps are being taken by the Federal government in many different areas toward making our national transport system more accessible. Most recently draft accessibility standards proposed for east coast ferry services and VIA rail services have been examined.

In addition, the Council of Ministers of Transport of the Federal, Provincial and Territorial governments have agreed to new initiatives in several important areas of interest to you. I would like to summarize these for you:
1. Guiding principles for access to inter-city buses are being developed.
2. Provincial Ministers with regulatory authority over interprovincial busing will urge bus companies to file adaptation plans with the Canadian Human Rights Commission by September 1985.
3. The Federal Government is prepared to commit $150,000 to fund an R&D program to develop a 46 foot inter-city bus with an integrated step-lift, wheelchair restraint system and flip-up seats.
4. It is proposed that the provinces look at short and medium term R&D into station-based loading devices, use of a narrow loading chair for manual lifting and market research.
5. The Council of Ministers also agreed to the creation of a Standing Committee on Transportation of Disabled Persons

to provide a forum for federal/provincial discussion of national transportation issues involving disabled persons. Their first task will be the development of a staged plan to provide reciprocity on para-transit services throughout Canada and to make recommendations which will, for example, allow para-transit operators to serve federal airports and rail stations.

6. Finally in response to recommendation 90 of the *Obstacles Report*, a memorandum of understanding has been signed by the Federal, Provincial and Territorial Ministers to allow disabled persons, who have a vehicle identification license plate or card to park in a reserved parking space anywhere in Canada. This agreement will also allow municipal authorities to ticket offenders in public parking areas. (Mazankowski, 1985, pp. 15–16)

(h) The development of an accessible roadcruiser bus

The Newfoundland inter-city bus system presented an important opportunity for the testing of community, industry and government ideas on how to make motor coaches accessible to persons with disabilities. The federal government had devolved regulatory responsibility for the inter-provincial bus system to the provinces. For disability advocacy organizations, advocating for change in the inter-city bus system was difficult because the case for accessibility had to be made in each of the 10 provincial jurisdictions. In the other provinces, the inter-city bus industry was operated by private industry, which was uninterested in, if not hostile to, the accessibility objectives of people with disabilities.

The attention drawn to the Newfoundland bus system by the *Obstacles Report* presented a way to apply indirect leverage to the entire inter-provincial bus industry — by demonstrating how to remove barriers in the bus transportation system. As Roadcruiser was in federal jurisdiction, there was a lever for gaining access to federal dollars for research and development on motor coach redesign and the development of lift equipment for motor coaches. In 1981, there were no lift-equipped motor coaches operating in the inter-city bus system in Canada.

People with disabilities were part of Roadcruiser's regular ridership. Fabian Kennedy states, "Disabled people used the Roadcruiser service from the beginning. Sometimes they travelled with an attendant, but they frequently depended upon Roadcruiser staff for assistance in getting on and off the bus ... including lifting [them] on and off the bus" (Kennedy, 1988, p. 2). Following the *Obstacles Report*, an Advisory Committee to address the recom-

APRIL D'AUBIN

mendation was established, and it included representation from the disability community, the federal and Newfoundland governments, Roadcruiser personnel and others. Irene McGinn, who was a member of the Coalition of the Disabled (a COPOH/CCD Newfoundland Member Group) and a COPOH/CCD Vice Chair, made a point of becoming involved in the work of the Roadcruiser Advisory Committee. McGinn participated on the Advisory Committee from April 1982 until April 1985. She was also appointed to the Management Committee of the Accessible Bus Demonstration Project.

In 1983, *Surmounting Obstacles*, the Third Report of the Special Committee on the Disabled and the Handicapped, was released. The report stated, "If funds can be found in 1983–1984 and subsequent years, the three year Roadcruiser Demonstration Project ... will be carried out" (Canada, 1983, p. 81). Funds were found, and an accessible Roadcruiser motor coach was constructed. Through the Management Committee, McGinn became integrally involved in the planning of accessibility for the motor coach, and with other consumers, tested the accessibility features of the motor coach as it was developed by the manufacturer. This involvement was important because it demonstrated to the Minister of Transport, Transport Canada, engineers, and the industry at large that people with disabilities have unique expertise regarding what makes a piece of transportation equipment accessible in the system it operates, and that expertise needs to be included in all stages of development of a policy, program or service.

Fabian Kennedy in *Report on the Roadcruiser Accessible Bus Demonstration Project* provides the following account of the proceedings on the historic day that the accessible motor coach went into service:

> The program to introduce an accessible bus service for disabled travellers in Newfoundland was formally announced by Mr. John C. Crosbie, then Federal Justice Minister, acting for the Minister of Transport at a press conference at Hotel Newfoundland in St. John's on January 28, 1985.
>
> Mr. Crosbie spoke about the new accessible service, the three-year Transport Canada demonstration project and new accessibility standards which had been developed for the Roadcruiser service....
>
> Irene McGinn, the Chairperson of the Advisory Committee and herself a wheelchair user, expressed the satisfaction of the Committee and the disabled community with the implementation of the new service. She said the introduction of the accessible

390

intercity bus, integrated into the regular Roadcruiser schedule, was the result of the efforts of the disabled community to achieve greater integration in transportation and all other aspects of society. She said that constant efforts were required to make people aware of the needs of disabled people and pointed out that, unlike the other speakers she spoke to the gathering from the main floor level. Because she was a wheelchair user she was unable to reach the raised dais with the other speakers. It had not been made accessible to wheelchairs, because nobody had thought about it.

After these official ceremonies ended, the people present left the hotel to inspect the accessible bus, which was parked outside. It was a windy, stormy day, one of the worst of that winter, nevertheless the bus demonstration went on as planned and Mrs. McGinn entered the bus in her wheelchair to demonstrate the accessibility of the vehicle.

The accessible bus made its first run in regular scheduled Roadcruiser service on February 1, 1985, leaving St. John's at 12:30 pm on Run 517. (Kennedy 1988, pp. 12–14)

The development of an accessible Roadcruiser bus was an important advocacy initiative in support of accessible bus transportation in Canada for a number of reasons:

1. It provided a way around the regulatory difficulties that came into play in the field of inter-provincial bus transportation and access to federal dollars for the work.

2. The advocacy organizations of people with disabilities were promoting the idea that they should be involved in all stages of development on any project that would have an impact on them. The appointment of Irene McGinn, who used a scooter, as a member of the Roadcruiser Advisory Committee on the Transportation of Disabled Persons and on the Management Committee of the Demonstration Project proved to be pivotal in successfully launching the Newfoundland Roadcruiser accessible bus.

3. The Roadcruiser accessible bus was a tangible example that it was possible to do what people with disabilities were advocating — safe, dignified access to mainstream transportation vehicles for people with disabilities.

Admittedly, adding one accessible bus to the system could not resolve all problems, but it was a first step. Because an accessible bus was not available on all runs, consumers found this a barrier to full participation. The addition of the accessible Roadcruiser to the Newfoundland provincial bus system did not make the whole system accessible; adding one accessible bus to the system was not sufficient. Furthermore, the project did not address important issues such as making rest stops accessible. However, like most developments in the accessible transportation story, the Roadcruiser project was an incremental step in a larger process (Kennedy, 1988).

(i) The road to accessibility —
An inquiry into motor coach service

At the urging of the Canadian Paraplegic Association, the National Transportation Agency [NTA] undertook an inquiry into the accessibility of extra-provincial motor coach services in Canada. The inquiry focused on the current level of accessibility, the need for accessible transportation and the need for a national accessibility standard for this industry. The inquiry released its report in 1993.

The panel of inquiry, which was chaired by the Hon. Erik Nielsen, the Agency Chairperson, included Patricia Danforth, a disability activist, and Rick Hansen, an athlete and campaigner for spinal cord research. The inclusion of Danforth and Hansen showed that the agency had acknowledged the unique expertise disability community members have on access issues.

Some of the inquiry's findings are as follows:

> The Agency found a general agreement that the adoption of a common standard was a necessary step toward increasing the level of accessibility of motor coach services.
> The Agency believes, that, if there are no mandatory requirements for accessibility, progress will be slow. The agency recommends that a national standard be agreed upon and adopted into law.
> The Agency believes that the national standard should be based upon fully-integrated services ...
> The Agency believes that the objective of a national standard should be full fleet accessibility over a reasonable period of time.
> Training and service requirements as well as certain low-cost equipment modifications should be implemented in the short term. (NTA, 1993, pp. vii–viii)

Despite these recommendations in support of regulation, no regulations have been forthcoming. Instead there is a voluntary code of practice and a complaints mechanism operated by Transport Canada.

Key Events That Tipped Policy Away from Improved Access

(a) De-regulation of transportation

In 1987, the federal government decided to de-regulate the transportation sector (Baker, 2005). The Hon. Don Mazankowski attempted to put a Canadian face on the de-regulation that he was proposing for the transportation system. He stated, "Any changes to existing regulations will only be made after genuine consultation of, and in co-operation with, the parties concerned. We believe in co-operation, compromise and compassion. We've always developed policies in Canada for Canadians and by Canadians ..." (Mazankowski, 1985, p. 10). As de-regulation threatened advances in accessible transportation, various advocacy groups worked to ensure that Mazankowski heard the consumer perspective on de-regulation (Baker, 2005).

Decisions of the CTC, then regulatory agency, had made significant contributions to the advancement of the disability community's goal of accessible transportation. The *Kelly* case and the *Adelia* case demonstrated to the disability community the role that a regulatory body could play in removing barriers to the full and equal participation of people with disabilities. A completely de-regulated federal transportation system would have jeopardized these CTC decisions and similar future CTC decisions anticipated by the disability community. The disability community and its allies made the public, the members of the opposition party, and the government aware that total de-regulation would have an adverse impact on the future of access for persons with disabilities.

There were internal and external pressures placed on the Minister of Transport to maintain regulation for access. As has been stated, the Minister of Transport established the Transportation of Disabled Persons Implementation Committee (TDPIC) to provide the community's viewpoints on how to implement accessibility standards. David Baker reports, "In October, 1986, the TDPIC voted to have the standards enforceable under the National Transportation Act.... This would necessitate the new National Transportation Agency (NTA) [which replaced the CTC] enforcing those standards" (Baker, 1987, pp. 13–14). The message to the Minister from his advisory committee was reinforced by external advocacy efforts from the community of persons with disabilities. Writing at the time of these actions, David Baker states,

> As a result of the recommendations, amendments were made to the National Transportation Act which will authorize the NTA to

393

remove 'undue obstacles to accessibility of disabled persons.' It would also allow the NTA to award disabled people damages when their rights had been violated under the Act. As a result, the existing CTC decisions will be continued, and a quick and inexpensive dispute resolution process has been provided. (Baker, 1987, pp. 13–14)

Externally, disability organizations maintained pressure on the minister and the government. There were representations to the House of Commons Standing Committee on Transportation. The amendment to the *National Transportation Act* occurred because the disability community exerted pressure at key intervention points — the Minister of Transportation and the House of Commons Standing Committee on Transportation, which includes government and opposition members and generates a public record that is available to the media and the citizenry.

Some people with disabilities need to travel with an attendant, because the attendant helps them to address barriers in the environment, and/or the attendant provides some form of disability supports to the individual. The self-representation advocacy organizations of persons with disabilities have urged that the airlines adopt a "one person, one fare" approach to the carriage of attendants. In 1994, the Minister consulted the industry and the disability community on a draft regulation that would reduce attendant's fares by 75%. In 1995, the Minister invited the passenger air industry to accept a voluntary "one person, one fare" policy. The ATAC took the position that a voluntary 50% reduction in attendant air fares was as far as it was willing to go to compromise on the attendant air fare issues. David Baker states,

> By this time it had become clear that ATAC lobbying had prevailed with the Minister. It was understood that the government was no longer willing to issue accessibility regulations. In November 1995, the NTA for the first time mused about using 'industry guidelines' as an alternative to regulations. Guidelines, it explained, would be minimum standards that air carriers would be encouraged to meet or exceed. In March 1996, the NTA released a 'Draft Code of Practice.' While the Code's provisions were to be voluntary, air carriers are advised that they are to meet or exceed them 'wherever possible'. Notable by its absence from the Code was any reference to the 'one-person one fare' issue. (Baker, 2005, p. 27)

A variety of codes followed this one: Ferry Accessibility for People with Disabilities, Passenger Rail Car Accessibility and Terms and Conditions of Carriage by Rail of Persons with Disabilities (the Rail Code), and Aircraft Accessibility for Persons with Disabilities, all were released by the CTA. Transport Canada issued the Intercity Bus Code of Practice.

(b) Replacing accessible equipment with inaccessible equipment

In 2001, people with disabilities began to notify the CCD that air carriers were replacing accessible aircraft with inaccessible aircraft. For example, carriers were replacing the Dash 8 with the Beech 1900D. Disability rights advocate Bill Crawford reported his experiences on the Beech 1900D:

> It is a very poor aircraft in terms of accessibility for people with disabilities. Well, first of all the staircase going up to the aircraft is excessively small. It is not very wide. Also inside it is very small. In the middle of the aisle there is a hump. You have to go up and over it and then you go back down over the hump to get into the back. It is very tiny. You have to turn side ways to go down the aisle. It is very small — compact. As a matter of fact, if a person had no mobility forget the Beech craft. I am sure the PAL lift cannot service the Beech craft. You absolutely have to leave your wheelchair in order to board the Beech. There is only one way out of Yarmouth by air and that is the Beech. Previously the DASH 8 was used in Yarmouth. The DASH 8 was more accessible. At least the PAL could load you. (CCD, 2002, p. 1)

On 14 August 2001, the CCD filed a complaint at the CTA because accessible aircraft were being replaced by inaccessible planes. In Decision No. 140-AT-A-2003, the CTA found that this practice did not present an undue obstacle to the mobility of persons with disabilities. This practice of introducing inaccessible craft continues to erode the accessibility of the transportation system. People with disabilities have fewer accessible flight options available to them (CCD, 2003a). The Agency has taken the approach that because there are other options in the system, the replacement of accessible equipment with inaccessible equipment does not constitute an undue obstacle to mobility.

A similar response was received from the Agency when people with disabilities made complaints about automated check-in kiosks that dispense boarding passes. When people with disabilities complained about these devices not having a voice output feature and therefore making them inaccessible to persons with visual impairments, the Agency's response was that these kiosks were not an undue obstacle to mobility because ticket agents were still available. There was a component of the check-in system that was usable by persons with visual impairments.

Case Example of an Accessibility Struggle

This section is a case example of efforts undertaken by one advocacy organization, the CCD, to prevent new barriers from being created in the federally regulated transportation system. The case study illustrates how voluntary codes of practice fail people with disabilities.

The CCD is a national self-representational, voluntary, advocacy organization of persons with disabilities. It works at the national level on issues identified by persons with disabilities. Its membership is made up of provincial and national organizations of people with disabilities. The CCD is a cross-disability organization, meaning that people with any disability are welcome to participate in its network. Its motto, "A VOICE OF OUR OWN", summarizes CCD's raison d'être.

In 2000, the Department of Transport funnelled $400 million to VIA Rail, a Crown Corporation, to improve its services. In April of 2000, the Minister of Transport's Advisory Committee on Accessible Transportation met with the Minister, the Hon. David Collenette, to seek a commitment from him that any new rolling stock would be accessible to people with disabilities. Following that meeting, the Minister wrote to VIA Rail and reminded the Corporation of its obligations with regard to access for persons with disabilities. On 16 November 2000, VIA Rail invited a select group of consumers to tour European rail cars that it was "considering" purchasing. Some of the consumers who were involved in the tour reported to the CCD that they were extremely concerned about the inaccessibility of the cars. Upon hearing these concerns, on 4 December 2000 the CCD filed a complaint with the CTA in an attempt to prevent the creation of a new obstacle to the mobility of persons with disabilities. The CCD applied to the CTA for an interim relief order to prevent VIA from entering into a contract to purchase the cars. Despite the obligations to provide accessible service as required in the *Canadian Charter of Rights and Freedoms*, the *Canadian Human Rights Act* and the *Canadian Transportation Act*, on 1 December 2000, VIA had purchased obsolete inaccessible European rolling stock that had been built for the Chunnel (the tunnel that connects Britain to Europe). Interestingly, on 8 December 2000, VIA had written to the CCD stating, "We believe that your resort to legal and regulatory avenues is premature." When it became known that VIA had purchased these cars, Eric Norman, a past Chairperson of the CCD, summed up the feelings of many people with disabilities when he stated, "We don't believe that $400 million of taxpayers' hard earned cash should be wasted on out-of-date obsolete coaches which do not meet the needs of Canada's travelling public" (CCD, 2000, pp. 3–4). CCD's objective with its CTA complaint was to prevent any deterioration in the level of accessibly in the rail system. Canadians will have to live with this deal for many years.

When it became clear that VIA had already purchased the cars, the CCD revised its CTA complaint, which was subsequently accepted by the CTA. As the cars had already been bought, the battle that remained was over how much redesign VIA would be required to undertake to make the cars accessible to persons with disabilities. The acceptance of the case by the CTA launched a David and Goliath struggle, with VIA Rail attempting to use its superior legal resources and wealth to prevent the CCD from advancing the complaint. For example, on 15 December 2000, VIA requested that, if an interim order was granted to the CCD by CTA, the CCD be required to put up a security equivalent to the purchase price of the cars. VIA also appealed a number of questions regarding the case to the Federal Court. Each trip to Federal Court drained CCD's financial resources. According to the legislation, a CTA complaint should be resolved within 120 days. Due to VIA's numerous trips to the Federal Court, all of which were decided in favour of the CCD, the complaint extended far beyond the 120 day limit.

On 27 March 2003, the CTA released phase one of its decision on CCD's complaint, making an unprecedented decision confirming that VIA's Renaissance cars do not meet the Agency's voluntary Rail Code and represent serious obstacles to the mobility of Canadians with disabilities. The CTA decision found that the Renaissance cars have significant barriers to the mobility of persons with disabilities:

- No movable armrests to allow transfer from a wheelchair to a seat in coach cars;
- No seating available for an attendant either beside or facing the area designated for passengers who use wheelchairs;
- Inadequate space to maneuver a wheelchair in the wheelchair tie-down area;

- Inadequate space in the tie-down area to accommodate both a person's wheelchair and a service animal;
- The bulkhead door is too narrow to permit safe and easy maneuvering of a wheelchair;
- Inadequate space for service animals;
- The washroom door for the sleeper unit is too narrow;
- The door of the accessible sleeper is too narrow;
- There is not enough space beside the toilet to allow a person to transfer from their wheelchair to the toilet;
- Riser heights of stairs and stair depth;
- Lack of closed stair risers;
- Due to a lack of space in the accessible suite, some wheelchair users may not be able to keep their personal chair with them in the suite; and
- The rail cars provided on the Montreal-Toronto overnight train have no accessible washrooms for persons using the wheelchair tie-down in economy coach cars.

In its decision the Agency stated,

> It is important to note that the majority of the obstacles identified above relate to those areas of the Renaissance trains that have been specifically designed to meet the needs of persons with disabilities. ... Considering the importance of these areas to persons with disabilities, it is clear that the foregoing obstacles have a significant impact on the mobility of persons with disabilities ... [I]n some cases, the obstacles may [actually] prevent some persons with disabilities from travelling on Renaissance trains. (CTA, 2003)

The Agency gave VIA 60 days to provide specific information with regard to structural, operational and economic implications of eliminating the obstacles under considerations before it makes its decision on the "undueness" of the obstacles. (The *Canadian Transportation Act* empowers the CTA to order the removal of "undue" obstacles to the mobility of persons with disabilities.)

VIA then appealed the CTA decision at the Federal Court of Appeal. In March 2005, the Court handed down its ruling on the appeal. In essence, the Court stated that CTA erred because it did not look at the entire network of passenger service and how that network could overcome the barriers caused by the Renaissance cars. Dissatisfied with that decision, the CCD sought and received the opportunity to appeal the decision to the Supreme Court of Canada.

Following the Federal Court of Appeal decision, the CCD continued to call on the Minister of Transport to intervene to make the cars accessible. The organization noted that in Election 2004 the Liberal Party asked Canadians to re-elect them because they would keep their promises and deliver on their commitments. It also noted the Ministry had promised the Renaissance cars would be accessible.

In its efforts to prevent erosion of accessibility in passenger rail, the CCD presented its public education message regarding accessibility to many players within the public policy environment: the Minister of Transport, Members of Parliament, organizations of persons with disabilities, and grassroots people with disabilities.

The CCD was disappointed by the Minister of Transport's wavering stance on accessibility. Before the cars were purchased, at an April 2000 meeting of the Minister of Transport's Advisory Committee on Accessible Transportation, on which the CCD has representation, the Minister agreed that the cars purchased by VIA should be accessible. At the next committee meeting, follow-up questions were posed to the Minister, as by then it was known that inaccessible equipment had been purchased. The Minister provided inconsistent responses to these questions and that continued in subsequent meetings. At one meeting, the Minister, the Hon. David Collenette, told the disability community that he had expressed the need for access to VIA; at a subsequent meeting he told the community to trust VIA to make the cars accessible.

The disability community's collective negative experience with retrofitted rolling stock makes this "wait and see" attitude unacceptable. The CCD organized a consumer meeting by conference call prior to another Committee meeting, so that groups attending the Committee meeting could be updated on CCD's findings regarding the inaccessible European cars. Disability organizations such as the Canadian Paraplegic Association wrote to the Minister to demonstrate community solidarity with CCD's actions on VIA rail. Throughout the duration of its litigation against VIA, the CCD reminded the Minister time and again about his commitments regarding access.

The CCD has also done public education on rail access with members of the Conservative Party and the New Democratic Party of Canada. The NDP Member of Parliament (MP) Wendy Lill stated, in her press release on 27 March 2003 following the CTA decision,

Canada should not support a rail system that leaves people in wheelchairs either on a siding or in peril, while those without a disability travel safely in first class. The Minister should have announced today that these cars are off the rails until they are safe and accessible. He should be telling VIA to buy different passenger cars, or come up with the funds to rebuild the Renaissance cars so all Canadians can use them without concern for their safety. Otherwise all promises by this Minister to Canadians are worthless.

The CCD devoted editions of its newsletter, *CCD Horror Gazette*, to inform its members and supporters about the VIA Renaissance cars issue. Individuals were encouraged to speak out to their MPs in support of an accessible rail system. The CCD also circulated media releases to inform Canadians about how the European cars would erode access in the rail system. Articles on the inaccessibility of the cars appeared in the *Globe and Mail* and the *Kingston Whig Standard*, and the CBC and the CTV have also covered the issue. The NDP MP for Windsor-St. Clair, Joe Comartin, held a press conference on 10 January 2001 to show solidarity with the disability community's efforts to achieve a barrier-free transportation system. On the complaint's one-year anniversary, the CCD commemorated the event by holding a press conference in Toronto. Wheelchair user Lucie Lemieux-Brassard, a member of CCD's Executive Committee, travelled by train from Montreal to Toronto to attend the Press Conference. A CBC camera crew met Lemieux-Brassard at the Toronto train station, and she told them how accessibility would be reduced when the European cars come into service. Lemieux-Brassard drew upon information the CCD developed throughout the duration of the case.

A delegation of CCD representatives, composed of consumers, engineers and a lawyer, toured the European cars, and each component of the delegation developed a report detailing their experience of inaccessibility of the cars. The aisle in the European cars is so narrow that many passengers who use wheelchairs will have to transfer from their own wheelchair to a special on-board wheelchair to move about in the cars. Ron Ross, a wheelchair user who toured the European cars on behalf of the CCD, wrote in his report on the cars that many consumers would refuse to ride in the new cars because of the necessity to be repeatedly transferred from their own wheelchair to the on-board chair. He felt that this would present a health and safety risk to some consumers. The CCD later published Ross's report in its quarterly newsletter, *A Voice of Our Own*.

The CCD lodged the CTA complaint in an attempt to stop the purchase of the cars so that a new disability-related barrier would not be introduced into Canada. With its $400 million windfall from the federal government, VIA had the opportunity to move Canada's passenger rail system in a direction that would begin to meet the demands of universal design. (Universal design makes systems usable by people with a wide range of functional characteristics.) Instead of taking this golden opportunity to embrace universal design as an operating principle for the corporation, VIA, a crown corporation, went outside of Canada and made an untendered deal on redundant European rail stock. It totally ignored the demands of the *Charter of Rights and Freedoms* and the *Canadian Human Rights Act* with regard to access. VIA's actions toward the disability community concerning the European car purchase were not above board. In retrospect, the community realized that the November 2000 consultation with select consumers about the European cars was only for show. The decision to buy the cars had already been made. At one point, VIA called CCD's complaint to the CTA "premature"; it was later revealed that VIA had purchased the cars prior to CCD's complaint without having gone public about the deal. The truth is that VIA used legal maneuverings and intimidation to challenge the CCD at every juncture of this case.

In June 2001, at its Annual General Meeting, the CCD Council of Representatives reviewed the work of its Transportation Committee on VIA Rail and agreed that the CCD would use every avenue available to it to prevent erosion of accessibility in the rail system. The CCD prioritized VIA's purchase of inaccessible rail cars for intensive advocacy work for several reasons. First, there is the slippery slope argument. If people with disabilities allow VIA to put new inaccessible rolling stock into service, other transportation modes may follow suit. For example, the CCD has spent years working to convince the bus industry it has a responsibility to bring accessible motor coaches into service and develop plans for implementing accessibility. The CCD does not want other transportation modes to backslide. Second, the Minister of Transport, David Collenette, made a commitment to the disability community in April 2000, affirming that VIA's new rolling stock, purchased with taxpayers' dollars, would be accessible. People with disabilities are also taxpayers and should share in the benefits of services developed for the public good. Third, accessible alternatives exist and are even built in Canada. Bombardier builds, and exports to the United States, accessible rail cars that comply with U.S. ADA requirements. Fourth, rail continues to be an important mode of transportation for many Canadians. One example is the use of the Montreal-Toronto-Ottawa route by business travellers. If with the addition of the European cars the rail system becomes less accessible, then Canadian workers with disabilities who use the Montreal-Toronto-Ottawa rail route for business travel, will face an additional barrier related to employment. Fifth, the acquisition of new rolling stock should move the Canadian transportation system forward and closer to becoming a barrier-free environment, not backward.

CONCLUSION

For people with disabilities, especially those involved in disability advocacy organizations, the advancement of accessible transportation has been a high priority. This chapter has emphasized the contribution of disability organizations to the field of accessible transportation and also reflects the role of other stakeholders. It examined events and issues that have tipped Canada toward and away from accessible transportation. It also identified the continuing obstacles and emerging barriers to the mobility of people with disabilities.

Directions for the Future

INTRODUCTION

As we conclude this volume, we have the opportunity to reflect on the progress in the disability policy field in recent years and on the challenges that persist on the horizon.

Six years into the new millennium, the disability policy field remains an enormously complex and fragmented area. Although characterized by a federalist policy approach, disability policy exists at all levels of jurisdiction, across sectors and ministries, and in different offices and programs. Most disability policies are embedded in general legislation, such as employment insurance or social assistance; there is little specified disability legislation, federally or provincially. The disability policy field has been described by Cameron and Valentine (2001) as non-coherent, fragmented, and not user-friendly. They question if the field achieves its objectives of equity and effectiveness, despite its orientation toward rights and entitlements.

We have demonstrated previously that there is no national disability policy in Canada; instead, there are a number of evolving federal position statements and vision documents, produced by the Office for Disability Issues in Social Development Canada. These are far-reaching and progressive documents that outline a view of Canada as inclusive and accessible. But unlike several other Western democracies, like the United States, Britain and Australia, Canada does not have federal umbrella legislation that offers assurances of equality and access. According to some researchers, disabled people in Canada are not disadvantaged by this (Cameron & Valentine, 2001). The combined effects of our human rights legislation, our *Charter of Rights and Freedoms*, and our universal health care system amount to an equally accessible environment for people with disabilities. Prince, in Chapter 7, disagrees. He identifies a pattern of erosion of financial support for disability programs in recent years and calls for a national program of disability-related services.

At the provincial level, only one province, Ontario, has legislation explicitly dealing with disability issues. In 2001, the *Ontarians with Disabilities Act* was passed to ensure accessibility of public buildings and to establish reporting requirements and oversight of access plans in the public sector. In 2005, the *Accessibility for Ontarians with Disabilities Act* supplemented the previous legislation by extending consideration to private-sector buildings and services. Also in Ontario, a ministerial post, Minister Responsible for Disability Issues, has recently been designated within the Citizenship and Immigration portfolio.

In Manitoba, a proposal to establish a Minister Responsible for Persons with Disabilities and a Centre for Coordinating Disability Policy is currently under consideration. In several other provinces (New Brunswick, Nova Scotia, Quebec, Manitoba, Saskatchewan, Alberta and British Columbia), there are designated offices within the provincial bureaucracy that provide infrastructure for disability issues and services. In the remaining provinces and territories, human rights inquiries are referred to provincial disability organizations, and responsibility for co-ordination of disability policy and services is not clearly delegated.

We referred earlier to the erosion of programs and supports for disability in Canada. This suggests that there was a time when things were better; in fact, there is a general perception that the disability policy field experienced its golden age in the 1980s. During that time, key achievements were made:

- The International Year of Disabled Persons was proclaimed in 1981, and the International Decade of Disabled Persons (1983–1992) was designated in 1982; both were high profile events in Canada;
- The landmark *Obstacles Report* was published by the federal government;
- The movement toward de-institutionalization began producing real results in terms of community living;
- People with disabilities were specified in the *Charter of Rights and Freedoms* as a group whose rights must be protected; and
- Disability groups proliferated and obtained unprecedented levels of membership and sponsorship.

These events, and many others, marked a period of tremendous accomplishment for disability advocacy that left this country with a legacy of normative, legal and institutional changes (Driedger, 1989).

However, since 1990 disability advocacy has not been so productive or prosperous (Neufeldt, 2003). Boyce and colleagues note that Canada in the 1990s saw a shift toward valuing economic growth and deficit restructuring over issues associated with the evolving welfare state. Cuts to social assistance, employment insurance, disability pensions and community-based training are evidence of this shift, and all of these unquestionably had stronger financial impact on persons with disabilities. Jongbloed (Chapter 15) noted this particular change, which shows a stark contrast to the preceding period (between 1945 and 1975) when there was greater concern for providing income support services to low-income groups. Prince (Chapter 7) also talks about the declining commitment of the federal government to persons with disabilities, as evidenced in the last Liberal budget as well as the recent Conservative budget.

Thus, as we assemble this volume, we are aware that we are at a turning point in disability policy in Canada. The following seven points represent the issues arising and the challenges ahead.

ISSUES ARISING — CHALLENGES AND OPPORTUNITIES

Supports and Services

Although there is some evidence that the prevalence of disability is decreasing (Statistics Canada, 2001a; Wolf, Hunt & Knickman, 2005), the need for *supports and services* to people with disabilities continues, and the feeling that the service environment is inadequate remains. Holt et al. (2000) and Pedlar et al. (2000) attest to the ongoing need for improved disability supports in the community. Canadian survey information tells us that people with disabilities experience disproportionate levels of unmet needs for service despite being high users of most health and social services (McColl et al., 2005). In this volume, a number of authors note the need for improvements in the service sector. McColl (Chapter 19) discusses the barriers that impede their access to health services. Prince (Chapter 7) contends that many people with disabilities lack vital supports, and that there is a declining commitment in government to provide those supports.

In the search for possible solutions, Yoshida and colleagues (Chapter 20) discuss self-managed attendant services, where people with disabilities have choice, flexibility, control and responsibility. Bickenbach (Chapter 5) notes that equality and full participation depend on the provision of services and supports.

Approach to Service Provision

What is the best way to provide people with disabilities with the needed supports and services? Some say the best way is to clearly understand the needs of particular groups of citizens and fashion services tailored to meet those needs — *a minority group* approach. Bickenbach, in Chapter 5, states that the minority model of disability was useful for creating a sense of solidarity in the disability community, but the approach is based on the idea that disability happens only to a few people. Others say the best way to provide needed services is to "level the playing field", so that society as a whole is made more amenable to the needs of all citizens — a *universalist* approach.

Which serves people with disabilities best? — the approach that segregates people with disabilities from the rest of society for the purposes of service provision but provides them with excellent, targeted service that is specialized to meet their needs; or the approach that considers people with disabilities as part of mainstream society and therefore provides them with services designed for the mainstream? Joiner (Chapter 6) argues that the minority group approach and universalism are not necessarily incompatible. The best answer is obviously somewhere between the two, but the rhetoric of this argument can be very divisive indeed.

Perhaps the area where this duality has been played out most openly is in the field of education for children with disabilities.

Until very recently, the prevailing culture insisted that children with disabilities should be integrated into mainstream schools, afforded opportunities to learn and grow with other children, and provided with the supports to be able to succeed in that environment. However, lately cracks have begun to appear — parents, teachers and student advocates have noted the extreme challenge of making this ideal a reality (Cole, 2005). A survey by Pitt and Curtain (2004) showed that students with disabilities find specialized education more accessible in terms of both physical and social aspects of access. They cited negative experiences in the mainstream education system due to the fact that the system had not fully embraced the notion of inclusion. van de Ven and colleagues (2005) suggest that what is needed in order to be successful in integration are continuity and reciprocity — a long-term continual relationship, characterized by a willingness on both sides to take risks and to problem-solve in a mutually respectful fashion.

Human Rights Perspective

This brings us to our next issue — the question of whether the *rights-based perspective* currently dominating our approach to disability issues in Canada is the right one for all issues. North American society generally is oriented toward individual rights and expectations. In Canada, this way of thinking became institutionalized in the *Canadian Charter of Rights and Freedoms* that accompanies our Constitution. As Bickenbach (Chapter 5) and Kerzner (Chapter 21) both point out, this approach assures individuals that they can depend on these basic expectations being met.

According to Crichton and Jongbloed, in the first edition of this book (1998), the dominant political ideology in Canada is liberalism. The government provides a framework of legislation within which individuals can successfully pursue their personal economic and social objectives. This approach pairs a belief in the rights of the individual with a historical commitment to collectivism. The legislative framework is expected to be regulatory, rather than restrictive. It is designed to advance the interests of individuals, to protect the investments of small business, and to ensure a reasonable standard of living for all, with built-in protections for those less fortunate. Thus, there is a tension in Canadian public policy between entrepreneurialism and welfare provisions, both aimed at seeking "peace, order and good government".

Interestingly, changes in the Canadian legal framework coincided with a change in the disability field as well. In the late 1970s, the social model of disability emerged to replace the prevailing medical (and in some cases, the persisting charitable) model. According to the social model, an environment designed without disability in mind is viewed as the cause of disability; that is, the focus of disability causation shifts from the individual to the environment. As Driedger (1989) puts it most aptly, disability changed from being considered a personal misfortune to a social injustice and an indicator of discrimination. Thus, the rights-based approach to ensuring needs became inextricably tied to the social model of disability.

However, the lack of progress in several important areas, such as income, employment and disability supports, suggests that this approach may not have been entirely successful (Piggott, Sapey & Wilenius, 2005). Whereas the rights-based approach is essential for issues of human rights (as defined by the federal and provincial human rights legislation — e.g., the right to freedom, assembly, affiliation, etc.), it may not work when there is no consensus that a right is involved. Jongbloed (Chapter 15) is certain that economic issues have never been clearly understood by Canadians as a right. She finds considerable ambivalence in Canadian political rhetoric about the welfare state and the economic rights of all Canadians.

Also of interest is that while the rights-based approach is typically an individually oriented approach, the social model is meant to represent a structural approach. The rights-based approach focuses on a particular individual and the extent to which his or her right has been violated. It typically results in some form of corrective justice for that individual, as well as in case law that may be of assistance to other individuals. However, the social model is intended to focus on the environment — to redesign society to be more inclusive and accessible to people with disabilities, to focus on broad systemic factors that prevent some groups from participating as equals. While this may be true, in practice the human rights approach is acted out one case at a time.

An individually oriented approach seems to be a very labour-intensive way to bring about reforms. Case law in the area of access to health services has been disappointing in the extent to which it has been generalized throughout the system. For example, successful human rights claims for sign language interpreters in health facilities have had no broader impact on the general availability of these services in the health care system (see McColl, Chapter 19). While it is indisputable that individual human rights cases represent important achievements in assuring equality for people with disabilities, there may be more far-reaching ways to make structural changes that would ensure access to needed resources for people with disabilities (Ellis, 2005).

Bickenbach (Chapter 5) suggests that one possibility is a focus on distributive justice, rather than solely on corrective justice. Distributive justice is the best approach when the issue is one of resource distribution; corrective justice is the best approach when human rights are the issue. Further, and perhaps equally important, the distributive justice approach does not necessarily polarize issues, pitting people with disabilities against the rest of society. Instead of placing a person with a disability in an adversarial relationship with others (as is the basis of the rights-based approach), an approach oriented toward more equitable distribution of goods and services may be more compatible with Canadian values of fairness and equality, and may result in more universal structural solutions. There may be some benefit in considering social responsibility, rather than rights, to reduce inequalities.

Social Model of Disability

This brings us to our fourth issue, already mentioned: the current dominance of the *social model* as a way of thinking about disability. Historically, medical and economic definitions of disability were dominant until the 1970s. For the first 70 years of the 20th century, most disability policies developed incrementally as needs were recognized. Military hospitals and pensions for war veterans were established, and compensation and training programs were established to meet the needs of injured workers. In most of the legislation introduced during these years, disability was viewed as an individual medical or economic issue.

As discussed in several other places throughout the book, a number of social forces, including the human rights movement and the International Year of Disabled Persons, led to the development of a definition of disability, which has come to be called the social model of disability, which situates disability in the environment. For a time this was viewed not only as the most acceptable, but as the *only* acceptable definition of disability. In disability circles, to persist in adhering to one of the earlier definitions of disability was considered disrespectful to the disability movement, and a sign of ignorance of the state of the art in disability theory.

However, recently the social model has attracted some critics. Several bold commentators noted that the experience of a physically disabled body was real, and the experience was not related to the environment. A number of authors point to the biological reality of impairment, and the necessity to consider both biology and sociology in order to have a full understanding of disability (Dowse, 2001; Goodley, 2001; Shakespeare & Watson, 2001). Dewsbury and associates (2004) coin the term, "the anti-social model of disability", to describe how the rhetoric of the social model has literally made the phenomenon of disability disappear in the minds of the public and of policy-makers.

Cameron and Valentine (2001) note that the social model has done little to significantly alter the public discourse or policy environment relating to disability in developed democracies. Dewsbury and colleagues (2004) suggest that this is because the social model merely replaces the language of medicine with the language of sociology; it still fails to address the real day-to-day issues that are of concern to people with disabilities. Prince (2004) points out that the field of disability studies is dominated by social issues, such as stigma, identity politics, role, power and social change. The social model has been so dominant in recent discourse that to challenge it feels as though it may be the beginning of a paradigm shift. If so, it is our hope that this book may contribute to some of the discussion that will surely ensue in this area.

Public Perceptions

The fifth issue on the horizon for disability studies is public *perceptions of disability*. As mentioned above, public perceptions are enormously influential in the policy development process. If the government perceives public sympathy for particular issues, it is relatively certain that those issues will have a policy profile. Prince (2004) and others have suggested that public pressure for disability issues may be waning. With the high visibility of tangible (and yet perhaps questionable) indicators of progress on disability issues, such as parking spaces and wheelchair washrooms, and the subsequent increased visibility of people with disabilities in the community, the public perhaps assumes that the overall situation for people with disabilities has improved in all respects.

A recent survey of attitudes toward people with disabilities released by the federal Office for Disability Issues substantiates these assumptions. The survey results show 83% of Canadians thought that significant progress had been made in recent years toward inclusion of people with disabilities. However, 82% thought there was at least some discrimination still afoot toward disabled people in Canadian society, and 43% felt prejudice was the most significant barrier encountered by people with disabilities. Yet, most reported no discomfort or awkwardness about people with disabilities.

In this volume, Wight-Felske and Krassioukova-Enns (Chapter 11) note that persons with cognitive disabilities are subject to stereotypes that label them incapable, and they are vulnerable to losing the right to participate. Stienstra and D'Aubin (Chapter 13) note discriminatory attitudes toward candidates for public office who have a disability. Frazee (Chapter 22) observes that for some, disability violates aesthetic taboos, and oppression persists through aesthetic judgments like these. McColl (Chapter 19) notes that stereotypes interfere with positive interactions between disabled people and health professionals. Finally, Prince (Chapter 10) comments on widespread and recurrent experiences of discrimination among disabled individuals.

What is the role of *advocacy organizations* in filling some of these public education gaps and promoting a more positive view of life with a disability? Numerous commentators have pointed to a decline in the effectiveness of the disability lobby in recent years, attributable to a number of possible factors. First, the entire policy environment has become increasingly constrained, as resources have become tighter and public programs have suffered from repeated cuts over many years. Boyce and colleagues (Chapter 16) note that Canadian disability organizations have experienced increased consumer demand for services and advocacy as a result of decreases in income, services and benefits. Even though people with disabilities have become more skilled at advocacy, and their causes are increasingly legitimate, there is a general decrease in popular support for public expenditures on any particular disadvantaged group.

Second, federal-provincial relations have shifted toward greater spending and programming autonomy for the provinces — a situation that several commentators have observed will not be in the best interests of the disability community (Cameron & Valentine, 2001; Torjman, 2001).

Third, disability organizations have become burned out and, perhaps, lost some of their energy for change (Neufeldt, 2003). Crichton and Jongbloed (1998), however, see this as the precursor to change — the phase in their development when disability organizations reconsider their mission and re-assess their ongoing mandate. Is this the stage that disability organizations in Canada have reached? If so, what appears to be a troubled time could also be re-interpreted as an exciting time of renewal and re-assertion.

Fourth, as Prince (Chapter 7) points out, the public may have become disenchanted with the disability agenda. Having seen a number of significant advances in recent years, there is the potential for a backlash if pressure persists. Finally, increased dependence on the private sector for delivery of public services has diminished the effectiveness of disability advocacy.

Some authors suggest that the disability community is not sufficiently well connected or politically sophisticated to be effective in advocacy. At the same time, there are others who state that the disability lobby has become co-opted by government, and has thus lost its edge (Neufeldt, 2003). By becoming too closely involved with members of the bureaucracy and too dependent upon government funding, the disability advocacy movement has eschewed some of the more effective tactics it employed in its earlier, more activist, days.

There has also been criticism levelled that the disability lobby is not unified or consistent. The heterogeneity of the community, which is at once its strength and its liability, is blamed for the lack of a consistent policy message. Joiner (Chapter 9) recommends citizen engagement through collaboration among disability organizations, thereby increasing not only numbers, but expertise and contacts.

For successful advocacy, Boyce and associates (2001) identify four conditions:

- Experience and expertise in the political arena;
- Organization and resources to support the advocacy effort;
- Effective and energetic leadership; and
- A readily recognizable identity.

Identity of the Disabling Community

This brings us to the sixth issue that requires some clarity if disability policy is to advance substantially in the coming years — the *identity of the disability community*. Cameron & Valentine (2001) have stated that the lack of a coherent, authoritative definition of disability is one of the major impediments to a successful lobby. Dowse (2001), too, notes the need for a strong identity and a consistent public perception for successful advocacy. Bickenbach (Chapter 5) points out the importance of being clear about what dimension of disability a particular law is addressing. He views it as appropriate to define disability as an individual impairment when the purpose of the law or policy relates to rehabilitation services or medical equipment. He also says that use of the social model is appropriate when dealing with issues of discrimination since discrimination is a function of the social perception of disability, not the state of a person's body or mind. If a physically disabled individual is unable to access a public building, this assaults the dignity of that person; however, as he points out, equality and full participation depend on the provision of adequate resources to meet needs.

Although we refer repeatedly to the notion of a disability community, Prince (Chapter 10) seeks to clarify what is meant by this. Does it mean a collection of organizations? A new social movement? A constitutional category? Or a political lobby? Crichton and Jongbloed (1998) pose a similar question. Is the disability community defined by shared interests and the potential for social mobilization, as is a social movement? Is it defined by its influence on society, as is a pressure group? Or is it defined by the service it provides to its members, as is a voluntary organization? Dowse (2001) and Lysack and Kaufert (1994) come to similar conclusion that the notion of a disability community may be misplaced as it suggests a level of coherence and identification that does not appear to exist among the many and varied groups representing people with disability.

In attempting to communicate the essence of disability, we usually resort to official definitions, and yet the literature is replete with discussions of the caveats of virtually any definition proposed. The challenge that remains is to establish an identity for the disability community that accomplishes the following:

(a) Is recognizable to the population and to decision-makers,
(b) Resonates with people with disabilities as reflecting their experience in society, and
(c) Adequately captures the problems they want addressed.

In the absence of such a definition, policy-makers, unfortunately, resort to historical practices and to the biomedical definition of disability (Cameron & Valentine, 2001).

Globalization

Finally, the trend toward *globalization* is seen as having a potentially negative impact on disability policy in Canada. Because globalization results in the utilization of inexpensive labour off-shore, it may lead to the loss of domestic jobs and a decrease in investment in Canadian enterprise, causing economically disadvantaged groups at home to suffer. As the economic environment becomes increasingly constrained for all Canadians, it is arguably more so for disabled Canadians (Sampson, 2003).

On the positive side, Canada (along with Sweden) has been central to the development of an international presence on disability issues (Driedger, 1989; Peters, 2003). Canadians with disabilities have the opportunity to contribute to peace and international justice initiatives in their capacity as developed consumer organizations. The plight of disabled people in troubled parts of the world is difficult for us to even comprehend from our Western perspective; yet, by looking beyond our borders, perhaps there is the opportunity to make our greatest contributions to disability issues, both internationally and domestically.

TIPS FOR POLICY ANALYSIS

We have suggested several times during this discussion that we are at a turning point in history for disability policy. We posit this based on a number of indicators: the life cycle of disability organizations, the development in disability policy to date, the constraints in the public service sector, the waning public support for minority group issues, and the lack of political attention to disability issues. On the positive side, however, are the recent Ontario legislation regarding access, proposals for structural changes in the bureaucracy in other provinces, and the federal Office for Disability Issues' efforts toward greater inclusion. Based on the issues discussed above, we propose the following guidelines and suggestions for analyzing policy pertaining to disability. These questions may be applied to various levels of policy, from legislation and regulations to programs of service or compensation, to positions statements or policy papers:

1. What is the objective of the policy? Is it aimed at promoting *equity*, *access*, or *support*?

2. What definition of disability is employed? Who is included, and who is excluded from the considerations spelled out in the policy? Consider the implications of the definition of disability from the following perspectives:
   • Recipients of goods and services;
   • Public perceptions of disability;

- Service provision; and
- Costs.

3. Does the policy refer to disability as a minority group issue or as a mainstream, universal issue? Does it propose to provide specialized services to people with disabilities if they meet some eligibility criteria, or does it apply generally to the public or to society as a whole? What are the advantages and disadvantages of this view of disability for the objective of the policy?

4. At what level of jurisdiction is the policy (federal, provincial, regional, municipal)? How does it correspond to other policies at that level? At other levels? Is it overlapping, inconsistent or detrimental to the implementation of other policies?

5. What is the history of the policy? How did it come about? At whose initiative was the issue brought to public attention? Who were the proponents and detractors of the policy? Is there a significant silent majority? If so, how are they likely to respond to the policy, and how easy or difficult would it be to mobilize them, either in support or in opposition?

6. Does the policy correspond to the mission of pertinent advocacy organizations? If so, how are they involved? What is their position, and how are they making it known? Are they working alone or together with other interested parties?

7. Does the policy aim to correct an injustice perpetrated on an individual, or does it seek to make Canadian society collectively a more supportive place for people with disabilities? Does it seek to enforce individual rights, or to outline collective responsibilities?

CONCLUSION

As we conclude this volume, we are aware that the future of disability issues and disability policy depends heavily on what happens on various fronts in the next few years. The health of the disability advocacy movement, the identity of the disability community, the ideological and philosophical direction of disability studies, and the penetration of disability issues in the public consciousness are all factors that will have a powerful impact on the future of disability and social policy in Canada. The authors of this book contributed their thoughts and their time to help paint a portrait of disability in the early 21st century for those involved in the disability field. With that, we look forward to a new era of disability policy and advocacy.

Bibliography and Index

BIBLIOGRAPHY

Abbas, J., Church, K., Frazee, C., & Panitch, P. (2004). *Lights... Camera ... Attitude! Introducing Disability Arts and Culture.* Toronto, Ont.: Ryerson University.

Abelson, J., & Eyles, J. (2002). Discussion Paper No. 7, Public Participation and Citizen Governance in the Canadian Health System. *Commission on the Future of Health Care in Canada.* Retrieved 6 February 2005, from www.hc-sc.gc.ca/ehglish/care/romanow/hcc 0545/html.

Abilities Magazine. (1992, Summer). Historic Omnibus Bill gets second reading. *Abilities Magazine,* 44–46.

Advocacy Resource Centre for the Handicapped (ARCH). (1988). Disabled Canadians at the polls. *Archalert, 4*(7), 5.

Advocacy Resource Centre for the Handicapped (ARCH). (1990). *Arch-Type,* 8(5). Toronto, Ont.: Author.

Alberta Committee of Citizens with Disabilities (ACCD). (1993). *The Alberta citizen special election edition, 1*(2). Edmonton, Alta.: Author.

Albrecht, G. L., Seelman, K. D., & Bury, M. (2001). Introduction: The formation of disability studies. In G. L. Albrecht, K. D. Seelman, & M. Bury (Eds.), *Handbook of disability studies* (pp. 1–8). Thousand Oaks, Calif.: Sage Publications.

Alston, P. (1992). The Commission on Human Rights. In P. Alston (Ed.), *The United Nations and human rights: A critical appraisal* (pp. 126–216). Oxford, UK: Clarendon Press.

Anderson, P., & Kitchin, R. (2000). Disability, space and sexuality: Access to family planning services. *Social Sciences Medicine, 51*(8), 1163–1173.

Antonak, R. F., & Livenh, H. (2000). Measurement and attitudes towards persons with disabilities. *Disability and Rehabilitation, 22*(5), 211–224.

Arbour, L. (2005, March). *Freedom from want.* LaFontaine-Baldwin Lecture, Quebec City, Quebec.

Aronson, J. (1993). Giving consumers a say in policy development: Influencing policy or just being heard? *Canadian Public Policy, 19*(4), 367–378.

Asche, A. (2001). Disability, bioethics, and human rights. In G. L. Albrecht, K. D. Seelman, & M. Bury (Eds.), *Handbook of disability studies* (pp. 297–326). Thousand Oaks, Calif.: Sage Publications.

Asenjo, F. G. (1988). *In-between: An essay on categories.* Boston, MA: Center for Advanced Research in Phenomenology and University Press of America.

Attendant Care Action Coalition (ACAC). (1986). *Options for independent living assistance.* Toronto, Ont.: author.

Attendant Care Action Coalition (ACAC). (1993, Spring). *Principles to guide the development of attendant services in Ontario 1990.* [Brochure].

Australian Institute of Health and Welfare. (2004). *Disability and its relationship to health conditions and other factors.* Australia: Author.

Avard, D. (2001). *Human genetics research and practice: Implications for people with disabilities.* Paper presented to the UN expert group meeting on disability sensitive evaluation and monitoring held at the United Nations Headquarters, New York. Retrieved 12 November 2005, from http://www.un.org/esa/socdev/enable/disid20013.htm.

Bach, M. (2002). Governance regimes in disability-related policy and programs: A focus on community support systems. In A. Puttee (Ed.), *Federalism, democracy and disability policy in Canada* (pp. 103–114). Montreal, Que. & Kingston, Ont.: McGill-Queen's University Press.

Bach, M. (2004). *Towards a movement for disability culture.* Unpublished.

Baker, D. (1986). Air accessibility standards: The Canadian model. In *Mobility in the global village* (pp. 1–9). Ottawa, Ont.: Transport Canada.

Baker, D. (1987). Amendments to the National Transportation Act. *Archtype, 7*(1), 13–14.

Baker, D. (1990). Anticipating the next generation of equality issues in employment for disabled people in Canada. In R. I. Cholewinski (Ed.), *Human rights in Canada: Into the 1900s and beyond* (pp. 41–55). Ottawa, Ont.: Human Rights Research and Education Centre.

Baker, D. (2005). *Moving backwards: Canada's state of transportation accessibility in an international context.* Winnipeg, Man.: CCD.

Barnes, C. (1991). A brief history of discrimination and disabled people. In C. Barnes (Ed.), *Disabled People in Britain and Discrimination: A case for anti-discrimination legislation.* London, UK: Hurst & Co.

Barnes, C. (1998). The social model of disability: A sociological phenomenon ignored by sociologists? In T. Shakespeare (Ed.), *The disability reader: Social science perspectives* (pp. 66–78). London, UK: Cassell Academic.

Barnes, C. (2002). Introduction: Disability, policy and politics. *Policy & Politics, 30*(3), 312–318.

Barnes, C. (2003a). Extended review. Disability and culture: Universalism and diversity. *Disability & Society, 18*(6), 827–833.

Barnes, C. (2003b). Rehabilitation for disabled people: A 'sick' joke? *Scandinavian Journal of Research, 5*(1), 7–24.

Barnes, C., & Mercer, G. (2001). Disability culture: Assimilation or inclusion? In G. Albrecht, K. Seelman, & M. Bury (Eds.), *Handbook of disability studies* (pp. 515–534). London, UK: Sage Publications.

Barnes, C., & Mercer, G. (2003). *Disability.* Cambridge UK: Polity Press.

Barnes, C., Mercer, G., & Shakespeare, T. (1999). *Exploring disability: A sociological analysis.* Cambridge, UK: Polity Press.

Barnes, C. & Oliver, M. (1995). Disability rights: Rhetoric and reality in the UK. *Disability & Society, 10*(1), 111–116.

Barnes, M. (2002). Bringing difference into deliberation? Disabled people, survivors and local governance. *Policy & Politics, 30*(3), 319–331.

Barton, L. (1998). Sociology, disability studies and education: Some observations. In T. Shakespeare (Ed.), *The disability reader: Social science perspectives* (pp. 66–78). London, UK: Cassell Academic.

Basnett, I. (2001). Health care professionals and their attitudes toward and decisions affecting disabled people. In G.L. Albrecht, K.D. Seelman, & M. Bury (Eds.), *Handbook of disability studies* (pp. 450–467). Thousand Oaks, Calif.: Sage Publications.

Batavia, A. I., & DeJong, G. (2001). Disability, chronic illness, and risk selection. *Archives of Physical Medicine and Rehabilitation, 82,* 546–552.

Beatty, P. W., Hagglund, K. J., Neri, M. T., Dhont, K. R., Clark, M. J., & Hilton, S. A. (2003). Access to health care services among people with chronic or disabling conditions: Patterns and predictors. *Archives of Physical Medicine and Rehabilitation, 84,* 1417–1425.

Bercovici, S. M. (1983). *Barriers to normalization: The restrictive management of retarded people.* Baltimore, Md.: University Park Press.

Beresford, P., & Campbell, J. (1994). Disabled people, service users, user involvement and representation. *Disability & Society, 9*(3), 315–325.

Bickenbach, J. E. (1993). *Physical disability and social policy.* Toronto, Ont.: University of Toronto Press.

Bickenbach, J. E. (2001). Disability human rights, law, and policy. In G.L. Albrecht, K.D. Seelman, & M. Bury (Eds.), *Handbook of disability studies* (pp. 565–584). Thousand Oaks, Calif.: Sage Publications.

Bickenbach, J.E., Chatterji, S., Badley, E.M., & Ustun, T. B. (1999). Models of disablement, universalism and the international classification of impairments, disabilities and handicaps. *Social Science & Medicine, 48,* 1173–1187.

Bockeneck, W. L. (1997). Primary care for persons with disabilities: A fragmented model of care for persons with spinal cord injuries. *American Journal of Physical Medicine and Rehabilitation, 76*(Suppl.), S43–S46.

Bordo, S. (1998). Braveheart, babe and the contemporary body. In E. Parens (Ed.), *Enhancing human traits: Ethical and social Implications* (pp. 189–221). Washington, DC: Georgetown University Press.

Bowe, F. (1979). Transportation: Key to Independent Living. *Archives of Physical Medicine and Rehabilitation, 60,* 483–486.

Bowers, B., Esmond, S., Lutz, B., & Jacobson, N. (2003). Improving primary care for persons with disabilities: The nature of expertise. *Disability & Society, 18*(4), 443–455.

Boyce, W. (1999). Participation of disability advocates in research partnerships with health professionals. *Canadian Journal of Rehabilitation, 12*(2), 85–94.

Boyce, W. (2002). A seat at the table: Persons with disabilities & policy making. Montreal, Que. & Kingston, Ont.: McGill-Queen's University Press.

Boyce, W., Krogh, K., Kaufert, J., Hall, B., LaFrance, C., & Enns, H. (2000). Strategies to support disability organizations in changing socio-political environments. *Research to action: Working together for the integration of Canadians with disabilities* ((pp. 151–156). Proceedings of SSHRC-HRDC Forum, Halifax, Nova Scotia, May 15–17, 1999.

Boyce, W., McColl, M. A., Tremblay, M., Bickenbach, J., Crichton, A., Andrews, S., et al. (2001). *A seat at the table: Persons with disabilities and policy making.* Montreal, Que. & Kingston, Ont.: McGill-Queen's University Press.

Braddock, D. L., & Parish, S. L. (2001). An institutional history of disability. In G.L. Albrecht, K.D. Seelman, & M. Bury (Eds.), *Handbook of disability studies* (pp. 11–68). Thousand Oaks, Calif.: Sage Publications.

British Columbia (BC) Ferries Inc. (2004). *Welcome to British Columbia Ferries.* Retrieved August 2005, from http://www.bcferries.com/.

British Council of Disabled People. (n.d.) *The new genetics of disabled people.* Retrieved 7 November 2005, from http://www.bcodp.org.uk/about/genetics.shtml.

Boadway, R. (2004). *Should the Canadian federation be rebalanced?* (Working Paper 2004 (1)). Kingston, Ont.: Institute for Intergovernmental Relations, Queen's University.

Brown, S.C. (1998). Demographics of disability. In M. A. McColl & J. Bickenbach (Eds.), *Introduction to disability* (pp. 29–43). London, UK: W.B. Saunders.

Buechler S. (1995). New social movement theories. *The Sociological Quarterly, 36*(3), 441–464.

Butler, J. (1993). *Bodies that matter: On the discursive limits of "sex".* New York, NY: Routledge.

Byron, M., & Dieppe, P. (2000). Educating health professionals about disability: 'Attitudes, attitudes, attitudes'. *Journal of the Royal Society of Medicine, 93,* 397–398.

Cairns, A. C. (1995). *Reconfigurations: Canadian citizenship and constitutional change.* Edited by D. Williams. Toronto, Ont.: McClelland and Stewart.

Caledon Institute of Social Policy. (1998). *Perspectives on partnership, Social Partnership Project.* Ottawa, Ont.: Caledon Institute on Social Policy.

Cameron, D. & Valentine, F. (2001). *Disability and federalism: Comparing different approaches to full participation.* Montreal, Que. & Kingston, Ont.: McGill-Queen's University Press.

Canada. (1981). House of Commons. Special Parliamentary Committee on the Disabled and the Handicapped. *Obstacles: Report of the Special Committee on the Disabled and Handicapped.* Ottawa, Ont.: The Committee.

Canada. (1983). House of Commons. *Surmounting obstacles: Third report of the Government of Canada response to recommendations arising from the International Year of Disabled Persons.* Ottawa, Ont.: Government of Canada.

Canada. (1985). House of Commons. *Equality for all: First report of the Parliamentary Sub-Committee on Equality Rights of the Standing Commit-*

tee on Justice and Legal Affairs. Ottawa, Ont.: Queen's Printer for Canada.

Canada. (1986a). Privy Council. *White paper on election law reform.* Ottawa, Ont.: Privy Council.

Canada. (1986b). House of Commons. *Toward equality: The response to the report of the Parliamentary Committee on Equality Rights.* Ottawa, Ont.: Queen's Printer.

Canada. (1986c). Department of the Secretary of State. Social Trends Analysis Directorate. *Report on the Canadian Health and Disability Survey, 1983–1984.* Ottawa, Ont.: Statistics Canada.

Canada. (1988). National Parliamentary Forum on Status of Disabled Persons. *3,300,000 Canadians: Insights from the Parliamentary Forum on the Status of Disabled Persons.* Ottawa: The Forum.

Canada. (1996). Federal Task Force on Disability Issues. *Equal citizenship for Canadians with disabilities: The will to act.* Ottawa, Ont.: The Task Force.

Canada. (1998). Federal, Provincial and Territorial Ministers Responsible for Social Services. *In unison: A Canadian approach to disability issues: A vision paper* (Available from http://socialunion.gc.ca/pwd/unison/unison_e.html). Hull, Que.: HRDC.

Canada. (2000a). Federal, Provincial and Territorial Ministers Responsible for Social Services. *In unison 2000: Persons with disabilities in Canada* (Available from http://socialunion.gc.ca/In_Unison2000/iu00100e.html). Hull, Que.: HRDC.

Canada. (2000b). Voluntary Sector Task Force, Privy Council Office. *Partnering for the Benefit of Canadians. Government of Canada — Voluntary Sector Initiative, 2000* (Available from http://www.vsr-trsb.net/publications/pub-june09_e.html). Ottawa, Ont.: Author.

Canada. (2001). House of Commons. Standing Committee on Human Resources Development and the Status of Persons with Disabilities. *A common vision: Interim report of the standing committee on human resources development and the status of persons with disabilities.* Ottawa, Ont.: The Committee.

Canada. (2002a). Federal/Provincial/Territorial Early Childhood Development Agreement. *The well-being of Canada's young children: Government of Canada Report, 2002.* Ottawa, Ont.: HRDC. Retrieved 13 February 2005, from http://www.socialunion.gc.ca/ecd/2002/b-5.htm.

Canada. (2002b). *User's guide: Participation and Activity Limitation Survey.* Ottawa, Ont.: Statistics Canada.

Canada. (2003a). Office for Disability Issues. *Defining disability: A complex issue* (RH37-4/3-2003-E). Ottawa, Ont.: Government of Canada.

Canada. (2003b). House of Commons. Standing Committee on Human Resources Development and the Status of Persons with Disabilities. *Listening to Canadians: A first view of the future of the Canada Pension Plan Disability Program.* Report of the Standing Committee on Human Resources Development and the Status of Persons with Disabilities. Ottawa, Ont.: Standing Committee on Human Resources Development and the Status of Persons with Disabilities.

Canada. (2003c). Office for Disability Issues. *Update: Advancing the inclusion of persons with disabilities: A government of Canada report* (Available from http://www.sdc.gc.ca/asp/gateway.asp?hr =/en/hip/odi/documents/advancingInclusion/aipdUpdate.shtml&hs=pyp). Ottawa, Ont.: HRDC.

Canada. (2004a). Governor General. *Speech from the Throne, February 2, 2004 to open the Third Session of the Thirty-Seventh Parliament of Canada*. Ottawa, Ont.: Author.

Canada. (2004b). Standing Committee on Finance. *Moving forward: Balancing priorities and making choices of the twenty-first century* (Available from http://www.parl.gc.ca/infocomdoc/documents/38/1/parlbus/commbus/house/reports/finarp03/08-toc-e.htm). Ottawa, Ont.: House of Commons.

Canada Assistance Plan of 1966, ch. 31, 1966–1967, S.C. (Can.)

Canada Pension Plan of 1965, ch. 51, 1964–1965, S.C. (Can.).

Canadian Abilities Foundation. (2004). *2004/2005 Edition of directory of disability organizations*. Toronto, Ont.: The Foundation.

Canadian Association for Community Living (CACL). (1997a). *Election update '97* (volume 1, number 3). Toronto, Ont.: Author.

Canadian Association for Community Living (CACL). (1997b). *Election update '97* (volume 1, number 4). Toronto, Ont.: Author.

Canadian Association for Community Living (CACL). (1997c). *1997 Federal election package*. Toronto, Ont.: Author.

Canadian Association for Community Living (CACL). (2004). *Budget 2004 — A national disability agenda to take shape* (Available from http://www.cacl.ca/english/mediaroom/pressrelease/2004/budget0404.html). Toronto, Ont.: Author.

Canadian Association for Community Living (CACL). (2005). *Tax fairness only one part of the picture: New investments need to secure the citizenship of persons with disabilities* (News Release, February 23, available from http://www.cacl.ca/english/mediaroom/pressrelease/2005/PressRelease_Budget05.html). Toronto, Ont.: author.

Canadian Association of Independent Living Centres (CAILC). (2004). *What is independent living?* Retrieved 13 December 2005, from http://www.cailc.ca/CAILC/graphic/whatisil/intro_e.html.

Canadian Centre on Disability Studies (CCDS). (2002). *Disability community capacity: A framework for preliminary assessment* (Analysis Paper to Human Resources Development Canada, Social Policy Unit). Winnipeg, Man.: Author.

Canadian Council on Social Development (CCSD). (2001). *Disability information sheet #2* (Available from http://www.ccsd.ca/drip/research/dis2.htm). Ottawa, Ont.: Author.

Canadian Council on Social Development (CCSD). (2002). *Disability information sheet: Supplemental tables*. Ottawa, Ont.: Author.

Canadian Disability Rights Council. (1991). *Annual report 1990–91*. Winnipeg, Man.: Author.

Canadian Education Statistics Council. (2004, March 1). *Children with special needs in Canada*. Paper presented at the Canadian Ministers of Education meeting.

Canadian Election Study (CES). (1997). *1997 Canadian election survey* (Available from http://www.ces-eec.umontreal.ca/surveys.html#1997). Survey conducted by Institute for Social Research (ISR), York University, Toronto, Ontario.

Canadian Hearing Society (CHS). (2000). *Submission to the Canada Transportation Act Review Panel: Recommendations for amending the Canada Transport Act* (Available from http://www.reviewcta-examenltc. gc.ca/submissions-soumissions/Nov16/The%20Canadian%20Hearing%20 Society.pdf). Toronto, Ont.: Author.

Canadian Paraplegic Association v. Elections Canada. (1992, Feruary 17) *Canadian Human Rights Tribunal (CHRT)*. Retrieved February 1992, from http://www.chrt-tcdp.gc.ca/search/view_html.asp?doid=116&lg=_ e&isruling=0.

Canadian Rehabilitation Council for the Disabled (CRCD). (1978). *Proceedings of a national transportation symposium*. Toronto: Author.

Canadian Transportation Agency (CTA). (1997). *Communication barriers: A look at barriers to communication facing persons with disabilities who travel by air*. Ottawa, Ont.: Author.

Canadian Transportation Agency (CTA). (1998a). *Code of practice: Passenger rail car accessibility and terms and conditions of carriage by rail of persons with disabilities*. Hull, Que.: Government of Canada.

Canadian Transportation Agency (CTA). (1998b). *Decision No. 365-AT-A-1998 APPLICATION by Henry Vlug, pursuant to subsection 172 (1) of the Canada Transportation Act, S.C., 1996, c. 10., concerning the insufficient number of TTY pay phones (telephone-teletype used by persons with a hearing impairment) and the absence of appropriate signage at the Vancouver International Airport*. Retrieved 13 December 2005, from http://www.cta-otc.gc.ca/rulings-decisions/decisions/1998/A/ AT/365-AT-A-1998_e.html.

Canadian Transportation Agency (CTA). (1997). *Code of practice: Aircraft accessibility for persons with disabilities*. Ottawa, Ont.: Author.

Canadian Transportation Agency (CTA). (2003). *Decision No. 175-AT-R-2003 APPLICATION by the Council of Canadians with Disabilities pursuant to subsection 172(1) of the Canada Transportation Act, S.C., 1996, c. 10, regarding the level of accessibility of VIA Rail Canada Inc.'s Renaissance passenger rail cars.*. Retrieved 13 December 2005, from http://www.cta-otc.gc.ca/rulings-decisions/decisions/2003/R/AT/ 175-AT-R-2003_e.html.

Canadian Transportation Agency (CTA). (2004a). *Air travel accessibility regulations — Summary* (Available from http://www.cta-otc.gc.ca/access/ regs/air_e.html). Ottawa, Ont.: Author.

Canadian Transportation Agency (CTA). (2004b). *Code of practice: Removing communication barriers for travellers with disabilities*. Ottawa, Ont.: Author.

Canadian Transportation Agency (CTA). (2004c). *100 Years at the heart of transportation*. Ottawa, Ont.: Author.

Capacity Assessment Office. (2005). *Guidelines for conducting assessments of capacity*. Toronto, Ont.: Ministry of the Attorney General of Ontario. Retrieved 18 November 2005, from http://www.attorneygeneral. jus.gov.on.ca/english/family/pgt/capacity/2005-05/guide-0505.pdf.

Cardol, M., DeJong, B. A., & Ward, C. D. (2002). On autonomy and participation in rehabilitation. *Disability and Rehabilitation, 24*(18), 970–974.

Castells, M. (1983). *The City and the grassroots: A cross-cultural theory of urban social movements*. London, UK: Edward Arnold.

Centre for Independent Living in Toronto (CILT) and Roeher Institute. (1997). *Final evaluation report. Self-managed attendant services in Ontario: Direct funding pilot project*. Toronto, Ont.: Author.

Centre for Research and Education in Human Services. (1988). *Independence and control: Today's dream, tomorrow's reality*. Toronto, Ont.: Ontario Ministry of Community and Social Services.

Centre for Research and Information on Canada (CRIC). (2001). *Voter participation in Canada: Is Canadian democracy in crisis?* Montreal, Quebec: Author.

Center for Universal Design, The. (1997). *What is universal design?*. Retrieved 13 December 2005, from http://www.design.ncsu.edu/cud/univ_design/ud.htm.

Chadha, E., & Sheldon, C. T. (2004). Promoting equality: Economic and social rights for persons with disabilities under Section 15. *National Journal of Constitutional Law, 16*(1), 27–102.

Chappell, R. (2004). *Social welfare in Canadian society*. Toronto, Ont.: Nelson Canada.

Charlton, J. (1998). *Nothing about us without us*. Berkeley CA: University of California Press.

Chatterji, S., Ustun, B., & Bickenbach, J. (1999). What is disability after all? *Disability and Rehabilitation, 21*, 396–398.

Chesson, R. A., & Sutherland, A. M. (1992). General practice and the provision of information and services for physically disabled people aged 16 to 65 years. *British Journal of General Practice, 42*, 473–476.

Cheyne, C., & Comrie, M. (2002). Enhanced legitimacy for local authority decision-making: Challenges, setbacks and innovation. *Policy & Politics, 30*(4), 469–482.

Childcare Resource and Research Unit. (2001). *Early childhood education and care in Canada 2001: Summary*. Retrieved, 10 January 2005, from www.childcarecanada.org.

Church, K. (1996). Beyond "bad manners": The power relations of "consumer participation" in Ontario's community mental health system. *Canadian Journal of Community Mental Health, 15*(2), 27–44.

City of Toronto. (1973). *Mayor's Task Force Report re Disabled and Elderly*. Toronto, Ont.: The Task Force.

Claxton, A. (1994). Teaching medical students about disability. *British Medical Journal, 308*, 805.

Coalition of Provincial Organizations of the Handicapped (COPOH). (1986). *Employment*. [Final report on the study group on employment and disability.] Winnipeg, Manitoba, Canada: Author.

Coburn, D. (2004). Beyond the income inequality hypothesis: Class, neoliberalism, and health inequalities. *Social Science & Medicine, 58*, 41–56.

Cohen, J. J., & Weiss, G. (Eds.). (2003). *Thinking the limits of the body*. New York: State University of New York Press.

Cohen, R. (1992). An interview with Dr. Bruce Halliday advance consideration. *Abilities, 13*, 123.

Cohen, S. (1985). *Visions of social control: Crime, punishment and classification*. Cambridge: Polity Press.

Cohen, S., & Scull, A. (1983). *Social control and the state*. Oxford: Martin Robertson.

Cole, A. (2001). *Genetic discrimination — Looking back to the future?* Toronto, Ont.: The Roeher Institute.

Cole, B. A. (2005). Good faith and effort? Perspectives on educational inclusion. *Disability & Society, 20*(3), 331–344.

Cole, A., & Knowles, J.G. (2001). Call for Submissions from the Centre for Arts Informed Research (CAIR) in the Department of Adult Education, Ontario Institute for Studies in Education, University of Toronto.

Coleman, W. D., & Skogstad, G. (Eds.). (1990). *Policy communities and public policy in Canada: A structural approach*. Toronto, Ont.: Copp Clark Pitman.

Communications Canada. (2002). *Public opinion research in the Government of Canada*. Ottawa, Ont.: Author.

Contandriopoulos, D. (2004). A sociological perspective on public participation in health care. *Social Science & Medicine, 58*, 321–330.

Corker, M., & French, S. (Eds.). (1999). *Disability discourse*. Buckingham: Open University Press.

Corker, M., & Shakespeare, T. (Eds.). (2002). *Mapping the terrain disability/ postmodernity: Embodying disability theory* (pp. 1–17). London: Continuum.

Council of Canadians with Disabilities (CCD), (1984). *Election 84 highlights*. Winnipeg, Man.: Author.

Council of Canadians with Disabilities (CCD). (1985). *Presentation to the Sub-Committee on Equality Rights*. Winnipeg, Man.: Author.

Council of Canadians with Disabilities (CCD). (1985/86). *Annual report* (p. 10). Winnipeg, Man.: Author.

Council of Canadians with Disabilities (CCD). (1989). *Human rights: Can't get no satisfaction*. Winnipeg, Man.: Author.

Council of Canadians with Disabilities (CCD). (1992). *Our own voices: Personal lives — Public diaries*. Winnipeg, Man.: Author.

Council of Canadians with Disabilities (CCD). (1999). *A national strategy for persons with disabilities: The community definition*. Retrieved November 2005, from http://www.pcs.mb.ca~ccd/nation~4.htm.

Council of Canadians with Disabilities (CCD). (2002, January 3). Obstacle to mobility: Beech 1900. CCD's *Horror Gazette, 5*(1).

Council of Canadians with Disabilities (CCD). (2003a). *CCD transportation file.*

Council of Canadians with Disabilities (CCD). (2003b). *A framework for a national disability related supports plan.* Winnipeg: Author.

Council of Canadians with Disabilities (CCD). (2004a). Council of Canadians with Disabilities challenge 2004 participation in the democratic process: A responsibility of citizenship. *A Voice of Our Own.* Retrieved 10 February 2005, from http://www.ccdonline.ca/publications/Voice/election2004.htm.

Council of Canadians with Disabilities (CCD). (2004b). *Liberal investment in disability issues welcome but must be re-profiled* [Press Release]. Winnipeg, Man.: Author.

Council of Canadians with Disabilities (CCD). (2005a). *Federal Court of Appeal tells Canadians with disabilities separate is equal* [Press Release, March 15]. Winnipeg: Author.

Council of Canadians with Disabilities (CCD). (2005b). *Canadians with disabilities once again left without supports* [News Release, February 23]. Winnipeg, Man.: Author.

Council of Canadians with Disabilities (CCD) & the Canadian Association for Community Living (CACL). (2005). *A call to combat poverty and exclusion of Canadians with disabilities by investing in disability supports* (Available from http://www.ccdonline.ca/ccpe.htm; http://www.cacl.ca/english/mediaroom/pressrelease/2005/docs/CACL_CCDCall ActionBudget05.pdf). Winnipeg, Man. & North York, Ont.: Authors.

Council of Canadians with Disabilities (CCD)/Canadian Organization of Provincial Organizations for the Handicapped (COPOH). (1979). *Proceedings of COPOH's national transportation conference.* Ottawa, Ont.: COPOH.

Council of Europe. (1996). *European Social Charter* (revised), ETS No. 163 (Available from http://conventions.coe.int/Treaty/EN/Treaties/Html/035.htm).

Crawford, C. (2003). *Towards a common approach to thinking about and measuring social inclusion.* Toronto, Ont.: Roeher Institute.

Crawford, C. (2004a). *Improving the odds: Employment, disability, and public programs in Canada.* Unpublished report for the Roeher Institute, Toronto, Ontario.

Crawford, C. (2004b). *Inclusive education for students with developmental and other disabilities: The general situation and implications for advocacy and policy development.* Unpublished report for the Roeher Institute, Toronto, Ontario.

Crawford, C. (2005, January). *Unmet needs for disability supports, and non-reimbursed costs of disability-specific supports: Technical paper.* Toronto, Ont.: Roeher Institute.

Crichton, A., & Jongbloed, L. (1998). *Disability and social policy in Canada.* North York, Ont.: Captus Press.

Cushing, P. J. (2003). *Policy approaches to framing social inclusion and exclusion: An overview.* Toronto, Ont.: Roeher Institute.

Cwikel, J. (1999). Different strokes for different folks: Is one standard of disability possible? *Disability and Rehabilitation, 21,* 379–381.

Daes, E-I. (1983). *Principles, guidelines and guarantees for the protection of persons detained on grounds of mental ill health or suffering from mental disorder* (E/CN.4/Sub.2/1983/17). Report by the Special Rapporteur to the UN Sub-Commission on Prevention of Discrimination and Protection of Minorities. New York: United Nations.

Dahl, T. H. (2002). International classification of functioning, disability and health: An introduction and discussion of its potential impact on rehabilitation services and research. *Journal of Rehabilitation Medicine, 34,* 201–204.

Degener, T. (2003). Disability as a subject of international rights: Law and comparative discrimination law. In S. S. Herr, L. O. Gostin, & H. H. Koh (Eds.), *The human rights of persons with intellectual disabilities: Different but equal* (pp. 151–184). Oxford, UK: Oxford University Press.

DeJong, G. (1979). Independent living: From social movement to analytic paradigm. *Archives of Physical Medicine & Rehabilitation, 60,* 435–446.

Dejong, G. (1997). Primary care for persons with disabilities: An overview of the problem. *American Journal of Physician Medicine and Rehabilitation, 76*(Suppl.), S2–S8.

Delli Carpini, M., Cook, F., & Jacobs, L. (2004). Public deliberation, discursive participation, and citizen engagement: A review of the empirical literature. *Annual Review of Political Science, 7,* 315–344.

Denzin, N. D. (1994). The art and politics of interpretation. In N. D. Denzin, & Y. S. Lincoln (Eds), *Handbook of qualitative research* (pp. 1–17). Thousand Oaks, Calif.: Sage Publications.

Department of Justice Canada. (1982). *Canadian Charter of Rights and Freedoms.* Retrieved 21 February 2005, from http://laws.justice.gc.ca/en/charter/.

Department of Justice Canada. (1985). *Equality issues in federal law a discussion paper* (Sessional Paper no. 331-4/6). Ottawa, Ont.: Author.

DePoy, E., & Gilson, S. F. (2004). *Rethinking disability: Principles for professional and social change.* Belmont, CA: Brooks/Cole.

Derksen, J. (2002a). An overview of how people with disabilities began to organize. *Council of Canadians with Disabilities, youth advocacy training manual.* Winnipeg, Man.: CCD.

Derksen, J. (2002b). *Council of Canadians with Disabilities Human Rights Committee presentation.* Winnipeg, Man.: CCD.

Despouy, L. (1993). *Human rights and disabled persons* (E.92.XIV.4). Human rights studies series 6. New York: United Nations.

Dewsbury, G., Clarke, K., Randall, D., Rouncefield, M., & Sommerville, I. (2004). The anti-social model of disability. *Disability & Society, 19,* 145–158.

Dickinson, H. (2002). Discussion paper no. 33: How can the public be meaningfully involved in developing and maintaining an overall vision for the health system consistent with its values and principles? *Commission on the future of health care in Canada.* Retrieved 6 February 2005, from www.hc-sc.gc.ca/ehglish/care/romanow/hcc0513/html.

Disabled Peoples' International (DPI). (2002). World Assembly. *Sapporo Declaration,* adopted by the DPI World Assembly and amended by the World Council. Retrieved 2 June 2006, from http://www.icrpd.net/en/toolkit/files/dpi_sapporo_declaration.htm.

Disabled Peoples' International Europe (DPI Europe). (2000). Position statement on bioethics and human rights. Retrieved 10 November 2005, from http://www.dpieurope.org/htm/bioethics/dpsngfullreport.htm.

DisAbled Women's Network Ontario (DAWN Ontario). (2004). *Vote for equality DAWN Ontario's issues-based voter education and awareness campaign election 2004.* North Bay, Ont.: Author.

Doe, T. (2003). *Studying disability: Connecting people, programs and policies.* Victoria, BC: Island Blue Press.

Donoghue, C. (2003). Challenging the authority of the medical definition of disability: An analysis of the resistance to the social construction paradigm. *Disability & Society, 18,* 199–208.

Doron, I. (1998). From lunacy to incapacity and beyond — Guardianship of the elderly and the Ontario experience in defining 'legal competence'. *Health Law in Canada, 19*(4), 96–114.

Dow, W. (1997, September). *The voluntary sector — Trends, challenges and opportunities for the new millennium.* Vancouver: *Volunteer Vancouver.*

Downie, J., & Caulfied, T. (Eds.). (1999). *Canadian health law and policy.* Markham, Ont.: Butterworths.

Dowse, L. (2001). Contesting practices, challenging codes: Self-advocacy, disability politics and the social model. *Disability & Society, 16,* 123–141.

Drake, R. F. (1999). *Understanding disability policies.* London: MacMillan.

Drake, R. F. (2002). Disabled people, voluntary organizations and participation in policy-making. *Policy & Politics, 30*(3), 373–385.

Drieger, D. (1987). Disabled peoples' international. *Rehabilitation Gazette, 28,* 13–14.

Driedger, D. (1989). *The last civil rights movement: Disabled peoples' international.* New York: St. Martin's Press.

Driedger, D. (1990). *History of the coalition of provincial organizations of the handicapped.* Winnipeg, Man.: Coalition of Provincial Organizations of the Handicapped.

Duckworth, S. C. (1988). The effect of medical education on the attitudes of medical students towards disabled people. *Medical Education, 22,* 501–505.

Dunleavy, P., and O'Leary, B. (1987). *Theories of the State: The politics of Liberal democracy.* Houndmills, UK: MacMillan Education.

Eadie, R. (2000, summer). A politician wanna be. *The Canadian blind monitor, 9.* Retrieved 15 December 2005, from http://www.nfbae.ca/publications/index.php?id=317.

Ekos Research Associates. (1998). *Lessons learned on partnerships* (Available from http://www.vsr-trsb.net/publications/ekosoc98/toc.html). Ottawa, Ont.: Voluntary Sector Roundtable.

Elections Finances Act, The. (1987). In C.C.S.M. c. E32, Paragraph 72(3)(a.1) RSM.

Elections Canada. (1989). *Report of the Chief Electoral Officer of Canada.* Ottawa, Ont.: Chief Electoral Officer of Canada.

Ellis, K. (2005). Disability rights in practice: The relationship between human rights and social rights in contemporary social care. *Disability & Society, 20*(7), 691–704.

Employment Equity Act of 1986, ch. 31, 1986, S.C. (Can.).

Enns, H. (1981, December). Canadian society and disabled people: Issues for discussion. *Canada's Mental Health,* 14–17 & 40–41.

Enns, H. (n.d.). Interview with Henry Enns. [Personal Communication].

Enns, H., & Neufeldt, A. H. (2003). *In pursuit of equal participation: Canada and disability at home and abroad.* Concord, Ont.: Captus Press.

Enns, R. (1999). *A voice unheard: The Latimer case and people with disabilities.* Halifax, NS: Fernwood Publishing.

Fagan, T., & Lee, P. (1997). 'New' social movements and social policy: A case study of the disability movement. In M. Lavalette & A. Pratt (Eds.), *Social policy: A conceptual and theoretical introduction* (pp. 140–160). London, UK: Sage Publications.

Fairweather, G. (1986). Mobility in the global village (pp. 1–10). *Proceedings of the Fourth International Conference on Mobility and Transport for Elderly and Disabled Persons,* July 21–23, 1986, Vancouver, B.C. Ottawa, Ont.: Transport Canada.

Fawcett, G. (1996). *Living with disability in Canada: An economic portrait.* Hull, Que.: Office for Disability Issues, Human Resources Development Canada.

Fawcett, G. (1998, May). *Untapped potential: Disability process and environmental barriers.* Paper presented at the National Workplace Equity Symposium for Persons with Disabilities, Ottawa, Ontario, Canada.

Fawcett, G., Ciceri, C., Tsoukalas, S., & Gibson-Kierstead, A. (2004). *Supports and services for adults and children aged 5–14 with disabilities in Canada: An analysis of data on needs and gaps.* Commissioned by the Federal-Provincial-Territorial Ministers responsible for Social Services. Ottawa, Ont.: CCSD. Retrieved 13 February 2005, from http://socialunion.gc.ca/pwd/gapsreport2004.html.

Feld, J. (1997, Fall). Sam Savona what a candidate! What a campaign. *Abilities.*

Finance Canada. (2005a). *The budget plan.* Ottawa, Ont.: Government of Canada.

Finance Canada. (2005b). *Budget speech.* Ottawa, Ont.: Government of Canada.

Fitzgerald, J. (1999). Bioethics, disability and death: Uncovering cultural bias in the euthanasia debate. In M. Jones & L. A. Basser Marks

(Eds.), *Disability, divers-ability and legal change* (pp. 267–281). The Hague: Kluwer Law International.

Foucault, M. (1976). *Mental illness and psychology* (First ed.). (Alan Sheridan, Trans.). New York: Harper & Row. (Original work published 1954).

Foucault, M. (1977). *Discipline and punish: The birth of the prison*. (Alan Sheridan, Trans.). New York: Pantheon Books. (Original work published 1975).

Foucault, M. (1978). *The history of sexuality: Vol. 1. An introduction*. (Robert Hurley, Trans.). New York: Vintage Books. (Original work published 1976).

Foucault, M. (1988). Technologies of the self. In L. H. Martin, H. Gutman, & P. H. Hutton (Eds.), *Technologies of the self: A seminar with Michel Foucault* (pp. 16–49). Amherst, Mass.: University of Massachusetts Press.

Fougeyrollas, P. (1991). The handicap creation process. *ICIDH International Network, 4*.

Fourth World Conference on Women. (1995). Beijing declaration and platform for action (Available from http://www.un.org/womenwatch/daw/beijing/index.html). *Report of the Fourth World Conference on Women, Beijing, 4–15 September 1995* (United Nations publication, Sales No. E.96.IV.13). New York: United Nations.

Fram, S. V. (1987). *Final report of the Advisory Committee on Substitute Decision Making for Mentally Incapable Persons*. Toronto, Ont.: Advisory Committee on Substitute Decision Making for Mentally Incapable Persons.

Frankish, C. J., Kwan, B., Ratner, P. A., Wharf Higgins, J., & Larsen, C. (2002). Challenges of citizen participation in regional health authorities. *Social Science & Medicine, 45*, 1471–1480.

Gadacz, R. R. (1994). *Re-thinking disability*. Edmonton, Alta.: The University of Alberta Press.

Gallegos, L.. (2004). *Sharing learning and building alliances — The legal dimension of inclusive development*. Comment during a break-out session at the World Bank Disability and Development Conference, Disability & Inclusive Development, 30 November–1 December 2004, Washington D.C., U.S.A.

General Social Survey (GSS). (1994). *The 1994 General Social Survey — Cycle 9 education, work and retirement: Public use microdata file documentation and user's guide*. Ottawa, Ont: Statistics Canada.

Globe and Mail, The. (2005, February 24). The Prime Minister opens the floodgates. *The Globe and Mail*, p. A18.

Goddard, J. (2005, October 6). *Capacity to grant or revoke a power of attorney*. Lecture to the Ontario Bar Association meeting, "Powers of Attorney: A Practitioners Toolkit".

Goodley, D. (2001). Learning difficulties, the social models of disability and impairment: Challenging epistemologies. *Disability & Society, 16*(2), 207–231.

Gordon, R. M., & Verdun-Jones, S. N. (1992). *Adult guardianship law in Canada*. Toronto, Ont.: Carswell.

Gosden, T., Forland, F., Kristiansen, I. S., Sutton, M., Leese, B., Giuffrida, A., et al. (2001). Capitation, salary, fee-for-service and mixed systems of payment. *Cochrane Database of Systemic Reviews*. Retrieved 20 July 2004, from http://gateway2.ovid.com/ovidweb.cgi.

Gosden, T., Sibbald, B., Williams, J., Petchey, R., & Leese, B. (2003). Paying doctors by salary: A controlled study of general practitioner behaviour in England. *Health Policy, 64*, 415–423.

Grabois, E. W., Nosek, M. A., & Rossi, C. D. (1999). Accessibility of primary care physicians' offices for people with disabilities. An analysis of compliance with the Americans with Disabilities Act. *Archives of Family Medicine, 8*, 44–51.

Graham, K., & Phillips, S. (Eds.). (1998). *Citizen engagement: Lessons in participation from local government*. Toronto, Ont.: Institute of Public Administration of Canada.

Graham, M. (1993, October 17). Sorry Tory tactic: Letter to the editor. *The Winnipeg Sun*.

Graycar, A., & Jamrozik, A. (1989). *How Australians live: Social policy in theory and practice*. Melbourne, Australia: Macmillan.

Green, L. (1995). Internal minorities and their rights. In W. Kymlicka (Ed.), *The rights of minority cultures* (pp. 257–272). Oxford, UK: Oxford University Press.

Griesdorf, W. L. (2004, May 17). *A review of the various tests for capacity*. Lecture to the Ontario Bar Association meeting, "Estates and Trusts: Conundrums in Cognition — Legal Issues of Capacity".

Groch, S.A. (1991). Public services available to person with disabilities in major U.S. cities. *Journal of Rehabilitation, 57*(3), 23–26.

Hahn, H. (1985). Towards a politics of disability: Definitions, disciplines and policies. *The Social Science Journal, 22*(4), 87–105.

Hahn, H. (1993). The political implications of disability definitions and data. *Journal of Disability Policy Studies, 4*, 41–52.

Hall, S. (1997). *Representation: Cultural representations and signifying practices*. London, UK: Sage in association with the Open University.

Halm, E. A., Lee, C., & Chassin, M. R. (2002). Is volume related to outcome in health care? A systematic review and methodologic critique of the literature. *Annals of Internal Medicine, 137*(6), 511–520.

Hanson, K. W., Neuman, P., Dutwin, D., & Kasper, J. D. (2003). Uncovering the health challenges facing people with disabilities: The role of health insurance. *Health Affairs's Web Exclusives, Datawatch: Disability and Insurance*, W3:553–W3:565.

Health Canada [Formerly Health and Welfare Canada]. (1993). *Pathway to integration: Final report, Mainstream 1992*. Report *to* ministers of social services on the Federal/Provincial/Territorial review of services affecting Canadians with disabilities. Ottawa, Ont.: Author.

Health Canada. (1997). Laboratory Centre for Disease Control. *Economic burden of illness in Canada, 1993*. Ottawa, Ont.: Author.

432

Health Care Accessibility Act. (1990). Retrieved 3 August 2004, from http://www.e-laws.gov.on.ca/DBLaws/Statutes/English/90h03_e.htm.

Health and Welfare Canada. (1980*). Disabled persons in Canada.* Ottawa, Ont.: Author.

Henderson, H. (2005, April 2). If Schiavo were a capital case, she would live. *Toronto Star,* p. L4.

Hennessey, J. C. & Muller, L. S. (1995). The effects of vocational rehabilitation and work incentives on helping the disabled-worker beneficiary back to work. *Social Security Bulletin, 58,* 15–28.

Herr, S. S. (2003). Self-determination, autonomy and alternatives for guardianship. In S. S. Herr, L. O. Gostin & H. H. Koh (Eds.), *The human rights of persons with intellectual disabilities: Different but equal* (pp. 429–450). New York: Oxford University Press.

Hickling Corporation. (1992). *Disability and transportation in Canada: Demographics, needs and opportunities.* Summary report. Ottawa, Ont.: Transport Canada.

Hinton, C. A. (2003). The perceptions of people with disabilities as to the effectiveness of the Americans with Disabilities Act. *Journal of Disability Policy Studies, 13*(4), 210–220.

Hogwood, B., & Gunn, L. (1984). *Policy analysis for the real world.* Oxford, UK: Oxford University Press.

Holden, C., & Beresford, P. (2002). Globalization and disability. In C. Barnes, M. Oliver & L. Barton (Eds.), *Disability studies today* (pp. 190–209). Cambridge, UK: Polity Press.

Holt, G., Costello, H., Bouras, N., Diareme, S. Hillery, J., Moss, S., et al. (2000). BIMOED-MEROPE project: Service provision for adults with intellectual disability: A European comparison. *Journal of Intellectual Disability Research, 44,* 685–696.

Hubbard, R. (1993). The eugenics of normalcy — The politics of gene research. *The Ecologist, 23*(5), 185–192.

Hubbard, R. (1995). Genomania and health (arguments against genetic prediction). *American Scientist, 83*(1), 8–10.

Hum, D., & Simpson, W. (1993). Employment equity and people with disabilities. *Policy Options, 14,* 30–32.

Human Resources Development Canada (HRDC). (1994). *Improving social security in Canada. The context of reform: A supplementary paper.* Ottawa, Ont.: Minister of Human Resources Development.

Human Resources Development Canada (HRDC). (1995). *Vocational Rehabilitation and Disabled Persons Act: Annual report 1994–1995.* Ottawa, Ont.: Author.

Human Resources Development Canada (HRDC). (1998). Strategic Policy. *Evaluation of the Opportunities Fund for Persons with Disabilities (Phase I): Final report.* Ottawa, Ont.: Evaluation and Data Development, Strategic Policy, HRDC.

Human Resources and Development Canada. (1999a). *Future directions to address disability issues for the government of Canada: Working together for full citizenship.* Ottawa, Ont.: Government of Canada.

Human Resources Development Canada (HRDC). (1999b). Evaluation & Data Development, Evaluation Services. *Lessons learned from evaluation of disability policy and programs*. Hull Quebec: Author.

Human Resources Development Canada (HRDC). (2000/1997). Evaluation & Data Development, Evaluation Services. *Disability policies and programs: Lessons learned. Final report*. Ottawa, Ont.: Author.

Human Resources Development Canada (HRDC). (2001). *Disability in Canada: A 2001 profile* (RH37-4/4-2001E). Gatineau, Que.: Author.

Human Resources Development Canada (HRDC). (2002a). *Advancing the inclusion of persons with disabilities: A Government of Canada report, December 2002* (RH37-4/1-2002E). Ottawa, Ont.: Author.

Human Resources Development Canada (HRDC). (2002b). *Knowledge matters: Skills and learning for Canadians*. Hull, Que.: Author.

Human Resources Development Canada (HRDC). (2002c). *Canada Pension Plan benefit rates 2002*. Ottawa, Ont.: HRDC — Income Security Programs Branch.

Human Resources Development Canada (HRDC). (2002d). Statistical bulletin, Canada Pension Plan/Old Age Security. Ottawa, Ont.: HRDC — Income Security Programs Branch.

Human Resources Development Canada (HRDC). (2003). *Evaluation of the Canada Pension Plan Disability Vocational Rehabilitation Program*. Ottawa, Ont.: Queen's Printer for Canada.

Hurst, R. (2000). To revise or not to revise? *Disability & Society, 15*(7), 1083–1087.

Hurst, R. (2003). The international disability rights movement and the ICF. *Disability and Rehabilitation, 25*(11–12), 572–576.

Iezzoni, L. I., Davis, R. B., Soukup, J., & O'Day, B. (2002). Satisfaction with quality and access to health care among people with disabling conditions. *International Journal for Quality in Health Care, 14*(5), 369–381.

Iezzoni, L. I., Davis, R. B., Soukup, J., & O'Day, B. (2003). Quarterly dimensions that concern most people with physical and sensory disabilities. *Archives of Internal Medicine, 163*(17), 2085–2092.

Iezzoni, L. I., McCarthy, E. P., Davis, R. B., & Siebans, H. (2000). Mobility impairments and use of screening and preventative services. *American Journal of Public Health, 90*(6), 955–961.

Ignatieff, M. (2000). *The rights revolution*. Toronto, Ont.: Anansi Press.

Imrie, R. (1997). Rethinking the relationships between disability, rehabilitation and society. *Disability and Rehabilitation, 19*(7), 263–271.

International Disability Alliance. (n.d.). *Who are we?*. Retrieved 25 November 2005, from http://www.internationaldisabilityalliance.org/.

International Labour Organization (ILO). (2002). *Managing disability in the workplace (ILO Code of Practice)*. Geneva: Author.

International Labour Organization, United Nations Educational, Scientific and Cultural Organization, & World Health Organization (ILO, UNESCO & WHO). (1994). *Community-based rehabilitation (CBR) for people with disabilities- Joint position paper*. Geneva: WHO.

International Labour Organization, United Nations Educational, Scientific and Cultural Organization, & World Health Organization (ILO, UNESCO & WHO). (2004). *CBR: A strategy for rehabilitation, equalization of opportunities and poverty reduction and social inclusion of people with disabilities (Joint Position Paper 2004)*. Geneva: WHO.

Inwood, G.J. (1999). Understanding Canadian *public administration: An introduction to theory and practice*. Toronto, Ont.: Prentice-Hall Canada Inc.

Irwin, S. H., Lero, D. S., & Brophy, K. (2004). *Highlights from inclusion: The next generation in child care in Canada*. Wreck Cove, NS: Breton Books.

Iser, Wolfgang. (2000). *The range of interpretation*. New York: Columbia University Press.

Ison, T. (1989). *Workers' compensation in Canada* (2nd ed.). Toronto, Ont.: Butterworths.

Jones, K. E., & Tamari, I. E. (1997). Making our offices universally accessible: Guidelines for physicians. *Canadian Medical Association Journal, 156*, 647–656.

Jongbloed, L. (2003). Disability policy in Canada: An overview. *Journal of Disability Policy Studies, 13*(4), 203–209.

Jordan, B. (1998). *The new politics of welfare: Social justice in a global context*. London, UK: Sage Books.

Joslyn, E. (1999). Disability and health care expenditure data: A wide range of user experience is more important that a standard definition. *Disability and Rehabilitation, 21*, 382–384.

Kanary, R. (1985). *Speech by Ron Kanary, Conference Chairperson, Transportation Plenary Presentation*. Report of COPOH 6th Open National Forum, Transportation and Independent Living, 14–17 March 1985, Montreal.

Kanary, R. (1986). Eligibility and reciprocity. In *Proceedings of the fourth International Conference on Mobility and Transport for Elderly and Disabled Persons*, July 20–23, 1986, Vancouver, B.C. Ottawa, Ont.: Transport Canada.

Kanter, A. S. (2003). The globalization of disability rights law. *Syracuse Journal of International Law and Commerce, 30*, 241–269.

Kennedy, F. (1988, December 19). *Report on the Roadcruiser Accessible Bus Demonstration Project in Newfoundland*. Ottawa, Ont.: Transport Canada.

Kirby, M. J. L. (2002). *The health of Canadians — The federal role volume 6: Recommendations for reform*. Retrieved 16 June 2004, from http://www.parl.gc.ca/37/2/parlbus/commbus/senate/com-e/SOCI-E/rep-e/repoct02vol6-e.htm.

Klein, J-L. (1992). « Le partenariat : vers une planification flexible du développement local ? » *Canadian Journal of Regional Sciences, 15*(3), 491–505.

Koch, T. (2001). Disability and difference: Balancing social and physical constructions. *Journal of Medical Ethics*, *27*(6), 370–376.

Kriegsman, D. M. W. & Deeg, D. J. H. (1999). Implications of alternative definitions of disability beyond health care expenditure. *Disability and Rehabilitation*, *21*, 388–391.

Kroll, T., Beatty, P. W., & Bingham, S. (2003). Primary care satisfaction among adults with physical disabilities: The role of patient-provider communication. *Managed Care Quarterly*, *11*, 11–19.

Lande, R. G. (1998). Disability law: Problems and proposals. *Southern Medical Journal*, *91*(6), 518–521.

Larana, E., Johnston, H. & Gusfield, J. R. (Eds.). (1995). *New social movements: From ideology to identity*. Philadelphia, Pa.: Temple University Press.

Lazar, H. (2000). *Working paper 3. The social union framework agreement: Lost opportunity or new beginning?* Kingston, Ont.: Queen's University School of Policy Studies.

Lee, K. K. (2000). *Urban poverty in Canada: A statistical profile*. Ottawa, Ont.: CCSD.

Legislative Assembly of Ontario Hansard. (1996). *City of Ottawa Act, 1996, Bill Pr34, Mr. Grandmaître Wednesday 29 May 1996*. Retrieved 13 December 2005, from http://www.ontla.on.ca/hansard/committee_debates/36_parl/session1/regsbils/t011.htm

Lin, Z. (1998, summer). Employment insurance in Canada: Policy changes. *Perspectives*, 42–47.

Lincoln, Y. S. & Guba, E. G. (2000). Paradigmatic controversies, contradictions and emerging confluences. In N. Denzin, & Y. S. Lincoln (Eds.), *Handbook of qualitative research* (2nd ed.) (pp. 163–188). Thousand Oaks, Calif.: Sage Publications.

Lindqvist, B. (2002, October). *All means all!* Key-note speech presented at the Osaka Forum, Osaka, Japan. Retrieved 20 November 2005, from http://www.disabilityworld.org/11-12_02/news/lindqvist.shtml.

Linton, S. (1998). *Claiming disability: Knowledge and identity*. New York: New York University Press.

Lippman, A., & Bereano, P. L. (1993, June 25). Genetic engineering: cause for caution. *The Globe and Mail*.

Lipset, S. M. (1989). *Continental divide: The values and institutions of the United States and Canada*. Washington, DC: Canadian-American Committee.

Lipovenko, Dorothy. (1986,6 November). Disabled jettison another handicap. *The Globe and Mail*, D2.

Lishner, D. M., Richardson, M., Levine, P., & Patrick, D. (1996). Access to primary health care among persons with disabilities in rural areas: A summary of literature. *Rural Health Policy*, *12*(1), 45–53.

Lysack, C. & Kaufert, J. (1994). Comparing the origins and ideologies of the independent living movement and community based rehabilitation. *International Journal of Rehabilitation Research*, *17*, 231–240.

MacKinnon, C. (1993). *Only words*. Cambridge: Harvard University Press.

Maguire, A. M., Powe, N. R., Starfield, B., Andrews, J., Weiner, J. P., & Anderson, G. F. (1998). "Carving out" conditions from global capitation rates: Protecting high-cost patients, physicians, and health plans in a managed care environment. *American Journal of Managed Care, 4*, 797–806.

Malcolmson, P., & Myers, R. (1996). *The Canadian regime*. Peterborough Ont.: Broadview Press.

Malkowski, G. (1990). We must continue to fight! *Arch-type, 8*(9), 24–25.

Malkowski, G. (1997). Running in the Federal Election. *CCD Election Monitor, 1*(2), 1–2.

Marine Atlantic Inc. (2003). *Welcome Aboard!* Retrieved 13 December 2005, from http://www.marine-atlantic.ca/.

Marks, D. (1999). *Disability: Controversial debates and psychosocial perspectives*. New York: Routledge.

Maxwell, J., Rosell, S. & Forest, P. G. (2003). Giving citizens a voice in healthcare policy in Canada. *British Medical Journal, 326*, 1031–1033.

Mazankowski, D. (1985). *Message from the Minister of Transport to the National Conference on Transport and Independent Living of CCD* (pp. 15–16). Report of COPOH 6th Open National Forum, Transportation and Independent Living, 14–17 March 1985, Montreal.

McCarthy, J., & Zald, M. (1987). *Social movements in an organizational society*. Oxford, UK: Transaction Books.

McColl M. A., & Bickenbach J. (1998). *Introduction to disability*. London, UK: W.B. Saunders.

McColl, M. A., & Boyce, W. (2003). Disability advocacy organizations: A descriptive framework. *Disability and Rehabilitation*, 25(8), 380–392.

McColl, M. A., Gerein, N., & Valentine, F. (1997). Meeting the challenges of disability: Models for enabling function and well-being. In C. Christiansen & C. Baum (Eds.), *Occupational therapy: Enabling function and well-being* (2nd ed.) (pp. 509–528). Thorofare, New Jersey: Slack.

McColl, M. A., Shortt, S., Boyce, W., & James, A. (2006). Making disability policy: Evaluating the evidence base. In D. Potheir & R. Develin (Eds.), *Critical disability theory: Essays in philosophy, policy and law*. Vancouver, BC: UBC Press.

McColl, M.A., Shortt, S., Jarzynowska, A. & James, A. (in press). Disability and unmet health care needs in Canada: A population level study. *Canadian Medical Association Journal*.

McRuer, R. (2003). As good as it gets: Queer theory and critical disability. *GLQ: A Journal of Lesbian and Gay Studies*, 9(1–2), 79–106.

McWhinnie, J. R. (1981). Disability assessment in population survey: Results of the OECD common development effort. *Rev. Epidémiol Santé Publique*, 29(4): 413–419.

Meekosha, H. (2001). Virtual Activists? Women and the Making of Identities of Disability. *Hypatia: Journal of Feminist Philosophy*, 17(3), 67–88.

437

Mehlmann, M. J., & Neuhauser, D. (1999). Alternative definitions of disability: Changes in a dichotomous vs. continuous system. *Disability and Rehabilitation, 21,* 385–387.

Mendelsohn, M., & McLean, J. (2000). SUFA's double vision: Citizen engagement and intergovernmental collaboration. *Policy Options, April,* 43–45.

Mendelsohn, M., & McLean, J. (2002). Getting engaged: The social union framework agreement and citizen engagement. In T. McIntosh (Ed.), *Building the social union: Perspectives, directions and challenges* (pp. 31–50). Regina: Saskatchewan Institute of Public Policy.

Mercer, S., Dieppe, P., Chambers, R., & MacDonald, R. (2003). Equality for people with disabilities in medicine. *British Medical Journal, 327,* 882–883.

Meyer, L. H., Peck, C. A., & Brown, L. (Eds.). (1991). *Critical issues in the lives of people with severe disabilities.* Baltimore, Md.: Paul H. Brookes.

Meyers, A. R., Branch, L. G., Cupples, A., Lederman, R. I., Feltin, M., & Master, R. J. (1989). Predictors of medical care utilization by independently living adults with spinal cord injuries. *Archives of Physical Medicine and Rehabilitation, 70,* 471–476.

Michaelakis, D. (2003). The systems theory concept of disability: One is not born a disabled person, one is observed to be one. *Disability & Society, 18,* 209–229.

Michalko, R. (2002). *The difference that disability makes.* Philadelphia, Pa.: Temple University Press.

Ontario. Ministry of Community and Social Services. (1983). *Support Services for Physically Disabled Adults.* Toronto, Ont.: Author.

Ontario. Ministry of Community and Social Services, Ministry of Health, & Ministry of Citizenship. (1991). *Redirection of long-term care and support services in Ontario: A public consultation paper.* Toronto, Ont.: Author.

Ontario. Ministries of Health, Community and Social Services and Citizenship. (1993). *Partnerships in long-term care: A new way to plan, manage and deliver services and community support — An implementation framework.* Toronto, Ont.: Author.

Monticone, G. T. (Ed.). (2004). *Long-term care facilities in Ontario: The advocate's manual* (3rd ed.). Toronto, Ont.: Advocacy Centre for the Elderly.

Moran, M., & Wood, B. (1996). The globalization of health care policy. In P. Gummet (Ed.), *Globalization and public policy.* Cheltenham, UK: Edward Elgar.

Morone, J., & Kilbreth, E. (2003). Power to the people? Restoring citizen participation. *Journal of Health Politics, Policy and Law, 28*(2–3), 271–288.

Muller, L. S. (1992). Disability beneficiaries who work and their experience under program work Incentives. *Social Security Bulletin, 55,* 2–19.

438

Munson, J. (2002). *Mental capacity under the Substitute Decisions Act: The assessor's role.* Prepared for the Capacity Assessment Office, Ministry of the Attorney General of Ontario.

Muszynski, L. (1989). Improving on welfare. *Policy Options, 2,* 26–31.

National Council of Welfare (NCW). (1989). *Welfare in Canada: The tangled safety net.* Ottawa, Ont.: Author.

National Council of Welfare (NCW). (1997, Autumn). *Another look at welfare reform: A report by the National Council of Welfare.* Ottawa, Ont.: Author.

National Council of Welfare (NCW). (2002). Welfare incomes, 2000 and 2001. *NCW Report 2002.* Ottawa, Ont.: Author.

National Population Health Survey (NPHS). (1998). *National Population Health Survey Cycle 3 (1998–1999): Public use microdata files documentation.* Ottawa, Ont.: Statistics Canada.

National Transportation Agency of Canada [NTA]. (1993). *The road to accessibility: An inquiry into Canadian motor coach services.* Ottawa, Ont.: Author.

Neufeldt, A. H. (2003). Growth and evolution of disability advocacy in Canada. In D. Stienstra, & A. Wight-Felske (Eds.), *Making equality: History of advocacy and persons with disabilities in Canada* (pp. 11–32). Concord, Ont.: Captus Press.

New Democratic Party. (1993). *Our commitment to persons with disabilities.* Ottawa, Ont.: Author.

New Democratic Party (NDP). (2002). *Federal NDP policy paper on disability issues.* Ottawa, Ont.: Author.

New Democratic Party (NDP). (2004). *Issues: Jack Layton on equality for Canadians with disabilities.* Ottawa, Ont.: Author.

New Democratic Party (NDP). (2005). *50 Ways in 50 days* (Available from http://epe.lac-bac.gc.ca/100/205/300/ndp-ef/05-03-08/ndp.ca/issues/default.htm). Ottawa, Ont.: Author.

New Economy Development Group Inc. (1996). *A study of innovative examples of local partnerships.* Ottawa, Ont.: HRDC.

Nosek, M. (1993). Personal assistance: Its effect on the long-term health of a rehabilitation hospital population. *Archives of Physical Medicine & Rehabilitation, 74*(2), 127–132.

Office for Disability Issues (ODI). (1998). *A way with words. Guidelines and appropriate terminology for the portrayal of persons with disabilities.* Hull, Quebec: Human Resources and Development Canada.

Office for Disability Issues (ODI). (2002). *Office for Disability Issues: Strategic plan 2002-2007.* Ottawa, Ont.: Human Resources and Development Canada.

O'Donoghue, F. (2001). Legislative and policy supports for inclusive education in Nunavut and the Northwest Territories. *Exceptionality Education Canada, 11*(2&3), 5–32.

O'Hara, K. (1997). *Citizen engagement in the social union.* Discussion Paper, Canadian Policy Research Networks (CPRN) roundtable on citizen engagement in the social union. Ottawa, Ont.: CPRN.

Oliver, M. (1990). *The politics of disablement: Critical texts in social work and the welfare state.* Basingstoke, UK: McMillan Press.

Oliver, M. (1996). *Understanding disability: From theory to practice.* New York: St. Martin's Press.

Oliver, M., & Barnes, C. (1998). *Disabled people and social policy: From exclusion to inclusion.* London: Longman.

One Voice. (1997). *Seniors election handbook.* Ottawa, Ont.: Author.

Ontario Ministry of Citizenship and Immigration. (2001). *Ontario Disabilities Act.* Retrieved 3 August 2004, from http://gateway.ontla.on.ca/documents/Bills/37_Parliament/Session2/b125ra.pdf.

Ontario Ministry of Citizenship and Immigration. (2005). *Accessibility for Ontarian's with Disabilities Act.* Retrieved 31 May 2005, from http://gateway.ontla.on.ca/documents/Bills/37_Parliament/Session2/b125ra.pdf.

O'Reilly, A. (2003). *The right to decent work of persons with disabilities, IFP/Skills working paper no. 14.* Geneva: International Labour Organization.

Organization for Economic Cooperation and Development (OECD). (2003). *Transforming disability into ability: Policies to promote work and income security for disabled people,* Paris. France: Author.

Organization of African Unity. (1981). African [Banjul] Charter on Human and Peoples' Rights, OAU Doc. CAB/LEG/67/3 rev.5, (entered into force 21 October 1986).

Organization of American States. (1988). Additional protocol to the American Convention on Human Rights in the area of economic, social and cultural rights. *Protocol of San Salvador,* OAS Treaty Series 69.

Organization of American States. (1996). *Inter-American Convention on the Elimination of All Forms of Discrimination Against Persons with Disabilities,* AG/RES. 1608, 7 June 1999.

Pal, L. A. (1997). *Beyond policy analysis: Public issue management in turbulent times.* Scarborough: Nelson.

Paris, M. J. (1993). Attitudes of medical students and health-care professionals towards people with disabilities. *Archives of Physical Medicine and Rehabilitation, 74*: 818–825.

Pascal, C. (1996). Executive Director of the Atkinson Charitable Foundation, Speech to the Canadian Centre for Philanthropy, Second Annual National Symposium. Ottawa

Patrick, M. (2002). Rights and recognition: Perspectives on multicultural democracy. *Ethnicities, 2*(1), 31–51.

Pearce, G., & Mawson, J. (2003). Delivering devolved approaches to local governance. *Policy & Politics, 31*(1), 51–67.

Pedlar, A., Hutchison, P., Arai, S., & Dunn, P. (2000). Community services landscape in Canada: Survey of developmental disability agencies. *Mental Retardation, 38,* 109–122.

People First of Oregon. (n.d.). *People first history*. Retrieved 25 November 2005, from http://www.open.org/~people1/about_us_history.html.

Perrin, B. (1991). *Extraordinary costs of disability: Conceptual considerations*. Toronto, Ont.: Office for Disability Issues.

Peters, Y. (2003). From charity to equality: Canadians with disabilities take their rightful place in Canada's Constitution. In D. Stienstra & A. Wight-Felske, (Eds), *Making equality: History of advocacy and persons with disabilities in Canada* (pp. 119–136). Concord, Ont.: Captus Press.

Pfieffer, D. (1999). The problem of disability definition: Again. *Disability and Rehabilitation, 21*, 392–395.

Phillips, S. (2001). SUFA and citizen engagement: Fake or genuine masterpiece? *IRPP Policy Matters, 2*(7), 1–36. Retrieved 14 February 2005, from www.irpp.org/pm/archive/pmvol2no7.pdf.

Pierson, C. (1991). *Beyond the welfare state?* University Park: The Pennsylvania State University Press.

Piggott, L., Sapey, B., & Wilenius, F. (2005). Out of touch: Local government and disabled people's employment needs. *Disability & Society, 20*(6), 599–611.

Pitt, V., & Curtain, M. (2004). Integration versus segregation: the experiences of a group of disabled students moving from mainstream school into special needs further education. *Disability & Society, 19*(4), 387–401.

Pivik, J. (2002). Discussion paper no.23, practical strategies for facilitating meaningful citizen involvement in health planning. *Commission on the Future of Health Care in Canada*. Retrieved 6 February 2005, from www.hc-sc.gc.ca/ehglish/care/romanow/hcc 0495/html.

Pleiger, D. (1990). Policy networks and the decentralization of policy making. *Bulletin of European Social Security, 37*, 55–56.

Priest, L. (2004a, December 18). Nursing homes no answer for the young. *The Globe and Mail*, A13.

Priest, L. (2004b, December 18). It's not where I should be. It feels degrading. *The Globe and Mail*, A14.

Priestley, M. (2003). *Disability: A life course approach*. Oxford UK: Polity Press.

Prince, M. J. (1992). Touching us all: International context, national policies, and the integration of Canadians with disabilities. In F. Abele (Ed.), *How Ottawa spends: 1992–93* (pp. 191–239). Ottawa, Ont.: Carleton University Press.

Prince, M. J. (2001a). Citizenship by instalments: Federal policies for Canadians with disabilities. In L. A. Pal, (Ed.), *How Ottawa spends: 2001–2002* (pp. 177–200). Toronto, Ont.: Oxford University Press.

Prince, M. J. (2001b). *Governing in an integrated fashion: Lessons from the disability domain*. CPRN Discussion Paper No. F/14. Ottawa, Ont.: Canadian Policy Research Networks.

Prince, M. J. (2001c). Canadian federalism and disability policy making. *Canadian Journal of Political Science, 34*(4), 791–817.

Prince, M. J. (2001d). Tax policy as social policy: Canadian tax assistance for people with disabilities. *Canadian Public Policy, 27*(4), 487–501.

Prince, M.J. (2002a). Designing disability policy in Canada. In A. Puttee (Ed.), *Federalism, democracy and disability policy in Canada* (pp. 29–77). Montreal, Que. & Kingston, Ont.: McGill-Queen's University Press.

Prince, M. J. (2002b). The return of directed incrementalism: Innovating social policy the Canadian way. In G. B. Doern (Ed.), *How Ottawa spends 2002–2003* (pp. 176–195). Toronto, Ont.: Oxford University Press.

Prince, M.J. (2004). Canadian disability policy: Still a hit-and-miss affair. *Canadian Journal of Sociology, 29*(1), 59–82.

Pronger, B. (2002). *Body fascism: Salvation in the technology of physical fitness.* Toronto, Ont.: University of Toronto Press.

Quinn, G. (1999). The human rights of people with disabilities under EU Law. In P. Alston (Ed.), *The EU and human rights* (pp. 281–326). New York: Oxford University Press.

Quinn, G., & Degener, T. (2002). Human rights and disability: The current use and future potential of United Nations Human Rights Instruments in the context of disability. New York and Geneva: United Nations. Retrieved 12 November 2005, from http://www.unhchr.ch/html/menu6/2/disability.doc.

Ratzka, A. D. (1993). The user cooperative model in personal assistance: The example of STIL, the Stockholm Cooperative for Independent Living. In B. Duncan & S. Brown (Eds.), *Personal assistance services in Europe and North America.* New York: Rehabilitation International.

Ravaud, J.-F., & Stiker, H.-J. (2001). Inclusion/exclusion: An analysis of historical and cultural meanings. In G.L. Albrecht, K.D. Seelman, & M. Bury (Eds.), *Handbook of disability studies* (pp. 490–512). Thousand Oaks, CA: Sage.

Reddel, T., & Woolcock, G. (2004). From consultation to participatory governance? A critical review of citizen engagement strategies in Queensland. *Australian Journal of Public Administration, 63*(3), 75–87.

Redden, C. (1999). Rationing care in the community: Engaging citizens in health care decision-making. *Journal of Health Politics, Policy and Law, 24*(6), 1363–1390.

Rekart, J. (1994). The hidden cost of government funding, front and centre. *Front & Centre, 1*(4).

Rice, J. J., & Prince, M.J. (2000). *Changing politics of Canadian social policy.* Toronto, Ont.: University of Toronto Press.

Rice, J. J., & Prince, M.J. (2004). Martin's moment: The social policy agenda of a new Prime Minister. In G. B. Doern (Ed.), *How Ottawa spends, 2004–2005, mandate change in the Paul Martin Era* (pp. 111–130). Montreal, Que. & Kingston, Ont.: McGill-Queen's University Press.

Ringaert, L. (2003). History of accessibility in Canada from the advocacy perspective. In D. Stienstra, & A. Wight-Felske (Eds.), *Making equality history of advocacy and persons with disabilities in Canada* (pp. 279–300). Concord, Ont.: Captus Press.

Rioux, M. H. (1997). Disability: The place of judgement in a world of fact. *Journal of Intellectual Disability Research, 41*(2), 102–111.

Rioux, M. H. (2000). *Bioethics, genetics and biotechnology — Promise or threat?* Speech presented at the Conference of the Australian Bioethics Association, Sydney, Australia.

Rioux, M. H. (2001). Bending towards justice. In L. Barton (Ed.), *Disability, politics and the struggle for change* (pp. 34–48). London: David Fulton.

Rioux, M. H. (2002). Social disability and the public good — Picking up the pieces of the Washington Consensus: The globalization of poverty. *Man & Development,* 179–198.

Rioux, M. H. (2003). On second thought: Constructing knowledge, law, disability and inequality. In S. S. Kerr, H. H. Kohl, & L. O. Gostin (Eds.), *Different but equal: The rights of persons with intellectual disabilities.* London: Oxford University Press.

Rioux, M. H., & Bach, M. (1994). *Disability is not measles.* Toronto, Ont.: The Roeher Institute.

Rioux, M. H., Muszynski, L., & Crawford, C. (1992). *Comprehensive disability income security reform.* Toronto, Ont.: The Roeher Institute.

Rioux, M. H., & Prince, M. J. (2002). The Canadian political landscape of disability. In A. Puttee (Ed.), *Federalism, democracy and disability policy in Canada* (pp. 11–28). Montreal, Que. & Kingston, Ont.: McGill-Queen's University Press.

Rioux, M., Zubrow, E., Furrie, A., Miller, W., & Bunch, R. (2002). Barriers and accommodations: Applying the human rights model of disability to HALS. *Abilities,* 56–57.

Roberts, E. V. (1989). A history of the independent living movement: a founder's perspective. In B. W. Heller, L. M. Flohr, & L. S. Zegans (Eds.), *Psychosocial interventions with physically disabled persons* (pp. 231–34). New Brunswick: Rutgers University Press.

Roberts, N. (2004). Public deliberation in an age of direct citizen participation. *American Review of Public Administration, 34*(4), 315–353.

Robinson, J. R. (2002). *Electoral rights: Charter of Rights and Freedoms.* Ottawa, Ont.: Library of Parliament, Law and Government Division.

Rodal, A., & Mulder, N. (1993). Partnerships, devolution and power-sharing: Issues and implications for management, Optimum. *The Journal of Public Sector Management, 24*(3), 27–48.

Roeher Institute, The. (1989). *Power of positive linking: How families can empower people who have a mental handicap through mutual support groups.* Toronto, Ont.: Author.

Roeher Institute, The. (1993a). *Direct dollars: A study of individualized funding in Canada.* North York, Ont.: Author.

Roeher Institute, The. (1993b). *Social well-being: A paradigm for reform.* Toronto, Ont.: Author.

Roeher Institute, The. (1994). *People with disabilities in transition.* Toronto, Ont.: Author.

Roeher Institute, The. (1997a). *A literature review on individualized funding. Self-managed attendant services in Ontario: Direct funding pilot project.* Toronto, Ont.: Author.

Roeher Institute, The. (1997b). *Disability, community and society: Exploring the links.* Toronto, Ont.: Author.

Roeher Institute, The. (1999). *Genome(s) and justice: Reflections on a holistic approach to genetic research, technology and disability.* Toronto, Ont.: Author.

Roeher Institute, The. (2001a). *Personal relationships of support between adults: The case of disability.* Toronto, Ont.: Law Commission of Canada. Retrieved 21 November 2005, from http://www.lcc.gc.ca/research_project/01_support_1-en.asp.

Roeher Institute, The. (2001b, December). *Striking a new balance: Proposal for a joint Federal- Provincial/Territorial disability supports investment initiative.* Toronto, Ont.: Author.

Romanow, F. J. (2002). *Building on values: The future of health care in Canada.* Ottawa, Ont.: National Library of Canada.

Rosenbach, M.L. (1995). Access and satisfaction within the disabled Medicare population. *Health Care and Financial Review, 17*(2), 147–167.

Rosenstone, S. J., & Hansen, J. M. (1993). *Mobilization, participation, and democracy in America.* New York: MacMillan Publishing Company.

Roth, W. (1983). Disability as a social construct. *Society, 20,* 56–61.

Roulstone, A. (2003). The legal road to rights? Disability premises, *obiter dicta,* and the Disability Discrimination Act, 1995. *Disability & Society, 18,* 117–131.

Ruether, S., St. Claire, T., & Coffman, J. (2001). Making room for citizens at the public policy table. *Journal of Health and Human Services Administration, 24*(4), 388–400.

Rummery, K., Eliis, K., & Davis, A. (1999). Negotiating access to community care: Perspectives of frontline workers, people with a disability and careers. *Health and Social Care Community, 7,* 296–300.

Russell, M. (2002). What disability civil rights cannot do: Employment and political economy. *Disability & Society, 17*(2), 117–135.

Safran, D. G., Tarlov, A. R., & Rogers, W. H. (1994). Primary care performance in fee-for-service and prepaid health care systems. Results from the medical outcomes study. *Journal of the American Medical Association, 271*(20), 1579–1586.

Safran, D. G., Wilson, I. B., Rogers, W. H., Montgomery, J. E., & Chang, H. (2002). Primary care quality in the Medicare program: Comparing the performance of Medicare health maintenance organizations and traditional fee-for-service Medicare. *Archives of Internal Medicine, 162,* 757–765.

Saloojee, A. (2002). Inclusion and exclusion: A framework of analysis for understanding political participation by members of racialized and newcomer communities. In *Bringing worlds together seminar proceedings: The study of the political participation of women in Canada and lessons for research on newcomer and minority political participation* (pp. 34–48). Ottawa, Ont.: Metropolis Project Team, Citizenship and Immigration Canada. (Available from http://canada.metropolis.net/events/Political%20Participation/AGENDA_e.htm)

Sampson, F. (2003). Globalization and the inequality of women with disabilities. *Journal of Law & Equity, 2*(1), 16–32.

Sanchez, J., Byfield, G., Brown, T. T., LaFavor, K., Murphy, D., & Laud, P. (2000). Perceived accessibility versus actual physical accessibility of healthcare facilities. *Rehabilitation Nursing, 25,* 6–9.

Sandvin, J. T. (2001). *Loosening bonds and changing identities; growing up with impairments in post-war Norway.* Norway: Bodo University Centre.

Savoie, D. (1999). *Governing from the centre: The concentration of power in Canadian politics.* Toronto, Ont.: University of Toronto Press.

Schechter, E. (1997). Work while receiving disability insurance benefits: Additional findings from the New Beneficiary Followup Survey. *Social Security Bulletin, 60,* 3–17.

Schriner, K. F., Rumrill, P., & Parlin, R. (1995). Rethinking disability policy: Equity in the ADA era and the meaning of specialized services for people with disabilities. *Journal of Health & Human Services Administration, 17*(4), 478–500.

Schriner, K., & Shields, T. G. (1998). Empowerment of the political kind: The role of disability service organizations in encouraging people with disabilities to vote ... the Motor Voter Bill. *Journal of Rehabilitation, 64*(2), 33–37.

Schur, L. A. (1998). Disability and psychology of political participation. *Journal of Disability Policy Studies, 9*(2), 3–31.

Schur, L. A., & Kruse, D. L. (2000). What determines voter turnout?: Lessons from citizens with disabilities. *Social Science Quarterly, 81*(2), 571–587.

Scotch, R. K. (1989). Politics and policy in the history of the disability rights movement. *Milbank Quarterly, 67*(suppl. 2), Pt 2: 380–400.

Scotch, R. K. (2000). Models of disability and the Americans with Disabilities Act. *Berkeley Journal of Employment and Labour Law, 21,* 213–222.

Scotch, R. K., & Schriner, K. (1997). Disability as human variation: implications for policy. *Annals of the American Academy of Political and Social Science, 549,* 148–159.

Scott, A. (1990). *Ideology and the new social movements.* London, UK: Unwin Hyman Press.

Scott-Hill, M. (2002). Policy, politics and the silencing of 'voice'. *Policy & Politics, 30*(3), 397–409.

Seebohm, P., & Scott, J. (2004). *Addressing disincentives to work associated with the Welfare Benefits System in the UK and abroad.* London: Social Enterprise Partnership.

Shakespeare, T. (1993). Disabled people's self-organisation: A new social movement? *Disability, Handicap & Society, 8*(3), 249–264.

Shakespeare, T. (1998). Choices and rights: Eugenics, genetics and disability equality. *Disability & Society, 13*(5), 665–681.

Shakespeare, T., & Watson, N. (2001). The social model of disability: An outdated ideology? In S. Barnartt & B. Altman (Eds.), *Exploring theories and expanding methodologies: Where we are and where we need to go* (pp. 9–28). London, UK: JAI.

Shankardass, K., & Bugaresti, J. (2004). Accessibility of doctors' offices in southwestern Ontario. Unpublished manuscript.

Shapiro, J. (1994). *No pity: People with disabilities forging a new civil rights movement.* New York: Random House.

Shields, T. G., Schriner, K. F., & Schriner, K. (1998). The disability voice in American politics: Political participation of people with disabilities in the 1994 election. *Journal of Disability Policy Studies, 9*(2), 33–52.

Shields, T. G., Schriner, K., Schriner, K., & Ochs, L. (2000). Disenfranchised: People with disabilities in American electoral politics. In B. M. Altman, & S. N. Barnartt (Eds.), *Expanding the scope of social science research on disability* (pp. 177–203). Stamford, Connecticut: JAI.

Slee, R. (2004). Meaning in the service of power. In L. Ware (Ed.), *Ideology and the politics of (in)exclusion* (pp. 62–81). New York: Peter Lang.

Smith, D. (1992). Whistling women: Reflections on rage and rationality. In W. Carroll, L. Christiansen-Ruffman, R. Currie, & D. Harrison (Eds.), *Fragile truths: 25 years of sociology and anthropology in Canada* (pp. 207–226). Ottawa, Ont.: Carleton University Press.

Smith, D. E. (1999). *Writing the social: Critique, theory, and investigations.* Toronto, Ont.: University of Toronto Press.

Smith, P. (2001). The impact of globalization on citizenship: Decline or renaissance? *Journal of Canadian Studies, 36*(1), 116–140.

Snow, J. (1993). Advocating for personal assistance in Ontario and in Canada. In B. Duncan & S. Brown (Eds.), *Personal assistance services in Europe and North America.* New York: Rehabilitation International.

Social Development Canada. (2002a). *Release of Advancing the Inclusion of Persons with Disabilities: A Government of Canada Report — December 2002* [Press Release]. Retrieved, 14 January 2005, from http://www.hrsdc.gc.ca/en/cs/comm/news/2002/021203_e.shtml.

Social Development Canada. (2002b). *Lessons learned.* Ottawa, Ont.: Office for Disability Issues.

Social Development Canada. (2004a). *Advancing the inclusion of persons with disabilities in Canada.* Ottawa, Ont.: Government of Canada.

Social Development Canada. (2004b). *Canadian attitudes toward disability.* Ottawa, Ont.: Government of Canada.

Somerville, M. A. (1994). Label versus contents: Variance between philosophy, psychiatry and law. *McGill Law Journal, 39,* 179–199.

Special Rapporteur on Disability of the United Nations Commission for Social Development. [SPD]. (2000, November 5–9). Let the world know: Report of a seminar on human rights and disability. Paper presented at the Almåsa Conference Centre, Stockholm.

Special Rapporteur on Disability of the United Nations Commission for Social Development. (2002). *Report on Third Mandate, 2000–2002* (E/ CN.5/2002/4). New York: United Nations.

Starfield, B. (1997). The future of primary care in a managed care era. *International Journal of Health Services, 27*(4), 687–696.

Starfield, B., Cassady, C., Nanda, J., Forrest, C.B., & Berk, R. (1998). Consumer experiences and provider perceptions of the quality of primary care: Implications for managed care. *Journal of Family, 43*(3), 216–226.

Statistics Canada. (1988). Disability Database Program. *Health and Activity Limitation Survey: User's guide.* Ottawa, Ont.: Author.

Statistics Canada. (1992). *Health and Activity Limitation Survey, 1991: User's guide.* Ottawa, Ont.: Author.

Statistics Canada. (1995). *A portrait of persons with disabilities: Target groups project.* Statistics Canada Housing, Family, and Social Statistics Division. Ottawa, Ont.: Minister of Industry, Science and Technology.

Statistics Canada. (2001a). *A profile of disability in Canada, 2001.* Retrieved 19 July 2004, from www.statscan.ca.

Statistics Canada. (2001b). *Canadian Statistics — Government transfer payments to persons.* CANSIM II, table 384-0009 [online statistical database].

Statistics Canada. (2001c). *Canadian statistics — Personal expenditure on medical care and health services.* CANSIM II, table 380-0024 [online statistical database].

Statistics Canada. (2002a). *2001 Census: Collective dwellings* (Available from http://www12.statcan.ca/english/census01/Products/Analytic/companion/ coll/contents.cfm). Ottawa, Ont.: Statistics Canada.

Statistics Canada. (2001d). *Participation and Activity Limitation Survey (PALS) 2001.* Ottawa, Ont.: Statistics Canada.

Statistics Canada. (2002). Housing, Family and Social Statistics Division. A profile of disability in Canada, 2001 (Catalogue No.: 87-577-XIE). Ottawa, Ont.: Minister of Industry.

Statistics Canada. (2003). Communications Division. *Canada e-book.* Ottawa, Ont.: Statistics Canada

Statistics Canada. (2005). *Participation in post-secondary education in Canada: Has the role of parental income and education changed over the 1990's?.* Ottawa, Ont.: Author.

Stienstra, D. (2003). "Listen, Really Listen, to Us". In D. Stienstra & A. Wight-Felske (Eds.), *Making Equality: History of Advocacy and Persons with Disabilities in Canada* (pp. 33–47). Concord, Ont.: Captus Press.

Stienstra, D., & Wight-Felske, A. (2003). *Making equality: History of advocacy and persons with disabilities in Canada.* Concord, Ont.: Captus Press.

Stiker, H-J. (1997). *A history of disability.* Foreword by D. T. Mitchell. Ann Arbor, MI: University of Michigan Press.

Stiker, H.-J. (1999). *A history of disability.* (W. Sayers, Trans.). Ann Arbor, MI: University of Michigan Press. (Original work published 1997.)

Stone, D. (1984). *The disabled state*. Philadelphia, PA: Temple University Press.

Strachan, D., & Tomlinson, P. (1987). *I am who I should be already*. A report on the proceedings of the National Symposium on Brokerage/Individualized Funding, Ottawa, Ontario, 1–49. Ottawa, Ont.: Health and Welfare Canada/Secretary of State

Sutherland, N. (1976). *Children in English-Canadian society*. Toronto, Ont.: University of Toronto Press.

Taber, J. (2004, January 24). Mercer puts Copps on the spot. *The Globe and Mail*, A9.

Tambay, J. L., & Catlin, G. (1995). Sample design of the National Population Health Survey. *Health Reports*, *7*(1), 29–38.

Tepper, S., Sutton, J., Beatty, P., & DeJong, G. (1997). Alternate definitions of disability: Relationship to health care expenditures. *Disability and Rehabilitation*, *19*, 556–558.

Tervo, R. C., Azuma, S., Palmer, G., & Redinius, P. (2002). Medical students' attitudes toward persons with disability: A comparative study. *Archives of Physical Medicine and Rehabilitation*, *83*, 1537–1542.

Thomas, C. (2004). How is disability understood? An examination of sociological approaches. *Disability & Society*, *19*(6), 569–583.

Ticoll, M. (1996, summer). The Human Genome Project — A challenge for the new millennium. *Entourage*, 10–12.

Timmons, V. (2003). Leadership for inclusive practice. *The CAP Journal*, *12*(1), 30–31.

Timmons, V. (2005). *Supporting families to enhance children's learning*. Unpublished chapter under review.

Titchkosky, T. (2000). Disability studies: The old and the new. *Canadian Journal of Sociology*, *25*(2), 197–224.

Titchkosky, T. (2001). Disability: A rose by any other name? "People-first" language in Canadian society. *Canadian Review of Sociology & Anthropology*, *38*, 125–140.

Titchkosky, T. (2003a). *Disability, self and society*. Toronto, Ont.: University of Toronto Press.

Titchkosky, T. (2003b). Governing embodiment: Technologies of constituting citizens with disabilities. *The Canadian Journal of Sociology*, *28*(4), 517–542.

Torjman, S. (1988). *Income insecurity: The disability income system in Canada*. Toronto, Ont.: The Roeher Institute.

Torjman, S. (1998). *Partnerships: The good, the bad and the uncertain*. Ottawa, Ont.: The Caledon Institute of Social Policy.

Torjman, S. (2001). Canada's federal regime and persons with disabilities. In D. Cameron, & F. Valentine (Eds.), *Disability and federalism: Comparing different approaches to full participation* (pp. 151–196). Montreal, Que. & Kingston, Ont.: McGill-Queen's University Press.

Torjman, S. (2002). *The Canada Pension Plan disability benefit*. Ottawa, Ont.: Caledon Institute of Social Policy.

Touraine, A. (1981). *The voice and the eye: An analysis of social movements.* Cambridge, UK: Cambridge University Press.

Townsend, P. (1975). *Poverty in the United Kingdom.* Hammondsworth, UK: Penguin.

Transport Canada. (1990). *Policy and Coordination. Transportation of disabled persons program: 1989–90 operational plan.* Ottawa, Ont.: Author.

Transport Canada. (1991). *Access for all: Transport Canada's Policy on Accessible Transportation.* Ottawa, Ont.: Government of Canada.

Transport Canada. (1998). *Intercity bus code of practice.* Ottawa, Ont.: Government of Canada.

Transportation Development Center (TDC). (1998). *Making transportation accessible: A Canadian planning guide.* Ottawa, Ont.: Transport Canada Safety and Security.

Treasury Board of Canada Secretariat. (1995, October). *Stretching the tax dollar, the federal government as 'partner': Six steps to successful collaboration* (Available from http://www.tbs-sct.gc.ca/pubs_pol/opepubs/tb_o3/fgpe1_e.asp). Ottawa, Ont.: Author.

Tremblay, M., Campbell, A., & Hudson, G. L. (2005). When elevators were for pianos: An oral history account of the civilian experience using wheelchairs in Canadian society. The first twenty-five years: 1945–1970. *Disability & Society, 20*(2), 103–116.

Turner-Stokes, L., Turner-Stokes, T., Schon, K., Turner-Stokes, H., Dayal, S., & Brier, S. (2000). Charter for disabled people using hospitals: A completed access audit cycle. *Journal of the Royal College of Physicians London, 34*(2), 185–189.

Tutor2u. (n.d.). *Notions of equity.* Retrieved 21 November 2005, from http://www.tutor2u.net/economics/content/topics/marketfail/notions_equity.htm.

United Nations (UN). (1998). *Principles and recommendations for population and housing censuses, rev. 1.* New York: United Nations.

United Nations. (2003). *Standard rules on the equalization of opportunities for persons with disabilities.* Retrieved 3 March 2005, from http://www.un.org/esa/socdev/enable/dissre00.htm.

United Nations Ad Hoc Committee. [UNAHC] (2002). *Report of the Ad Hoc Committee on a Comprehensive and Integral International Convention on Protection and Promotion of the Rights and Dignity of Persons with Disabilities* (A/57/357). New York: Author.

United Nations Ad Hoc Committee. (2003). *Report of the Ad Hoc Committee on a Comprehensive and Integral International Convention on Protection and Promotion of the Rights and Dignity of Persons with Disabilities* (A/58/246 & Corr.1). New York: Author.

United Nations Ad Hoc Committee. (n.d.). on a Comprehensive and Integral International Convention on Protection and Promotion of the Rights and Dignity of Persons with Disabilities. *Details of Ad Hoc Committee Proceedings.* Retrieved 2 November 2005, from http://www.un.org/esa/socdev/enable/rights/adhocmeetings.htm.

United Nations Advisory Committee for the International Year of Disabled Persons. (1982). *World Programme of Action concerning Disabled Persons, Recommendation 1 (IV) of the Annex to the Report of its Fourth Session.* Retrieved 17 November 2005, from http://www.un.org/documents/ga/res/37/a37r052.htm.

United Nations Committee on Economic, Social and Cultural Rights. (1994). General comment no. 5, persons with disabilities. *UN economic and social council, report on the tenth and eleventh sessions of the Committee on Economic, Social and Cultural Rights* (E/1995/22). New York: Author.

United Nations Commission on Human Rights (UNCHR). (1993). *Human rights and disability* (E/CN.4/RES/1993/29). New York: Author.

United Nations Commission on Human Rights. (1994). *Human rights and disability* (E/CN.4/RES/1994/27). New York: Author.

United Nations Commission on Human Rights. (1995). *Human rights and disability* (E/CN.4/RES/1995/58). New York: Author.

United Nations Commission on Human Rights. (1996). *Human rights of persons with disabilities* (E/CN.4/RES/1996/27). New York: Author.

United Nations Commission on Human Rights. (1998). *Human rights of persons with disabilities* (E/CN.4/RES/1998/31). New York: Author.

United Nations Commission on Human Rights. (2000). *Human rights of persons with disabilities* (E/CN.4/RES/2000/51). New York: Author.

United Nations Commission on Human Rights. (2002). *Human rights of persons with disabilities* (E/CN.4/RES/2002/61). New York: Author.

United Nations Commission on Human Rights. (2003). *Human rights of persons with disabilities* (E/CN.4/RES/2003/49). New York: Author.

United Nations Commission on Human Rights. (2004). *Human rights of persons with disabilities* (E/CN.4/RES/2004/52). New York: Author.

United Nations Department of Economic and Social Affairs, Division for Social Policy and Development. (1997). *The United Nations and disabled persons — An historical overview: First fifty years.* New York: United Nations.

United Nations General Assembly. (1948). *Universal declaration of human rights*, A/RES/217 A (III), 3rd Cong. New York: Author.

United Nations General Assembly. (1966a). *International Covenant on Civil and Political Rights*, A/RES/2200A (XXI), 21 Cong. (entered into force 23 March 1976).

United Nations General Assembly. (1966b). *International Covenant on Economic, Social and Cultural Rights*, A/RES/2200A (XXI), 21 Cong. (entered into force 3 January 1976).

United Nations General Assembly. (1971). *Declaration on the Rights of Mentally Retarded Persons*, A/RES/2856 (XXVI), 26 Cong. New York: Author.

United Nations General Assembly. (1975). *Declaration on the Rights of Disabled Persons*, A/RES/3447 (XXX), 30 Cong. New York: Author.

United Nations General Assembly. (1976). *International year for disabled persons*, A/RES/31/123. New York: Author.

United Nations General Assembly. (1981). *Convention on the elimination of all forms of discrimination against women*, A/RES/34/180 (entered into force 3 September 1981).

United Nations General Assembly. (1982a). *World Programme of Action concerning Disabled Persons*, A/RES/37/52.

United Nations General Assembly. (1982b). *Implementation of the World Programme of Action concerning Disabled Persons*, A/RES/37/53.

United Nations General Assembly. (1989). *Convention on the Rights of the Child*, A/RES/44/25 (entered into force 2 September 1990).

United Nations General Assembly. (1993). *The Standard Rules on the Equalization of Opportunities for Persons with Disabilities*, A/RES/48/96.

United Nations General Assembly. (2001). *Comprehensive and integral international convention to promote and protect the rights and dignity of persons with disabilities*. A/RES/56/168.

United Nations General Assembly. (2002a). *Accreditation and participation of non-governmental organizations in the Ad Hoc Committee on a Comprehensive and Integral International Convention on Protection and Promotion of the Rights and Dignity of Persons with Disabilities*. A/RES/56/510. New York: Author.

United Nations General Assembly. (2002b). *Ad Hoc Committee on a Comprehensive and Integral International Convention on Protection and Promotion of the Rights and Dignity of Persons with Disabilities*. A/RES/57/229. New York: Author.

United Nations General Assembly. (2003). *Ad Hoc Committee on a Comprehensive and Integral International Convention on Protection and Promotion of the Rights and Dignity of Persons with Disabilities*. A/RES/58/246. New York: Author.

United Nations General Assembly. (2004). *Ad Hoc Committee on a Comprehensive and Integral International Convention on Protection and Promotion of the Rights and Dignity of Persons with Disabilities*. A/RES/59/198.

United Nations Working Group to the Ad Hoc Committee on a Comprehensive and Integral International Convention on Protection and Promotion of the Rights and Dignity of Persons with Disabilities. (2002). *Report to the Ad Hoc Committee*. A/AC.265/2004/WG/1.

United States of America. (1990). *An Act to establish a clear and comprehensive prohibition of discrimination on the basis of disability ("Americans with Disabilities Act of 1990")*, S.933 — 101 Congress, 2nd Session.

Ustun, T. B., Chatterji, S., Bickenbach, J., Kostanjsek, N., & Schneider, M. (2003). The International Classification of Functioning, Disability and Health: A new tool for understanding disability and health. *Disability and Rehabilitation, 25*(11–12), 565–570.

van de Ven, L., Post, M., de Witte, L., & van den Heuvel, W. (2005). It takes two to tango: The integration of people with disabilities into society. *Disability & Society, 20*(3), 311–329.

Veltman, A., Stewart, D.E., Tardif, G., & Branigan, M. (2001). Perceptions of primary healthcare services among people with physical disabilities. Part 1: Access issues. *Medscape General Medicine, 3*(2), 18.

Verma, S. (1995). Competency and decision making capacity: A discussion of evolving concepts and problems with current models of assessment. *The Law Society Gazette, 29*, 252–267.

Wade, D. T., & Halligan, P. (2003). New wine in old bottles: The WHO ICF as an explanatory model of human behaviour. *Clinical Rehabilitation, 17*, 349–354.

Weber, M. (1947). *The theory of social and economic organization.* New York: The Free Press.

Weisstub, D. N. (1990). *Enquiry on mental competency: Final report.* Toronto, Ont.: Enquiry on Mental Competency.

Wickman, P. (1987). *Wheels in the fast lane ... a blessing in disguise.* Edmonton: Triwicky Enterprises.

Wight-Felske, A., & Stienstra, D. (2003). Introduction: Making equality and history. In D. Stienstra & A. Wight-Felske (Eds.), *Making equality: History of advocacy and persons with disabilities in Canada* (pp. 1–10). Concord, Ont.: Captus Press.

Williams, C. (2004). Poverty is not just about income — It's also about assets. *Notes for a presentation to the conference: Investing in Self-Sufficiency: Moving the Asset-Building Agenda Forward in BC.* Ottawa, Ont.: Canadian Policy Research Networks.

Williams, G. (1998). The Sociology of disability: Towards a materialist phenomenology. In T. Shakespeare (Ed.), *The disability reader: Social science perspectives* (pp. 234–244). London: Cassell Academic.

Willms, D. (2002). *Vulnerable children.* Edmonton, Alta.: The University of Alberta Press.

Wolbring, G. (2003). Disability rights approach toward bioethics. *Journal of Disability Policy Studies, 14*(3), 174–180.

Wolf, D. A., Hunt, K., & Knickman, J. (2005). Perspectives on the recent decline in disability at older ages. *The Milbank Quarterly, 83*(3), 365–395.

Wolfe, S. (1995). Beyond 'genetic discrimination': Toward the broader harm of geneticism. *Journal of Law, Medicine & Ethics, 23*(4), 345–353.

Wolfensberger, W. (1972). *Normalization: The principle of normalization in human services.* Toronto, Ont.: National Institute on Mental Retardation.

Woodill, G. (1992). Independent living and participation in research: A critical analysis [a discussion paper]. Toronto, Ont.: Centre for Independent Living in Toronto.

Working Group of the Direct Funding Pilot Project Self-Managed Attendant Services in Ontario. (1993). *A proposal for self-managed attendant services in Ontario: Direct Funding Pilot Project.* Toronto, Ont.: Author.

World Conference on Human Rights. (1993). *Vienna Convention and Programme of Action,* A/CONF.157/24 (Part I) Chap. III.

World Health Assembly. (1980). *International classification of impairments, disabilities, and handicaps: A manual of classification relating to the consequences of disease, published in accordance with resolution WHA29.35 of the Twenty-ninth World Health Assembly*, May 1976. Geneva: WHO.

World Health Organization (WHO). (2001a). *International classification of functioning, disability and health*. Geneva: Author.

World Health Organization (WHO). (2001b). *Innovative care for chronic conditions*. Geneva: Author.

World Health Organization (WHO). (2002). *The World Health Report 2002 — Reducing risks, promoting healthy life*. Geneva: Author.

World Health Organization (WHO). (n.d.-a). *Future trends and challenges in rehabilitation*. Retrieved 17 November 2005, from http://www.who.int/ncd/disability/trends.htm.

World Health Organization (WHO). (n.d.-b). *Disability and Rehabilitation Team (DAR)*. Retrieved 17 November 2005, from http://www.who.int/ncd/disability/index.htm.

World NGO Summit on Disability. (2000, March 12). *Beijing Declaration on the Rights of People with Disabilities in the New Century*. Adopted at the World NGO Summit on Disability in Beijing, People's Republic of China. Retrieved 21 November 2005, from http://www.dpi.org/en/resources/press_releases/Beijing.htm.

World Summit for Social Development. (1995). *Copenhagen Declaration on Social Development and Programme of Action* (E. Sales No. E.96.IV.8). New York: United Nations.

Yin, R. K. (1994). *Case study research: Design and methods*. Thousand Oaks, CA: Sage Publications.

Yoshida, K. K., Willi, V., Parker, I., Self, H., Carpenter, S., & Pfeiffer, D. (1998). Disability partnerships in research and teaching in Canada and the United States. *Physiotherapy Canada, 50*(3), 198–205.

Young, I. M. (1990). *Justice and the politics of difference*. Princeton, NJ: Princeton University Press.

Young, W. (1992). *History of the House of Commons standing committee on human rights and the status of disabled persons*. Ottawa, Ont.: Library of Parliament, Research Branch.

Zald M., & McCarthy J. (2002). The Resource Mobilization Research Program: Progress, challenge, and transformation. In J. Berger (Ed.), *New directions in contemporary sociological theory*. Lanham, MD: Rowman & Littlefield.

Zola, I. K. (1989). Toward the necessary universalizing of a disability policy. *The Milbank Quarterly, 67*(Suppl. 2), 401–428.

Zukas, H. (1979). *Center for Independent Learning (CIL) history*. Berkeley, CA: Center for Independent Living Inc.

INDEX

The Contributors

The contributors of this excellent volume on disability and social policy in Canada include Canada's best educators, researchers, practitioners and advocates:

JEROME E. BICKENBACH is a full professor in the Department of Philosophy and Faculties of Law and Medicine at Queen's University, and the holder of a Queen's Research Chair. He is the author or editor of several books, chapters of books and articles on various aspects of disability, focusing on the nature of disability and disability law and policy. He is a content editor of Sage Publications' 5 volume *Encyclopedia of Disability*. His research interests include disability quality of life, disability epidemiology, universal design and inclusion, modelling disability statistics, the relationship between disability and health, and the policy implications of summary health measures. (bickenba@post.queensu.ca)

EMILY BOYCE is a PhD student in Sociology at Simon Fraser University. Her interests include gender, disability and health, and feminist and poststructuralist theory. Her current research focus is the social construction of able-bodyliness, in terms of its discursive and cultural (re)production over time as a site of symbolic, material and embodied privilege. (Emilyboyce55@yahoo.ca)

WILLIAM BOYCE is Professor and Director of the Social Program Evaluation Group (SPEG) at Queen's University. He has a joint appointment to the Faculty of Education and Queen's Centre for Health Services & Policy Research. He conducts applied research and evaluations of programs in education, health, and rehabilitation for youth and disadvantaged groups in Canada and developing countries. He has numerous publications on disability and community-level policy to his name and is lead author on *A Seat at the Table: Disabled Canadians' Participation in Policy Making* (McGill-Queen's University Press).

APRIL D'AUBIN works for the Council of Canadians with Disabilities as a research analyst.

CATHERINE FRAZEE is a writer and educator who draws from her own experience of disablement in entering ethical and cultural dialogues about citizenship and personhood. A Professor of Distinction in Disability Studies at Ryerson University, she has lectured and published extensively on disability rights, disability arts and the disability experience. Her work is informed by many years of involvement in the equality struggles of marginalized groups, most notably during her term as Chief Commissioner of the Ontario Human Rights Commission from 1989 to 1992. Dr. Frazee was awarded an honorary Doctor of Letters from the University of New Brunswick in 2002. (cfrazee@ryerson.ca)

ADELE FURRIE is President of Adele Furrie Consulting Inc., a management consulting company that provides a range of research and analytical services to both government and non-governmental organizations. The foundation for the company is the extensive experience Ms. Furrie garnered from her national work in disability at Statistics Canada and her international work through consultancies. This work has been accomplished through the analysis of statistical surveys and administrative files, the design of survey questions to identify persons with disabilities and the construct of indicators to measure the nature and extent of barriers that prevent or impede their full participation. (adfurrie@magma.ca)

IAN JOINER is the Manager, Rehabilitation and Mental Health at the Canadian Institute for Health Information (CIHI) in Ottawa. At CIHI, Ian is responsible for key strategic, operational and analytical activities for three hospital-based reporting systems. He is a Registered Physiotherapist and is currently pursuing his PhD in Rehabilitation Science at Queen's University in Kingston, Ontario. For his PhD studies, his interest lies in assessing access to administrative and policy-making initiatives for people with disabilities and disability-related organizations. (ijoiner@cihi.ca)

LYN JONGBLOED is an associate professor in occupational therapy at the School of Rehabilitation Sciences at the University of British Columbia, Vancouver, Canada. Her research interests focus on the interrelationships between disability and the social, economic and political environments. (lynjon@interchange.ubc.ca)

LANA KERZNER is a lawyer with ARCH Disability Law Centre in Toronto, Canada. Since her call to the Ontario bar in 1994, she has represented persons with disabilities and their families while working in private practice and at Advocacy Centre for the Elderly. Currently her work focuses on areas of law including mental capacity, abuse, attendant services, health care, developmental services and telecommunications. Educating the public on disability law is integral to her work. Ms. Kerzner has authored public legal education materials on home care and abuse, and law reform submissions in which she advocates for the autonomy and equality rights of persons with disabilities. (kerznel@lao.on.ca)

RITA KLOOSTERMAN is Senior Research and Policy Analyst with the Canada Pension Plan Disability Directorate at Human Resources and Social Development Canada. (rita.kloosterman@sdc-dsc.gc.ca)

OLGA KRASSIOUKOVA-ENNS is Executive Director, Canadian Centre on Disability Studies. She has over 25 years of experience working in health, social and education fields and has particular interest and experience in interdisciplinary methodology, partnership development, disability policy and programs development and evaluation, poverty reduction and promotion of disability studies in Canada and internationally.

KARI KROGH is on disability leave from her positions as Assistant Professor in the School of Disability Studies at Ryerson University and Senior Research Fellow with the Canadian Institutes of Health Research. She developed innovative participatory research methodologies; investigated disability-related support and health policies; and acted as temporary advisor to the World Health Organization. She has received numerous academic recognitions, including the Royal Society of Canada's Alice Wilson award. After contracting a tropical virus, Kari developed a sudden on-set severe disability. She is currently engaged in "work without choice", navigating disability support bureaucracies and service systems. (kkrogh@ryerson.ca)

NANCY LAWAND has spent her career in the federal public service, developing and managing social programs and policy. Since the 1980s she has specialized in disability issues, initially as head of the Status of Disabled Persons Secretariat, then as the Disability Policy Lead for the Social Security Reform initiative, and since 1995, as Director of Policy for CPP Disability at Human Resources and Social Development Canada. (nancy.lawand@sdc-dsc.gc.ca)

DAVID LOCKER is Professor in the Department of Community Dentistry, Faculty of Dentistry, University of Toronto.

MARY ANN MCCOLL is Associate Director, Research at the Centre for Health Services & Policy Research, and Professor in the Department of Community Health and Epidemiology as well as in the School of Rehabilitation Therapy at Queen's University. Dr. McColl served as Head of Occupational Therapy at Queen's University from 1992 to 1998. Prior to coming to Queen's, she served as Director of Research at Lyndhurst Spinal Cord Centre in Toronto. Dr. McColl's areas of research interest include: disability, aging, access to primary care, community integration, spinal cord injury, health policy, spirituality, and qualitative research. (mccollm@post.queensu.ca)

IAN PARKER is one of the founders of the innovative Self-Managed Attendant Services Direct Funding Program in Ontario. He implemented its successful pilot (1994) and manages the program to the present day. He is also spokesperson for Attendant Consumer Action Coalition. Ian has had a disability and used attendant services for over 30 years. He was a pioneer in the attendant service/housing demonstration projects (1975) and has successfully advocated safeguarding attendant service activities from all medical and other external interference. Ian has lectured on the Independent Living movement at the University of Toronto. He lives in Toronto with his wife and daughter. (cilt@cilt.ca)

MICHAEL J. PRINCE is the Lansdowne Professor of Social Policy in the Faculty of Human and Social Development at the University of Victoria, Victoria, British Columbia. He was a faculty member at Carleton University, from 1978 to 1987, in the School of Public Administration. From 1997 to 2005 he served as Associate Dean and Acting Dean of the Faculty of Human and Social Development. Dr. Prince has been a consultant or advisor to all levels of government and four Royal commissions. His recent books are *Changing the Rules: Canadian Regulatory Regimes and Institutions* (1999) and *Changing Politics of Canadian Social Policy* (with James J. Rice, 2000). (mprince@uvic.ca)

MARCIA H. RIOUX holds several positions at York University — Graduate Programme Director of the M.A. (Critical Disability Studies), Chair and Professor in the School of Health Policy and Management and Director of the York Centre of Health Studies. Her research addresses health equity, universal education, international monitoring of disability rights, the impact of globalization on welfare policy, literacy policy, disability policy, and social inclusion. Dr. Rioux has lectured throughout the Americas, Europe, Africa and India and has been an advisor to a number of federal and provincial commissions, parliamentary committees, international NGOs and United Nations agencies. She is currently writing a book on law and disability and is engaged in a number of international research projects. (mrioux@yorku.ca)

RITA SAMSON is a lawyer with experience litigating and advising on human rights law and policy in both the public and private sectors. She has a Master of Arts degree in Understanding and Securing Human Rights from the University of London. Rita has worked with human rights and development NGOs in the United Kingdom and Canada. Currently, she is Project Coordinator of Disability Rights Promotion International, a collaborative project working to establish comprehensive and sustainable systems to monitor the human rights of people with disabilities worldwide. (ritasamson@hotmail.com)

DEBORAH STIENSTRA is Professor and Director of the Interdisciplinary Master's Program in Disability Studies at the University of Manitoba. She is especially interested in disability policy, as well as gender and policy, and leads several large research grants related to information technologies and end of life care for people with disabilities. (stienstr@cc.umanitoba.ca)

VIANNE TIMMONS is the Vice President Academic Development at the University of Prince Edward Island. Her research interests include inclusive education, family literacy and knowledge translation. Dr. Timmons has been working with teachers nationally and internationally in the area of inclusive education. (vtimmons@upei.ca)

TANYA TITCHKOSKY is Assistant Professor in the Department of Sociology and Equity Studies at the Ontario Institute for Studies in Education (OISE) of the University of Toronto. Prior to joining OISE, she taught courses in Disability Studies at St. Francis Xavier University. Her research aims to reveal how the meaning of disability is constituted through government documents, news media and everyday talk and interaction. She is author of *Disability, Self and Society* (2003) and *Reading and Writing Disability Differently: The Textured Life of Embodiment*, forthcoming from University of Toronto Press. (tanyatitchkosky@ oise.utoronto.ca).

473

AILEEN WIGHT-FELSKE is the Coordinator of Disability Studies, Department of Social Work and Disability Studies at Mount Royal College and an Adjunct Assistant Professor at the Community Rehabilitation and Disability Studies Program, University of Calgary. She has been a board member of various advocacy groups, including the Canadian Association for Community Living, and is currently a board member of the Canadian Centre on Disability Studies. Her research interests are in the areas of disability social policy and community capacity. (awightfelske@mtroyal.ca)

VICTOR R. WILLI has been the executive director of the Centre for Independent Living in Toronto (CILT) Inc. for 16 years. Victor's 40-year experience with being a quadriplegic has been invaluable in terms of learning how to live and thrive with a disability in a world of non-disabled persons, giving him a key area of expertise in both research and life experience. Victor is a Registered Social Worker but claims to be in remission now. (cilt@cilt.ca)

KAREN YOSHIDA is Associate Professor (Tenured) in the Department of Physical Therapy and the Graduate Department of Rehabilitation Science at the University of Toronto. She is a research member with the Centre for Research in Women's Health at the University of Toronto, and she is co-chair of the Gender and Disability Research Network, part of the National Network on Environments and Women's Health. She has worked in collaborative teaching and research partnerships related to Disability Studies for the past 15 years. Her current research focuses on issues of embodiment related to women living with disabilities and cultural representation(s) of disability. (Karen.yoshida@utoronto.ca)